Critical Probings: Essays in European Literature

RENEWALS 458-4574

DATE DUE

GAYLORD			PRINTED IN U.S.A.

Utah Studies
in Literature and Linguistics

edited by

Gerhard P. Knapp – Luis Lorenzo-Rivero
Wolff A. von Schmidt

Vol. 22

PETER LANG
Berne and Frankfurt/M.

Herman J. Weigand

Critical Probings
Essays in European Literature

From Wolfram von Eschenbach to Thomas Mann

with an Introduction by
Theodore J. Ziolkowski

edited by
Ulrich K. Goldsmith
with the cooperation of
Dietrich Goldschmidt

PETER LANG
Berne and Frankfurt/M.

CIP-Kurztitelaufnahme der Deutschen Bibliothek

Weigand, Hermann J.:
Critical probings, essays in European literature :
from Wolfram von Eschenbach to Thomas Mann /
Hermann J. Weigand. With an introd. by Theodore J.
Ziolkowski. Ed. by Ulrich K. Goldsmith with the
cooperation of Dietrich Goldschmidt. - Berne ;
Frankfurt/M. : Lang, 1982.
    (Utah studies in literature and linguistics ; Vol. 22)
    ISBN 3-261-04921-9

NE: GT

© Peter Lang Publishers Inc., Berne 1982
Successors of Herbert Lang & Co. Inc., Berne

Printed by fotokop Wilhelm Weihert KG, Darmstadt

TABLE OF CONTENTS

FOREWORD

Little needs to be said by the editors to introduce this volume. Professor Ziolkowski's eloquent and incisive analysis of Hermann Weigand's critical method and accomplishments is as valid today as it was at the time he wrote it. It is, moreover, seconded by Thomas Mann's evaluation of Weigand's skills in a personal letter. We are pleased to be able to reprint the two pieces as an introduction to the present collection of Professor Weigand's latest essays. This collection shows again that what *seem* to be scattered pieces in reality possess an inner unity, a unity which comes from the heart and mind of an exceptional, humane scholar. The presence among us of this critic and his work is both a consolation and an exemplary challenge. Whether he unravels the "texture of the self-revelation" of Kafka's narrator in "Der Bau" or exposes the vanities of Schiller's aristocratic great-grandson, who boasted eighty published volumes and is mischievously hidden in the texture of Thomas Mann's *roman à clef* — he makes us perceive unsuspected things. In his hands even textual criticism becomes imbued with the suspense of a detective story.

We have not separated the essays according to the language in which they are written as we consider the intermingling a demonstration of Weigand's ease and elegance of style in both English and German. The arrangement of the essays follows the model of the earlier collections, *Surveys and Soundings* (1966) and *Fährten und Funde* (1967), in that we have grouped the studies according to the authors treated, thus continuing several of the sequences of the previous volumes. The fact that Rilke is represented with five studies testifies to the author's continual preoccupation with this poet.

In the field of Rilke scholarship especially, Weigand has always been an original and independent interpreter. In his MLA Presidential Address on "The Poet's Dilemma" (here reprinted as No. 11) the meaning of Rilke's *Second Duino Elegy* is tightly and persuasively argued. At the same time some learned critics receive a firm, if courteous, rebuke for obscuring "an essentially simple situation by philosophical verbiage."

In all his studies Weigand's probings are performed within a wide comparative framework: in a seemingly casual manner threads are spun which establish connections with other works and authors in Western Literature.

The source of each essay is given in our list of Acknowledgments. We express our gratitude to the editors and publishers of the original texts, who have permitted us to reprint them. Only minimal alterations have been made.

We feel privileged to be able to include a new Rilke paper: Professor Weigand's "Seminar Lecture" on the forever enigmatic "Das Bett," which he wrote during the winter of 1980/81.

We are most thankful to those who made this publication possible: the staff of the *Utah Studies in Literature and Linguistics*, especially the Corresponding Editor, Professor Wolff A. von Schmidt, and the publisher, Mr. Peter Lang of Berne, Switzerland, whose speedy and efficient cooperation is sincerely appreciated. We acknowledge most gratefully the generous financial support granted by the Committee on Scholarly Publications at the University of Colorado.

Finally, we are, together with the author, most deeply indebted to his wife, Mrs. Mary Weigand, for her continuous and devoted assistance.

Laetissimi gratulationes agimus nonagenario!

Boulder, Colorado   Ulrich K. Goldsmith
Berlin, Germany   Dietrich Goldschmidt

ACKNOWLEDGMENTS

"Introduction." Professor Ziolkowski's article, "Hermann J. Weigand and a Letter from Thomas Mann: The Critical Dialogue," reprinted from *The Yale Review*, Summer 1967, pp. 537-549. With the permission of the author and of the editor, Sheila Huddleston. Copyright Yale University.

1. "Spiritual Therapy in Wolfram's Parzival," reprinted from *The German Quarterly*, LI (1978), 444-464. With the permission of the Editor, Professor Ruth K. Angress.

2. " 'Arbor Amoris': On the Transformation of an Image," reprinted from *Essays on European Literature: In Honor of Liselotte Dieckmann*. Ed. by Peter Uwe Hohendahl, Herbert Lindenberger, Egon Schwarz. St. Louis: Washington University Press. 1972. Pp. 167-177. By permission of Washington University.

3. "Hamlet's Consistent Inconsistency," reprinted from *The Persistence of Shakespeare Idolatry: Essays in Honor of Robert W. Babcock*. Ed. by Herbert M. Schueller. Detroit: Wayne State University Press. 1964. Pp. 137-172. By permission of the publisher and Prof. Schueller.

4. "Ein Brief", reprinted as "Ein Brief: Goethes Cupido-Gedicht" from *Lebendige Form. Festschrift für Heinrich E.K. Henel*. Ed. by Jeffrey L. Sammons and Ernst Schürer. München: Wilhelm Fink. 1970. Pp. 21-29. By permission of the publisher.

5. " 'Wandrers Sturmlied': Once More with Obiter Dicta," reprinted from *Creative Encounter: Festschrift für Hermann Salinger*. Ed. by Leland R. Phelps and A. Tilo Alt. Chapel Hill: U. of North Carolina Press. 1978. Pp. 105-116. By permission of Professor Richard H. Lawson, editor of Studies in the Germanic Languages and Literatures.

6. "Goethe's 'Harzreise im Winter': A Structural Analysis with an Excursus on Variant Readings," reprinted from *Lessing Yearbook*, VI (1974), 199-220. With the permission of the Managing Editor.

7. "Nietzsche's Dionysus-Ariadne Fixation," reprinted from *The Germanic Review*, XLVIII (1973), 99-116. With the permission of the Editor, Professor Joseph Bauke.

8. "Rilkes 'Römische Sarkophage' (*Neue Gedichte*)," reprinted from *Dichtung und Deutung: Gedenkschrift für Hans M. Wolff.* Ed. Karl S. Guthke. Bern: Francke. 1961. Pp. 153-162. By permission of the publisher.

9. "The Poet's Dilemma: An Interpretation of Rilke's Second *Duino* Elegy," Presidential Paper, reprinted from PMLA, LXXXII (1967), 3-13. With the permission of the Editor, Prof. Joel Conarroe, Exec. Director MLA.

10. "Rilke, 'Der Stylit': Eine Textinterpretation," reprinted from *Theorie und Kritik, Zur vergleichenden und neueren deutschen Literatur: Festschrift für Gerhard Loose.* Ed. by Stefan Grunwald and Bruce A. Beatie. Bern: Francke. 1974. Pp. 87-97. By permission of the publisher.

11. "Rainer Maria Rilke, 'Persisches Heliotrop'," reprinted from *Wissen aus Erfahrungen, Werkbegriff und Interpretation heute: Festschrift für Hermann Meyer.* Ed. by Alexander von Bormann. Tübingen: Niemeyer. 1976. Pp. 607-620. By permission of the publisher.

12. (hitherto unpublished) "R.M. Rilke: 'Das Bett', A Seminar Lecture." Author's copyright.

13. "Franz Kafka's 'The Burrow' ('Der Bau'): An Analytical Essay," reprinted from PMLA, LXXXVII (1972), 152-166. With the permission of the Editor, Prof. Joel Conarroe, Exec. Director MLA.

14. "Zu Thomas Manns Anteil an Serenus Zeitbloms Biographie von Adrian Leverkühn," reprinted from *Deutsche Vierteljahrsschrift für Literaturwissenschaft und Geistesgeschichte*, LI (1977), 476-501. Free from copyright restrictions.

Introduction

HERMANN J. WEIGAND AND
A LETTER FROM THOMAS MANN:
THE CRITICAL DIALOGUE

by Theodore Ziolkowski

The collection of Hermann J. Weigand's essays, *Surveys and Soundings in European Literature*, ably edited by A. Leslie Willson (Princeton University Press, 1966), exposes in bold relief a coherence of approach that may easily have escaped the attention of those readers who first became acquainted with the studies as they appeared over the years in various publications. A volume of essays, if it has any real justification, produces an impact that exceeds the sum of its parts. Usually many of the papers have appeared elsewhere and, as subject matter, are known; indeed, some may already be acknowledged as standard works. But as we re-read them in a collection, we see them from a different perspective, for the parts assume and reveal new and possibly unexpected dimensions sheerly by virtue of their configuration. Our interest shifts, I take it, away from the substance of the separate pieces to focus more broadly on the unifying consciousness that pervades the whole. If no such *Gestalt* emerges, the papers might as well have been left buried in the journals from which they were liberated by the solicitous efforts of an enterprising editor.

Weigand's work, of course, is well known. Internationally hailed as the *doyen* of Germanic studies in the United States, he dominated his field for a quarter of a century from his chair as Sterling Professor of Germanic Literature at Yale, where he produced several generations of aggressively devoted disciples. Now an Emeritus, he continues his writing with the energetic youthfulness that has long impressed, and often shamed, his colleagues and students. So the name on the title page is a warranty of scholarly excellence.

Even so, the essays as a collection will introduce a new Weigand to many readers. In an increasingly specialized age we have a tendency to bracket people — in scholarship and criticism no less than in government or sports. The restless mind that refuses to remain tamely within its discipline or specialty disturbs us, and we find it easier to overlook or ignore its achievements outside the area to which we have assigned it for our own convenience. Thus those readers who know Weigand as "the Thomas Mann expert" are often unaware of his masterly explorations of medieval literature. The author of papers on *Hamlet* and *Flamenca* may be unknown to those who have appreciated his studies of Schiller and Kleist. The German audiences who applauded his detailed and sophisticated analyses of Rilke's metrics or Wolfram's temporal sequences probably do not realize that Weigand is acclaimed in his own country as a cultural mediator writing on such general topics as *Faust* or "Gerhart Hauptmann's Range as a Dramatist." *Surveys and Soundings* presents us, then, with a profile view of Weigand's scope as a scholar and critic. The twelve essays constitute only a small portion of his work; they exclude not only clusters of papers on Heine and Wolfram von Eschenbach, but also entire areas with which Weigand dealt primarily in German: notably Kleist and Rilke. (A volume of papers in German has just been published by Francke Verlag in Berne, Switzerland, under the title *Fährten und Funde*.) Yet they are representative of his range, which summons up by association such names as Leo Spitzer, Erich Auerbach, and Ernst Robert Curtius. We should pause to remark the phenomenon. On the one hand, an impressive knowledge of medieval literature is balanced by a continuing critical engagement with contemporary works, to which Weigand was often the first to draw serious attention (e.g., Hermann Broch's *Death of Vergil*). On the other hand, the microscopic analysis of texts and sources alternates with a telescopic view of larger literary constellations ("Shakespeare in German Criticism," or the volume on courtly love).

Yet it is not the individual works to which attention needs to be called. Several of them have already become classics in their field. Weigand's "stroll in the medieval landscape" is so deceptively readable, twenty-five years after publication, that one almost forgets that it is a standard authority for the topos of the two-and-seventy languages of the world. The literary detective work on the sources of *Der Erwählte* has long since been absorbed into the corpus of Thomas Mann criticism. And Weigand's "program notes" to *The Death of Vergil*, written shortly after the novel appeared, still constitute the most incisive critical study of Broch's masterpiece.

But it is for more general reasons that the collection is now of interest, for any reader who peruses these papers from start to finish — from medieval to modern, through German, Provençal, and English literature — will detect a distinct "literary method" unifying the whole. This should not be understood in any rigid sense; Weigand can no more be tied down to a specific critical "ism" than to a narrowly circumscribed field of interest. But the essays display more coherence of approach than Weigand appears to concede when he singles out his concern with formal structure and with human psychology as the primary motivation of his endeavors. This unifying quality can be gotten at most generally, perhaps, through the notion of involvement — an involvement that establishes networks of tension in at least three directions: toward the work itself, toward the reader, and toward the writer.

Accompanying Weigand on his peregrinations through literature — and although he never theorizes about comparative literature, it has never occurred to him that his field is any but *Weltliteratur* in Goethe's sense of the word — one is struck first by the fact that he is a man to whom books matter: not Literature with a capital L, not critical theory, not principles of aesthetics, but individual poems, plays, and novels. To be sure, his documentation is impeccable and his scholarship exemplary. But there is never the feeling that Weigand is offering us merely, in the time-honored phrase, a contribution to knowledge. I would even go so far as to say that his works, all of which very sizeably enlarge our literary learning, do so only incidentally. The initial impulse, surely, is a subjective one, which breeds the undertone of personal experience that we note in every line. "Since I want to speak of Shakespeare as a living force in German literature rather than as an inexhaustible subject for the investigation of scholars, I shall limit myself in the main to the impact of one particular play," he notes at one point. And the delightfully learned survey of the two-and-seventy languages begins with the observation:

"Were this an isolated fact without any bearing on larger issues, there would be no point in stirring up dust to unearth it. But it is an important fact, one with wide ramifications." Weigand's work, in other words, is tempered by a sense of perspective, irony, and — not least — of reverence that distinguishes first-rate scholarship from the dead-earnest irrelevancies that all too often masquerade as scholarship.

At the same time, his critical involvement alerts Weigand constantly to the significance in works of the past for our own present. Thus a consideration of Schiller's philosophy of history concludes with a nimble leap that instantly enlivens the eighteenth-century theory with implications of actuality and immediacy. "The course of history has already invalidated Schiller's conclusions. But if his propositions are still on the agenda, we shall have to ponder the question whether it is the Russians who are the slowest people, or the Chinese, or some other nation still to emerge from the teeming equatorial belt." Chamisso's romantic tale of *Peter Schlemihl* gains an unexpected dimension when we are invited to regard it, in part, as "a great satire on salesmanship and on business ethics generally." The critic never eschews his responsibility of critical assessment. "Supposing the improbable, that the world of man should continue to exist for another thousand years, it is by no means unthinkable that Broch's *Death of Vergil* should continue to stand as the twentieth century's towering monument of a mystically oriented spirituality" — a judgment advanced long before Broch became fashionable on both sides of the Atlantic. By contrast, in his homage to the author of *Der Erwählte*, Weigand finds it necessary to take Thomas Mann to task for his "rather malicious delight in nibbling away at the defenses which guarantee the integrity of his native language" — an asseveration that prompted Thomas Mann to the long letter in response quoted at the end of this article. By the same token, the tradition of the past comes in for constant reappraisal. Thus Schiller's *Ode to Joy*, usually sacrosanct in the canon of German literature, "embarrasses a sensitive ear by its extravagant crudity." At a time when too few scholars venture to be critics and too few critics trouble themselves to be scholars, it is refreshing to voyage through literature with a navigator whose surveys and soundings are learned without pedantry, critical without vindictiveness, and everywhere responsive to the subtle currents of the individual works.

If there is any common denominator among the authors that Weigand has singled out for his attention, it is the possibility they offer for the play of intellect and wit — Wolfram von Eschenbach, Heine, Rilke, Thomas Mann. For Weigand, as a scholar and as a man, is delighted by the exercise of intelligence for its own sake. "The quest of sources is an intriguing game that keeps the mind in a state of taut alertness," he notes. But the "game" — a designation for scholarly research that is characteristic of Weigand's ironic perspective — is never an end in itself. "It is a legitimate literary enterprise as well when undertaken in the service of the basic question: in what manner and to what extent did the author achieve the transmutation of his materials into an integrated new work of art?" Thus the scholar and the critic are constantly referred to each other in their common search for meaning and value.

Characterizing the German scholar-critic Friedrich Gundolf, Weigand remarks that "he seems to have had the gift of total recall along with the magic touch of evoking in three-dimensional substantiality every figure that he discusses." It is tempting to turn this sentence upon Weigand himself. Certainly his uncanny memory contributes to the fullness of his writings. He has a limitless store of apt allusions that flood irrepressibly into his essays, opening new vistas and establishing almost kaleidoscopically new dimensions of meaning for every text. Recent scholarship has traced the sources of symbolism to Schiller's aesthetic theories, but how many critics have noted, like Weigand, the parallel between the early poems to Laura and Baudelaire's "Une Charogne"? No friend of abstractions, Weigand inevitably begins with a specific text or, even more characteristically, with a word or phrase that has piqued his curiosity. Working inductively from the text, by a process of gradual generalization and relevant allusion, he embroiders ever broader circles of meaning until the entire work lies explicated before us, radiant in its historical context and yet vibrant with relevance for the present.

This expository method is related to what could be called Weigand's involvement with the reader. He invites us to accompany him, step by step, in his own scrutiny of a particular text. The study of

Der Erwählte begins with a reference to Thomas Mann's account of
the composition of *Doktor Faustus*. "Taking our cue from these remarks, we shall begin by turning to chapter xxxi of *Doktor Faustus*.
. . . We expect that this chapter will supply revealing, if incomplete,
answers to [our] questions." In this manner, which includes all the
false starts and happy accidents of the search, Weigand solicits our
participation in an exploration that turns out to be rewarding not
only for its findings, but also for its methodology. (More than one
student found his way to Yale because of this very article and the
method that it embodies.) His exposition, exemplary in its clarity
and precision, succeeds in beguiling us, for a time at least, into the
pleasant delusion that we know what Weigand knows — that we are
in fact engaging in a lively conversation rather than listening to a
highly learned discourse. Weigand is probably accurate when he notes
in the Preface that he always had "only a vague idea of the particular
audience" he may persuade to accompany him "in his adventure."
But he has never reacted to this uncertain audience by retreating into
the ivory tower of professionalism, hedged in by the walls of jargon
and curtained by the illusory luxury of obscurity. Indeed, the word
"adventure" exemplifies his attitude, which involves the reader
through its liveliness and excitement.

　　Few scholars — and even fewer Germanists writing in English —
can match the lucidity, the vigor, and the economy of Weigand's
prose. Above all, he wants us to understand. Hence all the shibboleths
of academese are abjured; in their place we find a gratifying sense of
humor, which ranges from the impish through the ironic to the sar-
donic. He employs images that are sometimes witty, sometimes elegant, sometimes shocking — but never, under any circumstances,
dull, and always enlightening. Thus the rhythm of two strophes in an
early poem by Schiller tempts Weigand to orchestrate them: "a
whirling eggbeater to accompany the ladies' voices and a puffing toy
steam engine for the rude storming of the males." Who can approach
Schiller's poem with indifferent ears after such a characterization?

　　His memory, an unerring eye for detail, plus a capacity to visual-
ize everything that he reads — these qualities lead to the witty aper-
çus that enliven Weigand's studies, for he never suggests a generality
without its corresponding factual basis. Thus: "It is always in bold

fresco style that [Schiller] conjures up his pictures of Nature. He knew a lily from a rose, but it is to be doubted whether he could tell a violet from a pansy, an oak from a beech." A section of Weigand's interpretation of Schiller's essay on poetry is entitled, characteristically, "An Exercise in Optics"; for every abstraction tempts Weigand to seek its visualization, reducing the heady concepts to an immediately accessible scene. This same capacity reveals unsuspected sexual metaphors in the verse of the youthful Schiller, while a literal reading of references to the phases of the moon leads to a more precise statement of temporal sequences in the action of *Faust*.

At the same time, his obsession with visual detail is not a symptom of critical myopia. After establishing the essential facts, upon which all interpretation must rest, Weigand steps back to get a mythic view of the work in its largest dimensions. The last section of *The Death of Vergil* is exposed as a rendition of the Biblical creation in reverse; *Peter Schlemihl* is likened to *Faust* and other works based upon the legendary scheme of involvement with the devil, who is subsequently foiled by the powers of good. Detailed analyses of various works provide the background for the authoritative and general "Thoughts on the Passing of Thomas Mann."

It seems clear that we are faced here with what might well be termed — though Weigand would be loath to dignify it with the label "literary method" — a consistent approach to literature. This is borne out by his other writings as well: not only the articles, but the books on Ibsen, Thomas Mann, and courtly love. So it is hardly surprising, finally, that several modern writers have responded directly to this lively engagement with their works: notably Hermann Broch and Thomas Mann. Therefore I conclude with the translation of a hitherto unpublished letter from Thomas Mann, written in response to Weigand's article on *Der Erwählte* and published here with the permission of Professor Weigand and Frau Mann. The letter documents on the highest level the fruitful interplay, the "game", between the writer and his ideal reader, the scholar-critic. For it is not, as is readily evident, a statement — it is a running commentary that stands in precisely the same relation to the critical article as does the article itself to the novel. There is possibly no finer indication of the quality of Weigand's work and the spirit of his mind than this

letter, whose irony merely underscores the respect and admiration
that Thomas Mann felt for his critic. To this extent the letter can be
regarded as a mirror image of the critical approach that I have called
the unifying consciousness of *Surveys and Soundings in European
Literature.*

                                          1550 San Remo Drive
                                          Pacific Palisades, California
                                          29 April 1952

My dear Professor Weigand:

    Indeed, I most certainly *have* read your essay — and a very suc-
cessful "essay" it is! You were right to assume that I was curious
about it, and I am particularly grateful that you did not make me
wait for the arrival of the offprints. *The Holy Sinner* is an island that
now lies rather far back in the stream of my work, but it was a re-
markably amusing and novel sojourn that I had there, and to hear a
man like you talk about it — to talk about it in such detail and with
a precision that takes everything into account — that was quite ex-
hilarating. Really, you have done great honor to this somewhat pre-
sumptuous experiment of my old age — through the very extensive-
ness of your study: an honor so great, indeed, that it makes me run
the risk of not taking your warnings and misgivings sufficiently to
heart. This risk, to be sure, is intensified by a certain rash confidence
in my "feeling for the language" (which in my heart I cannot consider
"slipping") and by the thought that the linguistic escapades of *The
Holy Sinner* represent something wholly unique and unrepeatable —
a joyous stylistic buoyancy that is justified to a certain extent by the
state of suspension in which the entire work hovers. Your assumption that matters have come to such a pass with me, that this is now
gloomily to be regarded as the way of writing that my exile has
produced — this assumption would be too pessimistic. I shall never
again boast and swagger [Mann had used the Anglicism *bosten* and
swaggern] — of that you may be assured. And I am not even hopelessly committed to the wordform *ausfigurieren* [an Anglicism mean-

ing "to figure out"]. A few times, by the way, you see symptoms of degeneracy where none exists. "To show somebody the cold shoulder" is perfectly respectable German; and Goethe always, or almost always, uses *überall* for *überhaupt*. It is not an Anglicism, but merely a somewhat antiquated German. "Bringing up" a child [*Aufbringen*] has a rather similar smack, and it seems to me as though Goethe might in all innocence have used it for "raise" or "educate" — if he did not actually do so.

I also wanted to say something else. Nothing could have been farther from my thoughts than to imply that *The Holy Sinner* represents the fulfilment of Adrian Leverkühn's dream of an Art of the Future, liberated from all isolation. I know only too well that I am not the man for a fulfilment of that sort. This latter-day form of a legend is "late" in every sense of the word, as "late" as I myself am. That does not necessarily speak against it — or me. *Und dennoch sagt der viel, der Abend sagt* ["Yet he says much who whispers 'evening' "] is the way Hofmannsthal puts it. But I find it significant that the little book may not be published in "the East" — in Russian-occupied Germany, Czechoslovakia, Hungary — because it is "alien to the people."

I used the passage from Bishop Paulinus' epistle on the old St. Peter because I was enchanted by its magnificent Latin periodic style, which struck me as appropriate for the occasion. After all, my Roman gentlemen also "latinize" now and then in their manner of speech.

But to suggest that the "intensely intellectual" Faltonia (I would say *esprit fort*, but you might call it un-German!) has any similarity to "Mrs. Mann" or that the tone between her and Probus even vaguely resembles that between us — that is a total misconception. My good wife is clever and quickwitted, to be sure, yet she is anything but a bluestocking. A housewife through and through, she restricts her literary activity to writing letters to her children and grandchildren.

Do you really find that Hartmann von Aue handled the sinful love-scene between the children so much more discreetly than I did? After all, he is rather explicit about their "wrestling", and he left much more for me to do in some other places. The slaughter of the

fine dog was my own addition — partly to give the scene a more
bloody and terrifying structure, partly to give the narrator an opportunity to find this deed worse than everything else. Although he
despises nature because it permits such "physical" things to happen,
he does not take the sexual aspect overly seriously. Perhaps he has a
remote awareness of the fact that incest is actually nothing but a
priority taboo. It was acceptable for gods and kings and forbidden
only to the common crowd. Isis and Osiris were brother and sister,
and we tend all too easily to forget that Zeus and Hera were too.
Mythology teems everywhere with unions between brothers and sis-
ters, sons, mothers, and spouses. That is a phenomenon that extends
from the Near East right down to the Christian mystery of the Mother
of God. It is not for nothing that Sibylla prays: "Thou who art the
Highest's child, mother, and bride." —

Physicians are disqualified as readers of *The Magic Mountain* and
Egyptologists as readers of the *Joseph* cycle? And why on earth? I
have always had my best readers among doctors (*The Magic Mountain*
actually influenced lung therapy) and musicians. And I know of
more than one Orientalist who was delighted by *Joseph* from a very
professional point of view. While writing *The Holy Sinner* I turned
the pages of many a dictionary, tracked every word that I wrote hu-
moristically to its source, and I did it all as a gesture of friendly invitation to the philologist with a sense of humor — not least you yourself. And how you responded to this invitation, passing it on with a
recommendation to your younger colleagues!

Allow me here to say a word about the ostensible "second Leo-
nardo" and a dazzling pseudo-universality which in reality is always
only "skindeep." You are right, of course. True universality is not at
all possible in our time, and in my case there is even a certain brilliant
ignorance, which is perhaps too adept at using the "show window",
the display, the "manipulation of esoteric material," and which always appropriates knowledge only as a matter of expediency, for the
moment, and in order to play with it. And yet I should not like to
see the — if you will pardon the expression — Faustian expansivity,
that distinguishes my books from other contemporary works, represented as mere swindle. In its intent there is something genuine
about it, and whenever I have "made contact" with the various fields

of knowledge, I always did so with a peculiar empathetic intensity that reached the point of productive familiarity and astonished the specialists. In truth, during a long lifetime I have entered the mansions of many men — I have experienced a great deal, I have often been an intellectual parasite, and I can probably say that nothing human is alien to me. Even today it is possible to make a small cultural cosmos of one's life and work, in which everything is related to everything else, which despite all diversity constitutes a closed personal whole, and which a man can more or less hold up without shame for comparison with the great life-syntheses of earlier epochs. I believe that this "uncommon capacity for concentration," this high degree of organization in my life, has impressed people more than the display of encyclopedic learning.

But enough! The charm of your criticism lies precisely in the fact that you arouse interest by demasking. It is a kind of enlightenment that does not disenchant. And finally — to be distrustful of art and artistry, that is an attitude that can only strike me as familiar and congenital. Nietzsche once calls the artist an insufferably sensuous and vain monkey. Right he is!

You could not possibly track down all the sources where I "got my stuff." Apart from Gregorovius there was also the book by a Catholic writer in Munich named Joseph Bernhardt: *Der Vatikan.* From it I borrowed several papal decisions (by Leo the First, I believe) and attributed them to my Gregorius. The Old English names are taken from the volume on early English and Irish art in a series entitled *Handbuch der Kunstwissenschaft*, begun by Professor Fritz Burger and edited by Dr. A.E. Brinckmann (Potsdam: Akademische Verlagsanstalt). Also important were the texts in *Kleinere deutsche Gedichte des XI. und XII. Jahrhunderts*, edited by Albert Waag (Halle an der Saale: Verlag Max Niemeyer, 1916), particularly the "Vorau Lament of Sins" and the "Arnstein Song of Mary." Besides Hartmann, they were my principal Middle High German reading matter and word source; the expressions "ubele wuoftal" and the "wurmgarten," for instance, are taken from there. One item I appropriated almost verbatim:

Ein teil dû mirs sculdig bist
daz dû mir helvest umbe got:
wande dû den êwigen lop
durch die sundaere inphienge;
unde ne wêre nie niemen
mit sunden bevangen,
sô waeriz unergangen
daz got mit dir getân hât.

[In part you are obligated
to help me reach God:
for you received eternal praise
for the sake of sinners;
and if no one had ever
been enmeshed in sins,
then what God did to you
would have been left undone.]

In the original it is actually a man who is praying. So I altered the passage to read:

Ein Teil du mir's schuldig bist,
Sag ich mit Frauenlist etc.

[In part you are obligated,
I say with womanly wile]

I was quite taken with the passage in the Song of Mary (where a praying woman is speaking):

Stella maris bistû genant
nâ deme sterren, der an daz lant
daz muode schiff geleidet . . .

[Stella maris thou art called,
from the star that guided
the weary ship to land . . .]

which I expanded to fit the context for Sibylla:

So hast du auch bereitet
Ankunft dahin,
Ankunft bei mir
dem so genehmen Knaben,
dem muss ich Gedenken tragen
beides, bei Tag und Nacht,

da er mir Heil gebracht
mit seiner festhaltenden Hand.

[Thus hast thou also prepared
the arrival there,
the arrival in my home
for the lovely boy
whom I bear in mind
both day and night
since he brought me salvation
with his firm hand.]

You see, I am already doing the preliminary work for the young philologist that you exhorted!

I also want to mention a small volume that I picked up second-hand: *Deutsches Leben im 12. und 13. Jahrhundert. Realkommentar zu den Volks- und Kunstepen und zum Minnesang,* by J. Dieffenbacher (Leipzig: Göschen'sche Verlagsbuchhandlung, 1907). It supplied me with all sorts of material for venery, falconry, riding, tournaments, weddings, and so forth. Among my notes there is a whole list of Old German names for dogs, from which I chose "Hanegiff." I no longer recall where I got the names. In short, a weird blend of frivolity (the mêlée of centuries) and carefulness prevailed. And that was part and parcel, I suppose, of the initial conception of this rather special *opusculum*.

One last word about *Der Grüne Heinrich* [a novel by Gottfried Keller], which you imply is a gap in my education. Actually I was not unacquainted with the book when I read it "for the first time" in the hospital — that is to say: for the first time with full consciousness and enjoyment and with the admiration that I had reserved in my youth for Tolstoy, Turgenjev, Thackeray, Flaubert, the Goncourts, and Keller's own shorter prose, e.g. *Die Leute von Seldwyla*. The place for *Der Grüne Heinrich* was already more or less taken by *Wilhelm Meister*, rather as Stefan George's place was filled by Platen. I didn't need it. At least, I had believed that I didn't need it and was surprised by the pleasure that I derived from the first word to the last as I read it carefully at such a late date. I read the second version, as it appeared in 1926, newly edited from the manuscripts by Jonas Fränkel (Zürich: Eugen Rentsch), but I was not under the illusion that the novel appeared in this form for the first time in 1926. The same collection of Keller's works also contains the first version (Braunschweig, 1854), which stands in my library back to back with the final version. It is remarkable for the fact that in the later parts the narrative switches from the first to the third person. A curious case.—

Must I excuse myself for the length of this letter? I was deeply indebted to you!

With genuine gratitude

Yours sincerely

Thomas Mann

1.

SPIRITUAL THERAPY IN WOLFRAM'S PARZIVAL

Parzival's encounter with the hermit on Good Friday morning achieves the breakthrough that leads to the eventual fulfillment of the intricate story. At the same time our understanding of the situation is contingent on our knowledge of a host of incidentals many of which crop up only in the course of this Good Friday dialogue. These are fed to us like the pieces of a jig-saw puzzle which make sense only when fitted together. Full empathy with both men can be achieved only by rereading and rereading the scene with the grace of hindsight.

When the two men meet, Parzival's life lies open before us. We have followed it step by step, and Wolfram has even let it slip out that Parzival is heir apparent to custodianship of the Grail. As for the hermit, Wolfram has lifted the curtain sufficiently for us to know that Trevrizent is the brother of King Anfortas and of Parzival's mother Herzeloyde. When we ask, however, poised on the threshold of the climactic Good Friday encounter, what does Trevrizent know of the life of his nephew Parzival, and does he know who it is who has sought him out for counsel, we have no immediate answer, we are left in the dark. Even scholars who have worked on the *Parzival* for a lifetime may be expected to come up with very diverse answers to these questions. As the dialogue progresses, one item of information after another falls into place, the bits and pieces coming in a wholly haphazard order, akin to the exposition of analytic drama of which Ibsen was the outstanding practitioner. Only when interwoven with inferences made on solid grounds do they make a coherent pattern. First impressions have to be verified or corrected countless times.

It will be our first task to show that Trevrizent knew that the knight who failed his mission at Munsalvaesche was his nephew Parzival, and that he had a hunch amounting to inner certainty that the young man who came to seek his advice could be no other than his nephew. Since Trevrizent no longer resided at Munsalvaesche, the

Grail Castle, when that young knight came and defaulted, how was he to know that it was Parzival? In the course of the whole story we meet only one person qualified to communicate with the two members of the royal family who live on the edge of its precincts, namely Parzival's cousin Sigune, and his uncle Trevrizent. That person is Cundrie, the factotum and Grail messenger with the eponym La Surziere. She has vast, ill-defined powers that can only be labeled as magic. In appearance a repellent caricature of everything human, she is one of those priceless fabulous monsters of the Far East that is schooled to perfection in all the arts and sciences and is in full command of courtly decorum and protocol. In the course of the whole story we see her in action only twice, both times on an embassy to King Artus and the Round Table, the first time to denounce and ostracize Parzival from human society, the second time to summon back the rehabilitated hero to Munsalvaesche. Who sent her we do not know. It is most unlikely that the stricken king had any hand in these missions. Since we hear of no administrative agency we must look to an intuitive response on her part to a divine command. She is capable of traversing vast distances invisibly as shown by her contacts with the area of the magic castle, Schastel Marveil. Her relation to Sigune provides the only attested instance of her long-term activities. Sigune is her special ward. When Parzival happened by the cell in which she was immured with her dead lover some weeks before his encounter with his uncle, he heard from Sigune's own lips that the week's supply of food is brought to her every Saturday by Cundrie. This single fact provides the key, the only key to a number of mysteries. How can we picture that cell to have been built on piles halfway across a flowing brook except by virtue of Cundrie's white magic? Who knows — may she not avail herself of the aid of some of the evil and kindly spirits who live between the earth and the firmament? Some four years earlier we had found to our uncomprehending wonder Sigune seated in the crotch of a linden tree with her embalmed lover in her arms. Who but Cundrie La Surziere could be responsible for that disconcerting spectacle? If we accept these wonders we shall be more than ready to assume that she also communicates with Trevrizent. Long before Parzival made his ill-starred visit to Munsalvaesche, Trevrizent had withdrawn from the Grail company to his retreat in the wilderness, never to return. Yet he is able to tell Parzival that a young knight did come to Munsalvaesche unbidden and that his failure to ask the healing question turned hope into deepened despair. Assuming, as we must, that Cundrie communicated the disastrous news to Trevrizent on the instant, could she have failed to mention the name of the luckless knight? Facing the Round Table she had addressed him as Herr Parzival. She had also mentioned the name of his father Gahmuret and even that of his half-brother Feirefiz. This proves without question that Trevrizent knew the identity of the knight. As we shall see, he had good and sufficient reason not to mention his name to his young visitor.

Now for the second question: When does Trevrizent recognize his young guest as the nephew whom he has never seen? Perhaps it was rash to speak as I did above of a hunch amounting to inner certainty. An earlier age would have invoked what the Germans call "die Stimme des Bluts" — a mystical sense of kinship. Be that as it may, we shall confine our review to more rational factors. Let us consider the fact that Parzival had appeared before Sigune's cell and talked with her not so very long ago. He had been rueful and despondent. Could Sigune have failed to tell Cundrie this momentous piece of news when she came the following Saturday to deliver her week's supply of food? Is it not likely that Cundrie informed Trevrizent that after an absence of more than four years Parzival had again turned up in the vicinity? A sense of expectation may well have been building up in Trevrizent. Now when the young man halted before the hermit's cave, he must have produced a very favorable impression on the holy man by his direct and guileless approach: Sir, give me counsel, I am a man burdened by sin. The first question he raises after having been reproved for being abroad in arms on this holiest of days, exhibits him again as guileless and inexperienced in the ways of the world by asking a total stranger: Sir were you not scared when you saw a knight in arms? The chatty affability of Trevrizent's response shows him rather uncommonly eager to win the young man's confidence. As soon as Parzival has removed his armor and warmed himself by the brazier, while Trevrizent has lighted a candle, the light of Parzival's preternatural beauty begins to shine through the grime and rust left by the armor. In the course of the morning, when we are on the threshold of the moment of truth, Trevrizent holds the young man's gaze fixed in telling him that his complexion and features bear a striking resemblance to those of their late King, Frimutel, whom we later learn to be Parzival's maternal grandfather. Before the long day is done we learn how Parzival's father Gahmuret had recognized the adolescent Trevrizent by virtue of a family resemblance as the brother of his wife Herzeloyde.

We move to much surer ground when, having entered the chapel, Parzival raises the question of the calendar. Sir, he says, I have been here before. I recognize your reliquary. On this I swore a solemn oath. Leaning against the wall there was a decorated spear. This I borrowed, having splintered my own. The next day I fought two glorious jousts with it, so they tell me. I was not in my right mind at the time, having been spellbound by the image of my lovely wife conjured up in the snow by three drops of blood. At that time my life was all glory and honor and it turned overnight to shame and frustration. Could you tell me, sir, by any chance, how long it is since you missed that spear? Right gladly, says the hermit, reaching for his breviary or *psalter*, and without having to take time out for a complicated calculation he tells his guest that four and a half years and three days have passed since that spear was taken. Parzival is crushed by the realization of how great a part of his life he has wasted fruitlessly. Does it not surprise us that Trevrizent came up with his calculation so quickly? Since he kept a calendar we are entitled to ask: During the whole of his sojourn in the wilderness, what event would he have been most likely to register in his calendar as the most important? What could that event be but the abortive mission of Parzival to Munsalvaesche. And where would he find this event marked in his calendar? Exactly one day before the spear was taken from his chapel wall. Since the mystery of the spear's disappearance was never solved, though trivial in itself, it had become permanently associated in his memory with the calamitous visit. Having come this far, Trevrizent knowing the date of Parzival's visit to Munsalvaesche and knowing that his guest had haunted his retreat one day later, would not the inference be absolutely compelling that it must have been Parzival who took the spear? For Trevrizent not to realize that the two young men must be identical would have required a degree of blindness on his part that we could not possibly reconcile with his alertness. From this moment, therefore, before Trevrizent has had a chance to assuage the young man's wrath against God for His alleged treachery, and before the young man has uttered a word about his unremitting quest for the Grail, Trevrizent knows for certain with whom he is dealing. He is wise enough, to be sure, and experienced enough not to spoil things by a premature revelation of his own identity. Now that we have defined Trevrizent's perspective, we are able to follow the developing situation in all its phases.

There we see them, face to face, in the nipping cold of that Good Friday morning, the young horseman knowing only that he is facing a man reputedly holy; the hermit on his part knowing that this is his young nephew, Parzival, but betraying his knowledge by not a sound or gesture. He has his reasons, of course, for maintaining his incognito. He is eager to find out what kind of person his young nephew is. He knows enough to surmise that the young man may have been so bruised by his long warfare with God that only the utmost delicacy of approach to his nephew's troubles may keep him from utter, irremediable despair.

As for Parzival, we have already had evidence that very morning that he is no longer prey to an intransigent fury against God. When the barefoot pilgrim reproached him for riding in armor on that holiest of holy days, directing him to the nearby hermit for advice, Parzival had hesitated. Then, reflecting on the Creator's power to govern the movements even of beasts, he left the decision to his horse, saying to it: *nu genc nah der Gotes kür*, now go according to God's bidding. Feeling the touch of the spurs the horse takes him straight to Trevrizent's cave.

This softening up is not a sudden change in Parzival's attitude. It must have begun weeks ago when he chanced upon the new cell in the wilderness where he found his cousin Sigune immured with her embalmed lover. Recognizing him and seeing his distress, Sigune's pity had overflowed. All those curses she had heaped on his head on the morning after his abortive visit to Munsalvaesche she now retracted, speeding him in his quest with her good wishes. Formal curses in literature are never simply evil wishes. They have an objective power to bring harm. Correspondingly, the lifting of the curse brings a substantive blessing to the person affected. In letting Parzival find Sigune's cell, God's grace has touched him.

A word about the respective ages of the two men should be helpful here. Wolfram gives us no figures. Parzival, on the threshold of adolescence, may have been fifteen when he left his mother. After killing the red knight he spent a fortnight at Gurnemanz's castle acquiring all the arts of chivalry, undergoing as it were a mutation. Then, in far distant lands, by glorious feats of arms, he won the lovely Condwiramurs whom he cherishes above all other women in the world. More than a year passed in this way before he set out to see his mother again. That very day he was put to the test at the Grail Castle and failed. Then he wandered for four and a half years in fruitless search of the Grail. So we may think of him as twenty-one at this time. As for his uncle, by virtue of his many years of most rigorous privation and asceticism, he gives the impression of being a man of very advanced age. However, since Trevrizent met Parzival's father, Gahmuret, when he was a mere stripling and the other embarking on his fatal expedition to Baldac [Bagdad] when Parzival had been conceived but not yet born, Trevrizent cannot be more than forty. Since the temptation to follow up related strands of action will continue to tease us at every point of this paper, leading us to pursue the labyrinthine thread from one point to another and return to our starting point so late as almost to make us forget our main theme, we might snatch the opportunity here to ask: What was the total length of time of the tribulation and calamity suffered by King Anfortas and the Grail Company before God's wrath finally was appeased? Wolfram gives us no date for the *terminus a quo* when Anfortas suffered his grievous wound. This had not yet happened when Gahmuret encountered young Trevrizent in Sibilje. The time may have been right for it, however, after Trevrizent returned from his tour up and around the Adriatic on which his young friend Ither, the Red Knight, accompanied him. I like to think that his disregard of the law of celibacy and the playful practice of chivalry may have caused Anfortas to be stricken on the very day when Parzival, the predestined redeemer, was born. But I have nothing to go on except the thought that such a timing would have been superbly fitting. Enough of this. We now see the two men face to face.

Astonished at seeing a young knight in full armor approach his hermitage on Good Friday morning, Trevrizent expresses his concern at this violation of the most sacred taboo of the Christian community as he greets him, asking him to dismount and take shelter on this bitter frosty morning. — Since this is not a day for sport in the service of ladies, on what errand have you come? — Sir, this morning a grey knight referred me to you as a holy man who could give me counsel, for I am burdened with sin. — Right gladly, says the hermit. Dismount and tell me about the knight who directed you hither. — As Parzival rehearses the story of their meeting, Trevrizent recognizes an old friend in the knight and he fills Parzival in at length on his story, thus putting him at his ease. Encouraged by the flow of the hermit's ingratiating conversation, Parzival feels prompted to ask: — Sir, when you saw me riding in armor, were you not scared? — Oh, as for that, says Trevrizent, I am more used to being startled by the bear and the hart. I don't want you to think of me as boasting, but as for taking flight from man, I am still a virgin. In days gone by I was a knight like yourself, cultivating the pursuit of *Minne*, performing deeds of prowess, and also incurring sin. — Nothing would be more likely to win the young man's confidence than the realization that his father confessor has personal experience of his way of life. As the horse is to be stabled, Parzival remonstrates with the holy man for taking the bridle, only to be told that it would be poor courtesy for a welcome guest to argue with his host. — Poor as it is, we shall manage to find some fodder, wild grass and fern, for your mount. — Parzival is taken to a sheltered cave with a brazier of glowing coals. Here he disarms as his host lights a candle and gives him a cloak, a conventional mark of courtesy. As warmth returns to his body, the glow of his fair complexion begins to shine through the grime left by the armor he had been wearing for many days and nights in the forest. Now they go into a second cave which serves as Trevrizent's chapel. Seeing a green reliquary on the altar, Parzival exclaims, Sir, I have been here before. I once swore a solemn oath on this reliquary. — We do not need to go into further details, having seen in our introductory argument what a significant role the spear and its notation in Trevrizent's calendar played in convincing the hermit that his guest was indeed his nephew Parzival.

As Parzival realized for the first time how vast a portion of his life he has been wasting in the pursuit of a hopelessly elusive goal, sorrow and anger rise up in his gorge to focus upon a fierce denunciation of God as the prime source of his troubles. — I served Him and He has done me dirt. He laid a trap for me to bring me down to ridicule. Since that time I have shunned every place of worship where the seasons are recorded. Since He is reputed to be the helper, why doesn't He help me? — In a crescendo on the theme of the helper, spiralling to heights of emotional utterance that are the glory of Wolfram's verse, he lays his troubles at God's door. Trevrizent is shocked at his blasphemous words. — Let me hear your whole story, he entreats, but first sit down and let me set you straight on Him who has made heaven and earth and wields all the power over hell.

Soothed by his own passionate outburst, Parzival settles down to listen to his host's discourse. He is eager to find Trevrizent's argument persuasive. Has he not come in order to be shown that there is something radically wrong with himself? Trevrizent does not deliver a sermon. He entertains Parzival by an intimate chatty talk, touching on many of the highlights of the Christian view of the world. He tells that God so loved the world that He assumed human form to be born of a virgin in order to redeem mankind. Trevrizent dilates at great length on the sacred mystery of virginity, casting the story of Cain and Abel in the form of a conundrum calculated to sharpen his hearer's attention — who protests against it as an off-color joke — a singularly effective method for teaching schoolboys then as now the difference between plain talk and symbolic discourse. He uses emphatic language to stress the folly of a man who would bend God's will by headstrong antics and flying into a tantrum. — Anyone seeing you act in this way would judge you to be out of your mind. — By way of example he summons up with a few strokes the great battle in heaven when Lucifer with his cohorts Astirot and Belcimon, Belet and Rhadamanth, was thrust into outer darkness. What a thrill there is in hearing such names for the first time! Their ejection from heaven left a gap which God filled by the creation of man. Then came the fall, Eve's disobedience and her sin passed on to all her offspring. In his presentation of God's personality, Trevrizent stresses three characteristics. God is *ein triuwe*, the essence of streadfastness.

God is *ein warheit*, the essence of truth. God is *ein durchliuhtec lieht*, the light that penetrates opaque substances. Whenever a thought is born in man's heart, a divine beam noiselessly penetrates his breast and tests the thought before it turns to outward action. When Trevrizent turns to the theme of old pagan prophecy, telling of the foreordained coming of a redeemer, he surely takes his listener beyond his depth. What can the names of Plato and the Sibyl mean to a young man who has never been to school? We can be assured, however, that they reinforce Parzival's trust in the wisdom of his mentor. When Trevrizent has finished his quaint, thoroughly comforting discourse and Parzival has thanked him for setting him straight, it is time, at long last, for Trevrizent to come to grips with Parzival's specific trouble.

Having thanked Trevrizent for his assurance of God's trustworthiness, Parzival again ruminates on his having devoted all his life to the observance of good faith, contrasting it with his utter abandonment to misery. With this the time has come for Trevrizent to ask: Unless reluctance to talk restrains you, would you mind telling me the story of your troubles. I might be able to find a way out of this impasse for you which you cannot find by yourself. — So Parzival braces himself to make the first thematic statement of his predicament. Putting it very succinctly he says: My greatest distress concerns the Grail. Next to that I am consumed with longing for my wife who is the loveliest and most lovable young woman ever born. — With that the ice is broken; the theme of the Grail has been broached by Parzival for the first time. Trevrizent's rejoinder, however, takes up the second part of the complaint first. He commends Parzival warmly for loving his wife. Indeed his approval takes the form of hyperbole when he continues: You might be poised on the brink of hell in your woes, but if you remain steadfast in the love you have pledged to your wedded wife you will surely be rescued, all will certainly turn out well. — This is the second time Trevrizent has heard Parzival confess his love for his wife. The first time was when he spoke of the decorated spear which helped him win two victories while his mind was absent in a trance contemplating a vision of his beloved. If Trevrizent caught that fleeting remark, as he surely did, he has twice heard of Parzival's overwhelming love for his wife from his own lips.

What should provoke a hermit pledged to celibacy to single out this Christian virtue and bestow upon it a power of redemption that seems all out of proportion? Again we are up against unknowns. In the first place, we do not know whether Parzival's confession comes to him as news. Does Trevrizent know anything about that year which Parzival spent with Condwiramurs after delivering her from her importunate suitor? Had the Grail Messenger Cundrie herself any knowledge of Parzival's whereabouts during that time? We are never told this either. I prefer to think of the fact of Parzival's marriage coming to Trevrizent as a complete surprise. In any event, this provides the most plausible reason for Trevrizent's exaggerated expression of joy at the news. But why such a joy? Again it will take a very considerable length of time before this piece of the puzzle fits into place. We shall hear from Trevrizent's lips that a special injunction and dispensation regarding marriage applies to the King, custodian of the Grail; we shall hear of the deliberate flaunting of this rule on the part of King Anfortas and his younger brother Trevrizent, next in line of succession; it shall become evident that the sole heir left in direct line of succession is Parzival — only then will Trevrizent's joy stand out in full relief. As to the cardinal point of the divinely established law of succession Parzival has not forfeited his claim. Moreover he has lived in accordance with it, not by virtue of obedience to the law but in unconscious spontaneity from the fulness of his heart. Would not this realization be accompanied by a hope, be it ever so faint, that Parzival might still be restored to full grace and recalled to the Grail?

Turning now to Parzival's supreme distress, his longing for the Grail, Trevrizent chides him for entertaining so absurd a desire. — You must be in total ignorance of your quest since you do not know that the Grail can be found only by those who are predestined to its service. I know this and have seen it to be true. — Then you have been there? Parzival asks, and hearing Trevrizent's affirmative answer, he entreats him to tell what he knows, which Trevrizent now proceeds to do.

There is a company of Knights-Templar (Templeise) pledged not to sport but to life and death combat. They derive their nourishment from a stone the name of which Trevrizent gives in garbled Latin as

Lapsit Exilis. Before dilating on this he enumerates sundry miraculous virtues of the stone, all of them varieties of its power to recreate or preserve life. It accomplishes the rebirth of the fabulous Phoenix (of which Parzival is most unlikely to have heard). For a week after the stone has been seen the beholder cannot die. It preserves the youthful appearance and beauty of those gathered around it for an indefinite time, except that their hair may turn gray. With dramatic emphasis Trevrizent sums up its powers by saying: This stone is also known as the Grail. The next topic explains the source of the Grail's miraculous powers. Once every year, on Good Friday, its powers are renewed by a dove that brings from heaven a tiny white wafer which it deposits on the stone, whereupon it wings its way back heavenward. As in the folk tale of the magic table there is food to satisfy every appetite, as in paradise, not only the fruits of the earth, food and drink, but also the meat of birds and beasts. All the people destined to serve the Grail are brought from foreign countries as small children. Their divine nomination becomes known by their names appearing in writing on the polished clear surface of the Grail. The writing disappears after it has been read. In a very abrupt manner — the passage suggests an interpolation — Trevrizent now shifts to the prehistoric past: It was not always this way. When the great fight was going on in heaven a group of angels stood on the sidelines awaiting the outcome. These were banished from heaven and sentenced to minister to the Grail on earth. Whether they were subsequently granted a full pardon or banished forever from God's presence, Trevrizent professes not to know. By a later decree, God entrusted the care of the Grail to Christian hands. Sir, this is how matters stand.

That is the cue for which Parzival has been waiting. Sir, he says, if chivalry can win honor on earth and also a place in the Paradise to come, that has been the goal of my striving all my life. If God knows a good fighting man when He sees him, why, let Him nominate me to the service and let me show what I can do. This candid outburst moves the hermit to tears as he replies: Alas, if things were only so simple. High spirits alone do not avail for every task. Pride could all too easily bring your youth to a fall. Humility in the pursuit of higher things is needed to strike a balance. — With this preamble he takes up the tragic thread of the story.

There was and is a king, Anfortas by name. Hearing this name must make the blood rush to Parzival's cheeks. This name had engraved itself upon Parzival's memory when uttered during Cundrie's recital of the stricken king's desperate suffering and of the mute apathy of himself, the visitor, who had found neither word nor gesture of sympathy. Finding himself ostracized from the company of men of good will, taking farewell of his friend Gawan, he had groaned, *ei helfelôser Anfortas,/ waz half dich, daz ich bî dir was*? – Anfortas, his host continues, seduced by pride and the high spirits of youth, flaunted the law of virtue required of those who minister to the Grail. He indulged in adventuring, in the practice of courtly love. He came to grief and plunged us into mourning. All the knightly brotherhood are pledged to a rule of chastity. By dint of this they have had the strength to keep the mysteries of the Grail shrouded from an alien world. There is only one instance of a knight having found his way to the brotherhood without having been elected. He was a man devoid of sense and feeling. Unimpressed by the king's suffering, he passed on, burdened with sin as he was and adding more by his callous indifference. It is not up to me to denounce anyone, Trevrizent continues, softening his tone, but to think of all the grief and misery that he left on his trail! Before this knight there was another, Rois Lehelîn, who penetrated our outposts as far as Lake Brumbane. Challenged by the knight Lybbeals, he slew him and carried off his prized horse. In this way we got wind of the murder and robbery (rêroup).

Proceeding now with the utmost caution, the hermit ventures to ask: Sir, could you be Lehelîn by any chance inasmuch as your horse carries those Grail markings . . . ? Continuing in the same breath without giving the young man any chance to answer, he tells a long story of how the brand of the turtle dove became one of the insignia of the Grail horses. It was Anfortas who put the turtle dove on the saddles but Titurel the ancestor passed similar insignia, with which the shields were emblazoned, on to Frimutel, a brave hero who lost his life in battle. We revere him because he was devoted to his wife with such exemplary love as no man before him has ever shown. It gladdened my heart to hear you speak, sir, of the love you bear your own wife. I hope you will continue to follow Frimutel's example in this regard, and, as I look you in the face I am moved by the striking resemblance you bear to our late king. Now sir, do tell me where you are from and what is your lineage.

Above, in our introduction, we supplied proof to show that Trevrizent knew his guest to be Parzival all along. We are sure, therefore, that the question, Sir, could you be Lehelîn by any chance, could not possibly reflect the hermit's uncertainty. Here, in this tangle of a mare's nest, this Rattenkönig of a sentence which extends over twenty-four lines to the question of his lineage, we surely have the final proof that this question was a feint. Trevrizent feels that things are shaping up to a crisis. His question is a gambler's throw that might cause the young man to clam up. He does not want an answer at once. Floundering nervously over some ten lines on the matter of the stable brands as though the details mattered, quite gratuitously he brings the names of all three Grail kings into his discourse, and even more gratuitously, though very much to the purpose, all the details concerning King Frimutel. All atremble, if I read him right, he implores his guest to take him into his confidence. And indeed, Parzival understands what it is all about.

Psychologically speaking, those ten lines of babble about the turtledove markings to cover up a sense of shame at asking a disingenuous question as a stratagem to win his guileless visitor's confidence — then a question equating the young man with a knight fully a generation older, the despoiler of Herzeloyde's lands, and now the perpetrator of rêroup; then attempting to expunge rather awkwardly, almost apologetically, such unpleasant associations by returning to his commendation of the young man's marital status as following the example of an illustrious model — is this not intricate enough to make one imagine a blush that Trevrizent's sparse beard cannot hide suffusing the features of the holy father confessor?

Before listening to Parzival's answer, we must consider the impact of the name of Lehelîn on Parzival's mind. The question put him into a fix certainly, because — If you are not Lehelîn, how came you to be riding a Grail horse? — Thus one thing would lead to another. But there is something much more portentous about the question, the irony being that Trevrizent himself is not aware of this. If Wolfram had been a modern novelist he would have relished the opportunity to remind us of the terrible echoes the name of Lehelîn must have evoked in Parzival's mind. He would have taken us back to the day when the boy in fool's clothing, drunk at the sight of the Red Knight's glittering armor asked King Artus to give it to him. The situation was so absurd that Artus allowed himself to be persuaded by Keie's cynical humor to nod a 'yes' to the young fool's importunate demand. The youth had rushed back posthaste to Ither, calmly stationed in expectation of a challenger. Approaching, Parzival had uttered the cry: The King has told me I can have your armor. Take it off and be quick about it. — Ither, incredulously watching the fool's antic gesturing, frowned, saying: So this is the kind of courtesy the King extends to his kinsmen? — Shaking with impatience and greed, Parzival had blurted out: Stop your mutterings! Off with it! — At this, Ither, pointing the butt of his spear at Parzival, had given him such a poke in the ribs as to topple both him and his nag. And now, aflame with rage, Parzival had brandished his javelin crying: *Du maht wol wesen Lehelîn!* (You may well be Lehelîn). His infallible aim brought the javelin through Ither's open visor, scattering his brains as he fell. A moment later the young madman was already clawing at the clasps of his armor. "Lehelîn" — why that outcry? It was a pure inspiration. Three days ago he had heard Lehelîn's name from his mother as the despoiler of her lands. Lehelîn was the only human enemy he knew. That name involved an instant fusion of all the aggressive emotions possessing Parzival, and the murder was accomplished. We ask, would not Trevrizent's diffident question have reawakened in Parzival the terrible events of that day that marked his entrance into life, giving colors to them now so different from what he had seen in what we might call the trance of his frenzy? Wolfram cannot break the tension of Trevrizent's tangle to remind us of what he confidently expects us to remember. And, as for Trevrizent, he was not an eyewitness to the murder, he never heard the enraged outcry that precipitated the act.

In the pause that ensues after Trevrizent's question, the two men eye each other fixedly. Parzival is faced with a fundamental decision, to equivocate or to come clean. His whole future life depends upon this choice. He breaks the silence. Sir, he says, I am the son of a man who lost his life as a valiant fighter. Gahmuret was his name, by

lineage an Angevin. I ask you to remember him in your prayers. Sir,
I am not Lehelîn. If ever I committed that heinous crime of robbery
of the dead (rêroup) it was before I reached the age of discretion. I
confess myself guilty of that misdeed, however. I slew Ither of Kuku-
merland and laid him dead on the grass and took the takings.

The ice has been broken. Parzival acknowledges the deed as his
own. Hitherto, if ever he allowed his memory to stray into that area
of his transition from boyhood, he kept it sealed from sight as a complex of repression, belonging, as it were, to another being, tied by no
strand to his own identity. Now he recognizes this misdeed as an
inalienable part of his own self which he has to live with from now
on. The old saying, "It is only the first step that counts," comes to
mind. We, the readers, and Trevrizent too, look with full confidence
on what is yet to come. It is only a matter of time for the whole confession to pour out as a limpid stream.

Trevrizent heaves a deep sigh, deploring the bitter reward of getting entangled in the ways of the world. Now the moment for the
anagnorisis has come. — Dear Sisterson, he says, shifting from the
formal 'Ihr' to the familiar 'Du,' which he continues to use for the
rest of the visit, while Parzival continues the respectful 'Ihr' owing to
elders. — What advice can I give you in so terrible a case? You have
slain your own flesh and blood [a worse crime, evidently, slaying a
kinsman, than an ordinary murder]. What will you give God by way
of ransom? Your account is already preempted by God's claims on
your own person. (Does Trevrizent resort to this obscure formulation
because he sees in Parzival a guilt parallel to his own? As comes out
later when another piece of the puzzle falls into place, Trevrizent had
felt he could assuage God's wrath against his brother by committing
his whole life to the most austere penance, trying to perform an act
of vicarious atonement, forgetting meanwhile that he has the same
sin as Anfortas to answer for.) This leads him to pronounce a eulogy
on Ither, twenty lines in all which must have caused hot tears to run
down Parzival's cheeks. By another abrupt turn, switching from the
death of Ither, Trevrizent continues: My sister also lay dead as you
left, Herzeloyde, your mother. — (We have hardly time here to make
a mental note of the two facts that Trevrizent knew Ither intimately,
and that he must have been in communication with Herzeloyde to

know of her dreadful dream and her death.) — No, good Sir, Parzival interrupts, if I were Lord of the Grail that could not compensate me for the death of my mother. Tell me truly, are you my uncle, and is my mother dead? — I am no deceiver, Trevrizent replies. In the nightmare she suffered before your birth, you were the dragon that ripped her womb as he flew from her.—

Overcome with grief, Parzival now listens without a word of interruption to the tragic tale of Anfortas' woes. — There were five of us, Trevrizent begins, two of them now dead, your mother Herzeloyde and her older sister Schoysiane. Schoysiane died in childbirth and left your cousin Sigune for your mother to bring up. Still living, apart from my brother and myself, there is our sister Repanse de Schoye whose purity makes it her privilege to bear the Grail while all the false world could not budge it from the spot.

After Frimutel's death, Anfortas, the older of us, was crowned King. Reaching adolescence, he had to cope with the importunings of Minne. Flagrantly disregarding the obligatory taboo of our caste, he went adventuring in the service of a lady of his choice. On one such occasion he encountered a heathen knight from the Far East who coveted the Grail and had its name engraved on the point of his lance. In the charge that followed the heathen was killed, but his splintered spear lodged in Anfortas' groin. Despite the terrible pain, Anfortas managed to ride home. There the iron, with adhering bamboo splinters, was removed from the wound. The hideous affliction of the wound shook me so powerfully that I discarded my knightly status and my right of succession in order to devote myself to a life of the most rigid asceticism, hoping to placate God for my brother's sake. This was another calamity for the brotherhood, for now there was no successor to rule them. Anfortas was carried into the presence of the Grail. Seeing it, he could not die, and it was so ordained. Then the physicians came with their inventory of cures. First, antidotes to all known poisonous serpents were tried, but to no avail. Next we tried the water of one of the four rivers that flow out of Paradise from as close to the point of issue as our approach would permit. When this did not help, the golden bough was obtained by which Aeneas wended his way through the underworld under the guidance of the Sibyl because we thought the spear might have been tempered

with hell fire. Next to be tried was the blood of the Pelican that so
loves its brood that it pierces its breast in time of famine to feed
them. Then there was the unicorn, famed for its attachment to
maiden purity. We used its heart, and the carbuncle that grows under
its horn we immersed in the wound, all in vain. Finally, we resorted
to a root grown from the blood of a slain dragon, this root being
mysteriously akin to the constellation of the Dragon which exerts
special powers at the time of its culmination. Again to no effect. —
We content ourselves here with the mere mention of these items, inasmuch as Trevrizent-Wolfram's familiarity with the whole arsenal of
medieval medicine would warrant a commentary of source material
far beyond the scope of this paper.

— When we had exhausted all the cures known to medicine we
made another formal supplication before the Grail. Suddenly a written message appeared on its surface to this effect: Some day a knight
would come to Munsalvaesche. If he saw the degree of the King's suffering and was moved to ask him about his trouble the King would
be healed by divine power, but he would forfeit his kingship and the
newcomer would take his place. This contingent promise was coupled
with two strict warnings. Any attempt to give the knight the slightest
intimation of the power lodged in his question would nullify its
virtue. In the second place the question would have to be asked during the first night of his stay in order to be effective. There followed
an agonizingly long period of expectation. During this time we tried
all sorts of palliatives to ease the dreadful stench of the festering
wound. As for myself, finding the situation unendurable at last, I
retired to this wilderness. Eventually that knight, predicted as the
contingent deliverer, appeared. I have told you of the miscarriage of
his mission. He failed to open his mouth and inquire sympathetically
about the king's troubles. — Now it might be time for Parzival to
confess, but he remains mute.

Trevrizent's recital has come to an end, leaving them both to
sorrow and meditation. It is high noon, let us attend to our food,
Trevrizent says. You go and collect some fodder for the horse, wild
grass and ivy, while I shall grub in the snow for such fare as my cold
kitchen can provide. When the snow melts, I shall teach you to find
what we can eat. That is all your horse and you will have as long as

you keep me company. Even so, I have never had a guest whom I would have been more pleased to entertain with the choicest fare. While Parzival collects a bundle of fodder Trevrizent digs in the frozen ground. All he finds he hangs upon bare twigs. He never touches food before the nones, the traditional hour of Christ's death on the cross. After collecting his pickings they wash them in the flowing stream. Then, having seen to the horse, they return to the shelter with the brazier of coals. In munching his wild carrots and garlic Parzival feels more blissfully happy than if he were sitting at the board of Gurnemanz or even the feast provided at Munsalvaesche. Both of them are aglow with good feeling and assure each other by word and gesture of how happy they are in each other's company. Having eaten, they see to the horse once more. With genuine sympathy Trevrizent addresses the horse and apologizes to it, as to one groomed and nourished in the royal stables of Munsalvaesche, for having to put up with such wretched fare.

By this time the atmosphere of mutual good feeling holds Parzival in such tight embrace that he can no longer resist the urge to open his heart wide, even at the risk of casting a chill on his uncle's boundless good will, and let out his dread secret. Fumbling with a preamble, awkward and apologetic, he at last finds the clear and precise words for a full confession: He who came to Munsalvaesche and saw the inexpressible grief and failed to ask the question, that was I, wretched child that I am.

If Trevrizent is startled by this confession, it must be not by its content but by its timing, scarcely having dared to hope that it would all come out so soon. What is it you are saying? he exclaims. Then the sharp question: What were you doing with the five senses God gave you . . . ? In the context of the situation this sounds less like a reprimand than an exasperated wringing of hands at the irreversibility of time. Now, however, there follows no long lament. On the contrary, Trevrizent displays a fine sense of realism. – We must lament, you and I, but let us not go overboard in our sadness. There is a time for moderation in everything. That applies to you and me, the young and the old, otherwise the green vigor of your youth will turn brown and the white of my hair will turn drab. Dwelling on the metaphor, he expresses the wish that he might freshen the young man's green and see his high spirits restored so that he might still attain the prize and be reconciled to God. — I am truly ordained to counsel you and bring this about. — Here Trevrizent uses poetic language that is ambiguous enough to be read either as simply a confident assurance that God will fully forgive Parzival for all his blasphemous obstinacy or, beyond that, it might still be given to him to win the earthly prize that he covets. In the light of all the hints we have had, the fine quality of Parzival's guileless manhood, his spontaneous observance of the taboo against marital infidelity, his qualification by birth for the succession, is it not fair to assume that Trevrizent's hopes run high as regards both Parzival's career on earth and the life beyond? This is confirmed by the emphatic statement at the end of Parzival's stay with his uncle, that he absolved him from his sin on the one hand and on the other encouraged him not to follow his own example and become a hermit, but rather to continue steadfastly in his worldly station as a knight.

Having counseled moderation in sorrow as in all things, Trevrizent straightway puts his therapy to the test. Returning to the topic of Parzival's visit to Munsalvaesche he strikes a predominantly factual tone, supplementing the information already given. We learn of the effect that the culmination of the planets has on the wound. Saturn in particular, the highest, produces an intolerable chill. Its culmination coincided with Parzival's visit. The extreme palliative, never tried before, was to thrust the spear into the wound and bring it forth bloody. That was the significance of the bloody spear held aloft by the page who ran along the four walls of the great hall eliciting the moans and tears of the brotherhood. Presumably this remedy was applied just before Parzival was summoned to the king's presence. Parzival had seen two silver knives sharp enough to cut steel deposited on the king's table. They are another exhibit like the bloody lance. They were fashioned, Trevrizent explains, by a very cunning craftsman who learned the secret from the charm engraved on the sword that the king handed to Parzival. It was only these knives that were able to scrape the poisonous glaze off the spear that it had absorbed from the wound. Incidentally, the great frost that chilled the wound on that night affected the Earth, a less sensitive medium, only the next day when Parzival was caught up in a trance by the three drops of blood in the unseasonable snow.

The next topic to be dwelt on at length, within the framework of a general custom, is Parzival's parentage. Trevrizent tells of the betrothal and marriage of Herzeloyde to Castis, king of Waleis and Norgals. Bearing what is presumably a symbolic name, Castis sickened and died on the homeward voyage without having consummated the marriage, leaving Herzeloyde a virgin widow and queen of two lands. These events led to the tournament in which Gahmuret won her.

Having disposed of this topic, Trevrizent says for the first time in explicit language that it is mandatory for the king to have a wedded wife to whom he is faithful, whereas all other Grail Knights except those sent into foreign lands by divine decree are pledged to celibacy and the avoidance of sport in the service of ladies. This injunction I disregarded, he continues, and now at long last, having kept his own person in the background as much as possible, he has a confession of his own to make. Of this both Parzival and we readers have had no inkling up to this moment. We are treated to a long and colorful recital of Trevrizent's transgression. Pondering it, we might find it surprising that it is told without blushing and breast-beating. On the contrary, we feel something of the gusto of a man rejuvenated by the memory of his youthful exploits.

Roaming over the three continents, Europe, Asia, and Africa, in search of adventure for the glory of his lady, he came up in mountainous regions with wondrous encounters such as were still reported *bona fide* by Shakespeare's Othello and accepted as fact by his audience. Thanks to his brother's wealth and influence he went on these expeditions well equipped and accompanied. Slipping away, he carried his brother's seal as certification to some port where he could also leave his equipment on his return. We learn a great deal of geography in listening to Trevrizent's account. Another great surprise awaits us. While preparing to embark in Sibilje for the area north and east of the Adriatic, Trevrizent met Parzival's father, Gahmuret, who was setting out for Baldac to aid his liege lord the Baruk. They became fast friends. Trevrizent was still a beardless youth at that time, with the features and beauty that characterized all the members of the royal family. Gahmuret told him: You cannot be any other than the brother of my wife Herzeloyde. – After innumerable trick-oath denials, Trevrizent conceded the fact. They exchanged gifts. Trevrizent had his reliquary carved from a block of stone greener than clover (jade?) given him by Parzival's father while Gahmuret lent him their young kinsman Ither as a companion for his coming expedition. With the mention of Ither's name the tone of the rambling narrative changes as we would expect. Parzival is reminded of his great sin. For another sin he is charged with the death of his mother caused by his reckless departure. For good measure, Trevrizent also adds the sin of his having failed to speak sympathetically to Anfortas. Trevrizent treats this as the consequence of the crime unatoned for. Deepest remorse and its external symbol, penance by privation, will help him to win God's pardon. As the day draws to a close, Trevrizent has one more matter on his mind, the Grail horse that Parzival has been riding. How did he get it? Parzival reports the incident that happened to him shortly after he saw Sigune at her cloistered window. Trevrizent subjects him to a sharp cross-examination before being satisfied. Here as in other places we have a choice of two interpretations. Had Cundrie really failed to report to Trevrizent this piece of news that Parzival has again turned up in the vicinity after some four years, or, knowing about it, did he mean to test Parzival's mettle? Had Parzival been so crushed by becoming aware of his guilt that he would now passively follow his mentor's guidance? Or has he the courage to maintain his sense of right and wrong in terms of the code of chivalry by which he lives? I like to think that it was assurance on this point that Trevrizent sought by his cross-questioning. Parzival also has one more item on his mind, the mantle he was given before he was summoned into the presence of the King. — That was sent you by my sister Repanse de Schoye. She thought you would be wearing it as lord of Munsalvaesche.

The long day is done. They settle down to rest on such bedding as the cave affords. Parzival prolongs his visit to his uncle for fifteen days, spending it in meditation and penance. While the first day was rendered almost entirely in terms of dramatic and narrative dialogue, we are offered only the barest skeleton of a report on the remaining two weeks. Parzival asks his uncle a number of questions regarding what he saw on the night of his visit to the Grail Castle. He inquires among other things as to the identity of a very old white-haired man whom he glimpsed sitting in an adjoining room when the door opened. That was Titurel, the surviving founder of the dynasty, Trevrizent answered. Although he is paralyzed by gout they keep him alive (by exposing him to the Grail every week) to enjoy the benefit of his counsel. If we had been wondering who sent Cundrie La Surziere to Artus's court to excoriate Parzival on the third day, the person of Titurel provides a satisfactory answer.

Advising his nephew on the reverence owing to priests because of their sacred office, Trevrizent stresses the venerability of such priests as lead a life that conforms to their sacred trust. Although himself a layman, Trevrizent feels fully empowered by God to give formal absolution to his nephew. He does this on the day of Parzival's departure.

It is now five weeks before Pentecost according to the church calendar. Pentecost traditionally marks the festival of spring's full awakening. This Pentecostal season is fixed by divine decree to restore to the Grail community its golden age of purity and joy. In the interval Parzival engages in three more colossal contests against the most redoubtable incognito opponents who turn out to be his dear friend Gawan, the formidable Gramoflanz, and his own brother Feirefiz. These are not so much trials in the spiritual sense as they are spectacles of knightly prowess, glamorous exhibition games, if you will. Then, as once before, Cundrie appears before the Round Table to announce that Parzival is being summoned by divine decree to return to Munsalvaesche to heal the king by a word of sympathy and assume the rule of the kingdom. Guided by Cundrie and accompanied by his half-brother, Parzival proceeds to Munsalvaesche. Received in the Great Hall, he makes a triple obeisance in the direction of the temple where the Grail is housed, then asks the stricken King the simple question: Uncle what troubles you? Anfortas is instantly healed and Parzival takes over the realm. Meanwhile, Condwiramurs and the twins she has borne Parzival in his absence have been summoned by a divinely instructed embassy to proceed to Munsalvaesche. Going out to meet her, Parzival finds her encamped at the very spot where he had been spellbound by the three drops of blood in the snow. On the way to this joyful reunion he passes Trevrizent's retreat. The uncle greets him with transports of joy that find expression in a wild hyperbole echoing his Good Friday statement: You foolish man, you cannot force God's hand by flying into a wild tantrum. Now he says: So the unheard-of miracle has come to pass, and you have forced God's hand by your embittered persistence to do your bidding!

With this we have strayed beyond our topic. Let us briefly summarize our findings.

Wolfram makes it hard for us. He employs the method of a mystery story writer. We know next to nothing about Trevrizent, only his identity as a member of the royal family, his life as a hermit in the wilderness. On this Good Friday we learn about his life from his own lips bit by bit. Only as the long day draws to a close does the pattern of his life and its motivation assume a shape. It is not only he we do not know. We are also in the dark as to what he knows of Parzival. We are not given a chance to ask such a question at the beginning of their meeting. Gradually it dawns on us that he knows much more about Parzival than he lets on. Only when we get unmistakable evidence, again from his own lips, that he knows Parzival to have been at Munsalvaesche, failing his test, do we ask ourselves the question, never explicitly suggested by the author, *How* does he know? We can proceed only by inference, and the only channel of inference leads directly to the Grail Messenger Cundrie La Surziere. If, thanks to her supernatural powers, she communicates with Trevrizent at will at, let us say, the speed of a telegraph, does she fill in for him the picture of Parzival's doings? Does she prepare him for Parzival's visit on that Good Friday morning — forewarned is forearmed — by telling him that after having disappeared without a trace Parzival has at last turned up again in the vicinity? Parzival has talked to his cousin Sigune with whom she, Cundrie communicates every Saturday. Did such a message convey a glimmer of hope? We have a choice of answers. We take as our guiding criterion: Which interpretation makes better sense in terms of the overall design? And then there is the great moot area covering the year that Parzival spent as the husband of Condwiramurs. Is Parzival's kingdom of Brobarz so distant in space that knowledge of it escaped even Cundrie? If so, Trevrizent is taken by surprise by Parzival's spontaneous avowal of his deep love for his wedded' wife and its consequences for Parzival's qualification for the succession. I think the pattern of the events strongly favors this conjecture. I see it in Trevrizent's joyous and repeated response to this cue.

All this leaves us with a paradoxical situation. Wolfram structures the unraveling of the facts like the writer of mystery stories in which we have to fit the pieces together bit by bit to form a coherent pattern. The personal drama, on the other hand, is a matter of deep emotion and fiercely controlled tension. The prize is the redeeming of the young man's soul on the way to headlong perdition, and the method is one of the most cautious probing governed by wisdom. Any premature move on the part of the therapist might irremediably warp the process of healing. The mystification of the story and the tension of the human drama in which so much is at stake engage us at cross purposes so that we can get engrossed in sorting out the puzzle to the detriment of our committed empathy or allow our feeling to be played on without heed to the superb gamesmanship involved in the eventual triumph of the foreordained divine plan.

2.
ARBOR AMORIS
ON THE TRANSFORMATION OF AN IMAGE

Arbor Amoris. Der Minnebaum. If the sound of this beautiful title suggests echoes of Walther von Stolzing's Preislied in Wagner's *Die Meistersinger*, let such an association be eradicated once and for all. A glance at Volume 20 of the series Philologische Studien und Quellen,* will inform us that this is the study of a particular aspect of German religious life in the late Middle Ages. It fulfills the assignment of editing a hitherto unpublished text, of which copies in manuscript and early printings abound as parts of voluminous codices scattered throughout the whole German linguistic area. Copies, as the term is used here, includes major and minor modifications of a basic draft anonymously composed about 1300 but often ascribed to such names as Albertus Magnus, Bonaventura, and Thomas Aquinas in order to lend it additional authority. The original text is in Latin, as are the many modifications, elaborations, abbreviations, and other changes it undergoes for about a century in passing from hand to hand and from one generation to another. Appearing in the form of a tract, a meditation, a sermon, et cetera, it is meant to instruct and edify, sometimes didactic in tone, sometimes aspiring to mystical heights, and conforming in its appeal to the sociological stratum to which its communication is addressed. Urs Kamber's monograph may be regarded as a thoroughly competent piece of work carrying out a specific assignment, supplying insight into the thinking and the preaching of men consecrated to the cultivation of the Christian life in theory and practice. Scholastic and mystical interests intertwine in these pages.

The title requires a somewhat roundabout explanation. Although the subdivisions of a field of knowledge had been referred to as

---

*   Urs Kamber, *Arbor Amoris, der Minnebaum.* Ein Pseudo-Bonaventura-Traktat, herausgegeben nach lateinischen und deutschen Handschriften des XIV. und XV. Jahrhunderts (Berlin: Erich Schmidt Verlag, 1964).

branches, suggesting the underlying image of a tree at least as far
back as the neo-Platonist Porphyrius (third century A.D.), an ingenious scholar, Jacobus de Fusignano (d. ca. 1329), appears to have
been the first to compose a manual on sermon writing employing the
tree with its roots, its stem, and its branches as the central image do-
minating the composition of the sermon. We are reminded in some
versions of the manual that while Jesus enjoined his disciples not to
think in advance of what they would have to say when summoned
before the authorities because God would put the proper words into
their mouths, we latter-day preachers no longer enjoy this gift. We
cannot rely upon inspiration, and it devolves upon us to deliver our
message in a logical and orderly form. It was with this object in view
that the writers of sermon manuals selected the tree as their model.

About the same time, we are told, the idea took root of presenting the Christian life in its central aspect of the developing devotion
of the soul to God as its source under the symbol of a tree. In the
tract bearing the title *Arbor Amoris*, every aspect of the heart which
gradually rises from the bitter root of fear to a stem of many branches is related to some part of a tree's development. The dominant
method of development is that of allegory. A Biblical text concerned
with a tree is made the basis of the discourse, and every physical
feature of the tree and its environment is interpreted as symbolizing
some specific aspect of the soul's progress in its reach upwards toward God. The correlation between the physical and the spiritual is
performed with great finesse and strikes us as quaint. According to
the manner of the times, every statement is reinforced by one or
more pertinent quotations from the Bible, from the Church Fathers,
and from the later masters. Quotations of Biblical texts make up
more than half of the total. It is interesting to mention in this regard
that the most popular source of quotations throughout the fourteenth century was the Song of Songs. The abundance of these quotations is not necessarily a proof of superior learning on the author's
part, because every writer had numerous glossaries and concordances
at his command corresponding to the copious use of familiar quotations by even our most illiterate public speakers. The author of the
tract selected by Kamber for publication and comment, however,
must have been a scholar of more than average ability and aspiration.

After showing us how the tender cultivated shoot is grafted upon the wild rootstock, he follows its upward growth methodically. At a given point the young shoot sends forth two lateral branches, signifying two aspects of the first stage of the soul's love for its creator. Upward growth continues, the process of branching being repeated six times more, the last — the seventh — representing the attainment of the unattainable *unio mystica* of the soul with its creator (characterized by *mentis alienatio et rationis excaecatio*). For five of the seven stages of growth our author is indebted as regards both terminology and method to Hugo of St. Victor's (d. 1141) commentary on a very famous book — the treatise *On the Celestial Hierarchies* ascribed to Dionysius Pseudoareopagita who is identified with the patron saint of France, St. Denis. Dionysius was mentioned in the Acts of the Apostles when Paul preached to the Greeks in the Areopagus, taking as his theme their altar erected to an unknown god, and the Book of Acts tells us that Dionysius became Paul's disciple. Legend made Dionysius Paul's special and favorite disciple, and when Paul found himself raised to the third heaven, an experience of which he speaks in his First Letter to the Corinthians, Chapter II, tradition has it that much of the unutterable ecstasy he experienced was passed on to his favorite disciple. Now it happens that the intensities of love portrayed in five of the seven pairs of branches are peculiar to the highest order of the heavenly powers, the Seraphim, and far beyond the reach of human attainment. In addition to the text of the tract, Kamber's book reproduces a curious schematic picture which reveals both its ingenuity and naiveté to one who has digested the tract in full. Many of the later copyists and reworkers of the tract no longer understood the author's subtle scheme and cut down the text to simpler proportions, thereby losing its meaning.

The *Arbor Amoris* dates from about the year 1300. About a century later, German translations and adaptations began to appear. These have also been preserved in great numbers and, while some show a fairly close adherence to the Latin original, there are others that tend to revert to the habits of jungle growth. Some of the later ones are composed in a mixture of Latin and German for monks and nuns having enough of a smattering of Latin to make them superior to the common people. Except for the wit, we are reminded of the charming mish-mash of the Capuzinerpredigt in Schiller's *Wallen-steins Lager*, modeled after the macaronic style of Abraham a Santa Clara. Of the German versions, Kamber supplies us with a variety of sample texts and commentaries. After repressing feelings of a very different nature, I came to think of what a delightful text Kamber's book would make for a small seminar group of students well trained in Church Latin and familiar with a variety of medieval German dialects. As an exercise for catching on quickly to the nuances of language, once the central ideas have been mastered, it would be a challenging piece to work on, not without relevance to the student of middle high German.

To be sure, the pleasure derived from such an exercise is of a purely formal nature. As we read the first half dozen sentences of the tract, we find ourselves in a state of confusion hardening into shock as we proceed further. According to custom, every religious tract or sermon took as its starting point a Biblical text suited to the principal theme of the discourse. The text of our tract consists of three verses from the Book of Daniel, Chapter IV, verses 7-9 in the Vulgate, but numbered 10-12 in the King James version quoted below:

> . . . I saw, and behold a tree in the midst of the earth, and the height thereof was great. The tree grew, and was strong, and the height thereof reached unto heaven, and the sight thereof to the end of all the earth: The leaves thereof were fair, and the fruit thereof much, and in it was meat for all: the beasts of the field had shadow under it, and the fowls of the heaven dwelt in the boughs thereof, and all flesh was fed of it.

These verses deal with the vision of a tree. This vision continues for several more verses, but our tract ignores them as it ignores the whole setting of the vision and its consequences. I cannot state this point effectively without asking the reader of this paper to take his Bible and read the fourth chapter of the Book of Daniel from beginning to end. The whole chapter is couched in the form of a proclamation issued by King Nebuchadnezzar. It tells of the vision that troubled the King; it tells of his summoning Daniel, the most inspired of the captives taken from Jerusalem to Babylon. It reports the allegorical interpretation of the King's vision, prophesying dire consequences to

result from the King's impiety. It confirms that these consequences
actually came to pass, that the King lost his reason and grazed among
the oxen of the field; that God finally took mercy upon him, restoring him to his reason and to his seat of majesty. The proclamation
ends with an admonition to every one of the King's subjects to revere the God of Daniel as the one true God.

No modern writer of an edifying tract or sermon could have re-
frained from setting forth in outline the general context of the passage
that he had chosen to develop. He might have done so very briefly for
fear of his listeners being sidetracked by the profusion of visions
couched in pompous rhetoric with which the Book of Daniel abounds.
Not so our author of *Arbor Amoris*. Lifting from the context only a
part of the vision of the tree, ignoring completely the king, the prophet, and the setting of the whole episode as a proclamation, he un-
dertakes to develop an allegory of his own that has not a single point
in common with the allegorical interpretation enunciated by the prophet Daniel. He must suppress every association called up by the Biblical story in order to develop his allegorical construct of the love of
God implanted in the heart of man and culminating ideally in a
complete fusion of the human soul with the divine essence. Such a
method of procedure is monstrously perverse. The reader of the tract
is never so much as told of the origin of the textual passage. That the
author of the original tract knew the place from which his text was
lifted I regard as certain. But as to the generations of copyists and
manipulators who shortened, distorted, elaborated the tract to suit
their own degree of skill and the intellectual niveau of their audience
I have the greatest doubt. Unless I misread Urs Kamber's intention,
every manuscript of the tract *Arbor Amoris* begins with the same
textual passage. I am not clear as to whether the fourteenth century
parchment text which Kamber used as the basis of his edition mentioned the source of the text as Daniel IV: 7-9. Kamber does mention that some of the manuscripts attributed the text to Ezekiel, but
Kamber refrains so meticulously from critical remarks and humanis-
tic value judgments that, confined in the strait-jacket of scholastic
theology, we find it very difficult to breathe. Whether by temperament or assignment, the author seems to have felt no call to relate
the materials treated to fresher currents of thought.

Secular literature is ignored in the tracts except for the introduction of an occasional proverb. Kamber himself never casts a sidelong glance in that direction, whether by choice or ignorance it is impossible to say. Let us do a little exploring of our own in the secular area. The dates of Kamber's materials lie between 1300 and 1500. The manuals on the composition of sermons after the schema of the tree date from around 1300 and became so popular, we are told, as to lead to the coining of the phrase "Praedicare est arborizare." The prototype of the Latin *Arbor Amoris* tract is also dated around 1300, and its German counterparts, under the title *Der Minnebaum*, date from the fourteenth and fifteenth centuries. We are given the most definite impression that literature furnished no earlier instances of love as conceived under the image of a growing tree. By implication this would apply to secular as well as to divine love. Let us test this hypothesis by a more or less haphazard search for the occurrence of the *Arbor Amoris* as a motif in the masterworks of the *Blütezeit* around the year 1200, a century earlier than the starting point of Urs Kamber's investigation. I limit myself to Wolfram von Eschenbach and Gottfried von Strassburg. Since Wolfram's *Parzival* had appeared while Gottfried was still at work on his *Tristan*, this fact is sufficient to dictate the order of their presentation.

There is a gem of a passage germane to our subject in what is commonly referred to by Germanists as *Die Drei-Blutstropfen-Szene*. It occurs in Book 6, twenty-four hours after the rude termination of Parzival's venture at the Grail Castle, and forty-eight hours after his having taken leave of his beloved wife Condwiramurs. Parzival is astride his horse at the edge of the forest, the early morning air is chilled by a light, unseasonable snowfall. Seeing three drops of blood on the snow, he is reminded of his beloved's complexion and lapses into a love trance. A lookout of King Artus who is encamped close by, announces the presence of a challenger, and a young hotblood, Segramours, wangles the King's permission to try an encounter. In his state of trance, Parzival does not notice the jousting oncomer, but his horse has not lost its wits and automatically responds to the encounter by tumbling the young attacker, who scurries home for safety. A second challenger, the loudmouthed seneschal Keie, now determines to teach the stranger a lesson. The interval before his approach Wolfram employs to address a long reproachful apostrophe to Frou Minne for exposing so devoted a vassal as Parzival to such a predicament. Wolfram does not mince his words. He charges Frou Minne with all kinds of mischief. She is responsible for so much evil and disorder that, but for the fact that she is accompanied by Frou Liebe, Lady Delight, no right-thinking man would pledge himself to her service. Then, turning from generalities to a particular instance, Wolfram abruptly introduces the name of a famous poet of the preceding generation, Heinrich von Veldeke, the author of the German version of the story of Aeneas, reworked after the French *Roman d'Enéas*, which traces its line back to Vergil. Wolfram was very familiar with Heinrich von Veldeke's work, as numerous allusions to characters and situations indicate, including a considerable amount of his own poetic phraseology. He loved Heinrich, and now he suddenly evokes his name in the following passage:

> her Heinrîch von Veldecke sînen boum
> mit kunst gein iuwerm arte maz:
> hete er uns dô bescheiden baz,
> wie man iuch sül behalden!
> er hât her dan gespalden,
> wie man iuch sol erwerben.
> von tumpheit muoz verderben
> maneges tôren hôher vunt.
> was oder wirt mir daz noch kunt,
> daz wîze ich iu, vrou Minne.

> (292: 18-27)

> Herr Heinrich von Veldeke designed his tree
> with skill as conforming to your nature. Ah,
> how much better he would have done to in-
> struct us in how to retain you! Instead he
> split off for us to see only the section show-
> ing how to acquire you. Owing to inexpe-
> rience many a fool finds the prize only to
> lose it again. If that has been my fate or is
> still my destiny I shall hold it against you,
> Frou Minne.

Here there is presented to us the pattern of a *Minnebaum* symmetrically conceived as having two sets of branches, the one set show-

ing all the symptoms and artifices of acquiring love, the other the art
of retaining the treasure once acquired. Of these two, the master
craftsman has given us only the former. Wolfram reverses the temporal, logical sequence of the two states, couching the wish in the ex-
clamatory form of the contrary-to-fact conditional, either to allude
to a personal experience of his own or to simulate such a situation.
The threat that concludes the passage makes it seem more likely that
the personal element is make-believe. This sort of thing is one of the
most characteristic elements of Wolfram's personal style. Every
student of middle high German who comes across this passage for the
first time is bound to have trouble with it. The switch from the general to the specific, startling in itself, is reinforced by the coupling of
the rhyme scheme of the new sentence with that of the one just con-
cluded. There is the confusing reversal of the logical sequence. Moreover, the whole passage has the character of an impromptu interjec-
tion. Does not this last feature in particular almost compel us to assume that Wolfram's hearers were not unfamiliar with the schematic
designation of Frou Minne as a tree? The particulars of course which
led Wolfram to ascribe to Heinrich von Veldeke the Minnebaum-
craftsmanship in question refer to the story of Dido and Aeneas in
the early part of the story and the mutual infatuation of Lavinia and
Aeneas in the final part. The fact of Aeneas' abandonment of Dido
may be alluded to in the lamentation. Certainly, while all of Heinrich's brush strokes taken together work up to something like a phe-
nomenology of love in the making, there is precious little of this regarding the surviving counterpart — Aeneas and Lavinia after their
marriage. Let us now see how Gottfried in his turn handles the symbol of the *Minnebaum*.

We run across it in that early part of the *Tristan* story where the
youth is to be formally knighted. By a very clever device Gottfried
dodges the boring task of a full-dress description of a court festival.
With tongue-in-cheek modesty he observes that all this has been done
so well so many times that he could not match his predecessors if he
had twelve tongues in his mouth instead of one. This general observation gives him the lead for launching into a lengthy digression on the
contemporary scene of German literary art. The whole survey presents one of the finest exhibitions of Gottfried's superb rhetorical

eloquence. At the same time it discharges a whole volley of venomous shafts at his detested rival, Wolfram von Eschenbach, without
mentioning him by name. Gottfried's survey falls into two divisions:
The first discusses the composers of poetic narrative whom he
designates as colorists (*verwaere*). After that the writers of songs
whom he refers to as nightingales pass in review. Our concern here is
limited to the first group.

The poet whose name tops the list is Hartmann von Aue (Hartmann der Ouwaere). Gottfried lavishes praise upon him. Hartmann
must be accorded the chaplet of many colors bestowed upon the
winner of the poetic contest. There are some who would challenge
Hartmann's right to the crown, but Gottfried's innuendo leaves no
doubt as to the incompetence of their judgment in matters of poetry.
In the next passage Gottfried's studied equanimity gives way to a
fierce outburst of rage directed against the perverters of poetry. He
calls them frauds, tricksters, cheats, counterfeiters. Their tales are
fantastically incredible and parade an obscurity of diction that requires an interpreter. Gottfried dismisses them as purveyors of black
magic. While Gottfried speaks of these pseudo-poets in the plural,
there is not the slightest doubt that all his shafts are directed against
one single individual – Wolfram von Eschenbach, whose poetic temperament he felt as totally alien to his own. For our purposes it is
sufficient to remember that Gottfried launched a very vitriolic attack
against the author of the *Parzival* shortly after the book's appearance.
Having delivered himself of this blast, Gottfried continues his survey
by singling out for praise a second poet, Blikker von Steinach. Unfortunately, his work has been lost without a trace, and we have only
Gottfried's highly colorful imagery to whet our curiosity regarding
its style and content.

And now follows a key passage which, as in Wolfram's case, we
must quote in Gottfried's own language before supplying what is at
best a halting translation.

> 4723 Wen mag ich nu mer uz gelesen?
> ir ist und ist genuoc gewesen
> 4725 vil sinnic und vil rederich:
> von Veldeken Heinrich
> der sprach uz vollen sinnen:

wie wol sanger von minnen!
wie schone er sinen sin besneit!
4730   ich wæne, er sine wisheit
uz Pegases urspringe nam,
von dem diu wisheit elliu kam.
ine han sin selbe niht gesehen;
nu hœre ich aber die besten jehen
4735   die, die bi sinen jaren
und sit her meister waren,
die selben gebent im einen pris:
er inpfete daz erste ris
in tiut[i]scher zungen:
4740   da von sit este ersprungen,
von den die bluomen kamen,
da si die spæhe uz namen
der meisterlichen vünde;
und ist diu selbe künde
4745   so witen gebreitet,
so manege wis zeleitet,
daz alle, die nu sprechent,
daz die den wunsch da brechent
von bluomen und von risen
4750   an worten unde an wisen.

Whom else shall I single out for praise? There have been aplenty
distinguished by thought and artful discourse. Heinrich of Veldeke,
he spoke with full control of thought; how well he sang of Minne!
How beautifully he trimmed his thought! I venture to think that he
took his wisdom from the fountain of Pegasus from which all wisdom
took its origin. I have never known him personally. But now I am
told by the best among those who achieved mastery during his lifetime as well as those now living that are all in accord in attributing
to him this praise: he was the first to graft the cultivated sprig into
the wild rootstock of the German language. This subsequently sent
forth branches producing flowers from which the masters derived
their conceits and subtleties in such abundance. And this same art is
now so widely practiced and developed in such a variety of ways
that all who now compose spoken verse pluck their fill of flowers
and sprigs as regards both words and melody.

Here then, in Gottfried's literary survey, happily composed at
the very time when German medieval literature had reached the peak

of its excellence, we have not only a schematized allusion to the *boum* of Frou Minne that we found in Wolfram; here we find the three-dimensional full grown *Minnebaum* exhibited in all its glory of color and design. Here, strangely enough, Gottfried anticipates by a whole century the image of the cultivated shoot grafted into the wild rootstock of the German language. And strangest of all perhaps is the observation that Gottfried's antipathy to Wolfram did not hinder him from singling out for highest praise the very master who was Wolfram's avowed favorite. We may speculate about Gottfried's motives in making the name of this poet the climax of a long passage of dazzling virtuosity inviting comparison with his rival's manner.

But speculations aside, we have presented an incontrovertible demonstration of the fact that the motif of the *Minnebaum* had been brilliantly developed by the masters of secular poetry a hundred years before a theologian conceived the idea of making it the theme of a labored allegory.

In the case of the theological allegory, I was troubled by the fact that the question was never raised why that particular text from Daniel should have been chosen in preference to scores of other Biblical occurrences of shapely trees. Did Urs Kamber think of himself as writing for an exclusively select audience of theological scholars? Did he tacitly assume that they were all fully informed as to the enormous authority of the prophecies attributed to Daniel? Did he find it superfluous to mention that the concept of the Holy Roman Empire of the German Nation owed its foundation to that first vision of King Nebuchadnezzar recorded and interpreted by Daniel in Chapter I? A reference to the late Walther Rehm's illuminating study, *Der Untergang Roms im abendländischen Denken*, would surely not have been out of place. We should not tax him for studiously avoiding the correlating of the Book of Daniel with such secular themes as Goethe's "Das Märchen," Heine's "Belsazar," the legend of Saint Catherine of Alexandria, and possibly the legend of Wilhelm Tell. To do so would have been to stray beyond his field. But I ask the same question as to the implication of the allegory of the *Minnebaum*. Was Wolfram's and Gottfried's use of the *Minnebaum* unintentionally overlooked or was it studiously ignored? Has the necessity, or call it the blight, of ever-growing specialization cut a furrow through the

medieval field, forbidding the explorers of higher theology and so-
ciologically important *Gebrauchsliteratur* to cast so much as a glance
at the flourishing pastures on their left?

Finally, I would think it a matter of considerable interest to
know whether Wolfram and Gottfried were innovators in their symbolic use of the *Minnebaum* or whether they were the beneficiaries
of an established tradition. Some young scholar equipped to handle
Church Latin and the medieval German dialects with ease, and a
fluent reader of twelfth-century French might do well to keep on
his desk a special notebook labeled *Arbor Amoris*. I would not have
him go ahunting with a single-track mind, scanning a prodigious
amount of reading. It would be enough to keep some tiny corner of
his brain constantly alerted to the possibility of coming upon some
pertinent passage. Serendipity plays a considerable part in such a
quest, but if he is persistent and lucky, he may well find over a
course of years that he has amassed a considerable number of finds
germane to the subject. Papers originating in this way are written
with a minimum of effort and are likely to impress the reader with a
prodigious respect for the writer far in excess of his deserts. But a
sine qua non is a faith in *Frou Fortuna.*

3.
HAMLET'S CONSISTENT INCONSISTENCY

There are considerations that make a wholly satisfactory interpretation of *Hamlet* impossible. The text of the play was not edited
by its author. Shakespeare's *Hamlet* is based on an older play on the
same theme, and how much of the old text he was able to salvage
and bring into focus to fit his own purposes, we do not know. Moreover, the text has been tampered with in a major way, as I shall de-
monstrate. However, I shall not succumb to the temptation of indulging in any speculations; I shall base my interpretation of the
action and the characters strictly on the vulgate text of *Hamlet* as
we read it in our modern editions.[1]

I begin by pointing out some difficulties and discrepancies. First
of all, the time factor, in all its aspects, presents a major hurdle. I
do not, of course, mean the "unity" of the classical rules, for the
non-observance of which Dr. Johnson, in his Preface to his edition
of Shakespeare (1765) defended Shakespeare with elegant circumspection. I am referring, rather, to the duration of the action as a
self-consistent presentation. Old Hamlet was murdered while
sleeping in his orchard, as was his wont. That fixes the time of the
murder around midsummer. The curtain rises on the first act two
months later, when King Claudius and old Hamlet's widow, Queen
Gertrude, have just been married. Act I covers a day and two nights.
During the watch on the platform it is bitter cold. "It is a nipping
and an eager air," suggesting a wintry season. Acts II and III, com-
prising a space of two successive days, take us to a point of time
two months beyond Act I. To Hamlet's "my father died within's
two hours," Ophelia replies, "Nay, 'tis twice two months." By the
calendar it might be around New Year's, when the players arrive at
the court and Hamlet devises his trap to get "objective" proof of
King Claudius' guilt.

---

1 The quotations follow the *Hamlet* volume of the Yale *Shakespeare*, the
   revised edition of 1959.

In Acts IV and V there are five separate time strands, beginning simultaneously, running concurrently, and all terminating on the day of the catastrophe. But the imagination cannot conceive of these strands as being of the same length. The first of these strands concerns Hamlet. On the morning after Hamlet has sprung his trap, killed Polonius, overwhelmed his mother by a torrent of reproaches, and mocked his uncle with macabre jests about Polonius' corpse, he is shipped off to England. The next day he becomes the captive of pirates, who set him at liberty on the Danish coast in expectation of some good turn. Hamlet's absence from the court gives the impression of not having been more than a long weekend. There is nothing in his letters to Horatio and the king to hint at any appreciable lapse of time. The catastrophe that ends the play takes place on the day of Hamlet's return to the court. The second strand concerns Laertes. He gets word in Paris of his father's mysterious death and clandestine interment; he hastens back to Denmark in secret; he assembles a group of conspirators, and at their head storms into the king's presence with the intent to kill him and seize the crown. The king tells him that Hamlet murdered his father, and he and Laertes hatch the plot against Hamlet that finds its fatal denouement the next day. This series of events concerning Laertes the imagination cannot picture as elapsing in less than several weeks. The third time strand concerns Fortinbras' march over Danish territory to some fortified Polish stronghold, the success of his expedition and his return to Elsinore; this too on the day of the catastrophe. Such a campaign must be thought of as requiring considerable time. The fourth time strand deals with Rosencrantz and Guildenstern. They complete their voyage to England, without Hamlet, deliver the sealed commission which they think concerns the exacting of tribute, and are summarily executed according to the wording of the forged document substituted by Hamlet. England sends a return mission to report the execution of the king's order. It arrives within minutes after Hamlet, Laertes, Hamlet's mother and the king have succumbed to the poison. The fifth time strand, Ophelia's madness and accidental drowning, gives us even more trouble to fit into any coherent scheme. All this happens in late spring. Ophelia says, the violets all withered at her father's death. The landscape is ablossom with wild flowers, pansies, daisies, rue, columbine, dead men's fingers, that give color to these pathetic scenes. Thus, from the point of view of Ophelia, the time span from old Hamlet's murder, in midsummer or late summer, to Ophelia's death in late spring covers nearly a year, whereas Hamlet's embarcation, return to Elsinore and the fatal fencing match, take us to a season a little beyond four months after old Hamlet's death. No reconciling of these differences is possible. We must content ourselves with the observation that the course of the play was designed without regard for any coherent time scheme.

A totally different problem is that of Hamlet's age. Everything in the play up to the fifth act makes us think of Hamlet as a very young man, a youth in his late adolescence (T.S. Eliot to the contrary notwithstanding),[2] a student at Wittenberg, concerned particularly with the study of moral philosophy and the rhetorical arts, untried, inexperienced, but with a flair for philosophizing gravely on the general course of human affairs after the manner of Cicero, Seneca and Marcus Aurelius. But in Act V we are startled to hear from the lips of the gravedigger that Hamlet is thirty years old. The gravedigger took up the spade on the day when old Hamlet vanquished and slew old Fortinbras of Norway, and that was the day when young Hamlet was born. His age is corroborated by the turning up of Yorick's skull, who died twenty-three years ago, and Hamlet is moved by childhood reminiscences of frequent and intimate association with the beloved jester. How this image of Hamlet as a man of thirty got superimposed on that of the adolescent youth is a complete mystery to me. However, it ties in with another equally mysterious reference to thirty years. The player king and queen in "The Murder of Gonzago" are pictured as having been married for thirty years. We cannot but think of this reference as part of the passage inserted by Hamlet in order to make the parallelism between the player king and queen and his own father and mother glaringly obvious to all who saw the performance.

---

2   All the evidence points in this direction. The most specific references are to be found in Laertes' admonition to his sister (Act I, Scene 3) and King Claudius' remarks to Laertes about skill in fencing as something very highly prized by youth but rated much lower by mature men. Laertes and Hamlet are obviously in the same age group (Act IV, Scene 3).

But against this there stands the fact that before the fifth act no reader or spectator could have an inkling of such a parallelism being drawn; hence it is dramatically and theatrically ineffective. No experienced practitioner of the stage would have had recourse to such a device. I repudiate age thirty for Hamlet on other grounds. It is difficult to conceive of a queen in an Elizabethan play, at the age of fifty or thereabouts, as having preserved enough beauty, charm, vitality and sex appeal to incite her brother-in-law's covetousness and to win her response to his passionate advances within a matter of weeks after her husband's death. The play contains no hint, of course, suggesting that Gertrude was a party to her husband's murder or that there was a clandestine relation between her and Claudius before old Hamlet's death. There is no doubt, on the other hand, that Gertrude and Claudius are passionately attached to one another. If Gertrude were in her middle thirties, as could well be the case if we think of Hamlet as eighteen, the situation would resolve itself very simply. Hamlet's intense mother fixation, too, would be rendered infinitely more plausible.

So much of time, in the variety of its aspects. There are also discrepancies of a different nature to trouble us. Horatio's remark on the facial expression of the ghost, made to Marcellus and Bernardo on the first night of their watch, is at variance with what he tells Hamlet the next day. To Marcellus he said:

> Such was the very armor he had on
> When he the ambitious Norway combated;
> So frown'd he once, when, in an angry parle,
> He smote the sledded Polacks on the ice.[3] (I,1)

But when Hamlet, the next day, being told of the apparition, puts Horatio to a cross-examination and, in the course of it, asks, "What! look'd he frowningly?" Horatio answers, "A countenance more in sorrow than in anger." (I,2) There is a clear contradiction: Both statements contain the words "frown" and "anger," but the emphasis is reversed. What are we to make of this? Can it be intentional? Can it reflect on Horatio's integrity? Everyone with some experience knows

---

3   The remark about the armor might, of course, have been suggested by a portrait of the late king.

that memory is a faculty that not only preserves but also transforms the past. There is probably no court record but furnishes instances of this, particularly if the testimony concerns some incident charged with emotion. Can we think, then, of Shakespeare as having introduced this discrepancy as evidence of his own shrewd observation of men? I would dismiss such an explanation as fanciful. Though good psychology, it goes unnoticed by all but the most careful readers. Dramatically, therefore, it has no significance. Let us book it as a slip. It is important for us to explore all such leads, but we need an Ariadne's thread to bring us back out of the labyrinth.

Another discrepancy concerns Hamlet's way of living at Elsinore. Two days before being shipped off to England, he tells Rosencrantz and Guildenstern that he has "foregone all custom of exercises" (II,2) since the mood of melancholy settled down upon him. We get a very different impression from King Claudius' report to Laertes on Hamlet's reaction to hearing Laertes extravagantly praised for his skill at fencing. This report, he says,

> Did Hamlet so envenom with his envy
> That he could nothing do but wish and beg
> Your sudden coming o'er, to play with you. (IV,7)

And when Hamlet has accepted Laertes' bid and Horatio comments: "You will lose this wager, my lord," Hamlet replies: "I do not think so. Since he went into France, I have been in continual practice." (V,2) What are we to make of this contradiction? Hamlet is unpredictable enough, to be sure, to say one thing and do another, and it would be possible for spells of activity to alternate with moods of gloom, but at the time of Hamlet's first quoted remark, the image of Hamlet as under a spell of continuous gloom was firmly fixed in our minds. I think the contradiction is real. It is a mechanical piece of motivation devised to give plausibility to the situation that triggers the catastrophe.

A final question, not to be readily resolved, is the availability of Ophelia as a suitable marriage partner for Hamlet. Both her brother and her father tell her emphatically that a match between them is out of the question, Hamlet being of royal blood and under obligation to subordinate his personal preference to dynastic interests. Indeed, Polonius tells the king and queen that he put his interdiction

of Ophelia's easy commerce with Hamlet on these very grounds, and
their failure to qualify this rigorous renunciation by some semblance
of mitigation must be taken as tacit agreement with Polonius' version.
Against this stands the fact that the queen, tearfully strewing flowers
into Ophelia's grave, says these words of farewell:

> I hop'd thou shouldst have been my Hamlet's
>   wife.
> I thought thy bride-bed to have deck'd, sweet
>   maid,
> And not have strew'd thy grave. (V,1)

Yet these words uttered, now that the girl is dead, need not be con-
strued as more than the expression of genuine sorrow. The whole
matter of Ophelia's eligibility is, of course, linked to the rule governing succession to the throne. The succession was elective, not strictly
hereditary, and Hamlet might have eliminated himself as a candidate
for the succession by marrying a woman not of royal blood. As to
Claudius, he was a usurper only in so far as he had clandestinely
made away with the legal ruler. As to his having been duly elected to
succeed his brother and taken his widow to wife with the sanction of
the constituted authorities, the text of the play leaves no doubt.

We must now see what manner of person Hamlet was before the
shock of his father's death and his mother's hasty remarriage plunged
him into melancholy. We get a picture of Hamlet as a model of courtly behavior in speech, dress, and manners. We may well think of him
in terms of the eulogy that Ophelia pronounces in dwelling on his
former self. The background of Hamlet's education was the Catholic
religion. Hamlet assimilated the views of the conventional believer.
God, the everlasting, the creator, the fountain of moral law; the im-
mortality of the soul; heaven, hell, and purgatory; the necessity of
the rites of the church for the dying, were realities that he did not
question. Release from life might be yearned for; but suicide, forbidden by divine command, was ruled out, as we learn from Hamlet's
first soliloquy. The affairs of man are ruled by a guiding Providence.
Throughout his life Hamlet never wavers in his acceptance of these
traditional ideas. There is nothing to indicate, on the other hand,
that his relation to religious teaching transcended conventional acceptance. Religion never became a personal experience. I find no

trace of the mystic in Hamlet. Superimposed on this religious background is Hamlet's education in moral philosophy at the University of Wittenberg. We think of it as supplementing, but not in any way contradicting his religious education. He was too young to be inwardly aware of the divergent orientation of the teachings of the Church and that of the Stoic philosophers. Of Hamlet's temperament we can speak with assurance on the basis of its later manifestations. He was impulsive, highly emotional and passionate, but he was an idealist who believed in virtue and self-control. Like many young people of noble disposition, he had a leaning toward austerity. He affected a grave deportment, as conforming to the wisdom he sought to assimilate. Quite unformed as yet, untried, inexperienced, he loved to let his mind's eye roam over the human scene and generalize on human affairs after the manner of the ancient philosophers. We think of Hamlet as an apt pupil, a brilliant student, promising in the highest degree, gifted with a potential range of ideas and emotions vastly above the average. We may think of Hamlet as a prodigy of learning, for a prince particularly, if, by learning, we mean not scholarship but the positive and vital assimilation of the noble doctrine of Stoic philosophy. As to his family, he had a deep reverence for his father, and he was passionately attached to his beautiful mother. This attachment became a fixation of the most distressing urgency after his mother's remarriage, but of the adolescent's sex life at Wittenberg we know nothing.

All this has been very general. The only specific clue as to Hamlet's personality before his return to Elsinore concerns his relation to Horatio. Of this I must speak at length and with a fullness of insight derived from the text, because Hamlet's relation to Horatio, a slight acquaintance at their first meeting in Elsinore, grows into a bond of friendship that makes of Horatio, despite our scant knowledge of his background, the one dramatic figure most accessible to our imaginative penetration into the play, and his surviving presence as the mourner, knower, and ultimate revealer of the mystery of Hamlet's burden, derangement and erratic plunge, makes him the focus into which all the emotions aroused in us by the play are gathered.

Horatio was a fellow student of Hamlet's at Wittenberg. They knew each other by sight but did not frequent each other's company.

Horatio was a gentleman, but impecunious. He was not brought up at the court, as shown by his question, when he hears the noise of kettledrum and cannon: "Is it a custom?" He was somewhat older and more mature. He had evidently participated in one of old Hamlet's expeditions. He saw him once, he says. His description of old Hamlet in a very characteristic attitude —

> So frown'd he once, when, in an angry parle,
> He smote the sledded Polacks on the ice. (I, 1) —

cannot be based on hearsay. At Wittenberg Hamlet's eye caught Horatio. He admired him, adored him, made him the ideal of his emulative striving, but he nursed this emotion in the secret of his heart, too young and bashful, too aware of the contrast between his own highly emotional disposition and Horatio's cultivated control, to feel worthy as yet of his particular notice. In Elsinore Hamlet offers his friendship. The joint experience on the watch establishes a bond. Later, Hamlet makes Horatio party to the ghost's dreadful revelation and mandate. For two months Horatio has, we may presume, been watching his friend's development with growing concern. Now, on the day when chance and cunning have provided Hamlet with the Elizabethan equivalent of a lie detector, Hamlet unburdens himself to his friend in one of the most memorable passages of the play. His words unmistakably hark back to their student days at Wittenberg ("Since my dear soul was mistress of her choice / And could of men distinguish"), as he tells Horatio how much he has meant to him from that time on. He sketches a picture of Horatio's temperament and mature personality in which every word must be weighed. For reference to great personal misfortune suffered by Horatio, the play does not furnish us with any concrete instances. But for all the rest, Horatio's characterization might be taken as the paraphrase of a textbook sketch of the ideal man after the heart of the Stoic philosophers. Undoubtedly the picture fits the Horatio we see in the play in very large measure, except for the impulsive warmth that makes Horatio wish to end his life with Hamlet's in the scene of the catastrophe. But more important, it consists of traits altogether contrary to Hamlet's own, traits that are the opposite of his heady impulsiveness, his subjectivism, his emotional surrender to the situation in which he finds himself. Let us recall this dialogue in full:

Hamlet: Horatio, thou art e'en as just a man
             as e'er my conversation cop'd withal.
Horatio: O, my dear lord, —
Hamlet: Nay, do not think I flatter;
             For what advancement may I hope from thee,
             That no revenue hast but thy good spirits
             To feed and clothe thee? Why should the poor be flatter'd?
             No; let the candied tongue lick absurd pomp,
             And crook the pregnant hinges of the knee
             Where thrift may follow fawning. Dost thou hear?
             Since my dear soul was mistress of her choice
             And could of men distinguish, her election
             Hath seal'd thee for herself; for thou hast been
             As one, in suffering all, that suffers nothing,
             A man that fortune's buffets and rewards
             Hast ta'en with equal thanks; and bless'd are those
             Whose blood and judgment are so well comingled
             That they are not a pipe for fortune's finger
             To sound what stop she please. Give me that man
             That is not passion's slave, and I will wear him
             In my heart's core, ay, in my heart of heart,
             As I do thee. (III,2)

This passage, delivered with extreme emotion — it contains six run-on lines with full or major stops in the middle of the verse — this delayed piece of exposition, is the key to the tone with which Hamlet greets Horatio when he first lays eyes on him at Elsinore (I,2). When Horatio enters with Marcellus and Bernardo, immediately after Hamlet's first brooding soliloquy ("O that this too too solid flesh would melt"), Horatio offers the formal salutation, "Hail to your lordship!" Hamlet, not quite disengaged from his brooding, counters with an indifferent, "I am glad to see you well," before recognizing the identity of his visitor. Then, with a shout of incredulous joyful surprise, he exclaims: "Horatio! or I do forget myself." Horatio confirms it, with an obeisance to the prince: "The same, my lord, and your poor servant ever." Hamlet protests against such deference in his rejoinder: "Sir, my good friend; I'll change *that* name with you." (Italics mine.) Before exchanging courtesies with the two guards, Hamlet continues: "And what make you from Wittenberg, Horatio?"

repeating, a moment later, not yet mastering his surprise: "But what, in faith, make you from Wittenberg?" To Horatio's response of non-committal pleasantry, "A truant disposition, good my lord," Hamlet replies with impetuous warmth, revealing his admiration of Horatio's character:

> I would not hear your enemy say so,
> Nor shall you do mine ear that violence,
> To make it truster of your own report
> Against yourself; I know you are no truant.

Returning to the question: "But what is your affair in Elsinore?" he adds meaningfully: "We'll teach you to drink deep ere you depart." This last remark is an attempt, by way of irony involving a slur against Claudius, to establish an understanding between the virtuous man of moderation and himself, his emulator. In the exchange that follows, Hamlet reveals the depth of his grief without reserve:

Horatio: My lord, I came to see your father's funeral.
Hamlet: I prithee, do not mock me, fellow-student.
               I think it was to see my mother's wedding.
Horatio: Indeed, my lord, it follow'd hard upon.
Hamlet: Thrift, thrift, Horatio! the funeral bak'd meats
               Did coldly furnish forth the marriage tables.
               Would I had met my dearest foe in heaven
               Or ever I had seen that day, Horatio!

As Hamlet now launches into praise of his dead father, Horatio finds the cue to bring up the subject of his visit, the ghostly apparition that has haunted the platform of the watch three nights. Horatio's full account and Hamlet's intense cross-questioning contribute nothing essential to our further understanding of Hamlet's and Horatio's relation.

The case is very different, however, that night, when Hamlet, Horatio, and Marcellus keep the watch in expectation of another visit from the ghost. The scene preliminary to the ghost's renewed appearance commands our most attentive scrutiny. The sound of kettle-drum and trumpet is heard. Horatio, not brought up at the Danish court and a stranger to its customs, not a frequenter of the court even during this visit to his homeland, for Hamlet would unfailingly have spotted him during these weeks — Horatio inquires about the noise, and Hamlet informs him in a long speech of its significance. In this speech Hamlet is at pains to underscore his distaste of insobriety and noisy revelry, this, to cement his bond with the like-minded friend he is wooing. He is unaware, we surmise, that the strictures aimed at his uncle also apply to the regime of his father. We get the impression that nothing essential has changed with the new king's accession. Indeed, though it is not relevant to the present context, we cannot but assume that there has been no cabinet shift: Polonius undoubtedly was in charge of all high state matters and enjoyed old Hamlet's confidence. The passage explaining and condemning the revelry reads as follows:

Hamlet: The king doth wake to-night and takes his rouse,
Keeps wassail, and the swaggering up-spring reels;
And, as he drains his draughts of Rhenish down,
The kettle-drum and trumpet thus bray out
The triumph of his pledge.

Horatio: Is it a custom?

Hamlet: Ay marry, is't:
But to my mind, though I am native here
And to the manner born, it is a custom
More honor'd in the breach than the observance.
This heavy-headed revel east and west
Makes us traduc'd and tax'd of other nations;
They clepe us drunkards, and with swinish phrase
Soil our addition; and indeed it takes
From our achievements, though perform'd at height,
The pith and marrow of our attribute. (I,4)

But now, having delivered himself on the subject of his countrymen's national vice as the one spot on their otherwise shining armor, he goes on, pausing only to take breath, to develop an analogical situation in the lives of individuals. He makes sweeping generalizations, purporting to be gleaned from long and close observation of men, having the flavor of wisdom distilled by the sage. This speech of Hamlet's is remarkable on many grounds apart from its contents. Its formal structure lifts it out of the context of the scene. There is nothing like it, in fact, to be found anywhere else in the play. It is a single periodic sentence of thirteen and a half lines, holding off in the determination of its aim to the penultimate line bringing the predicate. This sentence, full of mazes, variational repetitions, concessive restrictions, pauses that allow the speaker to dwell on the ground already covered and to poise himself for the task still to be mastered, is a marvel of rhetorical artifice, almost incredible as an improvisation. It is calm, judicious, balanced, dispassionate. The distribution of the breath is under full control. The lines, despite their labyrinthine twists, flow along smoothly as natural units, with only one major pause in the middle of the eighth line, that is, right in the midpoint of the whole sustained utterance. It represents a rhetorical gymnast's feat of highest excellence. Let us follow it in its tortuous but unerring course:

> So, oft it chances in particular men,
> That for some vicious mole of nature in them,
> As, in their birth, (wherein they are not guilty,
> Since nature cannot choose his origin),
> By the o'ergrowth of some complexion,
> Oft breaking down the pales and forts of reason,
> Or by some habit that too much o'er-leavens
> The form of plausive manners; that these men,
> Carrying, I say, the stamp of one defect,
> Being nature's livery, or fortune's star,
> His virtues else, be they as pure as grace,
> As infinite as man may undergo,
> Shall in the general censure take corruption
> From that particular fault.

There follows a two and a half line coda of metaphor to sum up the elaboration tersely.

Let us remember the circumstances of this unique discourse. Hamlet is keyed up to a high pitch of excitement, in expectation of the apparition. He is awaiting the portent in the company of the man whom he adores as the ideal of moral mastery and whose friendship his soul yearns for. The ardor of his desire supplies him with the power to hold his own impulsive, passionate temperament in close tether, to speak as though Horatio's just and imperturbable temperament inspired his words. It is a speech to woo the listener by a supreme act of empathy into the mode of his mind. In this act, the form of sober, unerringly controlled gravity is of infinitely greater weight than the sententious content. [But we are not finished.] The degree of inner control governing the performance shows a strength of will in the envisaging and attaining of the projected goal that marks this supreme moment as different from all that follows. Up to this point the integrity of Hamlet's will is unbroken, despite the lacerating grief of his bereavement and shock. After the apparition and its dire communication and more dire mandate, Hamlet's will is broken. His personality is fragmented, never to be made whole again.

There is one more aspect about this speech, not to be overlooked. Picturing, as it does, the disintegration of a fine personality as the result of "one defect," one flaw in its composition, it is a cunning instance of tragic irony: the speaker unwittingly traces the course of his own doomed existence.

Some readers may protest that it is inadmissible to read into a Shakespearean speech all the implications warranted in the dialog of naturalistic drama. I repeat, this speech is keyed in a tone that sets it apart from the body of the play. As a fully controlled utterance, inspired by high emotion and a noble aim, it has a loftiness and significance that none of Hamlet's famous subsequent soliloquies can in any way approach.

In the interest of coherent presentation it seems best to trace the development of Hamlet's and Horatio's relation through the play without interruption. This cannot be done, to be sure, without certain assumptions that must be verified at a later point in my essay. I refer to the state of Hamlet's personality. After the apparition of the ghost with its dire communication and more dire mandate, Hamlet is stricken. He announces that it may suit his purposes to put on a show of erratic behavior. But, aside from his acting the madman, he is actually unstrung, unhinged, deranged. His personality disintegrates. In his own conduct he has lost his awareness of moral responsibility. He is a law unto himself. He has become psychotic, unpredictable in a way that shows he has lost the normal sense of the relative weight of things. Trifles assume for him an enormous importance, and enormities are dismissed by him as trifles. His state of mind is such that the safety of society would require his confinement in a mental institution, if death did not interpose as his deliverer.

From the time of their night on the watch together, Hamlet and Horatio are close friends. Hamlet has told Horatio all about the ghost.

He has also told Horatio that he has regarded him as his lodestar
since their student days. On the night when he proposes to put his
uncle's guilt to an objective test by the performance of a play depict-
ing an analogous murder, he enjoins Horatio to keep closest watch on
King Claudius' reaction. The King's call for lights and his abrupt departure do not, as a matter of fact, furnish any objective proof. The
sense of outrage by so blatant an insinuation might have caused even
an innocent king to lose his self-control. After the breaking-off of the
performance Hamlet does not see Horatio again until the day of the
catastrophe. We see the two friends first in the churchyard, where Hamlet amuses himself with matching his wits with the gravedigger and
with speculating very concretely on the transience of human ambition and human greatness. Horatio remains very much in the background during all this. Only when Hamlet says, "Why may not imagination trace the noble dust of Alexander till 'a find it stopping a
bunghole?" Horatio tries to put a damper on his macabre musings by
the reply: "Twere to consider too curiously, to consider so." Then,
observing the mourners at Ophelia's funeral and Laertes' wild abandonment to his grief, Hamlet leaps into the grave after Laertes in a
towering fit of passion that makes mockery of Laertes by escalating
the brother's hyperboles to new dimensions. After the two men,
grappling with each other in the grave, have been parted by the inter-
vention of attendants, Hamlet's fit has just as suddenly left him. He
leaves the stage, muttering incoherent remarks, and Horatio is sent
out to look after him.

The next scene, again showing Hamlet and Horatio, brings what
we expected to hear in the scene preceding. This was their second
meeting since Hamlet's return to Elsinore. Horatio had been prepared,
by Hamlet's letter, to hear some highly interesting things regarding
the beginning of Hamlet's voyage to England with Rosencrantz and
Guildenstern. But not a word of this in the graveyard, just whimsical
speculations on matters not of immediate personal concern. Why did
Horatio restrain his curiosity? Did he sense that Hamlet was not in a
state of mind for coherent personal communication? (The report of
Polonius' murder after their last evening together must have shocked
him.) Or did he feel it indelicate to prod the prince with questions?
We do not know. Some critics think that the sequence of the scenes

was tampered with; but if so, another change of scene would have been required after the graveyard scene to shape things up for the catastrophe. Leaving the scenes as they are, I find in their order additional evidence of a Hamlet become unpredictable.

Hamlet begins the story of how he found and read his uncle's sealed commission, consigning him to instant execution, and how he substituted and sealed a forged order in its place, commanding the execution of his uncle's ambassadors "not shriving-time allow'd," with the confession that it was in response to a rash impulse of curiosity. Generalizing in his wonted vein, he observed:

> And prais'd be rashness for it (let us know,
> Our indiscretion sometimes serves us well
> When our deep plots do pall. . . .)

Obviously the thought of the rash rapier pass through the arras flits through his mind and presumably that of Horatio as he listens. Was it a crime to have killed Polonius on sudden impulse? Oh no. To his mother he had made a casual expression of repentance (referring to the victim's identity rather than to the act) but he had added: "heaven hath pleas'd it so, / To punish me with this, and this with me, / That I must be their scourge and minister." In other words, he had been only an executive organ of Providence. In the same way now, in beginning the report of his cunning scheme, he lays its success to Providence:

> There's a divinity that shapes our ends,
> Rough-hew them how we will.

Horatio agrees to this general sentiment and then hears Hamlet unfold his tale and dwell on its hazards. Hamlet finds further proof of a special providential guidance in the execution of the scheme in the fact that he carried his father's seal. This type of reasoning may still be heard in many pulpits any Sunday, when some signal fortune or misfortune befalls that meets with the preacher's approval. It is surely a psychotic's (a paranoiac's) reasoning when it concerns not only the murder of two men (totally innocent of malice), but beyond that, the consigning of their souls to hell. Hamlet, no longer just an emissary of divine justice, plays at being God. The psychology of the cunning trick is clear beyond a doubt. The murder and consigning to

hell of Rosencrantz and Guildenstern is a symbolic substitution for
meting out that fate to his uncle. We can see him gloat in the telling
of it, and he evidently looks for a gleam in his friend's eye that spells
"Bravo!" But this expectation finds no echo in Horatio's tersely factual comment: "So Guildenstern and Rosencrantz go to 't." Hamlet's
rejoinder shows that he detected a tone of incredulous surprise, or
a reproach, in Horatio's summation. He flares up:

> Why, man, they did make love to this employment;
> They are not near my conscience. Their defeat
> Does by their own insinuation grow.
> 'Tis dangerous when the baser nature comes
> Between the pass and fell-incensed points
> Of mighty opposites.

The last sentence shows Hamlet shifting, in his defense, from the
moral issue to that of mere wordly status: these two are not VIPs.
They are expendable pawns in a game of two master players.

Again, instead of approval, Horatio utters only the noncommittal
exclamation: "Why, what a king is this!" This drives Hamlet into a
fit of hysterical frenzy. He becomes incoherent:

> Does it not, think thee, stand me now upon?
> He that hath kill'd my king and whor'd my mother,
> Popp'd in between th' election and my hopes,
> Thrown out his angle for my proper life,
> And with such cozenage — is 't not perfect conscience
> To quit him with this arm? and is 't not to be damn'd
> To let this canker of our nature come
> in further evil?

Once more Horatio's answer confines itself to a purely factual observation: "It must be shortly known to him from England what is the
issue of the business there." In other words: If you plan to see this
thing through, you have no time to lose. And, indeed, the return embassy from England arrives on that very day. Horatio neither encourages
nor discourages Hamlet. His wholly noncommittal responses throughout the scene certainly justify the conclusion that he is deeply
shocked and warrant the inference that he is skeptical of Hamlet's
resolution and apprehensive as to the disclosure of Hamlet's treachery.
Hamlet reaffirms his resolve, then changes the subject and expresses

his regret for having offended Laertes. But, characteristically enough, he does not arrive at a perception of Laertes' state of mind by way of natural sympathy, but rather by a process of reflection. This, too, seems to indicate that Hamlet's imagination as concerns his fellow men is deranged. It is as though some basic stabilizer or governor in his psychic machinery were no longer functioning.

With the arrival of Osric a radical change of mood sets in. The young courtier, come to report about the wager, obviously shows extreme affectation in dress, manners, and speech. But Hamlet's negative response to his person is cruel beyond anything we have seen. His withering contempt for Osric and his ilk is addressed not to him, but to his friend Horatio, in Osric's presence, as if he were an inanimate thing of no consequence whatever. The fencing match, however, does interest him, and he sends back his acceptance.

The two friends resume their dialog and Hamlet confesses to a misgiving that he cannot define. He brushes it aside with a confession to a belief in fatalism, a tranquil resignation to the guidance of events in the face of all the missteps that have brought him no nearer to the fulfilment of his mandate. "The readiness is all," sums up his state of mind. It has the ring of docile passivity, as believing his destiny to be shaped by higher powers beyond his control — fine words again, but issuing, in this concrete situation, from apathy and indifference.

The reconciliation scene with Laertes, preceding the match, is one of the strangest in this weird psychological drama. As though Hamlet were a marionette, he lets his uncle, the man he loathes like hell, touch him and put his hand into that of Laertes. Then Hamlet, speaking of himself in the third person, offers a bland apology to the man whose father he has baited, murdered, and made the butt of macabre jesting after his death and whose sister went mad and drowned on his account. A few words, uttered with apparent frankness, are to serve as an equivalent cancelling out these terrible injuries. These things must not be charged to Hamlet, he says, but to his madness. How strange that his madness should serve him as a ready excuse on this occasion, when he had never admitted to being mad. His simulated madness had served a variety of purposes: to disembarrass himself of Ophelia where the maze of his personal situation left him with no surplus energy to devote to the cultivation of amorous sentiments (I believe); to offset the emotional pressure of the mandate by throwing off the restraint of convention and indulging in any impropriety that came to mind; to put the court at sixes and sevens and to blight his uncle's life with a vague uneasiness. But to Rosencrantz and Guildenstern he had hinted that his madness was feigned, and by the example of the recorder, the next night, he had demonstrated to them, that his behavior was governed by a secret which he resented their attempts to pry into. Speaking daggers to his mother, he had protested to her that he was sane and offered to prove it by repeating his castigations. He had dared her to betray him by letting on to his uncle that his madness was only put on. There is no passage in the play to make us believe that Hamlet ever wavered in the assumption of his own sanity. Is it not frightening, then, to hear him placate Laertes with the excuse of insanity — frightening to think that Hamlet's judgment should allow him to conceive of Laertes as genuinely reconciled by the apology; frightening to think that a man should resort to such an excuse for the purpose of removing an obstacle to a fencing match on which he has his heart set at the moment to the exclusion of all other considerations? If Hamlet could be judged by the standards applying to a sane man, we would have to call his apology a perfidious lie, casually put forward as the condition for the gratification of a whim — the curiosity to find out how close he comes to matching Laertes' skill as a fencer. But the fact is that Hamlet's moral fiber has so radically disintegrated that, instead of judging, we can only pity him. When all is over, and the dying cover the stage, Horatio's outcry, "Now cracks a noble heart," and his desire to join his friend in death bares the depth of his grief, he is prostrated by his consciousness of the chain of events that has reduced a youth of infinitely rich endowment to an irretrievably psychotic wreck, a person so tortured, deranged, morally destroyed by the vicissitude of fate that his death can be felt only as heart-rending welcome release from an insupportable burden. Compassion for Hamlet, the victim of an ineluctable fate, is the upshot of this tragedy. Death as the ultimate deliverer provides the only element of reconciliation.

In tracing out Hamlet's relation to his one staunch friend, Horatio, the only relation that gives a thread of continuity to an otherwise wholly fragmented development, I have anticipated much that requires filling in to complete the picture.

To some readers Hamlet's mother fixation might have sufficed to bring about the total disintegration of his personality. The adolescent's pathological interest in his mother whose sex life fills him with desires that he cannot acknowledge to himself on the rational moral level — the "bad dreams" that haunt him — indeed play an enormous part in that whole tormenting relationship. And Ernest Jones' explanation that Hamlet cannot kill his uncle because, in a deep-down layer of his self, he identifies with him, cannot be dismissed as an idle speculation.

But there is the ghost. The ghost is built into the tragedy of *Hamlet* as an objective entity, and no interpretation of the drama can afford to ignore it. That Shakespeare, presumably a freethinker, took over the ghost, along with the traditional plot, as the prime mover of his most involved psychological tragedy is puzzling. The ghosts and other supernatural manifestations in Shakespeare's other tragedies, in *Richard the Third, Macbeth, Julius Caesar,* and *Antony and Cleopatra,* are of secondary importance and of a different quality. Shakespeare wrote his tragedies for audiences that believed in ghosts. They might not have found it difficult to find the appearance of the ghost of Hamlet's father credible. But as to himself, Shakespeare, it may have required a very special effort of the imagination to project this apparition as the prime mover of the wholesale catastrophe. Horatio, skeptical at the outset despite his acceptance of portents as reported by history, is overwhelmed by what he sees. When the ghost reappears during his watch with Hamlet and Marcellus on the platform, when it beckons Hamlet to follow him, Horatio, affrighted, tries most earnestly to dissuade Hamlet from following:

> What if it tempt you toward the flood, my lord,
> Or to the dreadful summit of the cliff
> That beetles o'er his base into the sea,
> And there assume some other horrible form,
> Which might deprive your sovereignty of reason
> And draw you into madness?

Prolonged exposure to the aura of the ghost (familiar to us in the analog of lethal radiation) might be thought of as destructive of sanity or tending in that direction, as Horatio warns. Hamlet's courage and idealism in the face of the warning are extraordinary:

> Why, what should be the fear?
> I do not set my life at a pin's fee;
> And for my soul, what can it do to that,
> Being a thing immortal as itself?

But after he has heard the dire message and the duty laid upon himself, he is a changed man. He vows to make himself the instrument of the mandate to the exclusion of all else, but even in doing so, his thoughts stray to his mother whom he has been enjoined not to taint his mind against and to leave to heaven and to her own conscience. And the realization that the mandate of revenge gives to his life a totally new orientation, abruptly shattering his projected life of serene contemplation and the cultivation of philosophic virtue, must have struck him with elemental force. The obligation imposed and automatically accepted and the natural bent of his inclination are irreconcilably at variance. When the shouts of Horatio and Marcellus rouse him, he is first a prey to indecision. Then, holding back the communication that is already on his tongue, he has a seizure. The wild humor of his shouting and dancing about, as he swears his companions to secrecy, shows that he is beside himself; and the realization of this, as he calms down, fills him, I believe, with a foreboding of similar attacks and makes him resolve to resort to simulated derangement in order to cover up similar fits in the future.

Even without the mandate that breaks his life in two Hamlet's life would have taken a course far different from what he had imagined as he pored over his books of serene philosophical wisdom. He was too young to know the force of his impulsive temperament. His mobile, tender emotionalism revealed itself in his outcry, "Alas, poor ghost," followed by the ghost's stern, "Pity me not," and the order to focus his thoughts on revenge. He was not born to realize the image of the "just" man that he saw in Horatio. He responded to situations with extreme passionateness as shown in his first soliloquy after the reception at court, before Horatio broke to him the news of the ghost's appearance. That soliloquy had seethed with hatred of his uncle and indignation against his mother, couched in hyperbole.

The image of his father as contrasted with his uncle was to him as "Hyperion to a satyr," anticipating the later castigation of his mother, when he conjoins the majesty of Hyperion, Jove, Mars, and Mercury in portraying his father and finds his uncle to incorporate "not twentieth part the tithe" of his excellence. This caricatures the situation. Except for the one black deed, unknown to the world, King Claudius compares favorably with most of the kings that we find in Shakespeare's tragedies and histories. We must think of him as a handsome man with a commanding presence. His words are kingly, spoken with poise and assurance. His way of feasting merely continues the tradition that prevailed during the reign of Hamlet's father. He is a man of energy, as shown by the intense preparations to head off an expected invasion and by his embassy to Norway. He is possessed of wisdom and moderation, as shown by his permission to young Fortinbras to spend his energies in a campaign against a common neighbor that had given trouble to Denmark. He has no sinister designs against Hamlet until Hamlet has given unmistakable evidence of a desire to destroy his person: he acts in self-defense with that self-evident exercise of power to which Shakespeare's image of all the English kings has accustomed us. When Laertes storms into his presence at the head of rebels intent on killing him and seizing the crown, he displays a coolness and majesty worthy of the best kingly tradition. "Let him go, Gertrude," he says to the Queen who has clutched Laertes' wrist:

> . . . do not fear our person:
> There's such divinity doth hedge a king,
> That treason can but peep to what it would,
> Acts little of his will.   (IV,5)

Later, in hatching his plot with Laertes, he dwells with sententious wisdom on the power of time to blunt the keen edge of purpose, echoing, as it were, Hamlet's own reflection put into the mouth of the player king, "Purpose is but the slave to memory":

> Not that I think you did not love your father,
> But that I know love is begun by time,
> And that I see, in passages of proof,
> Time qualifies the spark and fire of it.
> There lives within the very flame of love

> A kind of wick or snuff that will abate it;
>   . . . That we would do,
> We should do when we would, for this "would" changes,
> And hath abatements and delays as many
> As there are tongues, are hands, are accidents;
> And then this "should" is like a spendthrift's sigh,
> That hurts by easing.   (IV,7)

This king, with his one heinous deed, his insincere attempt at repentance, and his fine qualities of statecraft and representation, may strike us as something of a puppet but not as what Hamlet sees him. But Hamlet sees below the surface into the heart of things, Schopenhauer would have us believe. However, a fair reading of Shakespeare's text tells us only that Hamlet sees his uncle with the eye of hate and jealousy, as the man who enjoys his mother's intimacy. Far from being "just," Hamlet is "passion's slave," "his blood and judgment" are not "well co-mingled."

We have seen that Hamlet is subjective in his appraisal of his uncle. But all his relations have this coloring. Hamlet is a subjectivist by disposition, and when he begins to crack he raises subjectivism to a cult. Although he had reproved his mother for applying the word "seem" to his mourning, in the state assembly, the word "seem" turns up in his soliloquy immediately after:

> How weary, stale, flat, and unprofitable
> Seem to me all the uses of this world.

After he has abandoned himself to the irresponsible behavior and wanton insolence of his simulated madness, he tells Rosencrantz and Guildenstern, "There is nothing either good or bad, but thinking makes it so," and "This goodly frame, the earth, seems to me a sterile promontory; . . . this brave o'erhanging firmament, this majestical roof fretted with golden fire, why, it appeareth nothing to me but a foul and pestilent congregation of vapors." (II,2) The very form of his discourse shows that he is deliberately imposing the color of his particular unhappy situation upon the whole world. It is an emotional protest doing violence to his own reason. This wilful discoloration is, of course, a symptom of mental derangement.

In an earlier part of this essay I touched upon Hamlet's changed relation to Ophelia. He puts on an act of madness in her presence, but it derives, I believe, from a sense of desperate forlornness. With the mandate of revenge imposed on him, he cannot afford to pursue the cult of a tender passion. Projecting himself as stained with the blood of his mother's second husband, his future is blank. This gives him license to wallow in masochistic and sadistic cruelty. His own relation to Ophelia being destroyed, he is indifferent as to what becomes of her person. It might be inferred, of course, that her obedience to her father's injunction against giving him free access to her person had turned him against her. But the general evidence seems rather to point to a wilful abandonment of his relation to her, as part of his morbid negativism.

Hamlet's cult of subjectivism shows up most clearly in his treatment of the two "lads" who had been his most intimate companions before he left for the university. There is a tone of genuine warmth on both sides, during their first meeting, but this gives way very soon to a pathological suspiciousness on Hamlet's part, turning within the next twenty-four hours to intense malevolent hate. Critics, Goethe and Gundolf among them, have wholly disregarded the situation, choosing to see them through Hamlet's eyes as a pair of sycophants on which no sympathy is to be wasted. But there is not a shred of evidence to accuse them of bad faith toward Hamlet or to make us assume that they know the real nature of the sealed commission which they were instructed to present to the English king. Having been forewarned of Hamlet's madness, they could not but treat him with circumspection. Probably their names, traditionally Scandinavian, but sounding slightly funny to non-Scandinavians, and the coupling of their names in an amusing jingle,

> Thanks, Rosencrantz and gentle Guildenstern,
> Thanks, Guildenstern and gentle Rosencrantz,

is in part responsible. (The other pair of ambassadors, Cornelius and Voltimand, whose names do not lend themselves to lilting substitution, fared better.) On board ship, Hamlet has completely identified the ambassadors with him who sent them. As remarked above, his sending them to their doom unshriven is a symbolic substitute gratification of his vengeance. At the same time he must have gloated at the thought of the effect the return embassy, announcing the

fulfilment of his order, would have on his uncle. The diabolical
cunning of the plot has outraged the feelings of all readers who persist in salvaging Hamlet's nobility even in his madness. It did not fit
into Goethe's (Wilhelm Meister's) conception of Hamlet as "ein
höchst moralisches Wesen" (a man of highest moral integrity), and
in his reworking of the concluding acts in the interest, apparently,
of greater scenic compactness, he omits the whole episode. Gerhart
Hauptmann protests: Shakespeare cannot have written this episode.
This trick is too low for so noble a hero to stoop to.

In contrast to the diabolical scheming that eventuates in the
execution of Rosencrantz and Guildenstern – Hamlet's brain had
begun to work on this countermove before he left his mother's
chamber – the killing of Polonius was the work of a momentary
impulse. It had more the character of an event than of a deed (and
the same applies to Hamlet's killing of Claudius at the end). But this
killing, too, was performed as a symbolic substitute for the deed he
could not bring himself to accomplish. Hamlet, discovering that it
was Polonius, says: "I took thee for thy better." But can we believe
him? From his uncle, left kneeling, he had gone straight to his
mother's apartment. There would have been no physical possibility
for the king to steal in and eavesdrop. A sane man in Hamlet's place
could never have believed that it was the king he had killed. The
ever-present wish had governed his thrust, but he falsifies the scene
by making the wish appear to himself as a motive. This, to be sure,
is to apply the standards of sanity to a man whose mental unbalance
had gone very far. Insofar as Hamlet was insane, he may not have
been aware of the neat trick of transforming a wish into a motive.
In the castigation of his mother that follows, Hamlet most earnestly
asserts, to be sure, that it is not madness that governs his words. And
as regards his mother's transgression, he sees it in terms of those conventional standards of morality which have lost their validity for his
own wholly autonomous conduct. Himself now a man beyond good
and evil, a mere unhappy instrument of Providence, he lectures his
mother on the enormity of her crime. Then, in a sudden, wild shift
of mood, he dwells in a riot of riddling figures on imagery of filthy
cohabitation with counter-suggestive intent.

From all this there emerges a picture of Hamlet as an adolescent, who, burdened with a mandate that spells the ruination of his life regardless of whether he obeys or not, seeks escape from the storming of his brain in simulated madness, in a wilful flaunting of all standards of decent behavior, but who, in doing so, falls victim to forces within him that bring about the total disintegration of his moral personality. It is a gradual process. The simulated incoherence in his baiting of the senile Polonius affords Hamlet a grim amusement. He derives a much deeper satisfaction from the insolence of his behavior toward his uncle, licenced by the transparent mask. In his contacts with the players, on the other hand, he is not only warm, affable, free and easy, but it is as if he had forgotten all about his personal troubles. This is because the players offer an escape from reality. They are not persons in the everyday sense but impersonators of roles in a world of make-believe. In the impassioned eulogy addressed to Horatio, he struggles to cope with these disharmonious tensions of his own temperament. There we see Hamlet once more for a moment in the transfiguring aura of his youthful idealism. From that point on we follow with much pity and more amazement the total disintegration of his moral personality. The amazement regards the puzzling phases of the transformation that make Hamlet more and more immune to the motivation of common humanity. This, I think, is what T.S. Eliot has in mind with his somewhat cryptic phrase of the "objective correlative" that we miss in Hamlet in contrast to Shakespeare's other tragic personalities.

As I said above, all the philosophers notwithstanding, Goethe, Hegel and his school, Schopenhauer and Nietzsche, there is no reconciliation in the tragedy of *Hamlet* unless we find it in the abiding loyalty and heartbreaking compassion of the one friend, Horatio, the only one in the know as to the whole cycle of Hamlet's glorious promise and his disastrous disintegration.

4.
EIN BRIEF: GOETHES CUPIDO–GEDICHT

Lieber Heinrich, zu einem "Beitrag" langt es nicht mehr. Wenn mir aber in der Festschrift*, die Dir die Achtung und Zuneigung Deiner Schüler und Kollegen auf sichtbare Weise gewährleistet, ein Eckchen eingeräumt wird, so gestatte, daß ich Dich vor den Kessel führe, in dem ich rühre, und Dir ein Stückchen zeige, das obenauf schwimmt. Das Rühren im Kessel hängt damit zusammen, daß ich mir in langen Abständen die Hauptmasse von Kurt Eisslers zweibändigem Wälzer, *Goethe, A Psychoanalytic Study*, habe vorlesen lassen. Meine Einstellung zu einzelnen Partien schwankt zwischen fast ehrfürchtiger Bewunderung tiefer Einsicht und Weisheit und verärgerter Ablehnung einer bis auf die Spitze getriebenen doktrinären Algebra und Zahlensymbolik. Sein überragendes Wissen in Sachen der Goethephilologie steht außer Frage, aber zu einem zusammenfassenden Urteil fehlt mir der Überblick.

Laß mich Dir ein wenig von einem Gegenstand erzählen, der mich schon lange innerlich beschäftigt und der Dir gut vertraut ist. Versetzen wir uns in die Zeit von Goethes zweitem Römischen Aufenthalt, der vom Juni 1787 bis durch den April 1788 dauerte. Wie Du weißt, hat Goethe dieses Stück seines Lebens im dritten Teil seiner *Italienischen Reise* behandelt. Er hat sich bei der Abfassung auf zahlreiche Briefe gestützt, die er nach Fertigstellung seiner Arbeit größtenteils vernichtet hat. Geschrieben aber hat er diesen Teil erst im Jahr 1829, also mehr als 40 Jahre nach den berichteten Erlebnissen. Die *Römischen Elegien* sind, wenn auch erst nach Goethes Rückkehr nach Weimar entstanden, der dichterische Niederschlag des zweiten Römischen Aufenthalts. Dieser Aufenthalt bildet demnach die letzte Strecke von Goethes Weg zu den *Römischen Elegien*, die ein männlich-ruhiges, heiteres, sehnsuchtloses, besitzfreudiges Ethos atmen, das eine völlig neue Phase von Goethes Lebensgefühl darstellt.

---

*   für Heinrich Henel

Vieles auf dieser Wegstrecke muß uns für immer ein Geheimnis bleiben. Wir wissen aber, daß Goethe, der, laut eigenem Zeugnis, sich bis dahin in Italien von Frauen ganz ferngehalten hatte, sich diesmal in ein Liebesabenteuer verstrickt sah, und es ist gewiß, daß er bald darauf den Mut zu einem freien Verhältnis mit einer Römerin fand. Bei Gelegenheit eines mehrwöchigen Herbstaufenthaltes in Castel Gandolfo lernte Goethe eine junge Mailänderin kennen, deren "anfragendes Wesen" ihn sofort heftig entflammte. Wie es kam, daß er schon am dritten Tage, nachdem er von ihrer Verlobung erfahren hatte, den Ausdruck seiner Neigung in die Grenzen konventioneller Aufmerksamkeit zurückschraubte, erzählt er ausführlich, wenn auch nicht in allen Stücken ganz überzeugend. Daß ein Stachel sitzen blieb, ist nicht zu verkennen. Ob Eissler mit seiner These recht hat, daß Goethe bis dahin, also bis zur Mitte seines 39. Jahres, den vollen geschlechtlichen Verkehr überhaupt gemieden hatte, ist nicht mit Sicherheit auszumachen, aber vieles spricht für die Richtigkeit dieser Vermutung.

Erinnern wir uns, daß "Amor als Landschaftsmaler" und ein an Cupido gerichtetes Gedicht den ganzen unmittelbaren poetischen Ertrag von Goethes zweitem Römischen Aufenthalt ausmachen. Jeder Goethekenner, das wirst Du zugeben, wird die beiden Gedichte aus inneren Gründen in nahe Beziehung zueinander setzen. Das eine erzählt in schalkhaft allegorischer Vermummung von einem sich anspinnenden Liebesroman, oder sagen wir, von einem Schüler der Malerei, der alle Elemente der Landschaft mit den Augen der Liebe sieht. Das im Plauderton serbischer Trochäen geschriebene Gedicht gipfelt in der beglückenden Überraschung, daß das scheinbar von dem kleinen Liebesgott gemalte Mädchen aufsteht und auf den Schüler zukommt. Es schließt mit dessen Frage:

> Glaubt ihr wohl, ich sei auf meinem Felsen
> Wie ein Felsen still und fest geblieben?

Hier hat der Dichter seine betrachtende mit einer tätigen Rolle vertauscht.

Das zweite, das Cupido-Gedicht, bringt einen erschütternden Umschlag der Stimmung. Ich habe einmal in kleinem Kreise über dies Gedicht gesprochen. Da wurde mir von sich als maßgebend betrachten-der Seite vorgeworfen, ich nehme das Gedicht viel zu pathetisch. Es sei im Grunde auch nur ein im Mollton vorgetragener erotischer Scherz. Wir werden sehen. Ich sage, das Cupido-Gedicht entwickelt im Rahmen derselben mythologischen Konvention die desperat gefährlichen Folgen des fröhlich unbedacht begonnenen Abenteuers. Rücken wir uns vor allen Dingen den genauen Wortlaut des Gedichts vor Augen.

> Cupido, loser, eigensinniger Knabe,
> Du batst mich um Quartier auf einige Stunden!
> Wie viele Tag' und Nächte bist du geblieben,
> Und bist nun herrisch und Meister im Hause geworden.
>
> Von meinem breiten Lager bin ich vertrieben,
> Nun sitz' ich an der Erde, Nächte gequälet;
> Dein Mutwill' schüret Flamm' auf Flamme des Herdes,
> Verbrennet den Vorrat des Winters und senget mich Armen.
>
> Du hast mir mein Gerät verstellt und verschoben,
> Ich such' und bin wie blind und irre geworden.
> Du lärmst so ungeschickt; ich fürchte, das Seelchen
> Entflieht, um dir zu entfliehn, und räumet die Hütte.

Der kleine, anscheinend harmlose Gott ist zum Quälgeist geworden, der dem Dichter die Ruhe der Nächte und die Sammlung der Tage raubt, ja sein Leben gefährdet. Vermutlich bilden beide Gedichte den Niederschlag der so glücklich eingeleiteten und dann abrupt gestörten Bekanntschaft mit der schönen Mailänderin. Uns braucht die Frage nicht zu kümmern, inwieweit Goethe mit den Tatsachen frei geschaltet haben mag, um sie zu einem kleinen Roman umzugestalten. Aber es kann uns nicht entgehen, daß er noch im höchsten Alter mit besonderer Zartheit bei den Ereignissen verweilt. Man erinnert sich, wie Goethe bei Gelegenheit des Römischen Karnevals von einer letzten unverhofften Begegnung mit der inzwischen wieder genesenen, geliebten Person erzählt; wie er sie bei gestautem Verkehr mit Angelika Kaufmann im Wagen sitzen sieht, ein paar Worte tauscht und ihr die Hand zu einem letzten Lebewohl in den Wagen reicht. Nun erinnert man sich gleichfalls, daß Goethe das Römische Karneval schon ein Jahr nach seiner Rückkehr nach Weimar (1789) veröffentlicht hatte

und daß damals der schönen Mailänderin kein Seitenblick gelten
konnte, da der Leser nichts von ihr wußte. Man sucht und sucht, weil
das Erinnerungsbild nicht zu bannen ist. Endlich findet man die ge-
suchte Szene in dem zusammenfassenden Bericht für den Monat Februar, wo Goethe noch einmal auf Einzelheiten des Karnevals eingeht, um diesen Zug anbringen zu können.

Das ganze Gedicht ist eine Anrede an den göttlichen Knaben, Feststellung, Vorwurf und Klage über das über ihn hereingebrochene
Schicksal. Drei Strophen von gleichem Bau, mit der Apostrophe be-
ginnend; das Du und Ich in gespanntem Wechselverhältnis die drei
Strophen durchziehend. Höchst einfacher Satzbau: Nach der den ersten Vers füllenden Anrede bringt der zweite Vers eine Feststellung,
der dritte wieder eine im Ton der Ausrufung, die vierte formuliert
das Ergebnis. So geht es von Vers zu Vers weiter, jeder Vers ein selb-
ständiger Satz. Bis durch den 10. Vers wird das einfache syntaktische
Gebilde festgehalten. Nur die zwei Schlußverse weichen radikal von
diesem Schema ab. Durch Enjambement verbunden, bilden sie ein
zwar einfaches aber doch kompliziertes Satzgefüge. Es beginnt mit
einer Aussage: "Du lärmst so ungeschickt" (4 Wörter). Daran schließt
sich ein Folgesatz: "ich fürchte" (2 Wörter). Von diesem ist ein Ob-
jektsatz mit zwei Prädikaten abhängig: "das Seelchen entflieht . . .
und räumet die Hütte" (7 Wörter), wobei das erste einen Finalsatz
nach sich zieht, "um dir zu entfliehn" (4 Wörter). Der einfache syntaktische Aufbau gipfelt also in einer nicht zu überhörenden Steigerung.

Wie aber verhält es sich mit dem Bau der Strophen? Odenform als
Bezeichnung finde ich nicht zutreffend. In der deutschen Nachbildung
klassischer Odenmaße haben die einzelnen Verse der Strophe ver-
schiedene Taktzahl. Hier haben wir durchweg fünf Takte in jedem
Vers. An die Odenform erinnert das Fehlen des Reims bei strophi-
schem Bau. Prüfen wir die Verse der ersten Strophe näher, so finden
wir: Alle Verse sind fünftaktig und beginnen mit einer Vorschlag-
silbe (Auftakt). Der Gang der Takte im ersten Vers ist alternierend
bis auf den vierten Takt, der eine zweisilbige Senkung aufweist. Dieses Schema wiederholt sich in Vers zwei und drei. Der vierte Vers
aber bringt eine eigene Bewegung in den gemessenen Gang der Takte.
Hier nämlich hat nicht nur der vierte Takt zweisilbige Senkung, son-

dern der zweite und dritte Takt haben sie ebenfalls. Darauf war der Leser nicht vorbereitet. Er muß sich einen Ruck geben, um dem Rhythmus des Verses gerecht zu werden: "und bist nun herrisch und . . . ". Das "herrisch und" kommt so unerwartet, daß es eine stärkere Dynamik der Stimme verlangt, um die drei Silben überhaupt deutlich zu sprechen. Nach dem ersten, schwierigen Anlauf gerät dann der ganze Vers in Schwingung. Lese man dagegen zur Probe: "und bist nun Herr und Meister im Hause geworden," dann merkt man deutlich, was für eine explosive Wirkung die zusätzliche Silbe *isch* hervorgebracht hat. Dasselbe rhythmische Schema wiederholt sich, mit einer kleinen Abweichung, in der zweiten Strophe. Der vierte Vers bringt gleich im ersten Takt eine zweisilbige Senkung und wiederholt dies im zweiten, dritten, und vierten Takt. So bewirkt er im Versinnern eine gesteigerte Erregung. Die dritte Strophe folgt wieder genau dem Schema der ersten in der Anordnung der Takte. Wenn aber trotzdem die Wirkung der zwei letzten Verse als enorm verschieden von der entsprechenden Partie der zwei voraufgehenden Strophen empfunden wird, so ist der Grund dafür leicht einzusehen: Dort verliefen die Verse zäsurlos. Hier dagegen haben wir eine fünfmalige Hemmung des Atems. (Ich habe ein ganz klein wenig gemogelt. Der dritte Takt des letzten Verses der letzten Strophe hat nur einsilbige Senkung. Es heißt *entfliehn*, nicht *entfliehen*. Die Atempause ist an die Stelle einer zweiten Senkungssilbe getreten.)

Daß dieser Handhabung des Rhythmus ein Höchstmaß von Ausdruckswert innewohnt, scheint mir selbstverständlich, andernfalls wäre das Eingehen auf diese verstechnischen Finessen nur ein müßiges Spiel. Dies aber bringt mich zu einem Umstand, der mir dieses Gedicht brennend interessant gemacht hat. Ich hatte es mir auf Tonband vorlesen lassen und hörte es in der Folge so oft an, bis ich es ohne Anstoß nachsprechen konnte. Aber dann bekam die Sache einen Haken. Ich hatte nämlich gehört — und das war tatsächlich der Wortlaut der Textvorlage gewesen (*Goethes Gedichte in zeitlicher Folge*) —: "Du hast mir mein Geräte verstellt und verschoben." Wenn dem Rhythmus wirklich Ausdruckscharakter zukommt in dem Maße, wie ich es empfunden zu haben glaubte, wie konnte dann der Dichter, der dieses Schwingen und Pulsieren seines Bluts doch fühlen mußte, sich eine Abweichung erlauben, der ich keinen Ausdruckswert beizumessen imstande bin? Wie war das möglich? Ich konnte mich nicht damit abfinden und sagte mir: Da muß ein Fehler in der Überlieferung des Gedichts vorliegen. Es schien mir gar nicht unmöglich, daß eine spätere Abschrift von Goethes Hand das Versehen verschuldet haben könnte, aber ich bestand bei mir darauf, so kann es im Original nicht gelautet haben. Und ich habe recht behalten. Die Hamburger Ausgabe der *Italienischen Reise* schreibt "Gerät" ohne das fatale "e", und andere Ausgaben bestätigen das Resultat. Sollte ich einmal wieder nach Weimar kommen, so würde ich es mir aus der Handschrift bestätigen lassen.

Ich finde dies Gedicht so einzigartig in der Durchblutung der mythologischen Fiktion des göttlichen Knaben mit einem Leben, das nicht einen Augenblick Gefahr läuft, zur allegorischen Konvention zu verblassen. Wie reizend, dann wie herzzerreißend ist es geschildert, wie der flüchtige Besucher zum Dauergast, dann zum Quälgeist wird! Die Anschaulichkeit des verlassenen, breiten Lagers, auf dem der zappelige Junge nicht Ruhe hält; der von der Brunst des Eros Gequälte, die Nächte hindurch an der Erde sitzend, auf das flackernde Feuer starrend, das den für ein Lebensalter berechneten Vorrat an Manneskraft in einem kurzlebigen Brand zu verzehren droht; bei Tage sein Ordnungssinn aufgehoben, sein Tätigkeitsdrang lahmgelegt, so daß er befürchten muß, es gehe ihm diesmal ans Leben. Besonders schön die Koseform "Seelchen". Hier ist sie wirklich lebendig geworden, anders als damals, da er scherzend schrieb:

> Und daß die alte Schwiegermutter Weisheit
> Das zarte Seelchen ja nicht beleid'ge!

Da der Autor sich diesmal auf klassischem Boden befindet, hat das "Seelchen" vielleicht einen Abglanz von Kaiser Hadrians *animula, vagula, blandula* abbekommen.

Man empfindet das Cupido-Gedicht als das erschütternde Zeugnis einer letzten Wertherkrise, die Goethe durchmachte, unmittelbar ehe sich ihm ein ganz anders geartetes Liebesglück erschloß, die Erfüllung seines Trieblebens besitzfreudig und sehnsuchtslos in der Vereinigung mit einer römischen Partnerin. Aus den im dritten Teil der *Italienischen Reise* verwerteten Briefen geht mit Sicherheit hervor, daß sich Goethe um die Jahreswende 1788 in einem Dauerzustand

gesteigerter Erregung befand, der ihn veranlaßte, wiederholt von Ahnungen seines baldigen Todes zu sprechen. So schreibt er unterm Datum des 10. Januar, 1788: "Ich bereite mich zu meiner Auflösung,
damit ich mich ihr getrosten Mutes hingebe, wenn die Himmlischen
sie auf Ostern beschlossen haben." Solchen gelassenen Ahnungen
folgt dann im Februar ein an den Herzog gerichteter Brief, in dem er
diesem in verblümten aber völlig deutlichen Worten gesteht, daß sein
gegenwärtiges Leben die Erfahrung des geschlechtlichen Umgangs
kennt. Es versteht sich von selbst, daß die *Italienische Reise* keine
Spur einer Andeutung dieses Sachverhalts enthält. Dafür aber finden
wir unterm Datum des 14. März folgende Stelle:

> Ja ich kann sagen, daß ich die höchste Zufriedenheit meines Lebens in die-
> sen letzten acht Wochen genossen habe und nun wenigstens einen äußersten
> Punkt kenne, nach welchem ich das Thermometer meiner Existenz künftig
> abmessen kann.

Für den Leser, der Bescheid weiß, ist diese Stelle ein beredtes Zeugnis
für die heilsame Wirkung, die Goethe dem neuen Verhältnis zum
Leben verdankte.

Doch wir müssen zu dem Cupido-Gedicht zurück, das ja vor diese
Epoche fällt. Darüber gibt es noch sehr Merkwürdiges zu berichten.
Wo Goethe das Cupido-Gedicht in seinem vollen Wortlaut mitteilt —
es steht am Anfang der zusammenfassenden Partie, die über den
Monat Januar berichtet —, da folgt gleich auf die Verse ein Satz, in
dem der Autor dem Leser zumutet oder anempfiehlt, das kleine ero-
tische Gedicht symbolisch verallgemeinernd zu lesen und anstelle
des kleinen Liebesgottes sich alle erdenklichen Störungen vorzustel-
len, die die geordnete Existenz eines Menschen in Verwirrung bringen
können. Seine diesbezüglichen Worte lauten:

> Wenn man vorstehendes Liedchen nicht in buchstäblichem Sinne nehmen,
> nicht jenen Dämon, den man gewöhnlich Amor nennet, dabei denken, son-
> dern eine Versammlung tätiger Geister sich vorstellen will, die das Innerste
> des Menschen ansprechen, auffordern, hin und wider ziehen und durch ge-
> teiltes Interesse verwirren, so wird man auf eine symbolische Weise an dem
> Zustande teilnehmen, in dem ich mich befand und welchen die Auszüge aus
> Briefen und die bisherigen Erzählungen genugsam darstellen.

Mit dieser Miene des Mandarinen konnte Goethe das vor mehr als
vierzig Jahren geschriebene Gedicht dem Publikum vorlegen. Wohl-

gemerkt, er hatte es in keine Ausgabe seiner gesammelten Gedichte
bis dahin aufgenommen.

Nun aber zurück zu der Zeit, da es frisch vor ihm lag. Da freut er
sich in einer Briefstelle, daß das Liedchen den Freunden gefallen hat.
Er hatte es Herder mitgeteilt. Er nennt es sein Leiblied und sagt, es
werde in Musik gesetzt. Zu dieser Zeit ist der Frankfurter Musiker
Kayser bei ihm und komponiert die umgearbeitete Fassung des Sing-
spiels, *Claudine von Villa Bella.* Von dieser Arbeit spricht Goethe mit
großer Selbstzufriedenheit. Ja, er rühmt sich seiner Kühnheit, das
Singspiel in demselben Band mit dem Egmont drucken zu lassen. Keinem Italiener, sagt er, würde es einfallen, ein Trauerspiel zusammen
mit einem Libretto herauszugeben. Vielleicht befremdet uns die hohe
Meinung, die Goethe von seinem Singspiel hegte, das, mit Egmont
verglichen, doch nur ein Machwerk ist mit konventionellen Rollen
statt Gestalten.

Aber was hat das mit unserem Cupido-Gedicht zu tun? Vielleicht
sehr viel. Man liest in den Anmerkungen, Goethe habe den "Cupido"
dem Liederbestand der *Claudine* einverleibt. Das stimmt. Es wird von
dem verwegenen Räuberhauptmann Rugantino als Ständchen gesungen. Er verwendet es als Mittel in seinem Plan, sich der Lucinde zu
bemächtigen und sie zu entführen. Lucinde ist die Kusine der Schloß-
herrin Claudine. Aber wie? Er klimpert auf seiner Mandoline und
singt die erste Strophe. Der Gesang wird durch die Stimmen der aufmerksam gewordenen Mädchen unterbrochen. Es kommt zu einem
musikalischen Wechselgespräch mit dem Abenteurer, in dessen Verlauf das Liedchen wiederaufgenommen und schließlich zu Ende vor-
getragen wird. Wir bekommen es überhaupt nicht als zusammen-
hängendes Ganzes zu hören. Als Räuber vom Hausherrn entlarvt, ist
Rugantino skrupellos genug, Claudine als Geisel für die eigene Straf-
losigkeit mit gezücktem Dolch gefangen zu halten. Freilich zeigt sich
in der Folge, daß er der langgesuchte Bruder von Claudines Verlob-
tem ist und ein herrschaftliches Erbe zu erwarten hat. So findet das
Stück nach weiteren Komplikationen sein unvermeidliches "happy
end". Aber das Cupido-Gedicht kommt dabei um wie eine zerpflück-
te Blume. Es ist wie eine Vorwegnahme der Maxime:

> Gebt ihr ein Stück, so gebt es gleich in Stücken!
> . . . .
> Das Publikum wird es euch doch zerpflücken.

Wenn das Gedicht wirklich aus der Tiefe eines qualvollen Erlebnisses geboren ist und alles andre als einen Scherz in Rokokokostüm darstellt, wie war es möglich, daß Goethe auf den Einfall geriet, das kostbare Gebilde auf diese Weise zu verstümmeln? War es ihm vielleicht darum zu tun, sein Licht unter den Scheffel zu stellen? Machte es ihm Spaß, ein Bekenntnis in die Welt hinauszusingen, ohne daß die Leute etwas davon merkten? Man kennt die Wendung von dem "offenbaren Geheimnis", deren sich Goethe zu bedienen liebte. Steht uns in der Cupido-Einlage des *Claudine*-Singspiels ein solcher Fall vor Augen?

Dieses scheint sich zu bestätigen durch die Eintragungen Eckermanns unterm Datum vom 5. und 6. April, 1829. Die Gespräche der betreffenden Tage behandeln zuerst andre Dinge, ehe sie auf die redaktionelle Arbeit vom 3. Teil der *Italienischen Reise* und auf das Cupido-Gedicht zu sprechen kommen. Ich weiß nicht, wem ich den Hinweis auf Eckermann verdanke. Ich bin leider alles andere als Goethe-fest, und so überlasse ich es Dir, die *Gespräche* zur Hand zu nehmen und den eigentümlichen Duft und Ton zu erwittern, der das Cupido-Gedicht noch immer in Goethes Erinnerung umschwebt. Ich unterlasse es, aus den *Gesprächen* zu zitieren. Wenn Du aber beim Nachlesen darauf stößt, wie Goethe den Eckermann auf die Feinheiten des Rhythmus aufmerksam macht, dann wirst Du auch nachempfinden, welche Freude es mir gemacht hat, die Lesung "Gerät" hier als die richtige zu finden.

Ich bin zu Ende. Habe ich in dem, was ich Dir da vorgeplaudert habe, auch nur einen einzigen neuen Zug zur Sprache gebracht, auf den in der unübersehbar ausgedehnten Goetheliteratur nicht schon hingewiesen worden wäre? Ich weiß es nicht, und, abgesehen von dem schiefen Verhältnis, in das mich meine Unwissenheit gegenüber den Beiträgen versetzt, die mich polizeilich flankieren, kümmert es mich auch nicht. Wenn Goethe lebendig bleiben soll, so müssen wir, nachdem wir zuerst mit großer Mühe viel gelernt haben, eine Menge des Gelernten wieder vergessen, um das eine und andere bei günstiger Gelegenheit wieder neu für uns zu entdecken. Dabei kann man alt werden mit dem Bewußtsein, es werden in der Masse des Überlieferten, längst Durchstudierten, immer wieder frische Inseln auftauchen, uns mit dem Anblick von Neuland zu erquicken. Daß es auch Dir so geht, lange Jahre über das Ende Deiner Dienstzeit hinaus, wünscht Dir von Herzen Dein

Hermann

31. März, 1969

5.
"WANDRERS STURMLIED":
ONCE MORE WITH OBITER DICTA *

When and under whatever circumstances young Goethe may have
sat down to dash off the unpunctuated lines of "Wandrers Sturmlied"
on paper, sometime in 1772, whatever long period of incubation may
have preceded the decisive act, the poem that emerged breathes a
sense of immediacy that takes us to the heart of the creative process.[1]
We see the poet wandering through the countryside in a gusty spring
downpour of rain and sleet interspersed with an occasional glint of
sunlight, singing and shouting, athrob with a sense of life that makes
him feel kin to the elemental powers that buffet him about. He begins with a proclamation of his sense of intimacy with the powers of
nature, and this strain, continuing through the first six strophes, culminates in the twice-repeated proclamation of himself as "götter-
gleich." His mood is jubilant. It ascends to staggering heigths of euphoria and hybris.

The first line, an invocation of "Genius," "Wen du nicht verlässest, Genius," is repeated again and again with minor modifications
like a refrain, as his spirit surges. The verb that steers the keynote into an assertion, "wird," "wirst," dominates the grammatical structure

---

*   This essay is a revised version of a paper that first appeared in *Goethe-Jahr=
    buch*, 91 (1974), in German.
1   For the text of "Wandrers Sturmlied," appropriately grouped with other
    poems of Goethe's *Sturm und Drang*, I refer the reader to *Goethes Werke*,
    Hamburger Ausgabe, ed. Erich Trunz, I, 7th ed. (Hamburg, 1964), 33-36.
    Notes, some extended commentary, and a selected bibliography are found
    on pages 463-67. Recent notable additions to the bibliography would in-
    clude Gerhard Kaiser, "Das Genie und seine Götter. Ein Beitrag zu Wan-
    drers Sturmlied von Goethe," *Euphorion*, LVIII (1964), 41-58; and Hein-
    rich Henel, "Der Wandrer in der Not: Goethes 'Wandrers Sturmlied' und
    'Harzreise im Winter,' " in *Deutsche Vierteljahrsschrift*, LVII (1973),
    69-94.

four times and, despite the grammatical future, pervades the song with an abiding presence. The poem abounds in keywords that call for a perceptive ear: "entgegen," "decken," "um," "innen," "glühen," "Glut." They all recur. The first of these, "entgegen," an ambiguous word of relation, divides in English into two counterparts, toward and against. Here, in the first strophe, where it occurs as "entgegen singen," both meanings combine. There is movement toward and movement against. But the opposition, encompassed in song, is not hostile. It is the antiphonal rivalry of voices in a part-song, each striving to compete and assert itself as a cooperative element in a larger achievement. The poet is not alone in this striving. In the same sentence that invokes "Genius," he hails the lark above as a partner in this strenuous, jubilant exercise. The sense of immediacy in this gesture is complete. When we meet the word "entgegen" again, in strophe nine, as a challenge, it has the same antiphonal ring. Let us not forget this.

The second strophe, concerned with the mud and mire underfoot, begins with an image barely glimpsed. Genius will lift him over the slime with fiery wings. Is he not here thinking of the mythical winged steed, Pegasus, offspring of Poseidon and the Gorgon, hero of many adventures, associated with Parnassus, Helicon, the sacred springs and the Muses, since the Renaissance so prevalent a symbol of poetic inspiration down to Goethe's own age as to become a mere emblematic shortcut supplanting live imagery?

The second image here encountered is quite another affair. Within the sweep of one sustained rhythmic curve the poet sketches essentials of the aftermath of the Greek story of the Flood: we see Phoebus Apollo's vast figure bestriding the earth and discharging his arrows at the monster bred out of the steaming slime, and we see the poet emulating him in stance and power. But there is an element of obscurity about the utterance. The reader feels himself stumbling over detached verbal blocks, rather than skimming along the crest of a continuous wave. The poet must take the blame for this. He chopped up the one great line into six short phrases to be followed down the printed page. He followed the same practice in strophes nine and thirteen. In the present instance this leads to gross misunderstanding. Everyone falls into the trap of reading: "Wandeln wird er / Wie mit Blumenfüßen / Über Deukalions Flutschlamm." To my knowledge every commentator explains "Mit Blumenfüßen" as walking over flowers or light-footed. That is the touchstone for the universal misreading. But let us read the passage with an emphatic pause after "Wie," then more or less nonstop, and it will reveal hidden depths: "Wandeln wird er Wie: mit Blumenfüssen Über Deukalions Flutschlamm Python tötend, leicht, gross Pythius Apollo [wandelte]." "Wie" introduces a comparison, but not a literary simile comparing the poet's feet to flower-feet (whatever that may mean), but rather a comparison of the poet with the figure of Phoebus-Apollo in all his aspects. This sheds an entirely new light upon "Mit Blumenfüßen." Can we forget in the context of the universal Flood that Phoebus Apollo is not only the heavenly archer, but the sun god as well, the universal source of light, heat, and organic life? Wherever he bestrides the earth vegetation springs forth anew. Flowers spring up under his footsteps and caress his feet. Let me prove this by demonstration. (1) In this poem Phoebus Apollo is visualized as the sun god, source of life. (2) He is personified; we see him striding lightly over the mire. (3) In "Mahomets Gesang," another hymn of the same period, the movement of Islam, pictured as a mountain spring that grows to a mighty river, is also personified as a walker striding down the land to the ocean: "Städte / Werden unter seinem Fuß" (strophe 11). If it is questionable to speak of cities arising under his footstep, how natural, on the other hand, is it to speak of flowers sprouting under the sun god's footstep! (4) The condensation of the sentence into the compound "Blumenfüße" is effected without effort to form a conceit. (5) An automatic corollary of this condensation is the resulting image of the newly sprung flowers as caressing Apollo's feet. Such emotional response on the part of the flowers is not an embellishment; it is a substantial feature of the image. Summing up the present findings, we shall read: "Wandeln wird er wie . . . Apollo" and "Apollo wandelte mit Blumenfüßen."

Although I thought I knew this poem well, having been familiar with it for many years, I came upon the discovery here presented only very recently. Now, after the fact, I am aware that pressure tending toward this reading had long been building up in me by virtue of two passages in the final strophe: "Hoch flog / Siegdurchglühter / Jünglinge Peitschenknall" is a single six-beat phrase without room for the breath to pause, but is nevertheless chopped up into three lines. And the concluding part of the sentence, "Und sich Staub wälzt' / Wie vom Gebürg herab / Kieselwetter ins Tal," involves a comparison that as in the case of Apollo does not repeat the reflexive verb "sich wälzte," but implies it as clearly understood.[2] Persistent misapprehension of literary passages, such as we encounter here, is not altogether uncommon. Somewhere Nietzsche twits the Germans as being so addicted to song that they can only think of God as also singing: "So weit die deutsche Zunge klingt / Und Gott im Himmel Lieder singt." We may surely assume that Nietzsche read "God," or had the Germans read "Gott," as a nominative rather than a dative, tongue in cheek.

The slight alteration of the thematic line in strophe three to "Dem du nicht verlässest, Genius" (for *dem, den*) commits an atrocious lapse of grammar in favor of salvaging the rhythm. In this strophe the immediacy of the situation is suspended by predictive analogous reminiscences of divine tutelage. The rigors of camping out at night on a bed of rock are mitigated by the woollen pad of the wings of Genius. No one will think of these wings as detachable blankets; rather, Genius is envisioned as an angelic presence embracing the poet, sheltering him from the cold bare rock with wings tucked underneath, and protecting him against whatever dangers may lurk in the midnight grove, with guardian pinions spread out above. Seraphs, we remember, are equipped with three pairs of wings. "Decken" occurs as a term of protection against unspecified dangers. We shall meet this key word again in a most improbable context in strophe ten.

After this slight digression strophe four again alerts us to the spring tempest. It has now turned into a snow flurry. But the poet endows

---

2 I cannot help mentioning something totally irrelevant that haunted me while writing this paper. In his history of World War II (1971), the British historian, Liddell Hart, repeatedly refers to much valuable information on German plans and strategy supplied to the British after the war by General von Blumentritt. How would a general come by such a name? We can surely not think of him as Apollo's twin.

this with encompassing warmth. Note the *um*-of "umhüllen" which is soon to recur several times. There is an aura of warmth about him that attracts the Muses and the Graces and makes us think of the dance of summer insects around a moving object. Sensing their presence, the poet apostrophizes them in strophe five to reassure them. Pointing to the elements, water and earth, and the slime as their son, he endows them with positive value as elements of a creation in which everything is good and pure. That everything is affirmed as good and pure does not, of course, imply that everything is of equal value. We shall presently see that the poet is very conscious of a hierarchy of values. Here and in the following strophe the poet's pantheistic sense of at-oneness with the totality of nature reaches its climax.[3]

There is a pause. What follows before the mood of the poem has run its course, falls into three divisions: strophes 7 to 9, strophes 10 to 12, and strophe 13. Each of these intones its specific theme with a rhetorical question. Strophe 7 introduces a specific moving object as part of the outer landscape, "Der kleine schwarze feurige Bauer."

---

3   Casual reading has turned up interesting evidence to show how one of America's distinguished men of letters, James Russell Lowell, exploited his familiarity with "Wandrers Sturmlied" to advantage. There is a covert allusion to our poem in his *Biglow Papers*, part II, 1867. Ever since the publication of the Norsemen's voyages of discovery in three languages, in 1837, American scholars and amateur archeologists had been alerted to the search for evidence, particularly in the form of runes, of traces of pre-Columbian settlements. Lowell has one of his spokesmen, Parson Wilbur, send a communication to the *Atlantic Monthly* on the subject of runes, outlining that there are three kinds; first, those understood by the Royal Society of Copenhagen; second, those understood only by its distinguished secretary; and third, those not clearly understood by any of the authorities and therefore providing a great incentive "to enucleating sagacity." Of the third class, he reports, he is in possession of a specimen found in his own pasture. This he has deciphered to read as follows: "Here Bjarna Grimolfsson first drank Cloud-brother through Child-of-Land-and-Water." This inscription Parson Wilbur interprets to mean: In this pasture the Viking Bjarna inhaled his first tobacco smoke through a reed stem. We cheer Lowell for having fashioned two fine Icelandic kennings by virtue of "Sohn des Wassers und der Erde." The story, of which I have here given a condensed version, is to be found in Samuel Eliot Morison's *The European Discovery of America: The Northern Voyages A.D. 500-1600* (New York, 1971), p. 37.

Except for the skylark he is the first living organism to impinge upon
the visionary transformation of the landscape as the poet battles the
elements, and even the reality of the skylark has been questioned. Be
that as it may, the singing skylark and the little swarthy peasant,
brimful of energy, represent a plane of reality quite distinct from
Apollo, the sungod-archer bestriding the earth, and the Muses that
dance about him enlivened by his inner warmth. The figure of the
peasant is used to draw a contrast between his simple, rugged, close-
to-the-soil life and the poet's not-so-secure, but lavishly endowed,
infinitely enriched form of existence. There is a tremor of danger, of
apprehension betrayed by the question. Its emphatic repetition and
all that follows is designed to strengthen his reassurance on the
rebound. There is a contrast not only between the limited gifts awaiting the peasant, wine and the warmth of his hearth, and the limitless
gifts awaiting the poet, but also a subtle play of words involved in
the phrasing of their expectation. The peasant expects, awaits his
gifts; in the case of the poet, all the bounties of life are ranged about,
awaiting him. They are personified. They look forward to meeting
him in a joyous throng. The repeated use of *um* relative to the throng
encircling the poet is particularly notable.

   This strophe has invoked the wine god, Father Bromius, in association with the peasant. The name is Greek, and in the Roman tradition, which identified him with an old Italic divinity, he was commonly addressed as *Pater*, Father. Bromius, like Pater Liber, is only
one of his many names. In the age of Goethe almost everything
Greek was filtered through Roman tradition. Addressing him as
Father suggests a relation of affectionate intimacy. To replace the
name Bromius, which Goethe certainly encountered in Ovid's *Meta-
morphoses*, as pointed out by Arthur Henkel,[4] with Dionysus, as
some commentators of our poem have done, including Trunz,[5] only
leads to confusion. Thanks to Nietzsche, for a century it has been impossible to think of Dionysus without evoking the image of Apollo as

---

4   See Arthur Henkel, "Versuch über 'Wandrers Sturmlied,' " in *Die Gegenwart
    der Griechen im neueren Denken. Festschrift für Hans-Georg Gadamer zum
    60. Geburtstag* (Tübingen, 1960), pp. 59-76.
5   Erich Trunz, "Anmerkungen" to *Goethes Werke*, I, 464-65.

his dialectical counterpart, both of them members of a schematic ideology, in which Apollo stands for reason, consciousness, clarity, dialectics, individuation, whereas Dionysus is the god of the dark, subconscious, irrational, terribly eruptive creative powers, the god of divine frenzy and mass madness. There is absolutely nothing to warrant Goethe as having conceived of the god in these terms. In our poem the wine god is seen as a deity of subordinate rank. "Nur deine Gaben" stresses his limits and disqualifies him from the outset from participating in the highest values.

The eighth strophe invokes Father Bromius a second time in an atmosphere of strictures. Addressing him as the Genius of this age, "Jahrhunderts Genius," the poet disparages the age for contenting itself with the wine god as the symbol of its highest aspirations.[6] Now the time has come for our poet to reveal the source of his own inspired singing. It is Pindar, the most celebrated of the singers who immortalized the festival games of the Greeks in honor of their gods. Two letters to Herder of the year 1772 attest Goethe's boundless admiration for Pindar, and our poem, in both its free form and its rhapsodic content, obviously attempts to emulate the glow of inspiration, compared with which everything modern strikes him as tepid. What our modern poets try to achieve by an infusion of wine from

---

6   "Vater Bromius / Du bist Genius / Jahrhunderts Genius. . . ." More likely than not, this second, ill-tempered invocation of Vater Bromius was induced by a literary reminiscence lying very close at hand. In 1771, one year before the writing of "Wandrers Sturmlied," Wieland had published *Der Neue Amadis*, that mini-pornographic, mock-heroic, infinitely tedious epic, an exercise of lavish wit and ingenuity upon a wholly unworthy subject. In canto 13, strophe 26, Wieland had hailed Vater Bromius as the provider of some choice Burgundy, or, that being unavailable, a good Assmannshäuser. Knowing how Goethe lampooned Wieland's *Alcestis* in *Götter, Helden und Wieland* a few years later, we can imagine his feeling of disgust in leafing his way through *Der Neue Amadis*. As far back as 1883, Gustav von Loeper had pointed to canto 13 as a source for Vater Bromius. Readers of the second revised edition of *Der Neue Amadis*, posthumously published, will look in vain for any reference to Vater Bromius. Wieland deleted it in favor of a totally altered text. However, in the edition of 1839 (Leipzig: G.J. Göschen) of Wieland's *Sämtliche Werke*, the text of the poem is followed not only by Wieland's appendix of learned notes, but also by a complete list of variant readings showing Wieland's revision of the original text. The "Vater Bromius" variant can be found in vol. 15, p. 332.

without — that, and immeasurably more — Pindar achieved by virtue of his inner glow. The status of the wine god is further reduced by contrasting his gifts limited in quality and time with the limitless gifts of Phoebus Apollo, timelessly bestowed on all the world.

The poet's grief and vexation over the slackness of an age that cannot rise to heights of soul without the artificial stimulation of the wine god finds utterance in his cry, "Weh, weh!" In these words I do not hear the sound of an Old Testament curse, let alone a wail of self-pity; there is rather a tone of intense commiseration. A triple outcry of anguish is followed by a self-exhortation. At this moment the poet must have become aware of a meteorological change. A rift must have appeared in the clouds, showing sharp glints of sunlight. Phoebus Apollo, face him aglow! As in the first strophe, where along with the skylark the poet raised his antiphonal song against the bluster of the rain clouds, he now exhorts himself to make the antiphonal response to the sun god. The dread of failure looms in the background. To default at this test would be disastrous. He conjures up this contingency with apotropaeic intent. Here a new element, the cedar, is projected upon the scene, adding a third participant to the tense situation. The cedar is an element of the inner landscape, located in its stately grandeur at a distance behind the poet. He sees it with his inner eye. Biblical associations make it an object of high nobility. Within the triadic field of tension here depicted, the cedar assumes the role of honor in case the poet defaults. If the poet fails to face the god aglow, the lordly eye of Phoebus Apollo will disdainfully ("kalt") glide over and above the poet to come to rest ("verweilen") upon the cedar, which measures up to the test. Being evergreen, it is alive with an inner glow. It is in perpetual readiness to respond to Phoebus Apollo's encountering glance.

The cedar has given rise to much confused comment. I hold it as axiomatic that the cedar is introduced as a positive replacement for the poet in case he should default. It is contrary to all logic to think of the poet as failing because of weakness and the cedar failing because of self-sufficient pride. If both of them are to be dismissed as failures, what point is there in introducing the cedar at all? To say that the cedar can afford to do without Phoebus Apollo is to ignore the basic condition of all organic life. Some commentators think the poet might default, not because of weakness, but because of self-sufficient pride. These, stressing the attribute of pride as also pertaining to the cedar, would regard the cedar as no more than an emblematic metaphor for the poet, nailed by the disdainful glance of the sun god.

There is a catch, of course. We have the word "neidgetroffen" in the middle of the strophe. General consensus designates it as ambiguous. I discussed this in a paper many years ago.[7] Let me go over the ground again, sorting out the strands of possible interpretation. In our printed text, the apotropaeic passage, "Kalt wird *sonst* . . ." consists of seven lines. This picture is deceptive. The spoken reality reduces these seven lines to five.

> Kalt wird sonst sein Fürstenblick
> Über dich vorübergleiten
> Neidgetroffen
> Auf der Zeder Kraft verweilen
> Die zu grünen sein nicht harrt.

It is the rhythm that counts. In terms of rhythm, we have two pairs of four-beat, quick-march, trochaic lines, asyndetic, i.e., not connected, the first pair separated from the second by the two-beat line, "neidgetroffen." This line shores up the movement. It is ambiguous, pointing both backward and forward. As the reader observed, we left "neidgetroffen" altogether out of account in studying the emotional interrelation of the three principals.

What does "neidgetroffen" mean? What can it mean? It is a participial compound. The nominal element *Neid*, envy, can mean anything from covetousness to disdain to active enmity. That it need not mean covetousness in Goethe's language of this period is shown by the last lines of strophe one of his dramatic monologue "Prometheus," bidding defiance to Zeus: "Mußt mir meine Erde / Doch lassen stehn, / Und meine Hütte, / Die du nicht gebaut, / Und meinen Herd, / Um dessen Glut / Du mich beneidest." How can the lord of the thunderbolts be thought of as coveting the feeble flame of Prometheus' hearth! Yet, in presenting this example of *Neid* in the most general

---

7   Hermann J. Weigand, "Wandrers Sturmlied − 'Neidgetroffen,' " *Germanic Review*, XXI (1946), 165-72.

sense of ill-will and hostility, I find myself checked by the fact that
the whole first strophe is uttered by Prometheus as a taunt. It would
suit his mood of mockery to needle Zeus with the imputation of
petty jealousy. As for "getroffen," it is usually a word of action suggesting two participants, one shooting and one shot at, a subject and
an object of the action (although both activities can be thought of as
combined in one person).

Perhaps the best way to focus the problem is simply to ask: Who
is envious? Envious of whom? Remembering that *Neid* can stand for
any kind of ill-will, and that, compounded with *getroffen*, it may represent either a static emotion, a grudge lodged in some person, or a
dynamic current discharged from one person against another, we are
confronted with a confusing variety of choices. To take the simplest
case first: the readiest referent for "neidgetroffen" is Apollo's "Für-
stenblick." In that case the epithet would seem little more than an
expanded elaboration of "kalt," and this would certainly support my
contention that reasons of rhythm are primarily, if not exclusively,
responsible for the insertion of the two-beat compound. If, however,
we take the referent of "Neidgetroffen" to be "dich," which stands
closest to it, then Apollo's affect directed against the poet would be
highly dynamic. If this is what Goethe meant, why did he write
"neidgetroffen," we ask, and not "neidgetroffnen"? This is just the
kind of accusative that Goethe uses with signal effectiveness in "An
Schwager Kronos," another of the Storm and Stress hymns. Having
made elaborate rhetorical preparations in the third strophe from the
end, he charges the next run-on strophe with a whole battery of ac-
cusatives: "Trunknen vom letzten Strahl / Reiß mich, ein Feuermeer /
Mir im schäumenden Aug', / Mich Geblendeten, Taumelnden / In der
Hölle nächtliches Tor!" Since this device was demonstrably at Goethe's command, why did he not use it? We must therefore discard
this interpretation.

A third theoretical possibility lies open with regard to Apollo as
the envier. Many commentators have assumed that Apollo's *Neid* is
directed against the cedar. According to this view, the poet and the
cedar would be standing at opposite ends of the spectrum as it were,
the poet defaulting at the moment of the showdown from weakness,
whereas the cedar in brash, self-sufficient pride of stateliness and

beauty anticipates Apollo's springtime summons by virtue of its ever-greening life force. This could be brought into line with the Greek conception of "the envy of the gods," which asserts itself when man's good fortune becomes too much of a good thing. However, ignoring some strange variations of this general scheme, I find no reason whatever for the introduction of the cedar if it is not to stand as a positive foil against the hypothetically defaulting poet. To introduce the cedar by way of a warning that even the antiphonal zeal of a living creature may misfire vis-à-vis the gods, seems to me a switch of thought tantamount to a derailment.

There is one more possibility that we must explore. Must the personality harboring *Neid* be Apollo? May it not be the poet directing the shaft of his ill will against Apollo? As we follow this up there unfolds a highly complex dramatic situation. There is a multiple exchange of signals all taking place in a moment. Apollo's lordly glance sweeps over and beyond the poet, who sees himself "mutlos," dispirited, beaten. Seeing himself rejected, he glares with resentment at the god and observes that the contours of the god's eye have softened as it comes to rest approvingly upon the cedar. Accordingly, the poet's own expression of rage is modified to include a blend of jealousy against the preferred object of Apollo's favor. Since this whole exchange of signals takes place in the poet's imagination, and the cedar, unlike the skylark and the swarthy peasant, is only a part of the interior landscape, any naturalistic objection to the effect that the poet would have to have eyes in the back of his head to see the object upon which the god's benevolent glance alights, is pointless. This version, resolving the compressed compound, "neidgetroffen," into "von deinem Neid getroffen," does justice to the hypothetical confrontation of the Sun-god and the defaulting poet.

Here at the end of strophe nine it may be time to pause and recapitulate the points that have led to great divergence in the interpretation of the poem. It is apparent that many interpreters did not take "entgegen singen" in strophe one and "glüh' entgegen" in strophe nine as a friendly antiphonal response. Without this there would have been no grounds for charging the poet with pride and self-sufficiency. He may well be charged with hybris, but never with pride. All the way through he is under the protection of "Genius," whatever divine form this may take. The misinterpretation of Vater Bromius I find more difficult to explain. The reservation in strophe seven, "nur deine Gaben," makes it clear to me that Vater Bromius is conceived as a deity of subordinate rank, not to be compared in dignity or power with Phoebus Apollo, fit only to inspire an age that is destitute of inner glow. In strophe nine our analysis showed that while the ambiguity of "neidgetroffen" cannot be resolved, the logical sense of the strophe does not require it at all. It is, however, a rhythmical necessity of the first order.

To return to strophe seven and the peasant. More than twenty years ago, I trancribed and inserted in my copy of Max Morris, *Der junge Goethe* (1911), the following passage: "If the poor wretch, who is trudging on to his miserable cottage, can laugh at the storms and tempests, the rain and whirlwinds, which surround him, while his richest hope is only that of rest; how much more cheerfully must a man pass through such transient evils, whose spirits are buoyed up with the certain expectation of finding a noble palace and the most sumptuous entertainment ready to receive him!" The passage is from a letter communicated in book 3, chapter 10 of Henry Fielding's novel *Amelia* (1752). The pious sentiments here so eloquently expressed preface the information that the recipient, who has been expecting a legacy of 100,000 pounds, has been ignored in the will of his aunt just deceased, in favor of his avaricious sister. In connection with the passage quoted, in airing his pious sentiments tongue in cheek, the writer remarks that Cicero's *Tusculan Questions*, book 3, present a similar nobility of outlook despite the fact that Cicero was a benighted heathen.

The similarity of pattern between Fielding's sentence and strophe seven is so striking as to make one ask whether this is a mere coincidence. However, in view of the fact that sentences of such conditional correlative pattern might well be encountered in forensic argument or in treatises of eudaemonistic ethics, I scanned book 3 of the *Tusculan Questions* but without finding anything that bore a formal resemblance to Fielding's sentence. I assume it as probable therefore, almost to the point of certainly, that Goethe, who had become an avid reader of English novels during his sojourn in Strasbourg in 1771, had got his hands on *Amelia* and that, regardless of its tongue-in-cheek presentation, or even more probably because of it, the passage stuck in his mind, and its pattern found itself incorporated in "Wandrers Sturmlied." Such transpositions of key, including on occasion not only the borrowing of a formal pattern, but also the verbatim lifting of an alien content, are not unknown in literature.

Like strophes seven to nine, ten to twelve form a tightly knit group. Here, for the first time, the storm itself is apostrophized as a divine personality, Jupiter Pluvius. We must think of Jupiter here only in his specific capacity of rain god, not as supreme ruler of the Olympian twelve, for where would that leave Apollo, the source of all organic life? Similarly, the reference to the Castalian spring in this strophe as a mere tributary, in comparison to the rain god's torrent, should not specifically evoke the image of Apollo as god of the Muses, in addition to his other functions. To be sure, there is a monotheistic (albeit Trinitarian!) overtone in the poet's hailing of the rain god as: "Dich, von dem es begann,/ Dich, in dem es endet,/ Dich, aus dem es quillt," reminiscent of the biblical triad: "In ihm leben, weben, und sind wir" (Acts 17:28). Thoughts cascade pellmell in this strophe and the typological correspondence of the torrential downpour and the Castalian spring on the one hand, with the characteristic and the beautiful (strength vs. charm) as two distinct forms of aesthetic expression, as developed in "Von deutscher Baukunst" (1771), cannot be overlooked but should not be pressed too closely.

Like the preceding group that took off from the sight of the peasant, this group too begins with a rhetorical question: why does my song name you last? My song has been pouring you forth all the time. "Dich, Dich strömt mein Lied" is another antiphonal response to the divine power. He feels the deity's grasp as a fluid protection. He feels the downpour as a shielding cover, no different from the guardian pinions of strophe three.

In the next two strophes the confused ad hoc blend of ideological currents subsides into lyricism. These strophes with their weaving rhythms single out two of the most distinguished representatives of the idyllic and pastoral genre, Anacreon and Theocritus, as not having been vouchsafed the grasp of the torrential god. These two parallel strophes, keyed to an initial "nicht," weave the melodic pattern of a descending spiral rationing the breath as it is being released. But the first of these two, having completed its artful circumlocution and arrived at the name of the poet Anacreon as its goal, and calling for a full stop, suddenly jerks the voice upward to apostrophize the storm-breathing deity. Let the reader attempt to repeat this extraordinary feat of the voice and feel the crack in his throat! Was this intended as a danger signal? It is not repeated in the Theocritus strophe.

The last strophe brings another *tour de force* and a final crack-up. Despite the punctuation of the revised version (period and dashes), I can read this strophe, like strophe seven, sighting the peasant, and strophe ten, apostrophizing the storm god, Jupiter Pluvius, only as a deliriously ecstatic question in confident expectation of Pindar's antiphonal response across the ages. Abruptly follows a seizure, a threat of total collapse. Antiphonal song has turned into a plaintive cry for help from whatever divine quarter, to supply that minimum of glow that will sustain his reeling step to reach the hilltop and its sheltering abode. We could let our imagination wander to exploit the come-down in "meine Hütte," to picture a shanty so rude and primitive as to make the peasant's cottage with its wine and its hearthglow resemble a palace.

The British authors Wilkinson and Willoughby have made a case for reading a large dose of humor into "Wandrers Sturmlied."[8] I do not read the poem in those terms. There is hybris reaching its climax in strophes five and six; there is a desperate straining to sustain the mood of antiphonal song vis-à-vis the gods all the way into the final strophe, this followed by a threat of total collapse. There is self-irony in this, to my way of thinking, not humor. We know that Goethe had a great sense of poetic economy. He was loath in collecting his poetic works to lose anything salvageable. Yet he resisted including this great hymn in his first authorized edition of his poems in 1789, and again in the second authorized edition of 1806, dismissing it in the third part of *Dichtung und Wahrheit* in 1812 as "Halbunsinn." Only after an unauthorized printing in 1810 had made its existence known beyond the tiny circle of intimates favored with manuscript copies in the 1770s did Goethe include it with minimal alterations in the third

8   Elizabeth M. Wilkinson and L.A. Willoughby, "Wandrers Sturmlied, A Study in Poetic Vagrancy," *German Life and Letters*, n.s. 1 (1947-48), 102-16.

authorized edition of his poems in 1815. Would the poet have been disposed for so long a time to consign this remarkable poem to oblivion if he had conceived it as a *tour de force* of extravagant humor? Two years after writing the poem Goethe sent a copy to Fritz Jacobi (31 August 1774) with the comment: "Hier eine Ode, zu der Melodie und Kommentar nur der Wandrer in der Not erfindet." Quoted by Arthur Henkel[9] among others, and appearing as the well-chosen title of a recently published essay by Heinrich Henel,[10] "Der Wandrer in der Not" characterizes a frame of mind that rules out humorous intent.

---

9 Henkel, "Versuch," p. 61.
10 See n. 1.

6.
GOETHE'S "HARZREISE IM WINTER":
A STRUCTURAL ANALYSIS WITH AN EXCURSUS
ON VARIANT READINGS

This poem, if encountered for the first time without guidance, will give the reader a great deal of trouble. As with T.S. Eliot's *The Wasteland*, he finds stretches of arresting imagery and trains of thought that stir associations, but where is the key to a pattern that fits the pieces together? We may end up after the expenditure of considerable effort, in admiring the "Harzreise im Winter" as the finest lyrical fruit of Goethe's earliest years in Weimar, but the approach will be remembered as forbidding. Goethe himself on one occasion termed the poem "abstruse."[1] His contemporaries must have been similarly puzzled reading this distillate of a solitary expedition to the Brocken in early December 1777. Forty-three years later, he published an expansive account of this winter journey in response to the essay of an admirer, who, Goethe felt, had arrived at as fine an appreciation of the poem as could be achieved without knowledge of its personal background. Of prime importance for the reader is the information conveyed by Goethe's narrative commentary that he stopped off to make a visit incognito to a young man who had been pursuing the author of *Werther* with fan mail. Curiosity and pity prompted Goethe to seek out this recluse, this social dropout, as we would call him, a sufferer from the then modish malady of misanthropy and *Weltschmerz* which Goethe had unintentionally helped to make endemic by his *Werther*. It is also helpful to learn that Goethe had been accompanying his Duke and a few companions on a boar-hunting expedition in the foothills, before he branched off to pursue his solitary course to the mountains. As for the religious exaltation of Goethe's mood in attempting so novel and hazardous an exploit

---

1 Cf. Wolfgang Herwig, "Karl Ludwig Kannegießer: Über Goethes Harzreise im Winter," *Goethe. Neue Folge des Jahrbuchs der Goethe Gesellschaft* (Weimar 1962), p. 227.

as the scaling of a mountain in winter, the commentary is at pains to conceal its source as the great flame of passion for Charlotte von Stein, but the letters written to Charlotte during the trip only confirm what the poem itself proclaims in ecstatic language. With this bare minimum of background for introduction, the poem itself can take over and exercise its spell.

The title keys our expectation to the locale and the season. The grand opening strophe, couched in the wish-form like the introit of a celebration, makes a statement of intent. It firmly locates the speaker in time and space. The heavy morning clouds mark the time, and the poet's eye contemplates them from above. There is the vulture bedded motionless upon them, yet fully alert. The plain has been left far behind. The poet is well on his way to the goal of his journey. The calm equilibrium of the bird of prey stands as a symbol of the mood with which the poet surveys the scene on this morning. Equanimity, not the equanimity of somnolent revery, but equanimity reinforced by a heightened sense of life, is the message flashed by the bird's posture of equipoise. Only for a moment does the poet's eye dwell upon the somber grandeur of the view. It has yielded at once to an inner landscape, the counterpart of the expansive survey of his lofty stance. The poet's contemplation embraces the whole human scene, impersonally, dispassionately. He gives voice to fatalistic doctrine. Man is not the master of his fate. His life is preordained by higher powers. Choosing the language of pagan religious philosophy, he ascribes to "a god" what we would call the interaction of heredity and environment. Good fortune and misfortune are unpredictably distributed. The imagery in which this idea is clothed is borrowed from classical antiquity — the runner who wins the prize in the stadium; the frustrated individual waiting for the Parca to cut the thread of life. The language of the imagery dedicated to the man frustrated by misfortune mirrors the idea by tortuous word order, compression of phrasing, a most unusual distortion of pitch ("den die doch bittre Schere"), and a retardation of tempo that gives the last three words the interrupted cadence of single falling drops. As we remarked, this formulation of men's fates is remote and wholly impersonal. Without stripping it of its universal meaning, Goethe later reformulated the doctrine in terms applying to his own person in the famous first strophe of "Urworte. Orphisch" by use of the self-addressing "du": "Wie an dem Tag, der dich der Welt verlie-hen . . . "

The third strophe takes a breather from speculation to note the signs of the season. Whereas the eye had scanned the distance — clouds and the vulture — in the first strophe, it now focuses upon the immediate scene. Game animals, clothed in their shaggy winter pelts, huddle in the thickets, and when they stir, accumulations of snow, ice or rain slither down upon them, to which they react with a shiver. All this seems to be expressed by the ad hoc compound "Dickichtsschauer." The second sentence with reference to the marsh birds is not concerned with an observation. It registers rather a state of things that it notes as having come to pass. It is a true present perfect tense. The marsh birds have long since ceased to be heard or seen. (The variant readings of the last sentence pose an enigma too complicated to be dealt with in pursuance of the general analysis. It will be the concern of the excursus.)

With strophe four the inner landscape has again taken over, and the theme is the same as that of strophe two, the inequality of human fortunes *sub specie aequanimitatis.* The dichotomy is the same as in strophe two, good and evil, and the same sequence is followed. Again good fortune is symbolized by an image from classical mythology, the chariot of the goddess of fortune. The present strophe marks a variation of strophe two in two respects, material and formal. Whereas the fortunates of strophe two displayed competitive energy, the favorites of fortune here presented are indolently relaxed. As regards form, there are two parallel statements, the goddess of fortune with her train, and the prince followed by his retinue — this resembling the *parallelismus membrorum* found in the Psalms.

Let us dwell on the formal characteristics of strophes two and four to become fully aware of how they endeavor to express the soaring mood of equanimity that governs the intent of the poet's meditation. In sentiment and form both strophes might be translations from Greek antiquity. With unemotional tranquillity, the proposition is developed that individual man is not in control of his destiny. Good fortune and misfortune are sketched in turn, each clothed in imagery familiar to the ancient world, each limited to one

sentence, but the direct and simple statement of the plus side contrasts with the labyrinthine involutions of the minus side. The contrasting statements are produced by the conjunction "aber." Strophe
four makes its appearance as a slight variation of the basic theme.
The plus of good fortune again takes precedence in the arrangement,
the variation being its expansion into two parallel statements. It is
again followed by an adversative "aber." With this "aber," however,
we encounter a surprise. The adverse side of good fortune is indeed
pursued by what follows, but it is sufficiently involved to require a
strophe of its own instead of remaining linked to its partner as in
strophe two. Indeed, the one "aber" strophe, strophe five, will be
seen to divide into three to round out that situation. This formal
change of structure is a turning point, *the* turning point in the poem's
whole outlook. Something has happened. Unaccountably, the dispassionate, impersonal, unemotionally neutral mood of the poet's
soaring vision has been shaken by a tremor. Not only that; it has
been shattered. From now on, up to the final strophe, the climate
of equanimity is replaced by emotional involvement in a variety of
moods — moods embracing tender pity mingled with censure, robust
joy and ecstatic bliss.

     This change, as radical a change as is ever encountered in the
body of a poem, I would phrase as follows: Stimulated by the sight
of the vulture, the poet set himself the task to compose a formal,
ornate, rhetorical, static piece, an ode after the manner of Pindar.
But having got well under way, the poem suddenly asserted a will of
its own. It broke through its chrysalis and established its life as an
organism. Everything is changed, including the basic mode of utterance. Strophes one to four were a meditative monologue uttered in
isolation from other human beings. Now, however, the statement
gives way to questions. There is an urge to communicate. It finds its
outlet in a prayerful apostrophe to a loving deity who remains the
poet's emotional partner up to the final strophe. Needless to say, this
is not the pagan god of necessity or chance of strophe two. It is the
childhood God of the poet's Judaeo-Christian inheritance, a god
apostrophized as powerful, benevolently solicitous, with all of the
poet's license to reconstitute the universe in terms of the poet's
wish-dreams. Henceforth there is no more general speculation. It is

specific individual phenomena which become the poet's concern one after another: the man who drops out of sight, the joyous band of huntsmen, the poet's own person, the peak of the mountain range. Our analysis now follows these one by one.

The abrupt question, "Aber abseits, wer ist's?" suddenly shifts the focus to an individual moving object. He is, of course, part of the inner landscape. A series of movements, sharply focused, present themselves to the inner eye. The swaying bushes that hide him are in leaf. The grass over which his footstep has passed is resilient. He is swallowed up by the wilderness. Being forewarned by Goethe's commentary, we have recognized him as the recluse, the potential drop-out. The poet's heart overflows with sympathy. He casts about for help. The balm of love has turned into poison, hatred of the human race. To probing compassion, the poet adds censure of the sufferer's distorted moral focus. The effect is corrosive and threatens his moral destruction.

(The theme of *Menschenhass,* misanthropy, is very much in the forefront of Goethe's mind as a result of the public's response to Werther's suicide. There are the lines in "Prometheus:" "Wähntest du etwa, / Ich sollte das Leben hassen, / In Wüsten fliehn, / Weil nicht alle Knabenmorgen– / Blütenträume reiften?" Or think of "Rastlose Liebe": "Wie – soll ich fliehen? / Wälderwärts ziehen? / Alles vergebens! / Krone des Lebens, / Glück ohne Ruh, / Liebe, bist du!" Or "An den Mond": "Selig, wer sich vor der Welt / Ohne Haß verschließt." To these we might add the exhortation supposedly uttered by the spirit of Werther: "Sei ein Mann und folge mir nicht nach." All these instances show Goethe as pedagogically involved counselling youth to avoid the course of the drop-out.)

The case of the victim seems far advanced, beyond human help. With distress the poet lifts his voice to the "Father of Love" imploring his help to let heavenly music try where reason fails. He follows this by an allusion to help from above which showed Hagar a spring when she and Ishmael were about to perish from thirst in the desert (Genesis 21:17 ff.).

Having developed the memories stirred by his recent visit to the drop-out, the poet's mind is invaded by the hunting party from which he had slipped away. Suddenly a current of robust life replaces tender emotion. The language of the new invocation is unmistakably biblical: *Der du der Freuden viel schaffst.* It stems from Isaiah, being one of the famous passages interpreted by the Christian church as foretelling the coming of Christ and learned and recited by children in Christian lands throughout the ages at Christmas time. In the German bible, Isaiah 9:2,3 reads as follows:

> Das Volk, so im Finstern wandelt, siehet ein großes
> Licht, und über die da wohnen im finstern Lande, schei-
> net es hell.
>   Du machest der Heiden viel; damit machest du der Freu-
> den viel. Vor dir aber wird man sich freuen, wie man sich
> freuet in der Ernte, wie man fröhlich ist, wenn man Beute
> austeilet.[2]

"Der Freuden viel," "fröhlich," "Beute" — all this applies to *die Brü-der der Jagd.* At the same time it recalls the introit with its image of the vulture looking for *Beute.* Prey, booty, yield, loot, all these specialized terms of English usage have their equivalent in the more generalized German *Beute.* The poet's solitary quest is his equivalent of the boar hunt of his companions left behind. Would he not think of his successful encounter with Plessing as a first positive yield of his lonely venture? And would not his thoughts stray to his companions to wish them success in their turn? The studiedly shocking phrasing of their quest as joyously murderous lust is tempered by a reference to their youth and the excesses to which youth is prone.

This nine-line strophe is one very tightly knit sentence that resonates with a vibrating rhythm. The startlingly strong language emphasizes the poet's sympathy with the human victims of the marauding boars. What vehement partisan commitment! No equanimity here. The poet grimly takes the side of the poor peasants prevented by the cruel hunting laws from defending themselves efficiently against the destructive onslaught. What a difference between this indulgence in murderous lust and that lovely monologue, a few years later in *Faust*, where the beast and the fowl are embraced as brothers (the scene "Wald und Höhle"). To understand fully the outburst in

---

2   Many Bibles, then and now, have a perplexing variant, the inclusion of a "not." Therewith thou doest not multiply joy." It is obvious that the Bible of the Goethe household did not have this negative variant.

"Harzreise im Winter" we have to read a little between the lines. The poet's feeling was not at all the same as that of the hunters. The duke and his companions wanted the perpetuation of a grim and dangerous sport, while Goethe abominated the boars as a pestilential nuisance.

When the next strophe, continuing the mode of divine petition, focuses upon the poet's own self as its object, we know at once that we have arrived at the heart of the poem. It is his turn now to seek the blessings which he has invoked for others. Referring to himself as the solitary one, "der Einsame," in the third person, he never departs from this usage in the long passage devoted to himself. Solitude has always been a prerogative of romantic poets. Without straying into a limitless area of association, we may be permitted to recall that Dr. Johann Georg Zimmermann, the author of an inspirational work on solitude, *Über die Einsamkeit* (1756), sent a character sketch of Goethe before his arrival in Weimar to Charlotte von Stein, recommending his disposition as particularly congenial to her.[3] If, in the present strophe, it is no longer "Father of Love" who is apostrophized, but simply Love, can we doubt for a moment that the poet's expanding and relaxing thought was straying into the distance to commune silently with his beloved? In this strophe it is incidentals which govern all the accents. The landscape is suddenly aglow with color: golden clouds, the green of winter's ivy, to which the inner landscape contributes the rose. Are not inner and outer landscape fused at this point? But things have been happening. It was morning when the heavy clouds were rolling. What can it be now but evening when the clouds are tinged with a golden glow both real and symbolic? Have we been made aware of the passage of time at all? Indeed, we find a whole winter day has run its course. Time has been on the move. But what about the poet? Has he stirred from the spot where we first sighted him? Another delicate touch tells the story: his hair is moist. A symptom of emotion? More probably, he is steaming from the exertion of a whole day's ride over difficult terrain in the direction of his goal. Thus, suddenly, the illusion of a poet's day-dream against a static background has been swept away, and the signal given, movement takes over. It pulsates majestically.

---

3   Zimmermann's book was destined to play a remarkable role in Gottfried Keller's novel, *Der grüne Heinrich*, the second version, vol. 2, in the chapter "Schwindelhaber; Fortsetzung."

Five great sentences follow, each alive with a movement of its own. Instead of halting for the night, the wanderer pursues his course with redoubled energy by the filmy light of the moon, fording streams, making his way over rough ground, facing a barren heath. "Mit der dämmernden Fackel / Leuchtest du ihm / Durch die Furten bei Nacht, / Über grundlose Wege / Auf öden Gefilden." This the first movement, is a forward horizontal thrust. Five two-beat phrases of flexible rhythm precisely timed. In the second sentence the brilliance of the morning colors relegates the sense of movement to the background: "Mit dem tausendfarbigen Morgen / Lachst du ins Herz ihm." Movement, now vertical, upward, takes over again in the third sentence: "Mit dem beizenden Sturm / Trägst du ihn hoch empor." Sentences two and three, be it noted, form a chiastic pair; first a three-beat phrase followed by a two, then a two-beat phrase followed by a three. In the fourth sentence the upward sweep of the third is followed by a cascading sequence of three downward thrusts: "Winterströme stürzen vom Felsen / In seine Psalmen." Starting on a high note, three two-beat phrases of descending pitch. The fifth sentence finally, the paean of praise culminating in a prayer of thanks, has a playful horizontal movement: "Und Altar des lieblichsten Danks / Wird ihm des gefürchteten Gipfels / Schneebehangner Scheitel, / Den mit Geisterreihen / Kränzten ahnende Völker." Five three-beat phrases on a level, playfully joyful the first three, while the last two check the exuberance of the movement in order to behold with fitting solemnity the Brocken destined to become the rendezvous of demonic forces in the *Walpurgisnacht* of Goethe's *Faust*. The mountain has become for the poet an altar bearing his offering of praise. All this happened without a trace of personal initiative. The poet feels himself passively wafted along surrendering to the indulgent solicitude of loving powers.

The pilgrimage is completed. One does not ascend an altar. The poet beholds the peak. His gaze turns into apostrophe. The words that form on his lips are restrained, impersonal, dispassionate, unemotional. They make no attempt to establish a bond between beholder and object. They attribute to the colossus by way of factual descriptive statement that equanimity which in the initial strophe the poet had attempted to vindicate for himself. In facing the inscrutable mountain, the poet has recovered the equanimity which had vanished into thin air when he came to terms with the human scene. With this return to the beginning, the poem has rounded the circle of its development.

Let us summarize the features of the poem that we have tried to stress.

The first and the last strophe each presents in its own way a majestic thematic symbol of equanimity. Generalizations that borrowed their imagery from classical antiquity sustain the mood of equanimity through strophe four. Up to this point the form of meditation is the monologue, but from this point on a series of individual human features successively takes hold of the poet's mind — the drop-out, the band of hunters, his own person, the awesome mountain peak; there are no more generalizations. In keeping with this the form of utterance changes from a monologue to a groping desire for partnership which takes the form of prayer, and prayer remains the mode of communication up to the final apostrophe. We noted that while the cast of thought was pagan through strophe four, the remainder of the poem breathes a Judaeo-Christian spirit. There are three petitions involving successive objects followed by a paean of praise that culminates in a prayer of ecstatic gratitude. In the part of the poem which deals with the poet's own person we first become aware of the passage of time, then of movement, both of them by the employment of subtle means (the golden clouds, the perspiring brow). The apparently static character of the poem is here dispelled by a dynamic surge of movement. The poet has been operating in a trance as it were; he now moves in the real landscape. The total time span extends from early morning through a night into a second day. Along with the movement, the melodic and rhythmic features of the poem, somewhat halting in the first part, firm up in a way that makes the second half of the poem rise to supreme heights. Strophes one to four and strophe eleven constitute firmly disciplined rhetorical statement; everything in between is song.

EXCURSUS

The Variants

Strophe three of "Harzreise im Winter," all but ignored in our structural analysis, shall now engage our attention. "In Dickichts- schauer / Drängt sich das rauhe Wild, / Und mit den Sperlingen / Ha- ben längst die Reichen (Haben längst die Reiher) / In ihre Sümpfe sich gesenkt." Which is the correct reading? In the first authorized edition of Goethe's collected writings (Göschen, 1787-90), we read "die Reichen." A copy in a clear hand, made by Goethe for the printer's use, also reads, "die Reichen." [4] The first authorized Cotta edition of 1806 reads "die Reiher." So does the second Cotta edi- tion of 1815. When this variant was brought to Goethe's attention in 1820, he designated it as "ein wundersamer Druckfehler," a wondrous misprint. This should settle the matter. "Die Reichen" is the correct, doubly authenticated version. What forum is there to hear an appeal from the poet's own verdict? In all modesty we may nonetheless ask the question: Which is the *better* reading? Many of Goethe's early poems, after circulating in manuscript among his friends before print- ing, have undergone alterations, amounting sometimes to a "sea- change," in publication, and good modern editions of Goethe's works offer two or more versions side by side, giving preference to the earlier, more spontaneous. By way of example, we know how Goethe emasculated the glorious ending of "An Schwager Kronos;" and as for "An den Geist des Johannes Secundus," its humorously impudent imputation of his own impudicity to the chaste object of his veneration, Charlotte, made impossible the publication of the poem that was intended for her eyes alone. Instead of leaving well enough alone, he has turned it into "Liebesbedürfnis," a tame imita- tion that no one will look at a second time. In the light of such facts, our inquiry may be justified. It seems proper to begin by examining the appropriateness of both variants irrespective of their credentials. Let us begin with "die Reiher."

---

4   A facsimile of this manuscript is included in *Goethe. Viermonatschrift* — later Dreimonatschrift — (Weimar 1938), vol. 3, after page 126.

As our analysis showed, the first strophe after the orienting title (mountains and winter) presents a bank of brooding morning clouds against which is limned a motionless vulture. The speaker views this sight from above. After this introit the external landscape fades from view for the time being, obscured by reflections and mental imagery of classical flavor that survey the varying fortunes of men. In the third strophe the poet is momentarily roused from his reveries to note features of the actual landscape in which he is stationed. (We should say "through which he is passing"; however, as we saw, we have to follow the poem quite a long way before discovering any hint of the fact that he is on the move). He opens his eyes to survey the bleak landscape. He glimpses the tail end of one or another deer trying to find shelter in the thickets that shower moisture, rain, sleet, snow upon their shaggy winter pelts. This is a statement of visual observation. The next statement, referring to the reed birds and herons, is an observation only in negative terms. The poet's recollecting experience is at work to account for their absence. It presupposes familiarity with the habits of birds encountered in flocks and with individuals of striking stature. They have long since sought shelter in the protective swamps and marshes of the lowlands. Apart from stressing the lateness of the season, the strophe about the birds reinforces our consciousness of the poet as stationed in the uplands. It is all very plain except for the final line which is notable. Anyone familiar with the habits of herons will admire as peculiarly apt the term "gesenkt," lowered, settled in, for the almost vertical final stage of the descent to the ground of the heavy-winged birds. In this context it is appropriate to note that it was perhaps on the very day when Goethe wrote these lines that he used the same word, "gesenkt," as applying to himself in a long letter to Charlotte von Stein. Dating part of his letter of December 9 "Abends," he continues: Liebes Gold! Ich hab an keinem Orte Ruh, Ich habe mich tiefer ins Gebürg gesenckt . . ."[5] One would think that empathy with the big birds might have dictated the choice of that word. All this seems

---

5   *Goethes Briefe an Frau von Stein*, herausgegeben von Adolf Schöll, dritte umgearbeitete Auflage besorgt von Julius Wahle, I (Frankfurt a.M. 1899), 100.

perfectly fitting as the description of a landscape that is bleak, raw, and empty. These few lines along with the initial strophe are the only passage of the poem which shows the external landscape in clear focus, except for the scene of the final strophe.

Now, examining the second variant, "Und mit den Sperlingen / Haben längst die Reichen / In ihre Sümpfe sich gesenkt," what do we find? With "die Reichen," the rich folk, a wholly new element is introduced. There is something startling about this, to say the least. We began with an enumeration of congruent concepts: game animals and birds. Human beings, listed as the third member of the series, would have been unexpected, but the singling out of a specific class of such as coupled with the sparrows throws us off the track. What about the poor? Scanning the whole poem in rapid recollection, we find that, except for this isolated naming of the rich, not a single reference to a human being, rich or poor, appears on the landscape which the poet traverses. From Goethe's diary jottings and his expanded letters to Charlotte von Stein we know that during his two weeks' horseback ride through the Harz he passed through populous regions, meeting all manner of men and feeling himself drawn with a particular warmth to the poor, simple, honest, working folk, as contrasted with the professional and administrative class. However, not a trace of such sights or feelings is evoked in the poem. The Poem moves in a wilderness totally devoid of human beings. To continue: the following line brings the sentence to a bewildering close. Here we encounter symbolism. The swamps in which the rich have long since sought shelter are obviously a disdainful reference to towns with their creature comforts, mitigating the rigors of winter in a stuffy atmosphere of reduced vitality. If the "Sperlinge" are still thought of as reed birds, not as common house sparrows, their being coupled with the rich is limited to the simultaneity of their departure from the uplands. In that case we have not only symbolism but double-talk as well. The swamps in which the sparrows settle are not towns, but real swamps.

Thus the thought, without the abbreviation of double-talk, would have run: and along with the reed sparrows the rich folk have long since settled into their respective swamps. This is complicated, it is witty, it is satirical, it is confusing, and there has been absolutely nothing to prepare us for such a sally of fireworks. Everything up to this point was straightforward, sober, austere, and now we suddenly find ourselves entangled in a stylistic mode that is alien to everything that precedes this passage and, be it said at once, to everything that follows. This kind of departure from the stylistic mode of empathy into which we had settled is startling, incredibly so. If, having read these lines a second and a third time and becoming aware that we have fallen into a trap set by the poet, we catch ourselves up with a snort of amusement at the witty enumeration, symbolism, and double-talk, the mood of the poem is dissipated, and we shall not easily recapture it in being asked to return to the serious mytho-symbolical form of meditation in the next strophe. Let it be clearly understood: It is not the expression of an immense sense of liberation from the traffic of the civilized and well-to-do that gives offense — Goethe did feel this to a superlative degree — but rather the crass and destructive intrusion of wit à la Jean Paul into a wholly alien context. If this reading is found to be authenticated, it must be branded as "ein fremder Tropfen," a regrettable stain on one of Goethe's finest poems. Well, it is authenticated, doubly so (including the identification of the sparrows as reed birds), but perhaps not to the entire exclusion of a faint conviction that the reading "die Reiher" flowed from Goethe's pen in the original drafting of the poem. In any case, we shall have to ponder with no present hope of clear illumination what could have prompted Goethe to suffer such an aberration of his sense of style, to be so insensitive to the inner laws of his poem.

The Transmission

"Harzreise im Winter" was written in December 1777. Twelve years went by before it appeared in print in the first edition of Goethe's collected writings under the imprint of Göschen, 1787 till 90. This was a revised version of the original draft showing many stylistic variants that firm up the movement particularly of the first four strophes. Copies of the poem, as originally drafted, had been circulating among Goethe's intimates. There is or was extant a copy in the hand of Charlotte von Stein showing a considerable number of stylistic variants and some negligence in the writing of word endings. On August 5, 1778, Goethe enclosed a copy of the poem in a letter to his friend, Johann Heinrich Merck in Darmstadt. The letter alluded to the inclusion of the poem with this remarkable sentence: "Von den tausend Gedanken in der Einsamkeit findest Du auf beiliegendem Blatt fliegende Streifen." "Fliegende Streifen," flying streamers, flying wisps of cloud, gossamer threads? This designation envelops the poem in an aura of mystery. Merck, Goethe's senior by eight years, had been on intimate terms with the poet since 1771. As Goethe's friend, Merck established close relations to the ducal family of Sachsen-Weimar, notably to the dowager Anna Amalia. He performed many commissions for the duke, Karl August, and he was a welcome guest in Weimar in the spring of 1780. Unfortunately, his relations to Goethe deteriorated in later years. He got involved in a variety of questionable operations. Despondent over domestic troubles and the failure of financial operations, he shot himself in 1791. In *Dichtung und Wahrheit*, Goethe dwells on Merck's Mephistophelian temperament and he judges his one-time intimate in very harsh terms. Eventually Goethe destroyed all of Merck's letters recording the period of their friendship — for us a very regrettable loss.[6]

We have no hint how Merck reacted to Goethe's poem. Enormous interest attaches to the draft sent to Merck. This early copy, made seven months at most after the poem took shape, did it read "die Reiher" or "die Reichen?" My study took its lead from the extremely fine and perceptive apparatus of Erich Trunz, editor of the Hamburg edition of Goethe's works.[7] On page 477, Professor Trunz refers to a printing of the draft sent to Johann Heinrich Merck, without adding any specific data. Owing to a combination of circumstances, too frustrating to report, I spent a great deal of time in the attempt to locate this printed version. Was this a first printing not sanctioned by Goethe, as happened to some of his other

---

6   For a full account of Goethe's relations with Merck, see Hermann Bräuning-Oktavio, *Goethe und Johann Heinrich Merck. J.H. Merck und die französische Revolution* (Darmstadt 1970).

7   I used vol. I of the seventh edition (Hamburg 1964).

poems? If so, where and when did it appear? I thought I had arrived at a solution when I came upon a volume by Karl Wagner, *Briefe an Johann Heinrich Merck von Goethe, Herder, Wieland und anderen bedeutenden Zeitgenossen* (Darmstadt, 1835). This volume, introducing its substance with an extremely thin but ponderously worded sketch of Merck's life, contains Goethe's letter of August 5, 1778. After the sentence quoted above, on page 138, there is a footnote referring to the enclosed poem as follows: "Die Anlage enthält das unter der Ueberschrift: Harzreise im Winter, sr. Werke Theil II, S. 57 ff. mitgetheilte Gedicht mit der Aufschrift: 'Auf dem Harz im Dezember 1777' und mit folgenden Abweichungen von dem gedruckten." The rest of the footnote lists the variants found by Wagner. Taking "Anlage," as here used, as a synonym for "Einlage" or "Beilage," I expected to find the full text of the draft as a printed insert. Finding nothing of the sort, I surmised that a previous owner had extracted it as something particularly precious. For the time being, the list of variant readings brought no comfort, our moot line was passed over in silence. From this it had to be assumed that it coincided with the first authorized version, namely, "die Reichen." Despairing of my own efforts, yet unwilling to give up, I appealed for help to Professor Helmut Holtzhauer, Director of Nationale Forschungs- und Gedenkstätten der klassischen deutschen Literatur in Weimar. After a wait of six weeks there came, instead of a few lines, a *Forschungsbericht* of four single-spaced pages with explicit data and new leads. First of all, it became clear that Professor Trunz, usually so meticulous in the presentation of data, was in error in referring to the draft sent to Merck as being available in print. It has never been printed. Apparently Karl Wagner thought it a waste of paper to print the poem in full after having listed the variants. The original of Goethe's letter, Professor Holtzhauer wrote me, is not in Weimar. It is in the Houghton Library of Harvard University. (I have since held in my hand a xeroxed copy of that letter, and I wish to acknowledge this courtesy on the part of the Harvard Library authorities gratefully.) As for the even more precious draft of the poem, its whereabouts are unknown.

What next surfaced in the report of Professor Holtzhauer and his staff was a find of explosive significance. Checking on a number of footnotes relating to Goethe's works, and giving exact references, they found that the source of all of Wagner's references was the second Cotta edition of 1815. That this is indeed so I finally succeeded in confirming by getting my hands on the carefully guarded early editions in the Yale Beinecke Library, the Göschen edition of 1787-90 and the Cotta edition of 1815. What a new light this sheds on the situation! We remember that the Cotta edition of 1815, as well as Cotta edition of 1806, had our line read "die Reiher." In other words, if the draft sent to Merck read "die Reiher," just as did the Cotta edition with which Wagner compared it, it would not have been listed among the variants. Hence, supposing that Wagner compared his texts with diligent scrutiny, the draft sent to Merck must indeed have read "die Reiher," thus corroborating my conviction that whatever changes Goethe made later, the word "Reiher" originally flowed from his pen. That Wagner collated the two texts with care would appear from the fact that along with actual variants his listing included an undoubted slip of the pen ("du siehst" instead of "du stehst" in the first line of the final strophe). I cannot sufficiently express my gratitude to Professor Holtzhauer and his staff for their patient and successful pursuit of this complicated problem.[8] Thanks to the alertness of the Weimar archivists, we may regard our thesis as proved — always subject to the proviso that Wagner did not slip up in collating the two texts. There always remains the forlorn hope, of

---

8   I think I can trace Professor Trunz' error in referring to the draft sent to Merck as having been printed. Like myself, he presumably took "Anlage" to be a synonym for "Inlage," "Einlage," or "Beilage." That a different meaning attaches to "Anlage," as used by Wagner, became evident to me only in happening on another footnote on page 98 of his book, beginning "In Anlage befand sich." This is again a reference to a Goethe poem for which he lists variants. The use of the preterite in this case shows that Wagner understood "Anlage" to mean the body of manuscript material at his disposal in editing the present volume. Applying this definition as a criterion to his footnote about "Harzreise im Winter," we may now be certain that Wagner never intended to reproduce the poem in print. In the same footnote on page 138, Wagner's peculiar wording leads us astray a second time, in referring to the printed version as "das . . . sr. Werke . . . mitgetheilte Gedicht." In normal usage this could only refer to the first authorized printing, whereas Wagner again uses the second Cotta edition of 1815.

course, that the original draft of the poem, sold or given away, may again turn up on the market.

We cannot leave the topic of transmission without a few words about a copy of the poem in the hand of Charlotte von Stein. This, surely the oldest copy, part of a collection of Goethe poems in Charlotte's hand, was reported on by Heinrich Düntzer.[9] On page 99 of his essay, Düntzer compares the variants in Charlotte's copy with those in the copy sent to Merck. Apart from three wrong case endings characteristic of her spelling, substituting n for m, he lists two additional important stylistic variants. In the second strophe, Charlotte's copy reads: "Sträubt vergebens / Gegen die Schranken," as against Merck-Wagner's: "Er sträubt vergebens / Sich gegen die Schranken." Düntzer surmises without giving a shadow of proof, that these two escaped Karl Wagner's notice in making his collation, so that the two copies coincided on this point. This seems most unlikely in view of the fact that both variants occur at the beginning of a line. We saw, moreover, that Wagner's list of variants did not overlook a trifling slip of the pen, which he could easily have ignored. On the variant with which this paper is concerned Düntzer is silent. Recalling the fact that Düntzer made his comparisons half a century after the question of our variant was aired, we could make a variety of conjectures including the one that Düntzer had forgotten the controversy, and that the variant "die Reiher" vs. "die Reichen" escaped his notice. We are left without anything conclusive. However, Professor Holtzhauer is instituting a search for Charlotte's papers in the archives of the Stein family. (A later communication from Weimar now informs me that a search of the Stein Family archive has failed to turn up Charlotte's notebook of Goethe poems, and that no information on its whereabouts is available.)[10]

---

9 Heinrich Düntzer, "Die handschriftliche Sammlung Goethescher Gedichte von Charlotte von Stein," *Archiv für Litteraturgeschichte, 6* (Leipzig 1877), 96-110.

10 This public acknowledgment of indebtedness comes too late to reach Professor Holtzhauer. I mourn his untimely death on December 16, 1973.

The Showdown

In the three decades that elapsed after the first publication of "Harzreise im Winter" in 1789, was Goethe ever questioned about the meaning of our moot line? We do not know. In 1820 Karl Ludwig Kannegießer, director of the Gymnasium at Prenzlau and lecturer at the University of Breslau, published an appreciative analysis of "Harzreise im Winter" and sent a copy to Goethe.[11] Goethe was so pleased with this textual analysis, made without benefit of any specific knowledge regarding the biographical background of the poem, and with the fulsome praise of an admirer who was determined to exploit the possibilities of pedagogical edification to the utmost, that in the year following he composed and published an essay in response to Kannegießer's which is to be found in all major collections of Goethe's writings.[12] For the understanding of the poem as the precipitate of a specific experience, Goethe's commentary is of the greatest value. Together with brief diary jottings expanded into long letters to Charlotte von Stein, neither of which Goethe consulted in writing this essay, it tells of Goethe's secret, solitary expedition into the Harz, of his slipping away from his companions engaged in the boar hunt, of his incognito visit to an individual suffering from the Werther malady (Friedrich Plessing). It acknowledges his sense of euphoria, discreetly suppressing the fact that his love for Charlotte von Stein accounted for his religious rapture, and it mentioned his interest in mining, obscured in the poem by the symbolic phraseology of the final strophe, as one of the reasons prompting his hazardous excursion into the mountains. These few facts establish the links that constitute the experiential unity of this rhapsodic poem.

Apart from the satisfaction at the factual information here afforded, Goethe's commentary, written forty-three years after his solitary winter expedition, will be read with mixed feelings. It is

---

11 Kannegießer's text, also included in a collection of his essays, is now available in an annotated reprint by Wolfgang Herwig, "Karl Ludwig Kannegießer: Über Goethes Harzreise im Winter," *Goethe. Neue Folge des Jahrbuchs der Goethe Gesellschaft* (Weimar 1962), pp. 224-236.

12 For the text of Goethe's essay, see Erich Trunz, the Hamburg edition, I, 392-400.

evident throughout that Goethe's recollection of the facts cannot recapture the mood of 1777. (There are factual errors of no particular account — he gives the year as 1776 instead of 1777, and he dates his ascent of the Brocken as having occurred on December 7, instead of December 10, as his diary entry shows.) Much more important, Goethe involuntarily falsifies the circumstances and the mood that carried him forward. He speaks of setting out on the plain and riding into the uplands when he saw the motionless vulture outlined against the heavy morning clouds. This is the way Kannegießer had read the introductory strophe of the poem, and I dare say many other readers have done the same. However, a vulture, motionless bedded on the clouds, lets us see his back rather than his belly. How can he be looking for prey, it may be asked, through an obscuring bank of clouds? But there may be rifts in the clouds that he is pausing to exploit. Certainly the scene is more in keeping with the poem when we see the poet looking down upon the cloud bank and the vulture from above. In his account Goethe was evidently thinking of the start of his two weeks' journey, whereas the poem gives us the introit to an experience compressed to involve little more than twenty-four hours.

For another thing: whereas the mood of the poem's initial section is somber, austere, wholly impersonal, under the spell of Anagke, in viewing the fates of mankind, the mood of the commentator is cheerful and reads his sense of his own personal good fortune into the corresponding lines of strophes two and four. The commentator is so highly pleased with Kannegießer's elaboration, that we feel him savoring the incense and the aura of orthodox Christian piety which envelops the poet in Kannegießer's projection. He is loath to correct him on any point. As for the final strophe, to be sure, Goethe invokes the privilege of symbolism to interpret the veins of the brother mountains, not as brooks and rivers, but rather as the metallic veins of the brother mountains exploited by mines that account for the prosperity of the region. At that time no mine shaft had been sunk in the Brocken itself. The original reading of the poem, never published, "Du stehst, das Geweid unerforscht," replaced by "Du stehst mit unerforschtem Busen," spoke of the unexplored entrails of the mountain. ("Unerforscht" was readily taken by many later commen-

tators to mean "unerforschlich," inscrutable, leading to the misapprehension that it were the godhead he is apostrophizing.) With the
original reading entrails replaced by the conventional bosom, neither
Kannegießer nor any other discerning reader would have been likely
to hit upon Goethe's meaning. Thus, when Wolfgang Herwig, in his
perceptive notes to his reprint of Kannegießer's essay, stresses that
Goethe did not contradict Kannegießer on any point, we may certainly waive this exception.

We might, however, have thought of Goethe as furrowing his
brow at Kannegießer's strangely insensitive comment regarding the
plight of the animals exposed to the rigors of winter. Goethe does
not touch upon this. However, in pursuance of Kannegießer's observations on strophe three, Goethe formulates a pronouncement that
brings us back to our moot line, "die Reiher" vs. "die Reichen."
Plunging *in medias res*, Goethe says: "Wahrscheinlich ist ein wundersamer Druckfehler daher entstanden, daß Setzer oder Korrektor
die Reichen, die ihm keinen Sinn zu geben schienen, in Reiher ver-
wandelte, welche doch auf einiges Verhältnis zu den Rohrsperlingen
hindeuten möchten." (Probably a wondrous misprint arose by virtue of the fact that typesetter or proofreader, to whom "the rich"
did not seem to make sense, transformed them into herons, which
made a certain sense after all when thought of in connection with
the reed sparrows.) Goethe goes on to say that the present edition
reads "die Reiher," whereas the preceding edition read "die Reichen." By the preceding edition he is obviously referring to the original edition of 1789; for the time being he is forgetful of the fact
that both authorized Cotta editions, the one of 1806, as well as that
of 1815, have the version "die Reiher." Goethe does not waste another word on this matter. Again we notice that this dismissal of
"die Reiher" does not involve a correction of Kannegießer, but only
the correction of a misprint. In fact, taking up Kannegießer's designation of "Sperlinge" as "Rohrsperlinge," he makes it clear that he
had marsh birds in mind.[13] Here Goethe authenticates the reading
"die Reichen" a second time.

---

13 Harry Mielert, "Das innere Gesetz der 'Harzreise im Winter'," *Goethe.
Viermonatsschrift der Goethe Gesellschaft* (Weimar 1941), pp. 168-181,

When here the problem of variant readings has loomed again, it has taken on a wholly new aspect. It has disconcertingly shifted from a literary plane to a plane of ornithology and life science. Kannegießer had interpreted the reference to reed birds and herons as having settled in the marshes to mean that with the arrival of the cold season these birds bury themselves in the muck of the swamps, to hibernate in a state of rigidity until the returning warmth of spring restores their vitality. Incredible though this sounds, it was based on Aristotle's treatise on animals, Book 8, Chapter 16, Wolfgang Herwig's commentary tells us, and this doctrine had been passed on as a fact of natural history throughout the ages, to the end of the 18th century. We find this theory restated at greater length in Erich Trunz' critical apparatus (I, 479f.), when he tells us that in his lectures on natural history, Immanuel Kant, who knew everything about synthetic judgments *a priori*, told his students that the majority of birds dig their way into the ground at the coming of winter and hibernate like badgers or ants, without food, and that the swallows live in the water. It was not until 1814, Trunz continues, that a Heidelberg professor dismissed this theory as fanciful, citing, however, a host of learned authorities to the contrary.

Kannegießer, thus, imputed to the last line of strophe three, "in ihre Sümpfe sich gesenkt," the meaning that the reed birds, as well as the herons, were said by Goethe to bury themselves alive in the muck to hibernate there.

In the first part of this excursus we came as close as possible to proving that, as I put it, the word "Reiher" flowed from Goethe's pen when he first wrote "Harzreise im Winter." We now ask ourselves: was Goethe brought up to believe the preposterous notion of birds hibernating in the muck? Whatever may be said of the reed birds, could Goethe, twenty-eight years old when he wrote this poem, have thought of the herons as burying themselves in the swamps? This seems incredible, when every school boy knew that the storks left their nests on the roofs of the peasants' houses in the fall to return in the spring. How could long-legged birds like the herons manage such a feat as Kannegießer envisaged? Our professor of literature must have known from Schiller's "Die Kraniche des Ibykus" (1797), if from no other source, that at least the cranes, another species of long-legged water birds, migrate southward in the winter. Ibykus spots them overhead on his voyage from Reggio to Corinth as "Schwärme von Kranichen . . . , die fernhin nach des Südens Wärme / in graulichtem Geschwader ziehn." Did Goethe ever hold the notion that reed sparrows buried themselves alive? Who can answer this with certainty? Young Goethe had spent much time in the open country, but at the time of his coming to Weimar he had not yet engaged in any serious study of animal life. However, by 1785, eight years after writing "Harzreise im Winter" and four years before its publication, he had progressed far enough in his study of comparative anatomy of vertebrates, notably mammals, birds, and fish, to realize what changes in form and life habits are involved in the phenomenal modifications of an archetypal structure. This was when he rediscovered the intermaxillary bone of the human upper-jaw. As his insights increased with his observations in later years with regard to the correlation of form, function, and ambience, it is impossible to conceive that the mature Goethe could have read Kannegießer's elucidations of this part of his text without amusement. Far from agreeing with Kannegießer's interpretation of this line, Goethe must have dismissed it as absurd. We note, however, that apart from dismissing "die Reiher" as a wondrous misprint, Goethe did not say another word on the matter. Although Goethe is very expansive in this essay, his lips shut firmly at this point. It was no concern of his to set Kannegießer right on his weird notions of animal behavior. Perhaps he shrank from wounding him after so commendable a piece of exegesis. Goethe sat, inhaling Kannegießer's incense, with the smile of a sphinx.

We are now ready to tighten our net of conjecture in the hope of catching a fish. Perhaps things happened as follows:

Perhaps one of Goethe's intimates, shown the draft of the poem, took offense at the lines "Und mit den Sperlingen / Haben längst die Reiher / In ihre Sümpfe sich gesenkt." Perhaps he pictured this in terms of the obsolete notions voiced by Kannegießer more than forty years later. The image of herons struggling to bury themselves in the muck was indeed funny. It might have invoked the image of the ostrich who buries his head in the sand, except hat the herons did not stop at such half-way measures. I think of Merck or Herder as the type of critical mind that might have raised such a question, un-intentionally casting a ridiculous light upon our passage. In what peaceful terms Goethe had conceived it by way of contrast when, perhaps on the very day of writing the poem, he had applied the term *gesenkt* to his own person in writing to Charlotte: "Liebes Gold, ich hab an keinem Orte Ruh. Ich habe mich tiefer ins Gebürg gesenkt . . ." Was there a remedy to ward off ridiculous ambiguity? There was a flash of inspiration. By a trick of language no less wond-rous than the misprint, the whole passage could be salvaged and given a tang, moreover, that the original had lacked. The change of two letters did the trick. Perhaps the joy of the find prevented any aware-ness of the fact that the new version was a disruptive intrusion on the sustained mood of the poem. I say no more. My only regret in clos-ing this piece is that Goethe is not among us to say the last word.

7.
NIETZSCHE'S DIONYSUS–ARIADNE FIXATION

I belong among those machines that are liable to fly to pieces. (Nietzsche to Peter Gast, August 14, 1881). This self-characterization proved prophetic. The first intimation from Nietzsche to his friends that the catastrophe had occurred came in a letter to Professor Jakob Burckhardt of Basel, dated Turin, January 4, 1889, and reading as follows:

To my revered Jakob Burckhardt. That was the trifling joke on account of which I forgive myself the boredom of having created a world. Now you are [*sind Sie – bist Du –*] our great greatest teacher: for I, together with Ariadne, have to be only the golden balance of all things. All specific matters are in the hands of specialists who are more expert than we . . .

Dionysus

A second long letter, blending lucidity with madness, arrived the next day. The final postscript to this letter contained the sentence: "The *rest* for Frau Cosima . . . Ariadne . . . From time to time there is magic . . ." Here the cryptic apotheosis was deciphered: Ariadne was none other than the widow of Richard Wagner. Burckhardt shared the devastating news with Nietzsche's trusted friend Franz Overbeck, who rushed to Turin at once to pick up the pieces. Frau Cosima herself received a note reading: "Ariadne, ich liebe Dich," signed Dionysus. Two additional letters of Nietzsche's, addressed to her during those January days, are preserved in the Bayreuth archive.

The collapse of Nietzsche's mind produced nothing new. The elements of a web of fantasy, associating himself with the god Dionysus and Cosima with his mythical counterpart Ariadne, had long been germinating. What the breakdown did was to turn a play of fantasy into a delusion. As was to be expected, the Dionysus-Ariadne fixation became one of the most intriguing chapters in Nietzsche's biography. The vested interests of the Nietzsche archive, governed by the unscrupulous manipulations of Nietzsche's sister Elizabeth, contributed to much early misinformation. Against this, the two-volume work of Carl Albrecht Bernoulli[1] on Nietzsche and Overbeck (1908), provided a counterweight of verifiable solid information. In 1912 Hans Belart's book on Nietzsche and Wagner[2] and, in the nineteen-twenties, Charles Andler's six-volume study of Nietzsche,[3] contributed much to the clarification of the facts. More recently, after a spate of mythopoeic and oracular attempts to assign to Ariadne a symbolic function in Nietzsche's philosophy, Erich Podach's abrasively polemical monograph,[4] abounding in venomous innuendo, affords a glimpse into Nietzsche's notebooks (1963), and shows that the published text of Nietzsche's *inedita* referring to Ariadne cannot be trusted on all points.

All this refers to the late Nietzsche. To arrive at any real understanding of what is involved, we must briefly review young Nietzsche's relation to Frau Cosima. Nietzsche first made her acquaintance in 1869, the year he came to Basel as a professor of classical philology at the University. He experienced the fascination of her personality from the start. The Wagners were then living in Triebschen on Lake Luzern, close enough to Basel for Nietzsche to make twenty-three extended visits to their home before the Wagner household removed to Bayreuth in 1872. Allowing for Nietzsche's worship of Wagner's genius, it was Frau Cosima who sustained the lift of Nietzsche's spirits to a degree impossible to overestimate. As a trophy laid at her feet, Bayreuth preserves a sumptuously executed manuscript of one hundred and twenty-five pages, more than half of them blank, in Nietzsche's hand, bound in leather and embossed with metal. Spread over several pages, its title reads:

1   Karl Albrecht Bernoulli, *Franz Overbeck und Friedrich Nietzsche, eine Freundschaft* (Jena: E. Diederichs, 1908).
2   Hans Belart, *Friedrich Nietzsches Freundschaftstragödie mit Richard Wagner und Cosima Wagner-Liszt* (Dresden: C. Reissner, 1912).
3   Charles Andler, *Nietzsche, sa vie et sa pensée* (Paris: Editions Bossard, 1920-31).
4   Erich F. Podach, *Ein Blick in die Notizbücher Nietzsches* (Heidelberg: W. Rothe Verlag, 1963).

Five Prefaces
to Five Unwritten Books
For Frau Cosima Wagner
with Affectionate Devotion and in
Answer to Oral and Epistolary Questions,
Penned in a Cheerful Frame of Mind
During the Christmas Season of 1872

In these "Five Prefaces" Nietzsche cast himself in the role of tutor and mentor for a woman whom he admired above all other women, and to whom, even after his break with Wagner, he continued to pay homage. In these Prefaces Nietzsche appears as an eloquent, self-assured, dogmatic young teacher, priding himself on the privilege of guiding a woman of supreme intelligence, tact, and charm through the intellectual panorama of the present day, a task for which his schooling in the life of ancient Greece certified him, in his opinion, as a qualified interpreter. Except for a facsimile reproduction made in World War II, this manuscript was never published before Karl Schlechta included it in his edition of Nietzsche's Work.[5] No translation in English has been published to my knowledge.

The Prefaces are a highly interesting document containing many purple passages that correspond to Nietzsche's university lecture notes, which are part of the large octavo edition in nineteen volumes (1903-20), known as the Kröner edition. They are characterized by the idealistic, often ferocious extremism which reasserts itself in Nietzsche's last period. The philosophical matrix of all the thought developed is Schopenhauer's metaphysics. While it is outside the scope of this paper to attempt even a succinct analysis of their contents, these Prefaces harbor a number of ideas and situations which come to the fore again in the culmination of the Dionysus-Ariadne fixation. They will be referred to many times in this paper. At this point, however, we must limit ourselves to putting on exhibit one

---

5   Friedrich Nietzsche, *Werke in drei Bänden,* ed. Karl Schlechta (Darmstadt: Wissenschaftliche Buchgesellschaft, 1966). Vol. III, pp. 265-299. No English translation has been published to my knowledge. Except where otherwise noted, all quotations from Nietzsche, including the letters, are based on Schlechta's edition. All translations are my own. Most of these can be checked against available American translations by Walter Kaufmann.

single sentence which we run across in the Third Preface, entitled
"The Greek State." The impact of the sentence in question is in inverse
proportion to its innocuous, casual introduction. Taking the form of
a purely ornamental simile, it is designed to lend a touch of color to
Nietzsche's exposition of the distaste felt by the highborn free
Greek toward work, labor, toil of all sorts. Nietzsche inveighs against
the slogans "dignity of labor," "dignity of man," as modern inven-
tions of our soft and mendacious civilization. The Greek did not
require such slogans, and he had no use for them. As for the dignity
of labor, any exertion in the interest of preserving either the individual or the species was distasteful to the Greek's sense of the free play
of his powers, Nietzsche tells us. To reinforce this idea, Nietzsche
resorts to the following simile: "and as a father admires the beauty
and talents of his child, but can think of the act that gave it life only
with shamefaced repugnance (*mit schamhaftem Widerwillen, so er-
ging es dem Griechen*)." Nietzsche is saying, this is the way the
Greeks felt about it. This simile sparkles in a variety of facets that
dazzle and confound the beholder. It presents itself, in the first
place, as a self-evident proposition common to civilized men. In less
decorous language: sex is a nasty business at best. In the case of
many readers, our sentence might slip unexamined through customs,
as it were, as part of the cant of respectable bourgeois society in a
taboo-ridden age. Coming from the pen of Nietzsche's sister, for example, the statement would have sounded perfectly natural. But
could young Nietzsche, twenty-eight at the time, writing to a woman
of thirty-five, have phrased such a sentiment without expressing a
very personal feeling? I cannot believe it. And if the words mean
what they say, they reveal an attitude toward sex on his part that is
immature and abnormal. It is even stranger that natural tact should
not have forbidden his referring to so delicate a topic as sex in addressing a woman who had given birth to five children under circumstances that trained the disapproving spotlight of the world upon
her. We should observe, on the other hand, that both of them were
disciples of Schopenhauer and by virtue of this fact subscribers to
the doctrine that carnal lust is the motive power that spawns the continuing evil of individuation. They knew the lament of the dying
Tristan and Hans Sachs's melancholy reflection on man's frenzy: *in*

Flucht geschlagen, wähnt er zu jagen; hört nicht sein eigen Schmerz-
gekreisch, wenn er sich wühlt ins eigne Fleisch . . .[5a] Finally, in dealing with sexual procreation under the category of labor, could our
classical scholar's subconscious self have flashed across the screen of
his mind an image of Hercules performing one of his labors in im-
pregnating the fifty daughters of King Thespios in one night? Surely
the many facetious literary allusions to this labor of Hercules could
not have escaped his notice. And what does all this add up to? It
seems impossible that this young idealist should have sullied the
image of the woman whom he placed on the highest pedestal by indulging in erotic daydreams about her person. Jealousy of Wagner
was another matter. In view of Wagner's extravagant demands on
Cosima's exclusive attention, jealousy, avowed or unavowed, may
have contributed greatly to the strain which made Nietzsche curtail
his visits to the Wagners in the years to come more and more, and
which unquestionably accounts in large part for his constant psycho-
somatic illness.

To return to the beginning. When the machine of Nietzsche's
mind flew to pieces exactly sixteen years after the Christmas gift of
those "Five Prefaces to Five Unwritten Books" for Frau Cosima, his
inner relation to Frau Cosima had transformed itself into something
entirely new. He, for his part, had transcended the limits of mortality
by identifying himself with the god Dionysus, and Frau Cosima had
for him become Ariadne, with whom Dionysus celebrated his divine
nuptials after she had been abandoned by the mortal hero Theseus
on the island of Naxos. The correspondence of the myth to the human relationship which it supplanted in Nietzsche's mind amounts
to this: Naxos, the island locale of the Greek myth, stands for Triebschen, the home of the Wagners during Nietzsche's halcyon days. After
Wagner's death in 1883, Theseus-Wagner seems to have faded out of
the picture. These mythical identifications, encased in the solipsistic
shell of Nietzsche's mind for who knows how long, broke upon the
world as communicable fact in the letters quoted above.

5a „put to flight he fancies himself the pursuer; hears not his own cries of
anguish when he gouges his own flesh . . . "

Taking the mythical identifications of Nietzsche's collapse as given data, we shall make it our task to study the germination and growth of the mythical fixation before it became manifest for all eyes to see. This formulation of our purpose is admittedly a great overstatement. Our evidence at best will be fragmentary, and I do not propose to indulge in idle speculation. I believe, however, that we can get something in the way of insight by proceeding in an orderly way. To this end we shall look for evidence first in the body of Nietzsche's work, published and intended by him for publication. After this is done we shall look into Nietzsche's posthumously published papers for supporting evidence. As a third possible source there exists, of course, the vast body of letters, but in view of the fact that few public figures have been so singularly reticent regarding their personal sex life as Nietzsche, I regard it as highly unlikely that any light will be shed on our problem from this source.

Proceeding chronologically, we begin with *Beyond Good and Evil*, published in 1886, three years before the onset of Nietzsche's madness. By virtue of hindsight, we wonder what the earliest readers — Erwin Rohde, Franz Overbeck, Peter Gast — could have made of the handful of aphorisms that conclude this volume. Shifting to a much more subjective stance than the body of the book had assumed, they weave a spell of masquerading innuendo, obliterating all tangible outlines of the writer's personality in favor of a teasing, dazzling lyricism that culminates in an overwhelming narcissistic extended apostrophe to the elements of his own poetic imagery, all of which are substantized (*verdinglicht*), personified, or at least endowed with a faculty of perceptive response to their creator. As a poet, Nietzsche was one of the most unabashed devotees of the technique that Ruskin excoriated as the pathetic fallacy. After that final aphorism, Nietzsche breaks into verse, projecting his own image as that of a dweller in icy mountain wastes where the men he had known as friends are too weak to follow. There is a cryptic, enigmatic quality about those aphorisms which, by virtue of hindsight, can be read as confessing the fact that the writer harbors a secret that he is desperately eager to point to and touch upon but not to reveal — a quality of elusiveness for which our age of cold war has coined the term brinkmanship. If this game were being played for the reader's entertainment rather than the author's, we would refer to it as a kind of strip-tease performance.

Aphorism 288 discusses the art of concealing a higher intelligence by a mask of dullness and virtue. Aphorism 289 projects an image of the hermit-philosopher, a bear in his den, a dragon in his lair, one moving in a labyrinth, becoming more and more inscrutable even to himself, more imponderable, all the more fascinating on that account. This aphorism contains the sentence, "Does one not write books for the very purpose of concealing what one harbors within oneself?" After this dazzling spate of metaphors to emphasize the philosopher's unfathomable remoteness, the next, Aphorism 290, attunes its virtuosity to a softer key. It appeals to the reader's heart and invokes a feeling akin to pity for a form of existence so sublimely remote. To quote:

Every deep thinker is more afraid of being understood than of being misunderstood. The latter may grieve his vanity, but the former grieves his heart, his compassion, which always says: "Alas, why do you want your life to be as burdensome as mine?"

Aphorism 291 develops the old theme of morality as a mask; 292 projects the image of the philosopher as a meteorological phenomenon, a lightning storm; Aphorism 293 harps once more on the idea of pity. Branding the common run of pity as a mean symptom of a degenerate age, such as he had already done with the same emphasis in the third of the "Five Prefaces," he acknowledges pity as a positive value if it springs not from weakness but from an overabundance of inner wealth. It seems probable that Nietzsche included this well-worn thought at this point as a springboard for launching the theme which everything here discussed has been leading up to. One more step, however, has to be negotiated before venturing the leap: Aphorism 294, headed "The Olympian Vice," ranges philosophers in an ascending series according to the quality of their laughter, the highest being those capable of the golden, the Olympian laughter, which resounds even in the observance of solemn, sacred rites. With studiedly casual artfulness he continues:

Supposing that gods also philosophize, a conclusion which has forced itself upon me on many accounts, I do not doubt that they accompany this activity with a new and superhuman mode of laughter at the expense of everything serious...

Gods as philosophers, philosophers as gods — with this idea Nietz-sche has enticed us into a semi-mythical region where the con-tours of manlike gods and god-like men lose their distinction and blend.

What had just been thrown out as a playful hunch becomes some-thing like a matter-of-course affirmation in Aphorism 295, when our philosopher communes with philosophizing gods. Readers of the "Five Prefaces" will remember seeing him in the company of Hera-clitus, Pythagoras and Empedocles, as he had sketched them in the first of those "Five Prefaces." Did he not elevate Heraclitus to the rank of godhead by asserting that we need the testimony of history to vouch for so sublime an existence because the unaided imagina-tion would not be capable of creating so exalted a figure? Indeed, this aphorism is designed to introduce us to and familiarize us with the idea that the writer of these words, sharing the company and discourse of superhuman beings, has himself passed the threshold of the realm barred to human entry. His companion and divine men-tor in particular is Dionysus. This god he worshiped in his youth, and to him he brought his firstlings as an offering, he says, with a trans-parent reference to his first book, *The Birth of Tragedy*. Of this god he is the last disciple. The god has taught him arcane and esoteric wisdom in intimate companionship and by word of mouth. There must be something akin to an *unio mystica* between them. Boasting of his intimacy with the god, Nietzsche confesses to something like a sense of indiscretion in imparting fragments of the revelation re-ceived to his mortal friends. And one such fragment is presently of-fered, lifting by a trifle the veil that conceals the relations of Diony-sus to Ariadne.

But if we have been anticipating unpardonably in all this, our choice lay simply between quoting the aphorism in its entirety and speeding to follow it to its end point. Indeed, I venture to think that Aphorism 295 must be pondered many times and slowly for its in-cantation to work the effect intended by its author. For what could be stranger than its tantalizingly labyrinthine beginning! "The Ge-nius of the Heart" is the initial phrase. It is a puzzling phrase, and I shall try to elucidate it at once according to my lights. In the third of the "Five Prefaces" genius was one of the principal topics. There are many types of genius. The genius of art had been uppermost in young Nietzsche's mind, but the genius of the sage and philosopher had been a close rival of his interest, and a large part of the "Third Preface" focussed on the military genius as end and aim of the unconscious forces of nature at work in producing the state. In another place Nietzsche carried his generalities to the point of saying that the end and aim of all human existence is the bringing to birth of the Olympian man. This involves, of course, the heightening of every human quality to the point of genius. Long after the writing of these "Five Prefaces," Nietzsche adopted the term "Superman" to embody his ideal. At the time of the "Prefaces," Heraclitus had figured as a superman without the label, but his aloofness, austerity, and scorn of humankind had marked him with a limitation that fell short of universality, and which the later embodiment of the ideal in *Zarathustra* was designed to transcend. In addition to the genius of art, wisdom, and power, Zarathustra was intended to embody also "the genius of the heart," the most expansive and exalted generosity of the emotions. This had been underemphasized, to be sure, because the image of Zarathustra had concentrated on discipline, hardness, and cruelty despite the occasional revelation of a softer side to his nature. Now, in our Aphorism 295, Nietzsche, identifying himself with Zarathustra and, as we see, with Dionysus, is intent on compensating for this deficiency by intoning as loud and clear a paean as he can utter to the finest distillate of warmth, compassion, generosity, love. The hard metal of Zarathustra has been worked into a state of flux. Making allowance for all possible reservations, *Das Genie des Herzens* comes closest to the message of Beethoven's Ninth Symphony in the jubilant words of Schiller's hymn, *Seid umschlungen, Millionen!*

Now what have we here? He utters the phrase, *das Genie des Herzens*, and begins an elaboration of it that is labyrinthine and cryptic. Pausing in the middle of an already extended period, he repeats the thematic phrase and proceeds to develop its implications by a second series of involved clauses. He repeats the phrase a third time, to follow it by further explication, and for good measure he follows this procedure a fourth time, in order to break off with a feigned gesture of surprise as though he had caught himself in an embarrassing oversight. Apologizing, he gives the genius of the heart a name — his name, Dionysus, as though this had been too self-evident to require mention. So, by a sleight of hand, as it were, the austere Heraclitus, the superman Zarathustra, are recast in a divine embodiment in which Nietzsche almost partakes after the manner of an *unio mystica*. We would say emphatically that he does so already, if it were not for the fact that at the end of the aphorism he includes himself in the human scene. With this god Dionysus, the quintessence of charismatic charm, Nietzsche has talked many times in intimate conversation. *Zwiegespräche* is the term he uses for the conversation between the god and his initiate. Whenever these are mentioned, I use the term *duologue* to avoid confusion. Ariadne, though sometimes present, is never conceived in this connection as a partner.

And now we are given one small sample of that esoteric knowledge which Nietzsche had promised to pass on to his friends *sotto voce*, namely: in the presence of Ariadne, the god makes an apparently lighthearted but momentous pronouncement to his disciple:

"Under certain conditions I love man." And with these words he alluded to Ariadne, who was present. „Man is for me a brave, pleasant, inventive animal that has not its likes upon earth. It has a way of finding its bearings in every kind of labyrinth. I am fond of him and I often reflect on how I can improve him still further and make him stronger, wickeder, deeper than he is." – "Stronger, wickeder, deeper?" I asked, startled. "Yes," he said once more, "stronger, wickeder, deeper; also more beautiful." And in saying this the tempter-god smiled his halcyon smile, as though he had just delivered himself of an enchanting compliment.

At these words, turning to the reader with pretended indignation, Nietzsche charges the god with a lack of perceptiveness and reserve. "One sees here," he says, "that this god is deficient not only in modesty. Indeed, there are good reasons for surmising that the gods, taken generally, might do well to take a leaf out of our book. We humans are more humane." What is Nietzsche saying here but that the god, in having such an idea cross his mind, and venturing to pronounce it in Ariadne's presence, is not only tactless, but also imperceptive. For Nietzsche, Ariadne is the absolute embodiment of beauty. His feeling charges the god with an act of *lèse majesté*. What a long time it has taken him to come around to the point!

But there can be no question: Nietzsche has composed the whole panegyric on Dionysus as the genius of the heart for the sake of being able to deliver himself of an unqualified act of homage to the beauty of Cosima-Ariadne. In the same way, in a later book, we shall find Nietzsche paying this same compliment to his idol under more enigmatic circumstances. At this point we simply repeat our puzzled question: What could Nietzsche's most intimate friends and admirers have made of this aphorism as they read it for the first time in 1886?[6] We might indeed add: the final Aphorism, 296, with its jubilantly narcissistic tone, reflects Nietzsche's delight in the fact that he has just confessed to all the world to something that passed in and out of the ears of all who heard, without comprehension.

More than two years later, in *Twilight of the Idols* (1888), we see the same scene enacted with the same cast, in the chapter entitled "Forays of a Man Out of Season." Aphorism 19 presents a brief lecture on the theme that all our judgments and experiences of beauty — beauty of the world in general and human beauty in particular — involve an anthropomorphic bias. This is nothing new for anyone familiar with the conceptions of nineteenth-century science, even though it no longer sees the world in the anthropocentric, quasi-metaphysical terms of Goethe's famous essay on Winckelmann (1805). But we must hear it in full in order to see it converge upon a point, the *raison d'être* of its inclusion.

Beautiful and Ugly — Nothing is more conditioned, let us say, more *limited*, than our sense of beauty. He who would think of it as detached from the pleasure man derives from man, would immediately lose the ground from under his feet. "Beauty as such" is only a word, not even a concept. Beautiful man posits himself as the measure of perfection. In exceptional cases he worships himself in its contemplation. A biological species simply *cannot* avoid affirming itself in this manner. Its *fundamental* instinct — the instinct for self-preservation and self-expansion — radiates such sublimities. Man thinks of nature as offering a sumptuous display of beauty; he forgets himself as its cause. He alone has endowed it with beauty. Alas, only with a human, all-too-human beauty. At bottom man reflects himself in things: he regards everything as beautiful that reflects his

---

6   Because Walter Kaufmann's collection, *The Portable Nietzsche*, contains only a short portion of *Beyond Good and Evil*, not including the final aphorisms, I have translated Aphorism 295 in full, as an Appendix.

image. The judgment "beautiful" is the *vanity* of his *species*. The sceptic may
hear a faint suspicion whisper in his ear: has the world really been beautified
by the fact that it happens to be man who finds it beautiful? He has *humanized*
it, that is all. Nothing, absolutely nothing is a guarantee of the idea that it is
man in particular who furnishes the model of beauty. Who knows what a figure
man cuts in the eyes of a higher arbiter of taste? Daring, perhaps? Perhaps pro-
voking a smile? Perhaps a little arbitrary? . . . "Oh Dionysus, divine one, why
do you tug at my ears?" Ariadne once asked her philosopher-lover during one
of those famous duologues on Naxos. "I find a sort of humor in your ears,
Ariadne. Why aren't they even longer?"

Thus ends the aphorism. This time the god's comment on beauty
à propos of Ariadne does not evoke the disciple's mock-indignant
protest. He has understood. It is as if the god had been saying: Let us
suppose that the norm of human features included a pair of asses'
ears. In such a case the most exquisite beauty would be required to
conform to this state of things. The god is here obviously alluding to
Titania's predicament in "A Midsummer Night's Dream." For those
in the know, the particular point of the illustration chosen by the
god is that Cosima was admired for her very small ears, and this was
also a feature on which Nietzsche prided himself in his own person.
We shall find both these facts borne out by later passages, apart from
the fact that they are well attested by outside sources.

One more thing strikes us about this aphorism. In the earlier
book, Dionysus made his remarks on beauty *à propos* of Ariadne
during a duologue with his disciple-initiate. Now, for the first time,
these duologues are referred to as "those famous duologues on Naxos." The demonstrative "those" implies that they are well known.
They are characterized as famous, and the reference to their specific
locale (Naxos-Triebschen) rounds off the phrase. Why did Nietzsche
refer to them in this way, when these exchanges between god and
disciple transpired in absolute intimacy? Was he not thereby saying
that they were destined to become famous? For those who know the
"Five Prefaces," there comes to mind the initial theme in the "First
Preface" — Fame as a distinction to accrue to Nietzsche and to
endure throughout all eternity. Was he not now anticipating the time
when, having sloughed off his mortal shell, he would stand in the full
radiance of godhead for all to see?

"Those famous duologues on Naxos." This memorable phrase recurs in *The Antichrist*: Transvaluation of All Values, the final fanatical formulation of Nietzsche's repudiation of Christianity before his breakdown. Although this time Ariadne is not mentioned, and Dionysus is present only by implication as the guiding spirit of these duologues, the passage must nevertheless be quoted in its context because of the echoes it evokes. In the course of a long aphorism, number 39, Nietzsche musters all his resources of vitriolic venom to characterize Christianity as

this most peculiar (*fremdartigste*) of all phenomena (*Tatsachen*), a religion not only conditioned by error, but inventive to the point of genius, *only* in noxious, *only* in life- and heart-poisoning errors. Viewed from on high . . . this religion is a *spectacle for gods* — for those divinities who are at the same time philosophers, and whom I encountered, for example, during those famous duologues on Naxos. At the moment when they (*—and we!*) have overcome our nausea, they become grateful for the spectacle of the Christian: the wretched little star (*Gestirn*) which bears the name of Earth possibly deserves, solely because of *this* curious case, a divine glance, a divine interest . . .

Here the contrast is strikingly reminiscent of the first of those "Five Prefaces," which introduced us to three philosopher-divinities: Heraclitus, Pythagoras, and Empedocles, and made the disdainful reference to the diminutive "*Gestirn*," Earth, that harbored a breed of creatures who prided themselves on having invented cognition. In the case of a philosopher who disposes of time in so sovereign a manner as Nietzsche, the anachronism involved in the spectacle of Christianity being viewed by three great pre-Socratics must not faze us. This is the fourth time, incidentally, that Nietzsche takes us into a realm of myth where divinities are at the same time philosophers.

It is now time for us to scan the last of Nietzsche's works, the autobiography *Ecce Homo*, begun on his forty-fourth birthday, October 15, 1888, for traces of the Dionysus-Ariadne complex. Can we doubt that Nietzsche now feels aloof from everything human, like Heraclitus, when he writes, "At an absurdly early time, at the age of seven, I already knew that no human word would ever reach up to me. Has anyone ever seen me troubled on this account?" ("Why I Am So Clever," number 10). *Ecce Homo* contains one direct reference to Frau Cosima, the only such reference found in the whole body of Nietzsche's writings. Developing the idea that in the German social world everything significant in matters of taste derives from France, he exemplifies this by a reference to Frau Cosima, who had been educated in France. "In matters of taste, Frau Cosima had no rival among all the women of my acquaintance." ("Why I Am So Clever," number 3.)

As for Ariadne, her name makes its appearance where Nietzsche discusses his *Zarathustra*. He says, "Such things have never been uttered in poetry, never felt, never suffered. This is the way a god suffers. The answer to such solar isolation in its own light would be Ariadne. Who, except myself knows," he continues, "what Ariadne is? Of all such riddles up to now no one was in possession of the solution. I doubt that anybody here so much as suspected a riddle." ("Thus Spake Zarathustra" number 8). Here Nietzsche hints that Ariadne is a cryptogram, but he is still sufficiently in control to keep the identification of Ariadne with Cosima to himself. This passage represents the extreme instance of what I have called brinkmanship encountered anywhere. That cryptogram was deciphered only when Nietzsche went over the brink in his last letter to Jacob Burckhardt, January 5, 1889.

We find another veiled reference to the Dionysus-Ariadne complex in *Ecce Homo*, where Nietzsche quotes at length from the labyrinthine Aphorism 295 of *Beyond Good and Evil*, which we took such pains to analyze. Beginning with that memorable phrase, "The Genius of the Heart," he precedes the quotation by the peremptory injunction, "I forbid any surmise, by the way, as to whom I am describing in that passage." ("Why I Write Such Good Books," number 6.) Is not this his grimly humorous way of stating that not one of the few readers of the earlier book remembers the passage in which he had portrayed Dionysus, and himself as his reincarnation? This was another case of his playing hide-and-seek, exhibiting a side of his personality which radiated a mellow warmth, and countered this at the same time by a posture of imperious ferocity.

One more bit of evidence, not altogether trifling, regarding the Dionysus-Ariadne complex is found under the caption "Why I Write Such Good Books," number 2, where Nietzsche refers to his small ears as a feature of distinction: "Indeed, I venture to claim that I have the smallest ears." That Ariadne enjoyed the same distinction was expressed by innuendo when her divine lover tugged at her ears in lecturing on the anthropomorphic bias of the human ideal of beauty. We shall find further confirmation presently regarding the ears of Cosima-Ariadne. This completes our consideration of *Ecce Homo*.

We shall now supplement what we learned from the books issued and prepared by Nietzsche for publication by gleanings and snippets from the posthumous papers. The first item, however, to be taken up belongs more properly perhaps to the earlier category. Nietzsche's posthumous papers included a folder entitled "Dionysus-Dithyrambs." Of particular interest is the poem "Ariadne's Lament."[7] This long piece of free verse, rhymeless except for the last two pairs of lines, presents a weird problem. At the point where Ariadne's lament is done, it is superseded by the radiant apparition and the voice of Dionysus, answering her in prose. To quote:

> A flash of lightning. Dionysus becomes visible
> in emerald radiance.
>
> Dionysus:
> Be wise, Ariadne! . . .
> You have small ears, you have my ears:
> Slip a clever word in them!—
> Must two not first hate each other if they are
> destined to love each other? . . .
> *I am your labyrinth . . .*

There are two highly embarassing facts about "Ariadne's Lament." First, like most of the "Dionysus-Dithyrambs," the Lament had already been published in substantially identical form in *Thus Spake Zarathustra*, Part IV, under the caption "The Conjuror." By substantially identical I mean that such variants as we encounter are minimal and inconsequential. Being uttered by the conjuror as *his* lament, the poem contains a passage couched in masculine grammatical terms (a definite article and a relative pronoun) for which femi-

---

7   Karl Schlechta, *op. cit.* Vol. II, pp. 1256-59.

nines are substituted in the lament as uttered by Ariadne. (" . . .gib mir, *der* Einsamsten, *die* Eis . . . nach Feinden schmachten lehrt. . ."). Owing to the absence of grammatical gender for the corresponding forms in English, the difference cannot even be brought to the reader's attention in translation. There are also a few completely inconsequential transpositions of phrase. In the *Zarathustra* version, Zarathustra meets an old, debilitated man who simulates a fit, throws himself on the ground and delivers himself of what appears to be a long, delirious lament before Zarathustra, realizing that he has been tricked by the old conjurer-poet, takes his stick and thrashes him furiously. After Zarathustra has sufficiently vented his anger by blows, there follows a long exchange of words. Zarathustra rails at the conjurer as a fraud, a man of incredible histrionic talent who simulated the appearance of greatness without there being a shred of it in his personality. It is clear beyond the shadow of a doubt that the old conjurer, also labeled "the penitent of the spirit," stands for the aged Richard Wagner in Zarathustra's gallery of types.

And now for our second embarrassing problem: how is it possible to read these hysterical yearnings of a soul starved for love, these wild outcries of physical pain, these denunciations, defiant taunts, and masochistic baitings of an unseen tormentor-god, these self-lacerations, these posturings of pride, this fluctuation of the emotions brought about by surprise, this gesture of repulsion putting the adversary to flight, and the final passionate gesture involving unconditional mutual surrender — how is this to be read with empathy, when the identical words are tailored to fit a wholly dissimilar situation? In the old man it sounds like an orgiastic indulgence of the passions after the manner of epileptics. If we think of old Wagner specifically, the image of Kundry, frosted, awakening from her hibernation, moaning to be warmed by "the charcoal braziers of the heart," seems to float into the picture. If we think of Ariadne, on the other hand, as uttering all these cries, they make a specific kind of sense in view of the amused coolness of her partner-tormentor, when he finally appears to work her deliverance. All this pain, much of it stoically borne with pride and arrogance, and a sense of exultation in relishing the hurt — does it not suggest those savage initiation rites which precede the investiture of the neophyte in a primitive society?

After all, Ariadne, though a princess, was human. It would therefore be fitting for Dionysus, the god, to exalt her to his own status
by such an ordeal. This makes sense to me, particularly if my surmise
should be correct, that Nietzsche first conceived the poem as the
lament of Ariadne, and then found it convenient to put it, with the
minimal change of gender, into the mouth of the conjurer. Surely
there is an element of sexual conflict suggested in the relation of the
hunter-god to his quarry. The idea of the aggressor descending into
his victim's heart by means of a ladder evokes the quaint conceits of
medieval lyric verse; the victim's pride and defiance of her kidnaper
smack of feminine wiles; and the play of flight and return reveals a
love-hate relationship.

All this interpretation is admittedly subjective, and in my opinion does not warrant further speculation, particularly in view of the
fact that the quality of the verse strikes me as lacking in distinction.
Must "Ariadne's Lament" be booked as a symptom of a mind half
deranged? That is the question to which I do not venture an answer.

Let us now pass in brief review the Ariadne jottings of Nietzsche's
posthumous papers. Citations refer to the twelve posthumous volumes of the well-known Kröner edition, completed in 1919, now in
process of being replaced for the second time by a vastly expanded
critical edition. At approximately the time of the "Five Prefaces"
Nietzsche toyed with the idea of writing a drama on Empedocles,
inspired without doubt by the example of Friedrich Hölderlin, whom
Nietzsche had been the first of his generation to champion from the
days of his adolescence. Volume IX, pages 130-134, contains a
number of scenarios and a prose sketch of an introductory scene.
The scenario of Act Three couples the names of Theseus and Ariadne.
The scenario of Act Five ends with the question: "Does Dionysus
flee from Ariadne?" The question just quoted is indeed startling, but
the context is too fragmentary to warrant extended comment.

Volume XII, page 259, records a quotable aphorism: "A labyrinthine man, regardless of what he may tell us, never seeks the truth,
but only his Ariadne."

Volume XIII, page 250, yields a charmingly humorous sketch of
a Nietzsche-Cosima scene during the initial stage of their acquaintance, for he reports that it took place during his first sojourn on

Naxos. Nietzsche begins with a sample of a lecture he was allegedly delivering to Frau Cosima. Although its focus differs from the views Nietzsche held at the time, his memory certainly served him well in capturing the tone of their conversations in its happy blend of correct formality and free and easy banter. Having elaborated on his views, he continues:

Chatting in this way I gave full rein to my pedagogical bent, for I was tickled to pieces in having somebody who could stand listening to me. But at this very point, Ariadne could stand it no longer — the fact is that this happened on my first sojourn on Naxos — "But *mein Herr!*" she interrupted, "you are talking *Schweinedeutsch!*" — "German," I answered blithely, "simply German! Never mind about the swine, *meine Göttin!* You underestimate the difficulty of saying subtle things in German!" — "Subtle things!" Ariadne cried with horror. "But that was only positivism! Philosophy of the snout! A mish-mash of concepts and swill of a hundred philosophies! What are we coming to?" — and saying this she impatiently played with that famous thread which once guided her Theseus through the labyrinth. — Thus it came to light that in her philosophical education Ariadne was two thousand years behind the times.

Here there is a first mention of Theseus-Wagner in connection with Ariadne. In our pursuance of the Dionysus-Ariadne fixation as displayed in Nietzsche's late works there had been no mention of Theseus-Wagner. We wonder at what time the relegation of Theseus-Wagner to oblivion had begun. Wagner had died before the publication of *Zarathustra* Part I, we remember.

In Volume XIV, page 253, Aphorism 539, we have two series of satirical jottings at Wagner's expense:

Naxos.
From the conversations between
Dionysus, Theseus and Ariadne.
"Theseus is becoming absurd," said Ariadne,
"Theseus is becoming virtuous!" (The hero,
admiring himself, striking a pose of absur-
dity.)
Theseus' jealousy of Ariadne's dream. Dionysus,
without jealousy: "What I love in you, how could
a Theseus love that? One is not jealous when one
is a god, unless it be of gods."

* * *

> "Ariadne," Dionysus said, "you are a labyrinth.
> Theseus lost his way into you, he no longer has
> any thread. What good does it do him now that
> he was not eaten by the Minotaur? What eats him
> is worse than a Minotaur." — "You flatter me,"
> Ariadne answers, "but I do not want to feel pity
> when I love; I am tired of pity. All heroes shall
> perish by me. That is my last love for Theseus:
> I destroy him."

* * *

Final act. Nuptials of Dionysus and Ariadne.

The above page of day-dreaming about Naxos is particularly notable because of its inclusion of Theseus-Wagner in the mythical triangle, a fact which dates the musings that gave rise to these late jottings as prior to Wagner's death, February 13, 1883. Theseus cuts a sorry figure in the eyes of the principals, Dionysus and Ariadne, who speak of him with sarcastic condescension and mock pity, and Ariadne's tone of equanimity yields nothing to one of the celestials or a female Renaissance Borgia. As we saw, all the later developments of the Dionysus-Ariadne myth — in "The Lament of Ariadne," the virtuoso conclusion of *Beyond Good and Evil*, the ear-tugging episode of *Twilight of the Idols*, and the passage in *Antichrist*, recalling "those famous duologues on Naxos" — dispense with any mention of the human hero who seems to have vanished without a trace. Has he then been swallowed up by oblivion? Not quite: Nietzsche had one more ace up his sleeve. He demoted the one-time idol and hero to the role of the monster, for as such he is stamped in Nietzsche's pamphlet, *The Case of Wagner* (1888), in a concluding passage of towering rhetorical rage at the end of the "First Postscript":

. . . Ah, this old Minotaur! What has he not already cost us! Year after year they lead trains of the most beautiful maidens and youths into his labyrinth for him to devour — year after year all Europe intones the paean, "Off to Crete, off to Crete! . . ."

APPENDIX
Beyond Good and Evil. Aphorism 295.

The Genius of the Heart, of which that great concealed one is possessed; the tempter-god and born Pied Piper of consciences; whose voice knows how to descend into the nether world of every soul; who says no word, who casts no glance that does not harbor a device and fold of lure; among whose attributes of mastery is the art of seeming – and not what he is, but what is to those that follow him a *further* compulsion to press close to him, to follow him ever more inwardly and thoroughly – the Genius of the Heart, who silences everything loud and self-complacent and teaches it to listen; who smooths the rough souls and gives them a new desire to taste – to lie still like a mirror so that the deep heavens are reflected in them – the Genius of the Heart who teaches the clumsy and over-hasty hand to grasp with restraint and delicacy; who divines the hidden and forgotten treasure, the drop of kindness and sweet spirituality lodged under thick, cloudy ice, and is a divining rod for every grain of gold that long lay buried in its prison of much sand and mire; the Genius of the Heart, from whose touch everyone departs enriched, not showered by grace, not oppressed and delighted by gifts from without, but richer within himself, newer than before, burst open, touched and spied upon by a spring breeze, more uncertain, perhaps, more tender, more fragile, more fractured, but full of hopes that as yet have no name, full of new will and flow, counter-will and counter-flow . . . but what am I doing, my friends? Of whom am I speaking to you? Did I forget myself so far that I did not even mention his name to you? Unless it be that you did not guess by yourselves who this questionable spirit and god is who wishes to be *praised* in such a manner. Just as happens to everyone who has been a wayfarer and traveler in foreign lands from childhood on, so it happens that I encountered many a strange and not undangerous spirit, but above all him of whom I am speaking, and him again and again, no lesser a one than the god *Dionysus*, that great ambiguous tempter-god, to whose altar, in all reverence and secrecy, I once brought my firstlings as an offering – as the last man, I believe, to bring him an *offering*: for I found no one who understood then what I was doing. In the meantime I accumulated much, altogether too much knowledge, as to the philosophy of this god, and, indeed, by word of mouth — I, the last disciple and initiate of the god, Dionysus: and surely it is high time for me to begin at long last to give you, my friends, a bit of a taste of this philosophy in so far as I am permitted to do so? In a half-whisper, as is proper: for it will involve matters that are secret, new, strange, curious, uncanny. The very fact that Dionysus is a philosopher and hence, that also gods philosophize, seems to me a piece of news with a catch, one that might arouse distrust, particularly among philosophers — among you, my friends, this news will be rather less disturbing unless it be that it comes too late and out of season: for nowadays you are loath to believe in God and gods as I have been given to understand. Perhaps also, that in the frankness of my report, I have to go further than may always accord favorably with the strict habits of your ears? Assuredly the aforesaid god went further during such duologues, much further, and was always ahead of me by many steps . . . Indeed, if it were permitted, I would, according to the manner of men, endow him with many fine and virtuous names, I would make a great to-do of his intrepidity as a searcher and discoverer, of his honesty, candor, truthfulness, and his love of wisdom. But with all this venerable pomp and claptrap such a god does not want to be encumbered. "Keep this," he would say, "for yourself and the likes of you, and whoever needs it! I — find no reason to cover my nakedness!" — One is given to wonder: is this type of god and philosopher perhaps lacking in delicacy? — Thus on one occasion he said: „Under certain conditions I love man" — and with this he alluded to Ariadne, who was present: "Man is for me an agreeable, brave, inventive animal, which does not have its likes on earth, it has a way of finding its bearings in all labyrinths. I am fond of him, and I often reflect on how I can improve him still further and make him stronger, wickeder, and deeper than he is." "Stronger, wickeder, and deeper?" I asked, startled. "Yes," he said once more, "stronger, wickeder, and deeper; also more beautiful," — and with this the tempter-god smiled his halcyon smile, as though he had just delivered himself of a charming compliment. Here one sees at the same time: the divinity is deficient not only in delicacy —; and generally speaking there are good reasons for surmising that the gods as a whole might do well to take a leaf out of our book. We humans are — more humane . . .

8.
RILKES « RÖMISCHE SARKOPHAGE »
(Neue Gedichte)

WAS aber hindert uns zu glauben, daß
(so wie wir hingestellt sind und verteilt)
nicht eine kleine Zeit nur Drang und Haß
und dies Verwirrende in uns verweilt,

wie einst in dem verzierten Sarkophag
bei Ringen, Götterbildern, Gläsern, Bändern,
in langsam sich verzehrenden Gewändern
ein langsam Aufgelöstes lag —

bis es die unbekannten Munde schluckten,
die niemals reden. (Wo besteht und denkt
ein Hirn, um ihrer einst sich zu bedienen?)

Da wurde von den alten Aquädukten
ewiges Wasser in sie eingelenkt —:
das spiegelt jetzt und geht und glänzt in ihnen.

Wir sind gewohnt, Gedichte mit solchem Titel als Dinggedichte
zu bezeichnen. Ob diese Bezeichnung im Einzelfall zutrifft, darüber
läßt sich streiten, je nachdem man den Begriff des Dinggedichts enger
oder weiter faßt. Wir stehen auf sicherem Boden, wenn wir uns darauf beschränken zu sagen: Wie eine stattliche Anzahl der *Neuen Gedichte*, faßt auch dieses Gedicht einen Kunstgegenstand ins Auge, um
ihn nicht nur zu charakterisieren, sondern ihn auch in einen weiteren
Zusammenhang einzubauen, der ihn symbolisch erhöht. Diesmal
steht nicht ein Einzelfall künstlerischer Formung zur Betrachtung,
sondern ein Typus, ein beliebig oft hergestelltes Zweckgerät, wie die
Mehrzahlform des Titels besagt. Der Rilkekenner wird sich dabei sofort an das zehnte Gedicht der ersten Reihe der *Sonette an Orpheus*
erinnert finden:

EUCH, die ihr nie mein Gefühl verließt,
grüß ich, antikische Sarkophage,
die das fröhliche Wasser römischer Tage
als ein wandelndes Lied durchfließt.

Auch das fünfzehnte der zweiten Reihe, «O Brunnen-Mund...»,
steht unserm Gedicht sehr nahe, verbindet es doch die Vorstellungen

des fließenden Wassers, der Aquädukte und der Gräber. Unser Gedicht, das ja auch ein Sonett ist, liegt um mehr als fünfzehn Jahre den
Orpheus-Sonetten voraus: Ernst Zinn datiert es Mai/Juni 1906. Dem
zeitlichen Abstand entsprechend sind Ton und Aufbau unseres Gedichts ganz anders geartet als die aus befreiter Seele hervorquellenden
Jubelhymnen von 1922. Unser Gedicht erweist sich gegenüber dem
tiefer forschenden Blick als recht spröde, während ein flüchtigerer
Leser ahnungslos über manche Schwierigkeit hinweggleitet. Da ist
dann das erste Geschäft des Deuters das Aufspüren und Sichtbarma-
chen aller irgendwie fragwürdigen Einzelheiten. Dann aber wird man
sich um den Zusammenhang bemühen. Wir glauben, daß eine sorgfäl-
tige Analyse die Mühe lohnt.

Das Gedicht hat die Form einer Frage. Es beginnt mit einer Frage. Die Frage aber schwingt sich durch das ganze Gedicht hindurch,
wenn es auch den Anschein hat, als werde sie durch die Aussageform
der letzten drei Verse abgelöst. Denn das ganze Gedicht ist ein in der
Form der Frage durchgeführter Vergleich — ein Vergleich zwischen
«uns» und den römischen Sarkophagen. Von Anfang an ist es auf den
Vergleich hin angelegt. Die ersten vier Verse scheinen zwar nur von
«uns» zu handeln:

> WAS aber hindert uns zu glauben, daß
> (so wie wir hingestellt sind und verteilt)
> nicht eine kleine Zeit nur Drang und Haß
> und dies Verwirrende in uns verweilt.

Aber nimmt nicht gleich der zweite, eingeklammerte Vers auf
den Titel Bezug? Als «hingestellt» und «verteilt» werden wir bezeichnet, das heißt, wir werden unter dem Aspekt von Dingen, nicht von
Personen gesehen, die selbständig handeln. Irgendeine außer uns lie-
gende Macht hat über uns verfügt. Das Wort «verteilt» weist hin auf
einen Plan, eine Ordnung im Raum, eine Figur, an deren Zustande-
kommen wir auf passive, dienende Weise beteiligt sind. Eine Gleichsetzung zwischen «uns» und den Sarkophagen hat also bereits stattgefunden.

Dem Ton der Frage (die sich vorläufig nur mit «uns» beschäftigt)
haftet nichts Zweideutiges an. «Was aber hindert uns zu glauben...»

ist in Erwartung einer negativen Antwort gesprochen. Nichts hindert uns; oder, vorsichtiger: keine ersichtlichen Gegengründe stehen solchem Glauben im Wege. Die Frage vertritt also die Stelle einer positiven Aussage, eines Bekenntnisses zu einem Glauben. Doch klingt dies Bekenntnis mehr zaghaft, schüchtern tastend als zuversichtlich. Offenbar steht ein Wunsch hinter der Frage, ein Wunsch zu glauben, der sich nur leise zu äußern wagt.

Sobald wir nun aber dem sprachlichen Gefüge dieser Wunschfrage nachgehen, sehen wir uns in ein Netz negativer Bestimmungen verstrickt, das den Sinn der Frage auf heillose Weise zu verwirren droht. Schon «hindert» enthält die Negation eines «gestattet», und der dritte Vers bringt gleich drei negative Bestimmungen: Zuerst ein «nicht», dann «eine kleine Zeit» = eine nicht lange Zeit, schließlich ein zweideutiges «nur», das, auf «eine kleine Zeit» bezogen, heißt: nicht länger als..., aber, auf «Drang und Haß und dies Verwirrende» bezogen, heißt: nichts anderes als. Die Konstruktion ist undurchsichtig, schwer zu entwirren. Versuchen wir, um den Knoten aufzulösen, den nächstliegenden Weg, indem wir «nicht eine kleine Zeit nur» als Atemgruppe und logische Einheit zusammennehmen im Sinne von: eine lange, zumindest eine beträchtliche Zeit. Wie aber vermöchte die Tatsache einer langen Dauer in Anwendung auf den gleich zu bezeichnenden Inhalt ein Gefühl des Aufschwungs auszulösen? Bezeichnen nicht «Drang und Haß und dies Verwirrende» affektive Seelenzustände, die mit Hemmungs- und Abwehrgefühlen verbunden sind, mithin eine negative Bewertung in sich schließen? Ein Wunsch zu glauben, daß hemmungs- und abwehrbehaftete Affekte eine lange Zeit in uns verweilen, wäre eine Ungereimtheit. Die Möglichkeit also, «nicht eine kleine Zeit nur» als zusammenhängende Atemgruppe zu lesen, ist auszuschalten. Das «nicht» ist offenbar auf einen anderen Zusammenhang ausgerichtet, der sich später erschließen wird. Versuchen wir es also mit «eine kleine Zeit nur». Damit hätten wir eine sinnvolle Zusammenstellung, denn «eine kleine Zeit nur» kann doch wohl nichts anderes bezeichnen, als die kurze Spanne des irdischen Lebens (die, wie sich zeigen wird, in pointiertem Gegensatz zu dem «langsam» des zweiten Vierzeilers steht). Es wäre durchaus sinnvoll, den Glauben auszusprechen, daß die hemmungs- und abwehrbetonten Affekte nur die kurze Spanne unseres irdischen Lebens ausfüllen.

Für sich betrachtet, klänge solche Aussage der christlichen Vertrö-
stung auf ein besseres Jenseits zum Verwechseln ähnlich. Was fangen
wir dann aber mit dem «nicht» an am Anfang des Verses? «Nicht...
Drang und Haß und dies Verwirrende» als zusammengehörig zu lesen, ergäbe keinen Sinn; diese negativ gewerteten Affekte werden im
Gegenteil sehr deutlich als diese kurze Lebensspanne beherrschend
empfunden. Nur *eine* weitere Möglichkeit, den Satz zu konstruieren,
bleibt uns offen: Entschließen wir uns, das «nicht» mit dem «nur»
zu verbinden und den Satz also zu lesen: Was aber hindert uns zu
glauben, daß ... nicht nur Drang und Haß und dies Verwirrende –
eine kleine Zeit übrigens – in uns verweilen? Damit hätten wir erstens die Zeitbestimmung auf einen beiläufigen Nebenumstand der
Aussage reduziert (was ganz im Einklang steht mit Rilkes immer wieder geäußerter Grundanschauung von der Zeit als etwas Nichtigem),
und zweitens müßten wir uns darüber klar sein, daß das «nicht nur»
zu seiner Ergänzung ein «sondern auch» erfordert. Und wo stände ein
solches «sondern auch»? Unsere Antwort lautet: Die übrigen zehn
Verse des Gedichts sind die Übersetzung des logisch geforderten Ver-
bindungsgliedes in die Sprache der Bilder und des Gefühls. Auf alle
Fälle wäre mit dem Vierzeiler der Frage bereits angedeutet, daß noch
anderes, positiv zu Wertendes mit zur Bestimmung der menschlichen
Existenz gehört.[1]

An dieser Stelle wäre noch ein weiterer Versuch, das «nicht» des
dritten Verses zu konstruieren, zu erwägen und als unstatthaft abzu-
weisen. Verben des Hindern, Fürchtens, Zweifelns und dergleichen
werden in den klassischen Sprachen bekanntlich mit einer negativen
Partikel verbunden. Im 18. Jahrhundert ist dieser Sprachgebrauch
weitgehend im Deutschen nachgeahmt worden. Wo in der Lutherbibel
der Kämmerer aus dem Mohrenland den Apostel Philippus fragt:
«Was hindert, daß ich mich taufen lasse?» (Apg. 8, 36), hätten
Goethe und Schiller geschrieben: «was hindert, daß ich mich nicht
taufen lasse?» Neben dem Verweis auf Trübners Wörterbuch unter
«hindern» stehe hier noch ein ganz typischer Beleg aus Schillers Ab-

---

1 Es wäre nichts dagegen einzuwenden, neben der Hauptverbindung «nicht-
   nur» das «nur», im Nebenamt gleichsam (eine Art *apo koinou*), auch als zu
   «eine kleine Zeit» gehörig zu empfinden.

handlung *Über Anmut und Würde*: «Die Würde hindert, daß die Liebe nicht zur Begierde wird. Die Anmut verhütet, daß die Achtung
nicht Furcht wird.» (Schillers Werke, herausg. von Bellermann-Petsch,
VII, 155). Es wäre also zu fragen: Könnte das «nicht» des dritten
Verses sich nicht einfach im Gefolge des «hindert» eingestellt haben,
ohne eine Negierung zu bezwecken? Aber um diese Erwägung als
nichtig auszuschalten, genügt ein Hinweis darauf, daß das «nicht» des
Verses ja nicht von «hindert» abhängig ist, sondern von «zu glauben».
Somit bleibt als Ergebnis dieser etwas dornigen Untersuchung die
Lesung gesichert:

> WAS aber hindert uns zu glauben, daß
> (so wie wir hingestellt sind und verteilt)
> nicht — eine kleine Zeit — nur Drang und Haß
> und dies Verwirrende in uns verweilt...

Jetzt sind wir, bei aller Unbestimmtheit des Vorstoßes auf ein positiv
zu Wertendes der menschlichen Existenz, denn doch so weit, die
zweite Versgruppe ins Auge zu fassen:

> wie einst in dem verzierten Sarkophag
> bei Ringen, Götterbildern, Gläsern, Bändern,
> in langsam sich verzehrenden Gewändern
> ein langsam Aufgelöstes lag —

Die Achse dieser Verse (und aller noch folgenden) ist der Vergleich. Der antike Sarkophag — aus Marmor, mit Reliefskulpturen —
tritt in Sicht. In seiner Funktion und den damit verbundenen Zustän-
den und Vorgängen wird er in Beziehung gesetzt zum menschlichen
Sein. Dem «in uns» des vierten Verses entspricht das «in dem verzierten Sarkophag» des fünften; dem Verweilen das Liegen und Aufge-
löstwerden. Auch die Inhalte — die hemmungs- und abwehrbetonten
Affekte in uns und der geschmückte Leichnam im Sarkophag — stehen
in Parallele in mehr als einer Beziehung: Auf das Nicht-Dauern wird
in beiden Fällen ausdrücklich hingewiesen, während die negative
Bewertung der Inhalte uns nicht weniger deutlich nahegelegt wird,
ohne geradezu ausgesprochen zu werden. Verstärkt wird der Eindruck einer sehr weit gehenden Entsprechung der Inhalte durch das
nachdrückliche Hervorheben eines einzigen Unterschiedes: bei «uns»
handelt es sich um eine kleine Zeit, beim Sarkophag um ein Langsa-

mes. Nicht nur, daß das Wort «langsam» in zwei Versen an gleicher Stelle wiederholt wird; beim zweiten Mal steht es in einem Vers, der den Fluß der Rede durch seine Kürze verzögert. Er hat im Gegensatz zu allen übrigen nur vier Hebungen; anstelle der fünften steht eine volle Taktpause, die sogar als «Gedanken»-Strich sichtbar gemacht wird.

Ob aber die Entsprechung der zwei Bereiche in der zweiten Versgruppe noch über das bereits Festgestellte hinausgeht? Sollte etwa der Sinn des Verses

bei Ringen, Götterbildern, Gläsern, Bändern,

sich nicht in seiner ausmalenden Veranschaulichung nebensächlichen Beiwerks erschöpfen? Tatsächlich unterscheidet sich ja das schmükkende Beiwerk von dem verwesenden Körper durch seinen längeren Bestand. Sollten wir veranlaßt sein, auch zu dieser Unterscheidung eine Analogie im menschlichen Bereich aufzufinden? Das wäre durchaus denkbar, obgleich wir uns sofort sagen müßten, daß die Parallele sich kaum auf das Attribut «verziert» erstrecken dürfte. Gestehen wir es uns doch ein, die Gleichsetzung eines materiellen Behälters und seines diversen Inhalts mit einem immateriellen «wir» und dessen Inhalt ist ein höchst verzwicktes Unterfangen. Dem verwesenden Inhalt des Sarkophages entspricht zweifellos das flüchtige Triebleben unsrer irdischen Existenz, Seelisches steht hier in Parallele zum verwesenden Körper. Was aber entspräche in «uns» der Behälterfunktion des Sarkophags? Beileibe nicht der menschliche Leib, dem ja als Form über das Leben hinaus keine Dauer zukommt. Es ginge höchstens an, gewisse zierliche, relativ beständige Knochenbildungen des Skeletts mit dem schmückenden Beiwerk im Sarkophag in Beziehung zu setzen (etwa «die stille Krypta des Geschlechts» oder «des Fußgelenkes leichter Schmetterling», beide in «Hetärengräber» liebevoll gerühmt). Für die dauernde Form des Sarkophags aber findet sich in «uns» schlechterdings kein greifbares Gegenstück. Und dennoch verlangt die ganze Anlage des durchgeführten Vergleichs — dies sei vorgreifend gesagt — nach einer Gleichsetzung zwischen dem Sarkophag als Behälter und einem metaphysischen «wir» als Gefäß. Darauf wird zurückzukommen sein.

Betrachten wir nun den ersten anschließenden Dreizeiler:

> bis es die unbekannten Munde schluckten,
> die niemals reden. (Wo besteht und denkt
> ein Hirn, um ihrer einst sich zu bedienen?)

Die erste Hälfte leitet den Korrelativsatz («wie») des zweiten Vierzeilers durch einen Temporalsatz («bis») weiter, dem ein Relativsatz angehängt ist. Inhaltlich bezeichnen diese anderthalb Verse den Abschluß des Verwesungsprozesses, das völlige Verschwinden der menschlichen Überreste. Aber die Vorstellung des Verschwindens übersetzt sich dem Dichter in einen Vorgang geheimnisvoll visionärer Art. Das nicht mehr Wahrzunehmende ist geschluckt worden von Munden, von einer Vielzahl von Munden, die unbekannt sind, die niemals reden. Nicht nur geheimnisvoll, sondern geradezu beängstigend unheimlich mutet die dreimalige dunkle Vokalfarbe betonter Silben an:

> die unbekannten Munde schluckten...

Spürt man nicht, wie der Dichter im Sinnen über diesen Lauten sich festsieht, wie er in einen magischen Bann gerät, in einen autosuggestiven Zustand der Hypnose, in dem Auge, Ohr, Mund und Schlund gleichzeitig reagieren? Unbekannte Munde, dem äußeren Auge unsichtbare, im Irgendwo, die das schlucken, was sich aus dem Sarkophag ins Unsichtbare verflüchtigt hat. Und daran sich reihend die Vorstellung: Munde, die nur schlucken, nur organisch Gewesenes aufsaugen, die niemals reden. Das Grauen steigert sich zum Entsetzen. Die anderthalb Verse sind die Abbreviatur eines Alptraums!

Aber sind wir denn berechtigt, einen solchen Komplex affektiven Erlebens aus dieser kurzen Stelle herauszulesen? Heißt das nicht zügellos und willkürlich mit dem Dichterwort umgehen? Solchem Einwurf begegnen wir am besten, indem wir an die enorme, vielfältige Rolle erinnern, die dem Munde in Rilkes Vorstellungswelt zugewiesen ist. Wir brauchen den Umkreis der *Neuen Gedichte* nicht zu überschreiten, um auf eine Fülle von Beispielen für das Gesagte zu stoßen. Die Schlußverse des «Frühen Apollo» lenken den Blick auf den Mund,

> der jetzt noch still ist, niegebraucht und blinkend
> und nur mit seinem Lächeln etwas trinkend,
> als würde ihm sein Singen eingeflößt.

Da ist das Lächeln des Engels von Chartres («L'Ange du Méridien»)

> mit einem Mund, gemacht aus hundert Munden.

Da lesen wir im «Selbstbildnis aus dem Jahre 1906»:

> Der Mund als Mund gemacht, groß und genau,
> nicht überredend, aber ein Gerechtes
> Aussagendes.

Da heißt es von König Saul in der Zeit seiner Umnachtung («Saul unter den Propheten»):

> und sein Mund war wie der Mund der Traufen,
> der die Güsse, die zusammenlaufen,
> fallen läßt, eh er sie faßt.

Da schleudert der von der Hexe beschworene Tote («Samuels Erscheinung vor Saul») dem König die Frage entgegen:

> Willst du...
> in meinem Mund nach einem Siege suchen?
> Soll ich dir meine Zähne einzeln sagen?

In «Ein Prophet» ist der Mund des in den Dienst des Herrn Gezwungenen ein offener Krater, der fremde Worte hervorbringt,

> um sie in dem Ausbruch seines Mundes
> auszuwerfen, welcher flucht und flucht.

Da ertönt im «Jeremias» die verzweifelte Klage gegen seinen Herrn:

> Welchen Mund hast du mir zugemutet,
> damals, da ich fast ein Knabe war:
> eine Wunde wurde er: nun blutet
> aus ihm Unglücksjahr um Unglücksjahr.

Diese Beispiele mögen genügen zur Rechtfertigung unseres Satzes, die anderthalb Verse sind die Abbreviatur eines Alptraums. Strukturell betrachtet bilden sie eine Abschweifung vom Thema. Für den Augenblick ist der Sarkophag aus dem Blickfeld verschwunden. Die Munde (die es nicht angeht, mit dem Sarkophag zu identifizieren!), die unbekannten Munde sind an seine Stelle getreten und fesseln Sinn und Phantasie des Dichters. In den nächsten anderthalb Versen, die eingeklammert sind, versteigt sich die Abschweifung in eine neue Sphäre. Es ist, als ob die Phantasie ins Schleudern geriete. Die heftige

Frage nach dem Hirn ist wie ein verzweifelter Notschrei, den der vom
Alptraum Geschüttelte ausstößt. Es ist der Notschrei nach einem kosmischen Zentralorgan, das sich einst (ein zukünftiges «einst» im Gegensatz zu dem vergangenen des fünften Verses) der Vielzahl der
Munde bedienen wird. Wozu bedienen? Doch zu dem, was sie nie ge-
tan haben, zum Reden. Die Wo-Form verleiht der Frage eine unge-
stüme Heftigkeit. Sie macht aus der Existenz eines Überhirns ein
Postulat. Die Verdoppelung des Verbums, «besteht und denkt», steigert den Druck. Da äußert sich ein leidenschaftliches Verlangen nach
Bestätigung einer kosmischen Ordnung, um «das Verwirrende» in
seine Schranken zu weisen.

Der ganze erste Dreizeiler hat sich als eine Abschweifung vom
Thema erwiesen. Der Dichter ist der Hingabe an die Verführung des
Grauens erlegen, das aus den unteren Regionen heraufwehte. Dann
aber hat er sich, verzweifelt ringend, wieder in die Höhe zu arbeiten
gesucht.

Der letzte Dreizeiler führt zum Thema zurück.

> Da wurde von den alten Aquädukten
> ewiges Wasser in sie eingelenkt —:
> das spiegelt jetzt und geht und glänzt in ihnen.

Die Verse bringen das Gedicht, inhaltlich wie formal, zu einem
befriedigenden, ja beglückenden Abschluß. Fassen wir zuerst das
Inhaltliche ins Auge. Wieder muß die grammatische Erörterung hier
als Vorstufe zur Erschließung des Sinnes bemüht werden. Es handelt
sich um zwei Punkte. Erstens: «*von* den alten Aquädukten». Ist das
«von» als Agens oder bloß als Richtung aufzufassen? Beides ist möglich, aber es scheint mir als dem Charakter des Gedichts mehr entsprechend, die Aquädukte als Willensträger anzusprechen. Zweitens:
«ewiges Wasser in *sie* eingelenkt» ... Sie? Worauf bezieht sich das Pronomen? Das einzige seiner Pluralform entsprechende Substantiv ist
«Munde». Aber läßt die Vorstellung der unbekannten Munde, der
nur schluckenden, niemals redenden, aber möglicherweise dereinst
zum Reden gelangenden, sich in Einklang bringen mit der Vorstellung vom Eingelenktwerden ewigen Wassers? Dann müßte, wo nicht
der ganze Bau des durchgeführten Vergleichs zusammenbrechen soll,
eine Identifizierung der unbekannten Munde mit *dem* Sarkophag
anzunehmen sein, und gegen diese Gleichsetzung sträubt sich beides,

die grammatische Logik und die Phantasie[2]. Jeder Einsichtige wird, glaube ich, sich dazu verstehen, das «sie» ohne Zögern auf die Sarkophage des Titels zu beziehen. Die waren ja das ganze Gedicht hindurch pluraliter gegenwärtig gewesen, wie dies der Vers «so wie wir hingestellt sind und verteilt» bezeugte.

Damit ist, was die Sarkophage betrifft, volle Klarheit hergestellt. Diese Behälter waren angefertigt worden, um menschliche Überreste mitsamt dem ihnen beigegebenen Schmuck zu bergen. Diesem Zweck dienten sie, bis sich der menschliche Inhalt völlig aufgelöst und ins Nichts verflüchtigt hatte. Dann aber geschah es, daß ihnen (viele Jahrhunderte später) eine neue Aufgabe zugewiesen wurde, eine Aufgabe, die als ihre eigentliche und endgültige gegenüber der zeitweiligen, vorläufigen Bestimmung vom Dichter gefeiert wird. Jetzt stehen sie verteilt auf die Plätze der Ewigen Stadt als kostbare Tröge, durch die das nie versiegende Wasser aus den Gebirgen im Licht des Tages seinen Lauf nimmt. Sie sind Form, die einen Inhalt begrenzt, der kein Bleibendes ist. Sie sind gewürdigt, Durchgangsrinnen eines ewigen Fließens zu sein.

Die Sarkophage sind als Symbol menschlicher Existenz gesehen. Wie dort bei Fortdauer der Substanz Inhalt und Funktion sich radikal gewandelt haben, so — wagt der Dichter fragend zu glauben — könnte es auch im menschlichen Bereich zugehen. Angenommen, daß es so etwas wie eine menschliche Substanz gibt, die das Leben des Individuums überdauert, was hindert uns zu glauben, daß es einmal die Bestimmung dieser Substanz werden könne, im Plan einer höheren Ordnung als Träger oder Leiter ewiger Strömung zu dienen? Genaueres erfahren wir nicht. Wenn man nicht wüßte, wie ablehnend Rilke den christlichen Jenseitsvorstellungen gegenüberstand, so wäre nichts dagegen einzuwenden, die Symbolik unseres Gedichts in christlichem Sinne zu interpretieren. Ich glaube, wir werden diesem

---

2 In *Sonette an Orpheus* I, 10, werden die «antikischen Sarkophage» mit herrlicher Einfachheit als Munde begrüßt, als «wiedergeöffnete», «die schon wußten, was schweigen heißt», unter Anspielung auf das eigene Jahrzehnt des Schweigens, das sich zwischen Beginn und Abschluß der Duineser Elegien gelagert hatte; als singende, «die das fröhliche Wasser römischer Tage als ein wandelndes Lied durchfließt». Diese Bilder lassen sich auf unser ganz anders organisiertes Gedicht nicht übertragen.

Gedicht am besten gerecht, wenn wir den Keim seiner Entstehung in der Verbindung zweier Grundangelegenheiten von Rilkes dichterischem Schaffen sehen: einmal in dem Verlangen, die Erscheinungsformen der sichtbaren Welt in ihrer Wandelbarkeit als ästhetisches Phänomen zu rechtfertigen und zu rühmen, sodann in dem sich zu allen Zeiten in ihm äußernden Bedürfnis, die menschliche Existenz *sub specie aeternitatis* aufzufassen.

Werfen wir zum Schluß einen prüfenden Blick auf den formalen Charakter der letzten Versgruppe. Diese bringt in das ganze Gedicht eine neue überraschende Wendung. Es gehört zu den typischen Strukturmerkmalen der *Neuen Gedichte*, daß wir solchen Wendungen — meist gegen den Schluß — sehr häufig begegnen. Immer wieder befaßt sich das Gedicht mit der Schilderung eines Zustands oder Vorgangs, der an einem gewissen Punkt eine Unterbrechung erfährt oder durch ein neues, aktives, zumindest andersgerichtetes Element abgelöst wird. An solchen Wendepunkten findet man typischerweise ein «plötzlich», «auf einmal», «einmal nur», «aber» und Ähnliches. In unserm Gedicht vollzieht sich die Wendung durch eine syntaktische Schwenkung. Wir waren den Dehnungen und Windungen der in einen langen Korrelativsatz mündenden Frage gefolgt, die an zwei Stellen durch Einklammerungen unterbrochen war. Wir erwarteten, der Anlage des durchgeführten Vergleichs entsprechend, die Weiterführung des Satzes bis zum Abschluß des Vergleichs. Statt dessen hat ein plötzlicher Kurswechsel stattgefunden. Statt einer relativen Anknüpfung mit «worauf» gibt es einen neuen Einsatz mit kräftig-demonstrativem «Da». Das wirkt nach der eingeklammerten Frage, die, in der Versmitte einsetzend, den sicheren Gang des Gedichts inhaltlich wie formal ins Schleudern gebracht hatte, wie ein plötzlicher Ruck, der das bedrohte Gleichgewicht wiederherstellt. Unter Führung des «Da» treten die drei Schlußverse ihren eigenen Gang an. Sie schreiten den Weg gelassen zu Ende, mit Fülle und Wohllaut, mit federnder Bewegung, mit Majestät. Die ersten zwei erstrahlen durch ein Gepränge von Alliteration:

> Da wurde von den alten Aquädukten
> ewiges Wasser in sie eingelenkt.

Der zweite gibt durch Inversion des metrischen Akzents bei dem er-

sten, zugleich bedeutendsten Wort — «éwiges» — dem Vers eine ryth-
mische Beschwingtheit, die kein anderer Vers mit ihm teilt. Der dritte findet sein Gefüge in der majestätischen Aneinanderreihung dreier
Verben, dreier Tätigkeitswörter. Es ist bezeichnend, daß in unserm
Gedicht bloß das Ewige sich eine Fülle von Aktivität leisten kann, die
dem letzten Vers vorbehalten ist. Für den Bereich des Menschlichen
wie den des Sarkophags finden nur solche Verben Anwendung, die
ein Erleiden oder einen Zustand bezeichnen. Wir sind «hingestellt»
und «verteilt» (passiver Zustand). Drang, Haß und das Verwirrende
«verweilt» in uns (Zustand): Das im Sarg Befindliche verzehrte sich
(mediales Passiv), es «lag» darin (Zustand). In die Sarkophage wurde
ewiges Wasser eingelenkt (Passiv). Nur die kosmisch gedachten Kräfte der unbekannten Munde «schluckten» (aktiv) und das ebenfalls
kosmisch postulierte Hirn war mit einem Zustandswort («besteht»)
und einem Tätigkeitswort («denkt») bezeichnet. Das ewige Wasser
aber entfaltet eine dreifache Tätigkeit: es «spiegelt, geht und glänzt».

9

THE POET'S DILEMMA:
AN INTERPRETATION OF RILKE'S
SECOND *DUINO* ELEGY

To scan *The Duino Elegies* once more, forty years after the poet's death, smothered as they are under an avalanche of interpretations, is a hazardous venture. To do so for a body of readers including many who know this poetry only through the blurring medium of translation seems questionable. To single out one of the Elegies, moreover, and present its poetic statement as embedded in the matrix of a much larger whole, within the space of a short paper, seems impossible. The hope that a group of serious students, perceptive to all the nuances of Rilke's mythopoeic language, will find something not only new but valid in my exposition, prompts me to this essay. For those readers who have command of the secondary literature I wish to state that I have pondered and thoroughly digested many commentaries, including the latest and most voluminous by Jacob Steiner.[1]

I proceed on the assumption, scarcely open to challenge, that the *Duino Elegies* and the *Sonnets to Orpheus* constitute in their entirety one coherent poetic statement. The fact, known to all Rilke readers, that after the completion of the Second Elegy the poet remained frustrated, tongue-tied, and choked for ten years before the ice jam finally broke releasing a torrent of creative energy does not invalidate the conviction that everything that came out in the end was there from the beginning. We know that the *Sonnets* that flowed from Rilke's pen almost as a piece of automatic writing during a few January days in 1922 provided the catalyst that brought the *Elegies* to completion within a very short time. The *Sonnets* were published in 1922; the *Elegies* not until one year later. This is significant. The poet evidently wanted the *Elegies* to be read in the light of the message conveyed in the *Sonnets*.

---

1   Jacob Steiner, *Rilkes Duineser Elegien* (Stockholm: Almqvist & Wiksell, 1962).

As their title implies, the *Elegies* are written in a minor key. They sound a note of heartbreak, of infinite anxiety, anguish, doubt, and fear, although strains of ecstatic jubilation frequently interrupt the throb of the despairing heart. The *Sonnets* are written in a major key, sounding a theme of praise that brooks no qualification. They proclaim a panecstatic view of life. In the explicit language of the *Sonnets*, even lament is nothing but a muted form of praise. Praise of existence is a total musical statement as it were, requiring the minor themes of wailing and lament for its development. Among the *Sonnets* there is a specifically programmatic group that must be briefly glimpsed. Of the first cycle it includes, among others, one, three to nine, and the last, twenty-six. Of the second cycle, the first sonnet is particularly revealing. These sonnets deal with the god of song, with his mouthpiece, the poet, and with mankind. Formerly celebrated by Rilke as Apollo, the god of the lyre is now hailed as Orpheus. The substitution of Orpheus for Apollo as the deity that dominates the poet's mythical realm was prompted by two ideas. First, according to ancient tradition, Orpheus was the only mortal who penetrated the realm of Hades to move the dark divinities by his song and subsequently to return to the hither side. Secondly, he suffered martyrdom, being torn to pieces, fragmented, and his essence disseminated throughout the world by the waters that carried his remains. Much earlier, at the end of the *Stundenbuch (Book of the Hours)*, our poet had glorified the dying Saint Francis of Assisi in very similar terms: his essence communicated itself to all living things and became part of them. The suffering of Orpheus was a vicarious martyrdom for the benefit of all mankind. Analogies to the Christian doctrine of redemption are, of course, not to be overlooked.

Having proclaimed the divine singer, the *Sonnets* are primarily concerned with his mouthpiece. The poet *is* Orpheus. Under whatever names he may be known among men, the poet is a metamorphosis of Orpheus, a reincarnation of the divine singer. There is no need to memorialize the individual poet. Once and for all, it is Orpheus wherever there is song. The same sonnet, the Fifth, makes a point of defining genuine song as an undirected vibration in the space of the soul, in contrast to all song that focusses on any kind of specific wooing or yearning, notably the songs of the lover. Such song is rejected as missing the true mark, leaving no permanent imprint.

Already the Third Sonnet had broached with trepidation the problem of a mere man serving as the reincarnation of the divine voice. It is his ineluctable lot to diminish and wane. (We may find in this passage echoes of John the Baptist, designating Jesus as the one who must wax, while he himself must wane.) Facing his lot fills him with anxiety, but he moves and speaks in a sphere to which the non-poet has no access.

The Fourth Sonnet for the first time introduces the poet's breath as a symbol of his creative activity. This symbol, also used freely in the *Elegies*, finds its most elaborate development in the First Sonnet of the Second Cycle. In our Fourth Sonnet, remembering the harsh words with which in the Third the poet had dismissed the lovers' song of wooing, he invites the lovers to expose themselves on occasion to his breath. This stream of breath divides as it passes the cheeks of the lovers, caressing and enriching them, in order to reunite as it streams into the infinite beyond them.

This sonnet and the one that follows have cast the poet, the temporary and temporal mouthpiece of the divine voice, in a role that transcends all specific human concerns. His song is never a means, but an end in itself. The Sixth, again showing the poet as one moving among men but not as one of them, defines his superhuman capacities. In contrast to men, he is equally at home in the Here and in the Beyond, in the realm of life and the realm of death, in the sphere of time and that of timelessness. "More expertly would he bend the twigs of the willows [to shape the sides of the lyre] who has experience of the roots of the willow." All mysteries lie open before him. He cautions men against presuming to engage in practices that are reserved for him. The last line of this Sonnet defines the essence of song as praise.

The Seventh Sonnet characterizes praise as total and unqualified — the mould in the tombs of kings and the shadows cast by the gods notwithstanding. And the Eighth, in further development of the theme of praise, defines lament as a muted form of praise. A very striking, superbly developed image personifies lament as a minor deity, a nymph, guarding the source of tears against contamination.

"Our precipitation" he calls this spring of tears. There is something intentionally provocative, even bizarre, in the intrusion of this term of physical science into a sonnet. It is surely done to underscore the idea that the poet, a mediator between mankind and the universe, is conceived as an instrument of cosmic energies. In the *Elegies*, he again and again invokes the image of the poet as a sensitive transmitter of cosmic vibrations. In the space of the soul all phenomena appear transformed into pulsations. But lest this lead us too far afield, let us remark rather on the fact that the poet speaks of this precipitation as "ours." It is the poet's tears, the poet's formed utterance of lament, not human tears, that he speaks of. If we read these programmatic sonnets with particular care, we see that the line of demarcation separating Him, the incarnation of the divine singer, from mankind, beneficiary of his song and his suffering, is never forgotten. "Our" here, and recurring at the end of the sonnet as "a constellation of our voice," refers not to men and their sentiment but to those fellow poets whose formed sentiment has added to the constellation that sparkles in the space of the soul. Had Rilke wanted to be specific, he would have pointed to names like Keats and Hölderlin.

This bare sketch of a portion of the programmatic sonnets must be kept in mind throughout this paper. Regardless of what our analysis may ultimately establish, it supplies a warranty of my attempt to see in the second Duino Elegy an exposition, not of man's dilemma but of that of the poet. If it can be shown that the plural pronouns "we" and "our," wherever they occur in this Elegy, allow for a richer and more imaginative interpretation if taken to refer specifically to the poet's situation and not to that of mankind generally; if we shall find beyond this that a more inclusive "we" and "our" would involve the poet in embarrassing self-contradiction, the case must be conceded as proved. But by way of caution it must be added that for each Elegy the meaning of the use of "we" and "our" must be examined on its own merits. We are concerned here only with the Second Elegy, although, by implication, also with the First, written about the same time.

Whereas the competent student is invited to refer to the German text at every point of this discussion, I shall limit myself, generally speaking, to literal translation and elaborate paraphrasing of my own devising. Let us begin our discussion of the Second Elegy by a brief analysis of its structure. This Elegy consists of seven strophes. Strophe One is a meditation on the angel. Taking up the theme of the First Elegy, it contrasts the harmless familiarity of Tobit's companion in a remote apocryphal era with the lethal shock which his physical manifestation in the Here and Now would entail. Strophe Two apostrophizes the angels in a paean exalting their glory. Strophe Three returns to the mode of meditation. It culminates in a series of breathless questions. In Strophe Four the theme of the lovers, a major concern in the First Elegy, engages the poet's meditation. Strophe Five brings an abrupt change. His concern with the lovers has made their image crystallize in the poet's mind. He addresses the lovers with impassioned fervor. Strophe Six continues to address the lovers, but the poet's gaze has shifted from them to dwell on an inner vision of a type of lovers that bears only the faintest resemblance to the lovers of the here and now. And what of the final strophe? Is the poet here still addressing the lovers? Is he opening his arms, embracing them as it were, to let them share in his own fervent wish for a little patch of human tranquillity? Or — has the image of the lovers now faded? Has the poet resumed the mode of solitary meditation, thus completing the Elegy in the manner begun? I shall endeavor to show that only the latter reading makes sense within the framework of the Elegy, but its demonstration will require step by step examination.

   To begin:

> Every angel is terrible. And despite this, alas,
> I raise my song to you wellnigh deadly birds of the soul,
> out of my knowledge of you. Whither gone are the days of Tobit
> when one of the most radiant stood at the door of the simple dwelling
> a little disguised for travel and already no longer fearsome;
> a youth to the youth who peered out with curiosity.
> If now the archangel, charged with danger, were to take but one step
> down from behind the stars and hitherward, with a wild upbeat
> our own heart would slay us. Who are you?

Here we can confine ourselves to a brief explanation. Already the First Elegy, at its very beginning, had coupled the concepts of beauty and terror in referring to the angel: terror is beauty intensified to a

degree beyond the capacity of the human heart to bear, hence annihilating. The apocryphal story of Tobit, still familiar to readers of
the Catholic and Lutheran Bibles, is the charming tale of the travel of
a young man with his angelic companion to a distant land to collect
a commercial debt. They have an encounter with a big fish whose
viscera eventually serve to restore the eyesight of Tobit's blind father.
The allusion serves to contrast the here and now with a mythical
Jewish past, just as a mythical past of Attic Greece is conjured up
in the sixth strophe for purposes of contrast. There is a mysterious
emphasis in the poet's insistence that he has knowledge of the angels.
Whence does he derive his knowledge? The *Sonnets to Orpheus* in
their entirety provide a general answer, and one passage is furtively
specific on this point. The Seventh Sonnet ends with the statement:
"He [the reincarnation of Orpheus] is one of the enduring messengers
whose hand holding vessels filled with fruits of praise extends far
into the doors of the dead." But what is messenger ('Bote') other
than a literal equivalent of the Greek *aggelos* ('angel')? If the poet
is an angel, are not the *Elegies* shot through with a curious kind of
double talk in contrasting the inconceivable vastness of the angel at
every point with the status of the speaker, who is a poet? The fact is,
of course, that the poet is conceived as both divine and human, as
enduring and temporal, and the *Elegies* dwell in the main on his temporal aspect. Let us not forget to note the magnificent kinetic imagery
of the strophe's final statement. Within the compass of four successive beats four successive movements are delineated, a downward, a
hitherward, a vertical upward, and a vertical downward, the last two
of these spectacularly emphasized by the separation of the word
"hochauf-schlagend" by the final pause of a run-on line. We note the
occurrence of "our own" and "us," but these personal pronouns are
in this context too ambiguous for profitable inquiry.

Now follows the great paean, preceded by the question, who
are you?

> Early perfected, you favored darlings of creation,
> mountain ranges, dawn-lit ridges
> of all creativity, — pollen of blossoming godhead,
> joints of light, corridors, stairways, thrones,
> spaces of being, shields of rapture, tumults
> of turbulently ecstatic feeling and, all of a sudden, singly:

mirrors that draw back into their own countenances
the beauty that has emanated from them.

This passage, a profusion of imagery defying fixation, a miracle of
rhythmic elasticity in its changes of tone and tempo, can only be
profaned by extended talk about it. Analysis would — pardon the
figure — reduce it as in a garbage grinder. These angels are quasi-per-
sonalized projections of cosmic powers and agencies. The climactic
line, "tumults of turbulently ecstatic feeling," adumbrates equiva-
lents of spiral nebulae in the spaces of the soul. But there is a second
climax. Abandoning the dazzle of rapid-fire imagery, the final two
lines are devoted to the development of a single image.

The angels as mirrors. Personalized mirrors, with a countenance.
Mirrors endowed with the double faculty of radiating beauty and
gathering it back into themselves. For this gathering or drawing the
poet uses the word *schöpfen*, having the familiar association of *Atem
schöpfen* 'drawing breath.' The angels as mirrors are a source of their
own renewal. This is a wondrous power that sets the stage for the
meditations of the next strophe. Mirrors, as every student of Rilke
knows, are among the most varied and exciting elements of his ima-
gistic inventory. For Rilke, mirrors are surrounded by the same aura
of mystery as that which Lewis Carroll's Alice experiences — except
for a total absence of that quizzical humor which pervades the pages
of *Through the Looking Glass*. Did Rilke know *Alice*, I wonder? I
have not come across a single hint in his correspondence that would
answer this question.

Leaving such speculations aside, we come to a highly interesting
observation. Years before the image of the angels crystallized in the
poet's mind in this fashion, he had happened upon something closely
analagous in the human sphere. In the second volume of *Neue Gedichte* we find a poem entitled "Dame vor dem Spiegel" (*Lady Before Her Mirror*). After a late evening party the lady is seated before
her mirror in her dimly lighted boudoir. Via the extended image of
a sleeping potion carefully blended, she pours her tired features into
the mirror, then the fullness of her smile, finally she dissolves her
hair in the fizzing mixture. When the bubbles have fully risen and
the liquid cleared, she exposes her magnificent shoulder. Then she
deliberately drinks the contents of the mirror. What a lover would

toss off in ecstasy, she drinks cannily, with distrustful awareness. Only after the whole draught has been slowly drained, does she become aware also of the dimly lighted objects of her boudoir reflected in the mirror.

Here the contemplation of her features in the mirror has the function of a ritual of restoration by which the lady recovers the beauty she had expended during the social evening. To my knowledge, commentators on the Elegy have overlooked this poem. Without question, it is a prototype on the human level of the wondrous faculty of such renewal attributed to the angels.

For further elucidation of this mystery of recuperation and self-replenishment we must turn once more to the *Sonnets to Orpheus*. The First Sonnet of the Second Cycle apostrophizes breathing as an invisible poem. In the First Cycle, at the end of Sonnet Three and the beginning of Sonnet Four we found breath used as a symbol for the radiation of the poet's creative energy. This Sonnet is wholly devoted to the development of that symbolism. Properly read, it is seen to attribute to the poet the same power of recuperation and renewal that he attributes to his angels. The poet's breath and the space or spaces of the soul are conceived as a single communicating fluid entity. Every breath that goes out of the poet enriches this space of the soul. The waves he emits add up to a total sea, a most economical sea, enlarging the spaces. But it is a matter of give and take. The breath he takes in is permeated with the soul substance his breath has discharged into the space of the soul. Some winds brush his cheek as if they were his offspring. What adds to the startling quality of this sonnet is the intimacy of its utterance. The give and take are presented as an immediate personal experience. The only pronoun used is "I." — Again we must keep in mind the knowledge derived from the *Sonnets to Orpheus* in order to empathize with the point of view of the Elegies.

This peculiar virtue of the angels as constantly self-replenishing sources of cosmic energy is used by the poet as the springboard to launch him upon the central theme of this, the Second Elegy. Returning to his solitary meditation, he muses:

> For, as concerns us, when we feel, we volatilize; alas, we
> breathe ourselves out and away; from embers to embers

we give off a fainter fragrance. Peradventure someone will say to us:
indeed, you get into my blood, the room, the springtime
fills itself with you . . . What avails it, he cannot hold us,
we wane in him and about him. And what of them who are beautiful?
Oh, who guards them from wasting? Ever and ever a glow arises
and departs. Like dew from the morning grass,
our essence rises up and away, like heat from a
steaming dish. Oh smile, whither? Oh lifted eyes:
new, warm, receding wave of the heart − ;
alas for me: but this *is* we. Does the world space
into which we dissolve indeed take on our flavor? Do the angels
really recapture only what is their own, what has streamed out of them,
or, is there at times, by inadvertence as it were, a little
of our essence intermingled? Are we blended with their
features by but so little as that vagueness suffusing the faces
of pregnant women? They do not notice it in the swirl
of their return to themselves. (How should they?!)

The above strophe begins with "for," Rilke's favorite conjunction. Here it finds justification as the answer to the unspoken question: Why should I glorify the angels so extravagantly? Look at us by contrast. The first line of this strophe confronts us with the first crucial "we" of this Elegy. The latest commentator, most scrupulously meticulous in the weighing of the multiple meanings of every word, never stops to consider this question at all. For him it is a foregone conclusion that the strophe is concerned with the human condition. Let us ignore this, returning for guidance to the *Sonnets to Orpheus*. The Fifth Sonnet had defined the poet's human lot as a process of waning. *Schwinden* is the word used in that passage, while *verflüchtigen*, cognate of English 'fleeting,' rendered by me as 'volatilize,' is the first mention in our strophe of a process of waning, wasting, diminishing, ebbing away. *Schwinden* also recurs among the many synonyms in our strophe. The sonnet speaks of this diminishing, this waning, as the ineluctable lot of the divine singer's human reincarnation. It is something that must be faced by his hearers, and he gives expression to his own anguish in the face of this lot. Even more explicitly the Seventh Sonnet characterizes him as a sufferer: "His heart, oh transitory press of an infinite flow of wine for mankind." (The sacramental overtones are evident.) If the poet is indeed speaking of himself in this strophe of our Elegy, he also endows the

verb "feel" with a special sense. It does not signify human sentiment
but a creative emotional engagement. The very next line reintroduces
the term "breathing" as a synonym of this activity. There follows a
variety of illustrative examples to show that the emission of energy
leaves its source weakened. The line about the embers, authorities
tell us, alludes to the process of refining the precious substance of
the sperm whale. The transmission of the poet's vitality to a person,
or to an ambience, is transitory. He laments over the beauty of human beings suffering the same fate. After contemplating the homely
examples of the dew on the grass and the steaming dish, a high point
of anguish is reached in his apostrophe to the passing smile and the
uplifted eye. We see the poet poised, as it were, with outstretched
arms in the vain attempt to restrain every new, warm, receding pulse
of the heart.

Up to this point, it must be freely conceded, the strophe can be
read on two levels — superficially as reiterating the age-old lament on
the impermanence of the human condition; more deeply, as the
poet's peculiar sense of progressive depletion by the intensity of his
emissions — the breath, the pulse, the waves, the vapor. It is this
which prompts his agonized outcry, "but this is we!", and his burst
of questions. The questions are as corollary propositions to the basic
thesis. If it is the poet's precious volatile essence that drains away,
then it must impart its flavor to the medium into which it drains. If
this is so, the spaces of the soul must be so fully permeated and im-
pregnated by the poet's essence that this essence must also be blended
with the flow of energy that restores the features of the angelic mirrors. Imperceptibly, so far as they are concerned, but nevertheless
positively. This conviction, ventured at this point of the Elegy as the
faintest hypothesis, appears in the light of the *Sonnets to Orpheus*
as a hyperbole of understatement. But it is confirmed by the progress
of the Elegies themselves, when we follow them to the great finale
of the Seventh and the opening statement of the Tenth. However,
we need only to cross the gap separating this, the third strophe of
the Elegy, from the fourth to find ourselves confronted by a tone
of assurance.

At this point we must interrupt our progress in the Second Elegy
to take the briefest excursion into the Fifth. The theme of the Fifth

is the little troupe of acrobats that exhibit their open-air acts in the suburbs of Paris. The opening line glimpses their existence in the vaguely directed question: "But who, tell me, are they, these even more ephemeral than ourselves?" ("die . . . Flüchtigern noch als wir selbst"). "Ourselves" cannot be taken to refer to mankind. That would have required "the most ephemeral of us all." It becomes clear in the course of the Elegy that the poet includes the acrobats amoung the beings endowed with the creative impulse. He ranges them at the bottom of the series because the top yield of all their striving is an empty automatic virtuosity. But on the way to this he marks a notable exception. A half-grown boy, still learning the tricks of his art, ventures an inchoate smile in the direction of his mother, a smile erased by gushing physiological tears that anticipate any conscious pain induced by the hard impact of his leap. In this half-smile the poet perceives a volatile essence akin to his own. He apostrophizes the angel, charging him to procure a vase in which to preserve this smile, this "tiny-blossomed medicinal herb." Like an apothecary, using abbreviations, he is to label it with a flourishing sweep of his pen as *Subrisio Saltat.* 'Smile of Acr.' The analogy of this passage to the agitated questions concluding the third strophe of our Second Elegy is unmistakable.

We now turn to the fourth strophe:

> Lovers, if they understood this, could have wondrously strange things to utter
> in the night air. For it seems that everything
> secretly harbors us. Behold, the trees *are*; the houses
> we dwell in stand. It is only we
> who pass by everything like an airy exchange,
> and everything is engaged in a conspiracy of silence regarding us, —
> half, perhaps, from a sense of disgrace, and half as an ineffable hope.

There has been a shift of theme. The idea of the lovers has intruded upon the poet's meditation. What has brought them to his mind? Anything could, as a matter of fact. They are the most frequently recurring objects of his concern throughout the body of the *Elegies*. Their image hovers ever just below the threshold of his consciousness. The intensity of their passion is nearest to the intensity of his own experience. Yet he is not a lover because his assignment

directs his intensity elsewhere. Let us recall that the First Elegy had
called forth a bitter outcry of anguish on that score. There, having
enumerated a tree, a road, a habit, as items offering him a precarious
stability, he had rested his voice on the night as the greatest solace.
The night wafts the wind that gently wastes his features. The night,
though longed for, is gently disappointing. The night is a toilsome
task for the solitary heart to sustain. Is it easier on the lovers? This
was the question with which he interrupted his musing, only to give
the despairing answer: Alas, they only obscure one another's lot.
Then a bitter taste welled up in his mouth making him cry out: "Do
you not know it by now?" Then he had braced himself with the admonition to throw the emptiness out of his arms into the spaces,
thereby expanding the spaces, making them buoyant for the more
soulful flight of the birds. A bit later he had supplemented this admonition by saying: But if the yearning for a lover diverts you from
your fated task, sing the lovers: "not yet immortal enough by far is
their feeling with its aura of fame." Let us also revert to the *Sonnets
to Orpheus* for guidance. Had not the Fourth Sonnet of the First
Cycle invited the lovers to expose themselves on occasion to the waft-
ing of the breath (the poet's breath), which, though not aimed at
them, caresses their cheeks as it passes them by to stream into the
infinite? Has it not enriched them with its volatile fragrance?

It is with all this background that the statement is charged: "Lovers, if they understood this, could have wondrously strange things to
utter in the night air." If they understood what, we ask. If they understood that our — the poet's - volatile essence permeates and im-
pregnates all the spaces of the soul. The lovers do not understand
this. But what curious insight could they communicate if they did?
The answer is simple enough. They would realize that their words of
endearment, their songs of wooing addressed to each other, do not
stem from their particular situation. It is rather that the lovers are
the unconscious beneficiaries of the great store of formed emotion
accumulated in the space of the soul by the poets throughout the
ages. Can we not now reduce these subtle conceits to simple terms?
There comes to mind an often quoted saying of La Rochefoucauld's:
"If it were not for the poets there would be few lovers." There was
then, it seems, a furtive, knowing smile playing about the features

of the poet as he initiated the musings of the fourth strophe, so unlike the desperate, questioning eagerness with which the third
strophe had closed. The rest of the strophe dwells on the insubstan-
tiality of the poet's breath as contrasted with the substance of natural organisms and the less stable substance of the artifacts that make
up the human ambience. There is nothing difficult now about the
statement on which the strophe concludes. If the conspiracy of silence regarding the poet's breath in which all things engage is felt half
as a disgrace, that is because it has as yet permeated the space of the
soul but faintly. But what an ineffable hope there is in the thought
of filling them to saturation! Anticipating a note of jubilation in the
Seventh Elegy to confirm this, we quote: "So, after all, we have not
missed out on the spaces — these bestowing spaces, these our spaces.
(How fearfully vast must they be that millenia of our feeling have
not overfilled them?)"

We are now ready for the fifth strophe:

Lovers, you in your mutual appeasement,
it is you I ask concerning us. You grip each other. Have you proofs?
Lo, to me it happens that my hands become
aware of each other or that my used
face shields itself in them from wear. This contact
makes me sense myself a little. But who, on the basis of such slim evidence,
    would lay claim to *being?*
You, however, who wax by the partner's rapture
until overwhelmed he implores you:
no *more* —; you, who, cupped by each other's hands
become more abundant like vintage years;
you, who sometimes cease to be simply because the partner
completely takes over: it is you I ask concerning us. I know,
you touch each other so blissfully because the caress contains,
because the spot caressed by your tender touch does not diminish;
because you sense pure duration underneath. Thus you feel your embraces
    as almost
a warrant of eternity. And yet, when you have survived the thrilling terror
of the first exchange of glances, and the longing at the window,
and the first mutual passage through the garden just *once:*
lovers, *are* you then lovers still? When you each
lift the other to the lips, positioning, drink to drink:
alas, how strangely the drinker then disengages himself from the act.

Whereas the preceding strophe had shown the poet as relishing his mysterious secret of what makes the lovers tick, the strophe just quoted is keyed to a note of passionate agitation. The lovers, but now the object of meditation, have materialized before the poet's inner eye. The mood of meditation is abandoned, and the poet addresses the lovers directly. Being the source of their ecstasies, the poet wants something from the lovers in return. What is it that he would persuade himself as being in their power to bestow? It is assurance of a kind of being, apart from and over and above the volatile essence with which he flavors the spaces of the soul. In a three-fold series of superlatively sensuous descriptions he endows the lovers in every respect with characteristics that are at the opposite pole of all that he said about himself in strophe three. Whereas a sense of depletion, of waning and wasting away, marked his physical habitus, the lovers swell and expand under each other's caresses. Their bodies are taut with the rush of blood to the skin. Twice he implores their assurance in the identical words. The enigmatic question, "Have you proofs?", I would take to mean: Have you proofs of your own existence from which I could draw a semblance of assurance regarding my own existence as involving some sort of duration? Suddenly shifting from the "we"-form to "I," he makes a personal confession of the way he clutches at straws to get some assurance of being. There is a closed circuit when his hands caress each other or when he buries his face in them — the face worn, used up with seeing — to shield it from wear. During such habitual gestures, he would persuade himself, time has stopped and the depleting pulse of energy ceases to throb. By his own admission this is all very precarious. Let us not overlook, by the way, that this passage about his favorite gestures — gestures that are part of his poetic self-portrait in other contexts, too — is an elaborated cross-reference to what was merely thrown out as an indistinct hint in the First Elegy. Among the straws he clutched at for support was the fidelity of a habit indulged in, spoken of as if it were something alive and attached to its master. There, incidentally, he had used the plural "we" to introduce the subject, whereas the present passage has shifted to "I". In contrast to the very frail token of a closed enduring circuit that his gestures afford, the voluptuous solidity of the lovers is something to take heart in.

Soliciting the help of the lovers a second time in the identical words, he follows it up by another triad of statements regarding the sense of endurance, permanence, and even eternity felt by the lovers in the transports of their caresses. This series he introduces by an emphatic "I know," which again carries echoes of that brusque self-reproach in the First Elegy, "Weisst du's noch nicht" (is not your learning this long overdue?). Now follows a sudden about-face of mood, a collapse of what hopes he may have entertained for himself deriving from the example of the lovers. It is couched in the form of a long, periodic build-up, first developing the ecstatic, initial phase of love in another triadic series, then shifting to the reverse side of the medal, once more using the pattern of three verbal ideas. The third of the positive images evoked, "the first mutual passage through the garden just once," would, in a Victorian context, be read on the literal level. As such it would evoke an echo of Adalbert Stifter's whimsically developed postulate that love should proceed to the first kiss and then stop. (See his story *Feldblumen*.) But in Rilke's language, always suggestive of sex and surcharged with sex in this strophe of the Elegy, the walk through the garden probably symbolizes the first mutual exploring of the delights of the body. A reference to the garden as the body of the loving woman recurs at the very end of the Third Elegy, and I think it has the same meaning in its cryptic occurrence in the Fourth. The italics of "just *once*" in the text very strongly point in the same direction. In German folk song, as in the poetry modeled after it, we frequently find the garden used in this way.

But now the counter-movement sets in, elaborating the symbolic act of drinking. This is what happens to love, the poet reminds his lovers: the thrill of ecstasy degenerates into a physiological habit, deliberately, absentmindedly, and mechanically performed. So what is left of their boasted being? This realization brutally deflates all hopes that the poet had cherished for himself on the lover's account. Having described the course of love full circle, from the soul-shivering thrill of the first glances to the extinction of the divine spark in habituation, the poet, in the next strophe, invites the gaze of the lovers to dwell with him on a different spectacle.

Were you not astonished by the delicacy of human gestures
on Attic grave steles? was not love and parting
laid on their shoulders so lightly, as if it were made of a fabric
foreign to us? Remember the hands, how they
rest without pressure, although their torsos are full of strength.
These in their governance knew this sign language to say: to this point it
    is we,
it is given to us to touch each other's soul; stronger
is the bracing urge of the gods upon us. But that is the affair of the Gods.

In this strophe the poet still addresses the lovers. But his concern
is with images that symbolically portray a cultural climate of love
totally alien to the extremes of passion that abound in our world. He
conjures up the memory of such grave reliefs as he has seen in mu-
seums. Students of Rilke's poetry have gone to considerable trouble
to identify some such remnant of Greek art with the outline here
presented, but without very definite success. In a letter to Lou An-
dreas-Salomé dated 10 January 1912, a few days, that is, before the
first two Elegies took shape, he makes a somewhat vague allusion to
having seen such steles in Naples. What he recalled as a memory may
have been rather a wishdream projected by his yearning imagination.
It was certainly reinforced, moreover, by memories of the white
marble plaque representing Orpheus, Eurydice, and Hermes, copies
of which he saw in Naples and Paris and which supplied the stimulus
for his own long poem, "Orpheus. Eurydice. Hermes.", in the first
volume of *Neue Gedichte*. Here the grave steles seem to come to life
and speak. The delicate restraint of their typical gestures of love and
farewell they claim as their own, as inherent in their view of life.
They hint at also having been subject to paroxysms of passion, but
for this not they but the gods were responsible. We do not have to
scrutinize the accuracy of the poet's projection any more than we
would quarrel with Schiller's dictum a century earlier: "The Greeks
were Nature." Our task is to become Nature once more. Like beauty,
the projection of an ideal of tranquillity is its own excuse for being.
    And now the final strophe:

Could we but also find a pure, sheltered, slender
patch of human existence, a strip of fruitland that is our own
between torrent and barren ledge. For our own heart still surmounts us,
like unto those. And we can no longer retrieve it

via images that tranquillize or via
divine bodies that teach it moderation on a grander scale.

This tentative translation is literal enough to obscure the difficulties and blur the controversial points of the meaning. A searching analysis should assist us in arriving at a more satisfactory version. The very first line poses a problem: "Could we but also find . . . " Without question, "also" must refer to the Greeks as exponents of an ethos of tranquillity. But what does "we" stand for? It stands, of course, for the poet and the modern lovers he has just been addressing – such is the general tacit assumption. But if we were right in having assumed on a trial basis that the poet's use of "we" in this Elegy never includes anybody but the temporal incarnation of the divine voice, then it would be strange indeed to find the poet fraternizing in the end with the lovers he has been addressing. Throughout strophes four, five, and six the distinction between himself and the lovers had been sharply drawn – none the less sharply for the fact that with the human side of his self he would wish nothing better than to soften it. But our strophe itself presents insurmountable difficulties against the acceptance of an inclusive "we." The crux of the matter lies in the two-word phrase *wie jene* 'like those,' in the third line from the last. Who are those? Who can those be? If "we" includes the present-day lovers, "those" must be the Greeks. But can those same Greeks who expressed an ethos of tranquillity and who strictly differentiated between what feeling is their own and what is visited upon them by the gods – can they be spoken of as being still surmounted by their own hearts? There is a perverse blindness in twisting the poet's words to involve him in so glaring a contradiction and refusing to see it as a contradiction. There is no escaping from the dilemma if it does not occur to the interpreter that the "we" of the first line could have a restrictive rather than an inclusive meaning. Another small grammatical point should be mentioned at once. "Like those," our translation ran. But the Greeks of the steles had been referred to as "these," not "those." "We," linked with "like those," is the reef on which the inclusive interpretation founders.

Let us see whether our own reading will supply a touchstone for getting at the truth. The poet began the Elegy with a solitary meditation, which he interrupted to sing a paean of praise for the angels. He returned to his meditation to elaborate the theme of his *dwindling*. His meditation brought to his mind the theme of the lovers who benefit most directly from his *dwindling*. Having first intruded themselves as a theme, the lovers now loom up before the poet's inner eye as shapes to be addressed with impassioned vehemence. In the sixth strophe the poet's agitation has subsided; he still continues to address the lovers, but his attention is no longer centered on them. It is focussed upon those bygone beings of gentler stuff on which he had invited the lovers' eye to dwell along with his own. With this shift he had already made a half-turn away from the lovers, in citing the steles. Now, at the end of the sixth strophe, he is through with the lovers. They recede to the background. The seventh and last finds him returning to his solitary meditation in a rueful yearning for what cannot be.

If "we" stands for the poet, then "those" stands not for the Greeks but for the lovers lately addressed. "These," the Greeks, are at the moment much more immediately present than "those," the lovers. In our translation we must enlarge the cryptic phrase "like those" into a clause containing a verb, if the meaning is to become explicitly clear. The choice is between: For our own heart still keeps surmounting us as it did these (the Greeks), and: For our own heart still keeps surmounting us as it does those. (We are overwhelmed by our own heart as they were, versus: We are overwhelmed by our own heart as those are.)

This reading involves a biographical confession on the poet's part. Remembering the bitterness with which the First Elegy had characterized his every essay at love as abortive, he confesses that his infatuation with the temptation of love has not been conquered. Despite his no longer being able to plead the excuse of youth (*noch immer* 'still'), he is not cured. Like those passionate present-day lovers, he falls a prey to the illusion again and again.

To repeat and sum up the grammatical dilemma: the initial statement of the last strophe extends as a tightly meshed unit from "Could we but also . . . " to "like those." If the "we" includes the lovers, "also" must signalize the Greeks; must therefore lay the poet open to the charge of saying something in flagrant contradiction to what he allowed the Greeks to say regarding themselves in the pre-

ceding strophe. If, on the other hand, the initial "we" refers to the
poet only, the final "those" must refer to the present-day lovers, so
totally at variance with the ethos of the Greeks. Crediting the poet
with a consistent statement, we must translate: "For our own heart
still rises to flood tide as theirs does," or, keeping the object case
construction of the original: "For our own heart still surmounts us
as it does those." We observe then that this "we" refers less to the
poet in general as the incarnation of the divine spirit than to our
poet's personal situation and time of life. A possible objection to the
intimacy of this confession vanishes with the thought that this is simply the poet's way of saying: This is my way of responding to life, and
it will be so long as I draw breath.

The use of "still" as relating to the poet involves us in a difficulty
regarding the "no longer" of the third line from the end. "Still" and
"no longer" are correlative terms that normally apply to the same
frame of reference. In the present context, however, "no longer"
seems to me to refer rather to the contemporary cultural situation
than to a phase of the poet's personal life. To clarify this we have to
continue our analysis.

We have engaged in grammatical discussion. It is time to refer to
the symbolism of the strophe's opening statement. The "pure, confined, slender patch" of human tranquillity, vainly yearned for by
the poet — what looks like an optative clause is surely a contrary-to-
fact — as something to counterbalance his sense of wasting and depletion, is envisaged under the image of a fertile strip of land bound-
ed by a rushing torrent on one side and a barren ledge on the other.
Dauer im Wechsel was Goethe's formula for a synthesis of the two
opposite poles. But for Rilke *Dauer* presents itself as petrification,
fixation in lifeless habit, and *Wechsel* as the restlessly pulsating, ever
escaping moment of intimate experience. To every reader even superficially familiar with the whole cycle of the *Elegies* and the *Sonnets
to Orpheus* as well, the imagery of our passage must be felt as fitting
the Nile landscape so well that it must obtrude itself upon the imagination. Specific allusions to Egypt occur in the Sixth Elegy, the
Seventh, the Ninth, and abound in the Tenth. Having just spoken of
Attic Greece as an exponent of tranquillity, our poet engages in a
very bold sweep in superimposing, as it were, the landscape of Egypt

upon that of Attica, thereby making the whole of the ancient Near East appear for a moment like a single cultural landscape, which it never was, and never was to our poet. The boldness of this synthetic view is so questionable that so sensitive an interpreter as Romano Guardini never alludes to it. He must have been aware of it, I am convinced, but he resolutely excluded it as impertinent. I am here presenting a critical doubt on this passage which I could not stifle.

The final two and a half lines of the Elegy still confront us with a knotty problem of interpretation and translation. The German text: "Und wir können ihm nicht mehr nachschaun in Bilder, die es besänftigen . . . " presents as bold a deviation from German grammatical usage as would the literal English translation: "And we can no longer look after it into images that tranquillize . . . " Looking into the distance as an activity and the achieving of a specific end by such activity are the two poles of our statement. Looking after the heart that keeps rising and escaping out of bounds. Looking after the heart, i.e., sending the eye in pursuit of the heart to arrest it, to capture it, to retrieve it, to transform its pulse into something tangible. Is not this passage in its grammatical boldness a sort of shorthand crossreference to an earlier passage of the Elegy, the words of which conjured up an almost materially concrete image of the poet as poised with outstretched arms after the new, warm, receding wave of the heart? We have in the concluding statement of the Elegy an echo of this passionate outcry now transformed into a sad reflection of resignation.

What are these images that tranquillize and these divine bodies that teach the heart to attain a self-moderation on a grander scale? Much of what has been written on this seems to me to obscure an essentially simple situation by philosophical verbiage. Is there any need of going beyond our Elegy for the images that tranquillize? Has not the poet set just such images before us in the steles of ancient Attic Greece? But what of the divine bodies that perform the same function on a grander scale? Well, I take them literally as divine bodies, and I invite the reader to find this corroborated by Rilke's own earlier poetry. The two books of *Neue Gedichte* (1907 and 1908 respectively) are each introduced by a sonnet glorifying Apollo as the god of song in a sculptural manifestation. The first limits itself to the presentation of a marble head that was all promise, pointing to an ineffable fulfillment in a future still to be achieved. In those lips that seem to suck, the breath of poetry destined to emerge was still latent. The second had as its theme a torso totally irradiated by the head that was — by those eyes which had transmuted every curve, even every fractured surface of that mutilated stone into a dazzle of starlight — turned on the quailing beholder. And the poem entitled "Cretan Artemis," closely following upon the second Apollo poem, supplied another example of such divinity.

One last aspect of the Elegy's final statement calls for elucidation. "And we can no longer. . . " What does this mean? What does "we" stand for, we ask once more. Not for the individual poet, I think, not even for poets as a class, by no means certainly for the poet and the present-day lovers lumped together, but rather for the contemporary cultural ethos in which the speaker shares. Perhaps we became aware of "our" occurring in the same general sense when the poet remarked on the expressive gestures of the steles as though made of a stuff other than ours. If these two uses of the first personal pronoun plural are taken to invalidate the general premise of this essay, I have nothing to say. "No longer" I take to refer to the present age and the kind of art it excels in, despite the fact that its apparent correlative "still" referred to a specific phase of the poet's own life. Finally, the conjunction "and" that joins the final statement of the Elegy to the preceding must engage us for a moment. Reviewing the arguments concerning who is designated by "like those" — the Greeks or the modern lovers — if "those" had signified the Greeks the poet would almost certainly have continued with an adversative "but" rather than with a conjoining "and." Does not the poet here seem to say: our present art, nervous, experimental, extreme in all its aspects, fails in its efforts to present a synthesis between the pulsing of living experience and the yearning for duration. It is not impossible, on the other hand, to associate even the "no longer" with the poet's time of life, making it a true correlative of "still." In that case the poet would be taken to say very much the same thing as the foregoing but with the addition: the art of the ancients no longer speaks to me with the same vitality that inspired me in my younger days. For better or worse, I am now committed to the art of the moderns which no longer looks to the representative art of the ancients for guidance.

Recapitulating our translation of the Elegy's last strophe on the basis of this extended analysis, we would tentatively phrase it as follows:

Could we but find a pure, contained, ever so modest
patch of the human domain, a strip of fruitland really our own

between torrent and barren ledge. For our own heart still wells up and over-
powers us

as it does those. And we can no longer send our eyes
in pursuit to arrest it, retrieve it, and transform it into images that tranquillize or into

divine bodies that teach it restraint on a grander scale.

10.

RILKE: DER STYLIT
Eine Textinterpretation

VÖLKER schlugen über ihm zusammen,
die er küren durfte und verdammen;
und erratend, daß er sich verlor,
klomm er aus dem Volksgeruch mit klammen
Händen einen Säulenschaft empor,

6 der noch immer stieg und nichts mehr hob,
und begann, allein auf seiner Fläche,
ganz von vorne seine eigne Schwäche
zu vergleichen mit des Herren Lob;

10 und da war kein Ende: er verglich;
und der Andre wurde immer größer.
Und die Hirten, Ackerbauer, Flößer
sahn ihn klein und außer sich

14 immer mit dem ganzen Himmel reden,
eingeregnet manchmal, manchmal licht;
und sein Heulen stürzte sich auf jeden,
so als heulte er ihm ins Gesicht.
Doch er sah seit Jahren nicht,

19 wie der Menge Drängen und Verlauf
unten unaufhörlich sich ergänzte,
und das Blanke an den Fürsten glänzte
lange nicht so hoch hinauf.

23 Aber wenn er oben, fast verdammt
und von ihrem Widerstand zerschunden,
einsam mit verzweifeltem Geschreie
schüttelte die täglichen Dämonen:
fielen langsam auf die erste Reihe
schwer und ungeschickt aus seinen Wunden
große Würmer in die offnen Kronen
und vermehrten sich im Samt.

Dies Gedicht, geschrieben in Paris im Frühsommer 1908, veröffentlicht in *Neue Gedichte* im Herbst desselben Jahres, behandelt einen Gegenstand aus dem Umkreis frühchristlicher Historie und Le-

gende, einem Bereich, der Rilkes Phantasie von seiner frühesten bis
zu seiner spätesten Zeit befruchtete. Da Rilkes Gedicht ein histori-
sches Phänomen zur Voraussetzung hat, tun wir gut, uns mit den
Grundzügen des überlieferten Sachverhalts zu befassen und die Vor-
lage in unsere Analyse miteinzubeziehen. In der elften Ausgabe der
Encyclopedia Britannica findet man unter dem Titel «Simeon Sty-
lites» Angaben, die sich mit dem folgenden decken: Ein syrischer
Mönch namens Simeon (390-459) lebte bis zu seinem dreißigsten
Jahr in einer klösterlichen Gemeinschaft. Von der Brüderschaft wegen seiner übergroßen asketischen Strenge ausgestoßen, erbaute er
sich einen sechs Fuß hohen Pfeiler, um darauf zu predigen. Diese
Freiluftkanzel genügte ihm auf die Dauer nicht. Von Jahr zu Jahr
erbaute er sich höhere Pfeiler, bis er es schließlich im zehnten Jahr
zu einer Höhe von sechzig Fuß gebracht hatte. Mit einem Geländer
umgeben, wurde dieser Pfeiler seine Wohn- und Wirkungsstätte, die
er dreißig Jahre lang nicht verließ. Seine Jünger versorgten ihn mittels
einer Leiter mit Speise und Trank. Simeon war predigend und kir-
chenpolitisch tätig. Sein Zeitgenosse Theodoret hat, auf persönlicher
Bekanntschaft fußend, seine Lebensgeschichte geschrieben. Dieser
erste Pfeilerbewohner hat bis ins achtzehnte Jahrhundert viele Nachfolger gefunden. – Simeon war also ein fanatischer Kirchenmann.
Seine Wirkung auf das Volk zeugt von unleugbar charismatischer
Begabung, und ein starker Einschlag von Exhibitionismus ist unver-
kennbar. Die Verwandtschaft von Rilkes «Stylit» mit dem ersten
Säulenheiligen beschränkt sich auf die allgemein religiöse Orientie-
rung des Helden und auf seine luftige Wohnstätte. Mit dem Persön-
lichkeitstypus des historischen Simeon hat Rilkes Held nicht einen
Zug gemein. Was aber Simeons Nachfolger betrifft, so wird mancher
Leser sich an die amerikanischen Fahnenknopfhocker der dreißiger
Jahre erinnert fühlen.

Betrachten wir nun Rilkes Gedicht, wie es sich dem inneren Sinn
des Aufnehmenden darstellt.

> Völker schlugen über ihm zusammen,
> die er küren durfte und verdammen ...

Dieser Eingangssatz von atemverschlagender Knappheit bringt einen
Menschen und seine Lage auf eine Formel. Gegenstand des Gedichts

ist ein absoluter Herrscher über viele Völker, Herr über Leben und
Tod, nicht etwa ein Kirchenfürst mit der Gewalt der Schlüssel. Derselbe Satz bezeichnet ihn als vom Untergang bedroht. Die Bedrohung
ist so stark in den Vordergrund gerückt, daß sie die logische Folge des
Vortrags umwirft. Sich überstürzend meldet der Satz zuerst das Was
und erst dann das Wer. Die Art der Bedrohung kann aus diesem Satz
nur undeutlich erfaßt werden. Es handelt sich jedenfalls nicht um
eine Verschwörung von Einzelnen gegen einen Alleinherrscher. Wir
könnten allenfalls an einen Massenaufstand denken, aber wir bekommen bei dem Zusammenschlagen der Wogen nur das Bild eines Er-
trinkenden. Schon der nächste Vers:

und erratend, daß er sich verlor,

verdeutlicht die Lage. Die Bedrohung ist nicht physischer, sondern
seelischer Art. Das Sichverlieren ist eine Gefahr, die dem auf der
Höhe der Macht Ausgesetzten droht. «Die Sich-Verlierenden läßt
alles los», – so hieß es in dem Gedicht «Der Ölbaumgarten» von dem
an seiner Sendung Scheiternden. Damit wissen wir schon, dieser Ge-
fährdete kann sich seine Stellung als Alleinherrscher nicht erkämpft
haben, sie muß ihm als Erbe zugefallen sein, und er findet sich der
Verwaltung dieses Erbes nicht gewachsen. Ihm fehlt die Robustheit
des Willens zur Selbstbehauptung. Er ist ein Neurastheniker des Gefühls. Er ist kein Kämpfender, aber er ist auch kein passiv Verzwei-
felnder, denn er sinnt instinktiv auf Flucht. Flucht wohin? In dem
Völkergewoge ist ihm jeder Ausweg ins Horizontale verstellt. Nur
eine Rettungsmöglichkeit bietet sich: die Flucht nach oben, – das
«oben» sowohl physisch wie symbolisch verstanden.

Die seelische Notlage des auf seiner Höhe der Macht Exponierten,
des der Wucht der Verantwortung nicht Gewachsenen, ist ein Thema,
das uns schon auf einer älteren Stufe von Rilkes Kunst entgegentritt.
Bereits im dritten Teil des *Stundenbuchs* (1903) finden wir eine
Variante desselben Themas. Dort endet das dritte Buch mit einer
Seligpreisung der Armen, die sich in einer nie enden wollenden Fülle
von Bildern ausströmt, um schließlich den heiligen Franz von Assisi
als die Verkörperung jener Armut zu verkünden, die «ein großer
Glanz aus Innen» ist. Eingeleitet ist dieses Thema des Reichtums.
Unsere Reichen, heißt es, die Reichen von heute, sind nicht reich.

Fortfahrend werden in einer Folge von Absätzen die wirklich Reichen ferner Zonen und Zeiten den heutigen Reichen entgegengestellt.
Einer dieser wirklich Reichen wird eingeführt als

> ... des Ostens weißer Gossudar,
> dem Reiche eines Gottes Recht erwiesen;
> er aber lag mit abgehärmtem Haar,
> die alte Stirne auf des Fußes Fliesen,
> und weinte, – weil aus allen Paradiesen
> nicht *eine* Stunde seine war. (SW I, 354)

Wie der Stylit ist der Held dieses Passus ein absoluter Herrscher über
weite Reiche, dessen Verehrung für seine Völker die Gestalt göttli-
cher Anbetung annahm. Wie der Stylit ist dieser Herrscher ein Neurastheniker der Verantwortung. Er ist alt geworden. Wir sehen das
Bild des Erschöpften, wie er auf dem Marmorparkett seines Palastes
hingestreckt weint. Das ist einer, dem es zu Bewußtsein gekommen
ist, daß er sich über die Verantwortlichkeit für seine Völker verloren
hat. Ohne Zweifel glauben wir hier den Keim zu dem späteren «Stylit» zu entdecken. Freilich macht sich gleich ein wesentlicher Unterschied zwischen den beiden bemerkbar. Jenes Bild des weißen Gos-
sudars des Ostens beschränkt sich auf eine sentimentale statische Gebärde. Dieses Statische, ein charakteristisches Merkmal von Rilkes
früher Kunst, ließe sich durch unzählige Beispiele belegen. Hier genüge der Hinweis auf ein Musterbeispiel dieser Art. Es beginnt mit
dem Vers:

> Schau, wie die Zypressen schwärzer werden ... (SW I, 163)

Man vergleiche die Urform dieses Gedichts mit der höchst interessanten Umarbeitung, die das Gedicht später erfahren hat, ohne indessen
den statischen Charakter der Urform verleugnen zu können. Rilkes
reife Kunst hat diese Statik überwunden und durch eine stets vibrie-
rende Dynamik ersetzt. Die *Neuen Gedichte* schildern nicht mehr
eine bloße Haltung oder Gebärde, sondern einen Vorgang. Dafür
bietet «Der Stylit» ein hervorragendes Beispiel.

Ganz kurz sei hier noch darauf hingewiesen, daß die Erkenntnis
um die Gefahr des Sichverlierens im Kern von Rilkes tiefster Art des
eigenen Erlebens begründet ist. Das Sichverlieren als ein Vorgang von
Verausgabung seelischer Kräfte ist in dem Gedicht «Der Dichter» –

es steht ebenfalls in dem ersten Band der *Neuen Gedichte* — bereits auf die Formel gebracht

> Alle Dinge, an die ich mich gebe,
> werden reich und geben mich aus.

Es würde zu weit führen zu zeigen, wie dieses Gefühl des Sichverströmens, der Hingabe an die Dinge, dem ein Gefühl der Verminderung der eigenen Kräfte entspricht, in den *Duineser Elegien* und den *Sonetten an Orpheus* zu einem Hauptthema der dichterischen Aussage wird. Ich habe dies an anderer Stelle aufzuzeigen versucht[1]. Das Motiv der Kraftäußerung als eines Kraftentzugs findet sich bereits in der christlichen Heilsgeschichte: Jesus, von einer Heilungsbedürftigen, die auf ihn vertraut, unwissenderweise am Saum seines Gewandes berührt, spürt den Heilungsvorgang als eine Verminderung seiner Kraft (Lukas 8 : 46). Die Analogie zu diesem Empfinden bietet sich im modernen Leben, ohne daß man sich dessen bewußt wird, in dem Phänomen des Akkumulators, der elektrischen Batterie. Man erinnert sich, wie der zur Mystik neigende alternde Strindberg die Wunderkraft von Heiligenbildern auf diese Weise zu erklären sucht: Wenn Tausende von Menschen einem Heiligenbild über lange Zeiträume hinweg ihre Verehrung zollen, so sammelt sich in diesem eine Fülle von Kräften an, die sich unter Umständen wunderwirkend entladen. Solche Spekulationen gehören zu der Atmosphäre der Zeit, in der Rilke dichtete. Kehren wir nach diesen durchaus nötigen Abschweifungen zu unserem Gedicht zurück.

Wir wissen jetzt Bescheid über unseren Helden in seiner Lage der Bedrohung, in seiner Erkenntnis der Gefährdung und in seiner Flucht. Es ist der Druck der Lebensangst, der ihn nach oben treibt. Wie die Flucht aber vor sich geht, das erfahren wir in einem Bild von grotesker Komik. Wie dieser Fürst, an dessen Händen der kalte Schweiß der Lebensangst klebt, an einer Säule, vermutlich Überbleibsel einer Tempelruine, emporklettert, das erinnert an die Gelenkigkeit eines Affen. Es ist ein Einschlag von skurriler Groteskerie in diesem reali-

---

1 "The Poet's Dilemma: An Interpretation of Rilke's Second *Duino Elegy*," in *PMLA*, Band 82, Nr. I, März 1967 and in the present volume, above pp.

stisch gar nicht vorzustellenden Vorgang. Die Säule hat keine Vor-
sprünge, wie etwa die gotischen Zierblumen, zu denen das Gespenst
in Goethes «Totentanz» sich zu dem Türmer hinaufhäkelt, oder
sollte man sich diesen Mann vorstellen wie eine menschliche Fliege,
behutsam an einer runden Mauer emporklimmend? Solche Vorstellungen liegen ganz fern. Es geht im Nu in die Höhe, wie in einem
pneumatischen Lift. Er ist oben. Dazu macht der Pfeiler selbst eine
Bewegung nach oben mit. Wir sehen ihn geradezu wachsen:

der noch immer stieg ...

Man fragt sich unwillkürlich, ob Rilke die Ästhetik von Theodor
Lipps gekannt hat, deren zweiter Band (1906) die Einfühlung in die
architektonischen Grundformen der Klassik als ein dynamisches Spiel
verfolgt. Bei dieser ganzen, in einem magischen Nu sich vollziehenden
Bewegung haben wir noch nicht Zeit gehabt, auf ein anderes Element
zu achten:

klomm er aus dem Volksgeruch ...

Damit ist ein zweites Motiv seiner Flucht signalisiert. Zuzugebender
Maßen ein Nebenmotiv. Der Volksgeruch, der Dunst der kleinen
Leute, dringt ihm in die Nase und verunreinigt seinen Atem, sein in-
times physisches Sein. Denken wir dabei nicht unwillkürlich an Julius
Cäsar, den bei dem schweren Dunst des ihn umringenden Pöbels eine
Ohnmacht anwandelte? Denken wir nicht ebenfalls an jenen Kaiser
der Südöstlichen Inseln, dessen dichterisches Inerscheinungtreten
freilich noch zu erwarten stand, als Rilke seinen «Stylit» schrieb, den
Kaiser, der in seiner aristokratischen Vornehmheit den Menschenge-
ruch als etwas so Widerliches verabscheute, daß er seine abgöttisch
geliebte Gattin ermorden wollte, die sich daran besudelt hatte? (Hofmannsthal: *Die Frau ohne Schatten.*) Kein Zweifel jedenfalls, der
Ekel des Vornehmen gegenüber der gemeinen Menge ist mit zu be-
rücksichtigen als ein treibendes Motiv der Flucht unseres Helden, und
damit ist ein weiteres Merkmal der Identifizierung des Dichters mit
seinem Helden gegeben, wie jedem Rilke-Kenner deutlich sein muß.
Ich kann es mir nicht versagen, darauf hinzuweisen, wie nah es gelegen hätte, den Vers, von dem unsere letzten Betrachtungen ausgin-
gen, so zu formulieren:

klomm er aus dem Volksgewühl ...

Das wäre klassizistisch wohlanständig gewesen, und keinem Leser wäre es eingefallen, eine andere Lesart vorzuschlagen oder zu vermuten. Aber wieviel echtester Rilke wäre mit dieser einen Silbe verloren gegangen!

Die nächsten fünf Verse berichten in schlichter Sprache, was den Helden, der sich sein Alleinsein erkämpft hat, auf seine Höhe treibt. Gleich zu bemerken: von allem, was noch kommt, nimmt er nicht die geringste Notiz. Sein Sinnen, seine Betrachtung hat es jetzt nur mit dem Herrn zu tun, dem Anderen. Es entwickelt sich ein polarer Bezug zwischen seinem immer mehr zu einem Punkt zusammenschrumpfenden Ich und dem ins Übergroße wachsenden All. Dem Lauf der Erzählung vorauseilend, werden wir darauf aufmerksam, wie das Alleinsein, die Einsamkeit im All, auf die Dauer das Gleichgewicht seiner Persönlichkeit untergräbt. Er redet immer mit dem ganzen Himmel, er heult nach allen Richtungen hin, er ist ein Ekstatiker geworden, der, verelendet an Leib und Seele, seine Kräfte im Kampf mit dämonischen Ausgeburten seiner Phantasie verausgabt. Damit ist alles gesagt, was unsere innere Anteilnahme an dem Helden angeht. (Die Frage nach seiner physischen Ernährung überhaupt aufzuwerfen, verbietet sich im ganzen Zusammenhang unseres Gedichts.) Aber es wäre durchaus verfehlt zu meinen, daß damit die dichterische Aussage erschöpft wäre. Der zwölfte Vers hat einen Wechsel der Perspektive eingeleitet, so unvermittelt schroff das noch eben Festgehaltene nach Art eines Vexierbildes verwandelnd, daß wir meinten geträumt zu haben. Auf einmal hat sich ein Volksgewimmel in einer weiten Landschaft mit einem großen Fluß vor das innere Auge gedrängt. Hirten, Ackerbauer, Flößer — wo sind sie hergekommen? Sie sind einfach da. Schaulustige Gaffer mit einem aufwärtsgerichteten Blick auf den Punkt in die Höhe. Nach befriedigter Schaulust verlaufen sich die Gaffer, aber das Gedränge wächst von Jahr zu Jahr, und wieder gibt es eine Überraschung: Die Sensationslust muß sogar die Vornehmen in einem weiten Umkreis von Ländern ergriffen haben, denn wir sehen auf einmal Gruppen von Hofleuten und Kronenträgern in kostbaren Gewändern und blankem Waffenschmuck. Diesen wird Platz gemacht, wie es sich gebührt, so daß unser Blick in dem abschließenden Absatz des Gedichts das Bild eines Freilufttheaters umfaßt, dessen Zuschauer nach Rängen gegliedert sind, wobei, wie

es sich von selbst versteht, die Vornehmsten die vorderste Parkett-
reihe besetzen.

In dem Abgesang aber — diese Bezeichnung gebührt dem Schluß —
hat die Perspektive von neuem gewechselt. Jetzt ist der Blick des
Aufnehmenden dem Helden bis dicht auf den Leib gerückt. Er sieht,
wie der verzweifelt Schreiende sich unter gräßlichen Zuckungen win-
det. Er sieht die offenen Wunden des ausgemergelten Leibes. Er sieht
große Würmer aus ihnen hervorstarren, sich mit langsam ungeschick-
ten Bewegungen von dem Körper ablösen und fallen, um bei einem
letzten Abwärtsgleiten der Perspektive wahrzunehmen, wie sie von
dem Samt der Kronen der fürstlichen Gaffer aufgefangen werden und
in überrealistischer Anschaulichkeit sich darin paaren. So schließt das
Gedicht mit einer grotesken Orgie animalischer Begattung.

Der Held ist während des ganzen Vorgangs ohne Bezug auf das
Publikum geblieben. Aber der Vorgang findet seinen Sinn in seiner
Bezogenheit auf die gaffende Menge.

Vielleicht hält das Erinnerungsbild des Hörers oder Lesers den
gräßlichen Vorgang als ein Einmaliges fest. Das wäre weit gefehlt. Es
würde stimmen, wenn es geheißen hätte:

> Aber *als* er oben, fast verdammt ...
> schüttelte die *quälenden* Dämonen.

Statt dessen aber heißt es *wenn*. Der ganze Zusammenhang stellt den
Satz unter den Aspekt täglicher Wiederholung, und die als täglich bezeichneten Dämonen verleihen dem Vorgang die Bedeutung eines
täglich zelebrierten gräßlichen Opfers.

Abschließend wäre über den Sinn unseres Gedichts zu sagen: in
unserem Gedicht laufen zwei Stränge zusammen, erstens, die tiefe
aber doch bedingte Einfühlung des Dichters in einen Helden von sehr
ausgefallener Geistesverfassung; und zweitens, ebenso wichtig, der
Hohn des Geistesaristokraten gegenüber der verständnislosen stumpfen Menge. Es ist derselbe unausgesprochene Hohn, der dem Gedicht
«Kreuzigung» sein Gepräge verleiht, wo die stumpfen Henkersknech-
te bei dem Schrei des Gekreuzigten die Ohren spitzen und mit sach-
licher Neugier «ein ganzes Spiel» erwarten.

Im Verlauf unserer Analyse des Gedichts als eines Vorgangs, der
sich dem inneren Sinn des Aufnehmenden mitteilt, ist der logisch-

syntaktische Aufbau des Gedichts deutlich geworden. Eine Gliederung in drei Teile hat sich dabei ergeben. Auf die kürzeste Formel gebracht lauten diese: erstens der Held, zweitens das Publikum, drittens der Bezug. Wir haben es bisher geflissentlich vermieden, die technische Seite des Gedichts auch nur mit einem Seitenblick zu streifen. Dieser Seite wenden wir jetzt unsere Aufmerksamkeit zu. Wir wären versucht gewesen, damit anzufangen, hätten wir nicht befürchten müssen, daß mancher flüchtige Leser das Gedicht als ein minderwertiges Produkt einer ausgearteten Phantasie beiseite gelegt hätte.

Das Gedicht besteht aus dreißig auftaktlosen alternierenden Fünfhebern. Nur muß dies dahin eingeschränkt werden, daß einige wenige Verse — es sind im ganzen vier — um eine Hebung verkürzt sind. Darauf ist später zurückzukommen. Für das Auge gliedert sich das Gedicht nicht in Strophen, sondern in Versbündel von verschiedener Länge. Es sind im ganzen sechs. Jedes der fünf ersten besteht aus fünf bzw. vier Versen, während das abschließende, das ich als den Abgesang bezeichne, acht Verse enthält. Auf den ersten Blick scheint es sich bei dieser Gliederung um reine Willkür zu handeln, denn die logisch-syntaktischen Haltepunkte der Aussage werden dabei völlig ignoriert. Sehr bald aber merkt man, das gliedernde Prinzip dieser Aussage ist lediglich der Reim. Jedes der ersten fünf Versbündel ist durch einen a-b-Reim zu einer Gruppe zusammengeschlossen. In den Gruppen zu vier Versen kommt jeder der beiden Reime zweimal vor; in den Gruppen zu fünf stellt sich einer der beiden Reime dreimal ein. Die Anordnung der Reime wechselt nach Belieben. Reimpaare, Reimverschlingung und Reimumklammerung sind aufzuweisen. In dem Abgesang ist es freilich anders. In seinen acht Versen wird ein kompliziertes System von vier Reimen aufgebaut, die sich sogar für den äußeren Sinn sehr stark von den fünf voraufgehenden Gruppen abheben. Es sieht danach aus, als habe der Rilke der *Neuen Gedichte* den Endreim als das wesentliche Merkmal dichterischer Aussage bezeichnen wollen. Hat er nicht die langen Blankversgedichte, die am Ende des ersten Bandes dieser Sammlung stehen, bei ihrer ersten Veröffentlichung in der *Neuen Rundschau* (1905) mit dem Titel «Gedichte in Prosa» versehen? Die Gliederung in sichtbare, durch den Endreim zusammengehaltene Gruppen, die unser Gedicht aufweist, ist jedenfalls kein vereinzeltes Phänomen. Einen der interessantesten

Fälle solcher Präsentierung für das Auge bietet das Gedicht «Die Fensterrose». Der erste Blick besagt, daß es sich um ein Sonett handelt mit dem üblichen Schema von zwei Vierergruppen, die durch zwei Dreiergruppen ergänzt werden. Das ist aber pure Augentäuschung. In Wirklichkeit, das heißt dem Sinn nach, hebt das Gedicht an mit einer Aussage in zwei Versen. Daran schließen sich vier Dreiergruppen, die in Rhythmus und Melodie als echte Terzinen anzusprechen sind. Nur in dieser Form prägt sich das Gedicht dem Gedächtnis ein. Für das Schriftbild ist aber, wie im «Stylit», der Reim maßgebend. Man fragt sich, was den Dichter zu so auffallend manierierter Schematisierung seiner Gedichte bewogen haben kann. Man erinnert sich, wie Rilke wenige Jahre später zu wiederholten Malen betonte, daß *Die Aufzeichnungen des Malte Laurids Brigge* «gegen den Strich» zu lesen seien. Ist es nicht plausibel anzunehmen, daß dasselbe Versteckspiel für die Gedichte gilt? Man hört sie gegen den Strich. Ein Blinder würde nie darauf verfallen, sie so aufzuzeichnen, wie sie sich auf dem Papier dem Auge darbieten. Was ist demnach über die Hörwirkung unseres Gedichts zu sagen?

Für das Ohr hat das Gedicht eine sehr einfache Gliederung. Man hört das Gedicht bis Vers 22 als eine strömende Einheit. Siebenmal im Verlauf der ersten zweiundzwanzig Verse setzt der Vers mit einem «und» ein. Vor dem Abgesang aber sammelt sich der Atem in einer Pause von eindrucksvoller Dauer. Vorbereitend wirkt schon die Tatsache, daß der zweiundzwanzigste Vers ein Kurzvers ist. Nun setzt der Abgesang ein mit einem energischen «aber». Der Abgesang gibt sich seiner Hörform nach als Zielpunkt des ganzen Verlaufs. Hier, wo von dem Höreindruck die Rede ist, wäre beiläufig zu bemerken, daß unser Gedicht, im Gegensatz zu Rilkes sonstiger Art, sehr sparsamen Gebrauch von Alliteration und Klangmalerei macht. Einziges Beispiel wirkungsvoller Alliteration, noch durch Enjambement verstärkt:

> klomm er aus dem Volksgeruch mit klammen Händen ...

Klangmalerei finden wir nur in Vers 3 und 4 des Abgesangs:

> einsam mit verzweifeltem Geschreie
> schüttelte die täglichen Dämonen:

Der Abgesang ist von geradezu enormer Hörwirkung. Dies läßt sich auf die verschiedenste Weise demonstrieren. Verliefen die ersten

zweiundzwanzig Verse in lässiger syntaktischer Folge, so bietet sich
der Abgesang als eine geschlossene Satzperiode von streng symmetri-
schem Bau und virtuos durchgeführter Satzmelodie. Die ersten vier
Verse bilden den Vordersatz, einen iterativen Temporalsatz, die folgenden vier den Nachsatz. Wie straff das Ganze zusammenhängt,
zeigt sich schon daran, daß das Hauptverbum des Satzes an den Anfang des fünften Verses zu stehen kommt, während das Subjekt sich
erst im :siebenten Vers einstellt. Eine solche Satzperiode operiert in
ihrem syntaktischen Bau mit Spannung und Lösung. Die Spannung
betrifft die erste Hälfte, die Lösung die zweite. Einen besonderen
Beitrag zu der Spannung des Vordersatzes bietet das proleptische
Pronomen «ihrem» des zweiten Verses, das erst durch das Substantiv
«Dämonen» des vierten Verses in seiner Beziehung erkannt wird.
Doch der Hauptanteil an der Hörwirkung des Abgesangs fällt ohne
Zweifel den Reimen zu. Man hat im Bisherigen bei jedem zweiten
oder dritten Vers eine Reimantwort erwartet und gefunden. Hier
dagegen stellt sich in den vier Versen des Vordersatzes überhaupt
kein Reim ein. Dies versetzt das Ohr in einen Zustand merklicher
Spannung, der sich von Vers zu Vers steigert. Und nun bringen die
vier Verse des Nachsatzes die antwortenden Reime: zuerst einen
Reim auf den dritten Vers, dann einen auf den zweiten, dann auf den
vierten und schließlich auf den ersten, so daß die Spannweite des
ersten Reims über acht Verse reicht. Das Ohr war auf den erwarteten
Reim eingestellt. Es wußte, der ganzen Anlage der Periode nach mußte er kommen. So bestätigt sich die Erwartung in einer wundervollen
Folge von Gleichklängen für das Gehör. Wir tun gut, noch auf einige
Nebenwirkungen aufmerksam zu werden. Die Verse zwei bis sieben
haben durchgehend zweisilbigen Reim, der Reim von Vers eins und
acht dagegen ist einsilbig. Dieser Kontrast hebt den am weitesten
gespannten Reim von den übrigen ab. Ferner, die Verse sind alternie-
rende Fünfheber, aber der letzte Vers ist um eine Hebung verkürzt.
Solche Kurzverse können in anderem Zusammenhang geradezu träu-
merisch-retardierend wirken. Man denke an den Schlußvers des
«Panther»:

und hört im Herzen auf zu sein.

Hier dagegen bringt der Kurzvers des Schlusses noch eine weitere
Straffung des Tempos. (Zwei im Voraufgehenden unberücksichtigt

gebliebene Kurzverse, Vers 13 und 18, erleichtern die Atemführung in dem ununterbrochenen Fortgang der ersten zweiundzwanzig Verse. Darüberhinaus vermag ich ihrer Kurzform keinen spezifischen Ausdruckswert zuzuerkennen.)

Bei dem Kontrast zwischen Form und Inhalt des Abgesangs fühlt man sich erinnert an ein Wort Thomas Manns von der nahen Verwandtschaft des Obszönen und des Heiligen.

Unser Gedicht führt zu einer Beobachtung, die den genugsam bekannten Bezug von Rilkes Schaffen zu den neuesten Experimenten zeitgenössischer Malerei in ein helles Licht rückt. Hat man bemerkt, wie sich unterhalb der Oberfläche der bildhaften Schau, gleichsam subkutan, ein System von Linien abzeichnet, das als symmetrische Figur skizziert zu werden verdiente? Zuerst sind es die gewölbten Linien der zwei sich auf einen Mittelpunkt zu bewegenden Wogenkämme. Dann, im Augenblick ihrer Berührung, schießt eine Vertikale in die Höhe. Diese Bewegung findet ihren Abschluß in einer Horizontale, einer Fläche, auf der die Bewegung zum Stillstand kommt oder vielmehr zu kommen scheint. Im weiteren Verlauf nämlich, der das Agieren des Ekstatikers schildert, sind Ansätze zu einer fächerartigen Wölbung nach oben gegeben — sein Reden mit dem ganzen Himmel — und eine entsprechende fächerförmige Ausstrahlung nach unten in seinem herabstürzenden Geheul. All dies erinnert an die Technik der abstrakten Malerei, die die Körperwelt in ein System von Linien auflöst. Freilich wird die Kunst des Nebeneinander die Dynamik der Gestaltung immer nur in einem Moment des Geschehens festzuhalten imstande sein. Es dürfte sich lohnen zu untersuchen, in welchem Maß ein derartiges System von Linien in anderen Gedichten aus Rilkes Reifezeit anzutreffen ist. Für die «Römische Fontäne» ist dies bereits vor langer Zeit in vorbildlicher Weise geschehen[2].

---

2   Leopold Liegler: «Das Rilke-Problem», *Plan*, Kunst — Literatur — Kultur, 2. Jahrgang, Nummer 2, Wien, 1947.

11.
RAINER MARIA RILKE: PERSISCHES HELIOTROP

ES könnte sein, daß dir der Rose Lob
zu laut erscheint für deine Freundin: Nimm
das schön gestickte Kraut und überstimm
mit dringend flüsterndem Heliotrop

den Bülbül, der an ihren Lieblingsplätzen
sie schreiend preist und sie nicht kennt.
Denn sieh: wie süße Worte nachts in Sätzen
beisammenstehn ganz dicht, durch nichts getrennt,
aus der Vokale wachem Violett
hindüftend durch das stille Himmelbett —:

so schließen sich vor dem gesteppten Laube
deutliche Sterne zu der seidnen Traube
und mischen, daß sie fast davon verschwimmt,
die Stille mit Vanille und mit Zimmt.

Dieses Gedicht gehört zu der Fülle neuer und neuartiger Produktion, die Rilke unter dem Titel «Der Neuen Gedichte anderer Teil» veröffentlichte. Es entstand nach den Angaben in Ernst Zinns Register im Frühsommer 1908[1] und gehört zu dem Zeitraum, wo *Die Aufzeichnungen des Malte Laurids Brigge* ihrer Vollendung entgegenreiften und die ersten zwei *Duineser Elegien* (1911-1912) wiederum eine radikal gewandelte Art der lyrischen Aussage in des Dichters Schaffen ankündigten. Es ist schwer anzufangen. Es wäre ein purer Verlegenheitsausweg, die Fülle der Blumengedichte aus Rilkes Reifezeit Revue passieren zu lassen, um das Spezifische des diesmaligen Vorwurfs aufzufinden. Beginnen wir lieber gleich mit dem Titel. Persisches Heliotrop: wer fühlte sich bei diesem Titel nicht daran erinnert, daß in den Gärten von Schiras und Isfahan die Blumen dunkler

---

1 Rainer Maria Rilke, Sämtliche Werke in sechs Bänden, hg. vom Rilke-Archiv in Verbindung mit Ruth Sieber-Rilke, besorgt durch Ernst Zinn, Inselverlag, 1955 bis 1965, Bd. I, S. 630. Alle weiteren Hinweise auf Gedichte Rilkes erfolgen nach dieser Ausgabe.

und berauschender duften als irgendwo sonst in der Welt! Wer zufäl-
ligerweise die vergröberte Großform des kalifornischen Heliotrop
kennt, wird schon am Titel begreifen, daß es sich hier um die erlesen-
ste Verkörperung der Idee des Heliotrop handeln müsse. Schon beim
Eingang ist also unsere Erwartung auf etwas sehr Kostbares eingestellt. Die ersten zwei Verse führen uns allerdings vorerst in einen
Vorraum der Überlegung, wo die Rose in Sicht tritt. Erst dann wird
die Titelblume, auf den ersten Blick als polarer Gegentyp der Rose
erkennbar, präzis beschrieben, mit Namen genannt und beherrscht
fortan den Vierzehnzeiler bis zum Ende des Gedichts. Dieser Ablauf
enthält aber in seinen ersten sechs Versen soviel Verblüffendes, rätsel-
haft Verschlungenes und Verschlagenes, daß wir gut daran tun werden, vorerst den Aussagemodus des Gedichts und seine Gliederung
ins Auge zu fassen. Das Gedicht beginnt mit einer Erwägung des
Sprechers, die kaum als Möglichkeit aufgetaucht, sofort als der gegen-
wärtigen Situation entsprechend erkannt, einen Willensimpuls auslöst, der mit den beiden Imperativen «nimm» und «überstimm» das
Schema des vorgeschriebenen Handelns bezeichnet. Daran reiht sich
ein weiterer Imperativ, «Denn sieh» (Vers 7), der nicht wie die vori-
gen beiden zu einem Tun, sondern zu sinnender Betrachtung eines in
der wahrnehmbaren Welt nicht auszuschöpfenden Vorgangs auffor-
dert. Dieses Sich-Versenken in die Betrachtung dauert bis zum Ab-
klingen der seelischen Schwingung, die das Leben dieses Gedichts
ausmacht.

Das ganze Gedicht steht im Zeichen der Anrede-Form. Der Spre-
cher setzt sich mit einem Du auseinander. Was haben in diesem Zusammenhang die hypothetische Erwägung, der imperativische Impuls,
die sinnende Betrachtung für einen Sinn? Besteht die Grundsituation
etwa darin, daß ein Freund den Dichter aufsucht und ihm seine Ver-
legenheit darüber gesteht, wie er seiner Angebeteten in taktvollster
Form seine Verehrung oder Huldigung ausdrücken könne? Zu solcher
Auffassung wäre, der Titel vorzuschlagen: Guter Rat. Das wäre eine
Banalisierung des Gedichts, die doch keinen Augenblick in Erwägung
gezogen werden kann. Die ganze Tönung der Sprache ist viel zu intim
für eine Situation, in der sich ein Mann von einem Freunde Auskunft
in Liebesangelegenheiten erbittet. Nein, das Du dieses Gedichts ist
selbstverständlich das lyrische Du. Der Dichter ergeht sich im Zwie-

gespräch mit dem eigenen Selbst. Er ist es, der eine Möglichkeit er-
wägt, sie blitzschnell als richtig bestätigt empfindet und die Lösung
findet, die dem Sonderfall adäquat ist. Da aber nach den an das eigene Ich gerichteten Imperativen, «nimm» «überstimm», ein «denn
sieh» hinzukommt, das, zwar von den voraufgehenden imperativi-
schen Formen nicht zu unterscheiden, dennoch von einer unverkenn-
bar verschiedenen Gefühlstönung getragen ist, muß es uns klar werden, daß dieses «denn sieh» nicht nur den Charakter eines Selbstge-
sprächs trägt, sondern zugleich die geliebte Person als ideelle Ge-
sprächspartnerin mit einbezieht, daß mithin das ganze Gedicht nicht
nur für sie gedichtet, sondern zugleich an sie gerichtet ist und die
Überschrift «Liebesbrief» tragen könnte. Unwillkürlich denkt man
dabei an Goethes «Mit einem gemalten Band». Mit der Übersendung
der blühenden Topfpflanze verbunden, wäre es von der Geliebten als
der kostbarere Teil der Sendung zu würdigen. Sie erfährt damit die
beglückende Auszeichnung, die in ein subtiles Wortgewebe übertra-
gene Umarmung des Senders mit- und nachempfinden zu dürfen. Mit
der Wahl des Heliotrop huldigt der Dichter dem spezifischen Frauentyp seiner Freundin. Muß es gesagt sein, der Liebesbrief trägt nicht
den Charakter einer Werbung, er bringt vielmehr die innigste sinnlich-
seelische Vereinigung der beiden Liebespartner zum Ausdruck.

Nun aber wird es endlich Zeit, den gar nicht ohne weiteres ver-
ständlichen Sinn der ersten sechs Verse ins Auge zu fassen. «Es könnte sein, daß dir der Rose Lob / zu laut erscheint für deine Freundin:».
Diese Verse erscheinen in der einleitenden Überlegung von eindeuti-
gem Charakter zu sein. Das als «zu laut» empfundene Lob der Rose
charakterisiert das Wesen der Rose durch volltönende Klangmalerei
mit der nebeneinander gestellten Verdoppelung des volltönenden
Vokals. Grammatisch gesprochen haben wir ein Substantiv mit vor-
angestelltem Genitivattribut. Um seinen Sinn befragt kann das nur
heißen: das vom Dichter der Freundin durch Überreichung der Rose
zugedachte Lob. Der Genitiv ist, grammatisch gesprochen, ein Instrumentalis bzw. Subjectivus, das erstere, wenn die Rose bloß als ein
Mittel der Huldigung aufgefaßt wird, das letztere, wenn sie, poetisch
personifiziert gedacht, der Freundin die Huldigung darbringt. Mir
scheint, die implizierte Personifizierung der Rose als der Königin der
Blumen, der Rilke in zahlreichen Gedichten wie «Die Rosenschale»,

«Das Roseninnere», dem für ihn selbst bestimmten «Grabspruch», überschwenglich gehuldigt hat, wäre voll und ganz auf unsere Eingangsverse anzuwenden. Doch schon in den allererersten Worten regt sich der Zweifel, ob die königliche Blume in Glanz und Üppigkeit auch die passende Abgesandte wäre, dieser seiner Freundin von seiner Liebe zu reden. Das Bedenken macht sich sofort geltend, daß die Freundin einem Frauentyp angehört, dem der Charakter der Rose nicht entspricht. Daß sie schön ist, versteht sich von selbst und wird obendrein durch die Bezeichnung «das schön gestickte Kraut» ausdrücklich hervorgehoben, aber für ihren Schönheitstyp würde sich das von Rilke so oft bevorzugte Wort «verhalten» empfehlen. Der flüchtige Blick des Uneingeweihten könnte sie sogar als unscheinbar übersehen: ein Kraut, dessen schwanke Stauden an das geschwungene Linienmuster einer Stickerei erinnern. Liegt eine bewußte Ironie darin, daß der Dichter sich bei der Wahl dieser Blume ausdrücklich auf den Instrumentalis festlegt («*mit* dringend flüsternden...»)? Es handelt sich aber keineswegs um ein absolutes Werturteil. Wie bei der Aufteilung menschlicher Erfahrungsgebiete in polare Gegensätze überhaupt geht es um Typen, die in einem bestimmten Schema einander gegenseitig bedingen und auf dieser Grundlage ihren jeweiligen Plus- und Minuswert erhalten. Man denke etwa an die Kontrapunktierung von Tag und Nacht im zweiten Akt von Wagners *Tristan und Isolde*. Für die Polarität der Typen in unserem Gedicht bietet die Psychologie die geläufigen und hier bestimmt zutreffenden Bezeichnungen «extravertiert» und «introvertiert».[2]

In den Imperativen «nimm» und «überstimm» ist die Aufforderung zu einem Wettbewerb gegeben. Dazu tritt eine neue Figur ins Spiel, der Bülbül. Da haben wir es. Mit dem Auftreten des Bülbül, der Nachtigall, befinden wir uns, dem Titel gemäß, auf persischem Boden. Jeder in der neueren Literatur Geschulte weiß, daß in der persischen Literatur des Mittelalters der Bülbül als der Liebhaber der Rose auftritt und sie mit seinem Singen umwirbt. Seit Goethes *Westöstlichem Divan* (1819) ist dieser Topos der orientalischen Literatur in die Metaphernsprache der deutschen Dichtung übernommen worden, und

---

2   Es versteht sich von selbst, daß in anderem Zusammenhang auch eine Rose als introvertiert aufgefaßt werden kann.

Goethes jüngere Zeitgenossen, in erster Linie Platen und Rückert, haben sofort das Vorbild des Meisters als Anlaß benutzt, in der persischen Formen- und Bildersprache auf eigene Hand zu dichten, während Heine die neue Manier parodierte.[3] In ihren Dichtungen ist die Anspielung auf das Liebespaar Nachtigall und Rose immer wieder anzutreffen, auch sind die weitläufigen Studien Hammer-Purgstalls, denen Goethe seine Einführung in das Altpersische verdankte, von den Nachfahren reichlich benutzt worden. Zufällig ist mir gerade ein autoritativer Ausspruch über diese Dinge zur Hand. Alexander von Humboldt, der berühmte Weltreisende, der nicht nur das ganze naturwissenschaftliche Wissen seiner Zeit überragend beherrschte, sondern auch in allen humanistischen Studien zu Hause war, schreibt im zweiten Band seines *Kosmos*, Seite 43 (ich zitiere nach der Originalausgabe der 1840er Jahre): «Der Lieblingsgegenstand der persischen Dichtung, die Liebe der Nachtigall und der Rose, kehrt immer ermüdend wieder, und in den konventionellen Künsteleien der Blumensprache erstirbt im Morgenlande das innere Naturgefühl.» Schon 1826 hatte Karl Immermann eine Reihe satirischer Epigramme zu Heines Prosa-«Nordsee» beigesteuert, die die neue Manier in Deutschland spottend glossieren. So schreibt er unter dem Titel «Östliche Poeten»: «Alter Dichter, du gemahnst mich, als wie Hamelns Rattenfänger; / Pfeifst nach Morgen, und es folgen all die lieben, kleinen Sänger.» Ein zweites: «Von den Früchten, die sie aus dem Gartenhain von Schiras stehlen, / Essen sie zuviel, die Armen, und vomieren dann Ghaselen.» Ein drittes: «Sonsten sang, beim Mondenscheine, Nachtigall seu Philomele; / Wenn jetzt Bülbül flötet, scheint es mir denn doch dieselbe Kehle.» Bekanntlich reagierte Platen gereizt auf diese Sticheleien, und Heine rächte sich dafür mit mörderischem Witz in den *Bädern von Lucca*.

Das Auftreten der neuen Figur in unserem Zusammenhang zeigt, daß es sich um zwei Paare, den Dichter und seine Freundin, und den Bülbül mit seiner Geliebten, der Rose, handelt. Fragt man, was Rilke veranlaßt habe, die Nachtigall persisch zu kostümieren, so liegt der

---

3   Neben wiederholter Verkoppelung von Rose und Nachtigall erscheint im *Divan* Bulbul als Nachtigall viermal, einmal im «Buch Timur», zweimal im «Buch des Schenken» und einmal im «Buch der Parabeln».

Grund doch gewiß in der Mißhelligkeit der deutschen Sprache, die dadurch entsteht, daß der Name *die* Nachtigall den Geschlechtsunterschied zwischen dem männlichen Sänger und seiner Geliebten verwischt. Das Verhältnis der beiden Paare erweist sich sofort als die Rivalität der zwei männlichen Werber. Es ist ein Wettkampf, ein Sängerkrieg, in dem die beiden Rivalen sich messen und der Dichter, seinem Instrument, dem «dringend flüsternden Heliotrop», vertrauend, sich unterfängt, seinen Gegner niederzusingen. Diese Wendung kommt uns durchaus überraschend, noch überraschender aber die Tatsache, daß der Partner der Rose unleugbar mit schnöden Worten abgefertigt wird. Was hat es für eine Bewandtnis mit diesem Bülbül, «der an ihren Lieblingsplätzen sie schreiend preist und sie nicht kennt?» Der schmetternde Gesang des Bülbül mit seinem Getue geht dem Dichter offenbar auf die Nerven. Nur ihm? Gewiß doch auch der angesungenen Partnerin, »die er nicht kennt». Damit bleibt die Rose von jedem Makel unberührt, der der nicht feinfühligen Werbung des sie belästigenden Freiers anhaftet. Mit knappster Ökonomie konstatiert der Dichter hier seine persönliche Einstellung, die der literarischen Tradition zweier Jahrtausende direkt zuwider läuft. Seit Ovids *Metamorphosen* war der griechische Mythos der Verwandlung der geschändeten und verstümmelten Philomele in die Nachtigall zum Gemeingut westlicher Tradition geworden. Die Nachtigall gilt oder galt für den gefiederten Sänger kat' exochen. Diese von aller Welt geteilte Bewunderung der Nachtigall verwirft nun der Dichter und lehnt sie mit verletzenden Worten ab.

Wie kommt Rilke dazu, so ausfällig zu werden gegen einen harmlosen Vogel? Die Antwort ist einfach: es ist nicht der Vogel, sondern die lyrische Sängerzunft, an der er Kritik übt. Die Nachtigall zu feiern war einmal neu. Wer es jetzt tut, ist kein Neuerer, ist auch kein routinierter Meister, ist nur ein Nachbeter des Gewesenen. Das einmal Gebrauchte wird zum Vielgebrauchten, wird schließlich zum Abgebrauchten und Verbrauchten. So verhält es sich mit den Formen der Dichtung, ihren Rhythmen und Klangwerten, ihren Bildern, so verhält es sich mit allen Nuancen der dichterischen Sprache. Man denke sich nur den Versuch, ein Gedicht wie «Persisches Heliotrop» in eine Anthologie des neunzehnten Jahrhunderts einzuschmuggeln, um einzusehen, wie unmöglich es wäre. Der Neuerer, der seine Aufgabe, die

Ausdrucksmöglichkeiten des menschlichen Empfindens zu erweitern, wirklich ernst nimmt, vermeidet in allen Nuancen seiner Kunst das Hergebrachte, Abgeschmackte. Im Fall der Nachtigall wünschte man sich einen Super-Computer, der sich die Aufgabe stellte, jedes Vorkommen des Wortes *Nachtigall* in der Lyrik der westlichen Kultur zu registrieren, dieses Vorkommen hübsch systematisch nach Sprachen, Zeiträumen, Dichtern zu ordnen, und eine Fülle statistischer Ergebnisse auf graphischem Wege dem Auge vorzuführen. Da dies für den Augenblick unmöglich ist, seien ein paar Hinweise auf konkrete Einzelfälle gestattet. Ohne Zweifel erreicht die Verehrung der Nachtigall in dem dritten Viertel des 18. Jahrhunderts einen Höhepunkt in dem «Lied an die Nachtigall» des jungen Hainbund-Dichters Ludwig Hölty. Ich setze es hierher.

> Geuß nicht so laut der liebentflammten Lieder
> Tonreichen Schall
> Vom Blütenast des Apfelbaums hernieder,
> O Nachtigall!
>
> Du tönest mir mit deiner süßen Kehle
> Die Liebe wach;
> Denn schon durchbebt die Tiefen meiner Seele
> Dein schmelzend «Ach».
>
> Dann flieht der Schlaf von neuem dieses Lager,
> Ich starre dann
> Mit nassem Blick und totenbleich und hager
> Den Himmel an.
>
> Fleuch, Nachtigall, in grüne Finsternisse,
> Ins Haingesträuch,
> Und spend im Nest der treuen Gattin Küsse,
> Entfleuch, Entfleuch!

Mit seiner feierlich archaisierenden Sprache, den Imperativen «geuß», «fleuch», «entfleuch» und dem extremen Gefühlspathos der Beschwörung besingt das Lied die Nachtigall in einem Zustand gehoben bürgerlichen Ehelebens. Man möchte sich fragen, ob nicht schon zu Höltys Lebzeiten nur ein durchaus naives Publikum dieses Lied ohne einen Anflug von Lächeln habe hören oder lesen können. Für uns liegt in dem Anhören der überaus sympathischen Vertonung von Johannes Brahms eine entzückende Komik in diesen Liebesklagen.

Das war Erlebnisdichtung. Ein halbes Jahrhundert später hat wohl kein deutscher Dichter die Nachtigall öfter besungen als Heinrich Heine. Für ihn aber ist sie zur Formel geworden, die er meisterlich handhabt. Das Moment des Erlebnisses ist dabei ausgeschaltet. Es kostet wenige Minuten festzustellen, daß in den vierundvierzig spezifisch für den Gesang geschriebenen Gedichten, die Heine 1830 unter dem Titel «Neue Lieder» veröffentlichte, die Nachtigall sechzehnmal vorkommt und daß eine Philomele die Zahl auf siebzehn erhöht. Wie aber steht es um Rilkes eigene Verwendung der Nachtigall in Dichtung und Prosa? Man kann ein Rilkekenner sein, ohne sich im Augenblick an einen einzigen Fall zu erinnern. Es wäre ein tristes Bemühen, die Tausende von Seiten der Gesamtausgabe zu überfliegen, um nach der Nachtigall zu fahnden. Glücklicherweise aber gibt es jetzt eine fast druckfertige Computer-Konkordanz zu Rilkes Dichtungen. Die Arbeit ist unter der Anregung und Leitung von Professor Ulrich K. Goldsmith an der University of Colorado in Boulder unternommen und ausgeführt worden. Eine briefliche Anfrage brachte den präzis dokumentierten Bescheid: in den zu Rilkes Lebzeiten vom Dichter selbst veranstalteten Sammlungen seiner Gedichte, einschließlich jenes Teils seiner frühen Produktion, den er auch späterhin noch mit Vorbehalt gelten ließ, kommt der Name der Nachtigall dreimal vor. In dem jetzt vorliegenden umfangreichen Nachlaß ist die Nachtigall fünfmal erwähnt. Darüber hinaus erscheint in einem Jugendversuch in russischen Versen die Nachtigall mit ihrem russischen Namen als *solowjei*. In den Versuchen aus Rilkes Spätzeit, sich das «neue Atemfeld» des französischen Verses zu eigen zu machen,[4] findet sich der *rossignol* dreimal.

Verweilen wir einen Augenblick bei den Stellen im eigentlichen Werk. Das *Stundenbuch*, in seinem letzten Teil, dem *Buch von der Armut und vom Tode*, klingt aus in eine Preishymne auf das Urteil wahrer Armut, den heiligen Franz von Assisi. Da steht er auf dem Markt als «der braune Bruder deiner Nachtigallen». *Das Buch der Bilder* enthält einen Zyklus, «Die Zaren». Der Anfang des zweiten Stücks spielt

---

4   Zeile 7 des Gedichtes «Jetzt wäre es Zeit, daß Götter träten aus / bewohnten Dingen ...», Band II, S. 185. Nach Ernst Zinns Angaben entstanden Mitte Oktober 1925.

an auf einen urzeitlichen russischen Mythos, dem zufolge die Nachtigall als Riesenvogel in den Kronen von neun Eichen gelagert die Nacht mit ihrem Schreien durchdringt, während sich die Männer zum Kampfe mit ihr salben. Ein drittes und letztes Mal begegnet uns die Nachtigall im Werk in «Der Neuen Gedichte anderer Teil». Es ist das letzte Stück des Zyklus «Die Parke». Nachdem der Dichter mit einer Virtuosität ohnegleichen das Rühmen der Parkanlagen des ancien régime vollzogen hat, verschattet sich sein Blick in Trauer über den Verfall einst gepflegter Stätten. Von diesen heißt es: «Jeder Vogelruf ist wie verrufen, / wie vergiftet jede Nachtigall». Auf die Stellen des Nachlasses hier einzugehen, erübrigt sich. Sie bestätigen bloß den erlangten Gesamteindruck.[5] In der Überzahl der Bilder, die Rilkes Füllhorn entströmten, findet die Nachtigall nur einen bescheidenen Platz. Bei ihrem Auftreten freilich fehlt es an jeder Spur von Gereiztheit.

Was Rilke zu seinem Ausfall gegen die Nachtigall in «Persisches Heliotrop» reizte, war vermutlich nicht nur die überbetonte Sonderstellung dieses Vogels in der Lyrik des Abendlandes, sondern wohl auch ihr aufreizender Gesang selbst, der die Stille der Nacht störend durchbricht. Am Ende unseres Gedichts ist es die Stille, die das schreiende Preislied des Bülbül überstimmt hat. In diesem Zusammenhang kann ich es mir nicht versagen, auf einen großen Zeitgenossen Rilkes hinzuweisen, der Rilkes Abneigung gegen den Gesang der Nachtigall teilt und diesem Gefühl in einem Gedicht Ausdruck verleiht, das den hysterischen Wonnerausch des jungen Hölty in einer Parodie von nüchternster Sachlichkeit verulkt. In der hoffentlich falschen Befürchtung, daß Christian Morgensterns Lied, überschrieben «Palmström an eine Nachtigall, die ihn nicht schlafen ließ», durch die Flut politischer Satire verdrängt oder in Vergessenheit geraten sein könnte, setze ich es hierher.

---

5   Die genauen Angaben Professor Goldsmiths, für die ich ihm zu großem Dank verpflichtet bin, lauten wie folgt: Die Stellen aus dem Werk: I, 364, 429, 607; die Stellen aus dem Nachlaß: II, 41, 61, 379; III, 722, 750. – Die «Nachtigall» auf russisch und die französischen Stellen: IV, 959; II, 566, 639, 681.

Möchtest du dich nicht in einen Fisch verwandeln
und gesanglich dementsprechend handeln? –
Da es sonst unmöglich ist,
daß mir unternachts des Schlafes Labe
blüht, die ich nun doch notwendig habe!
Tu es, wenn du edel bist!

Deine Frau im Nest wird dich auch so bewundern,
wenn du gänzlich in der Art der Flundern
auftrittst und im Wipfel wohlig ruhst,
oder, eine fliegende Makrele
sie umflatterst, holde Philomele,
(–die du mir gewiß die Liebe tust!)[6]

Fassen wir jetzt das ganze Verhältnis der beiden in so knappen Worten geschilderten Liebespaare, des Dichters und seiner auf lautes Lob nicht eingestellten Freundin einerseits wie des Bülbül mit seiner zudringlichen Werbung um die Rose andererseits, zusammen, so geschieht es eigentlich ganz von selbst, daß Bülbül und Rose einen durchscheinenden Symbolcharakter annehmen, der auf ein zweites menschliches Liebespaar hinweist oder, da die Aussagen über den Bülbül, «an *ihren* Lieblingsplätzen *sie* schreiend preist und *sie* nicht kennt», grammatisch gleicherweise auf die Rose wie auf die Freundin des Dichters zu beziehen sind, kommt damit etwa die Andeutung einer Rivalität beider Männer um dieselbe Frau mit ins Spiel? Ist es etwa Eifersucht, die den Dichter seinen Rivalen als – sagen wir – aufgeblasenen Heldentenor erblicken läßt? Wohl jedem Leser, der diese Verse auskostet, wird das flüchtige Bild eines Vertreters dieses Typs dabei vorgeschwebt sein, vielleicht sogar eine konkrete Erinnerung wie die an den von dem Komponisten in Hofmannsthals *Ariadne auf Naxos* geäußerten Vorsatz: «dem Bacchus eintrichtern, daß er ein Gott, ein seliger Knabe, kein selbstgefälliger Hanswurst mit Pantherfell!» Gewiß ist all dieses und mehr aus dem dichten Sprachgewebe herauszuholen. Geht man aber noch einen Schritt weiter und spürt der Möglichkeit nach, das Gedicht als den Niederschlag einer Episode aus Rilkes Pariser Leben aufzufassen, so hat man mit dieser Frage das Gebiet des Interpreten überschritten und befindet sich auf dem Boden biographischer Forschung.

---

8   Christian Morgenstern, Alle Galgenlieder, Bruno Cassirer Verlag, 1933, S. 131.

Für die Interpretation des nun doch schon recht ausführlich behandelten Passus bleibt uns zu guter Letzt noch ein grammatisches Nachspiel vorbehalten. Betrachten wir noch einmal die Überlegung, die den Gesang des Gedichts einleitet: «Es könnte sein, daß dir der Rose Lob / zu laut erscheint für deine Freundin.» Wir hatten in diesem Eingang die Rose als Mittel oder als Trägerin des der Freundin zugedachten Lobes aufgefaßt. Nachdem wir jetzt aber das Verhältnis des Bülbül zur Rose frisch im Gedächtnis haben, verschiebt sich der Sinn der Wendung «der Rose Lob». Jetzt hören wir beim Erklingen dieser Worte das Lob, das der Rose gespendet wird von ihrem Anbeter, dem Bülbül. Damit hätte sich der instrumentale bzw. subjektive Genitiv in einen Objektivus verwandelt. Wir hätten damit dieselbe Konstruktion wie etwa in A.W. Schlegels von Schubert vertonten «Lob der Tränen» (die Tränen werden gelobt) oder des Erasmus «Lob der Torheit» (die Torheit wird gelobt). Für die anfangs von uns verstandene Funktion des Genitivs bieten sich Fälle wie Schillers «Des Mädchens Klage» (das Mädchen klagt) oder Uhlands «Des Sängers Fluch» (der Sänger flucht). Damit stehen wir vor einem verblüffenden Ergebnis. Wie schon der junge Lateinschüler gelernt hat, ist die Konstruktion eines Substantivs mit Genitivattribut doppeldeutig. Die beiden Bedeutungen sind logisch nicht miteinander vereinbar und was der Sinn ist, entscheidet der Zusammenhang. Welches ist nun die richtige Bedeutung in den Eingangsversen, das Lob, das die Rose erteilt, oder das Lob, das der Rose zuteil wird? Darauf wäre zu antworten, an der in den zwei Eingangsversen uns zuerst aufgegangenen Bedeutung ist festzuhalten, bezeichnet sie doch durch das «zu laut» den Persönlichkeitstyp der Freundin, und eine andere Bedeutung würde uns überhaupt nicht in den Sinn kommen, wenn wir nicht weiterläsen. Unzweifelhaft richtig ist es aber, daß der logische Sinn der Wendung in den anschließenden Versen eine Umkehrung durchgemacht hat. Dieser, der ersten Lesung logisch konträre, Sinn wäre aber ebenfalls auf die Freundin uneingeschränkt anwendbar. Es ist nicht zu leugnen, die grammatische Konstruktion hat unter der Hand einen Salto mortale vollzogen. Es ist die bekannte Wirkung des Vexierbildes; man stellt den Blick darauf ein, und plötzlich schlägt der Hohlkörper um in ein festes Gebilde. Beim Vexierbild wird keiner sagen können, die eine Sicht ist richtig, die andere falsch. Beide

Male ergänzt das Auge die Linienführung der Fläche durch eine Illusion. Auch in unserer grammatischen Konstruktion erfahren wir das Phänomen solchen Umschlags. Das Phänomen des psychologischen Umschlags ist bekanntlich ein Faktor von überragender Bedeutung für die Sicht, in der Rilke die Erscheinungen der Welt erlebt. Es würde zu weit führen, hier darauf einzugehen. Gleicherweise müssen wir uns mit einem bloßen Hinweis auf verwandte Spiele grammatischer Art begnügen. Ich meine die Konstruktion apo koinu, wo die Mittelachsenstellung eines Satzteils, der, je nachdem er als Ergänzung des Voraufgegangenen oder als Ansatz einer noch zu entwickelnden Aussage aufzufassen ist, eine andere grammatische Funktion erfüllt.[7]

Was jetzt noch kommt, ist das Preislied, das den Vorsatz des Dichters, den schmetternden Gesang des Bülbül mit dem Instrument seiner Wahl zu überstimmen, zur Tat macht. Eine Pause setzt das geflüsterte Lied von der Einleitung ab, indem der sechste Vers des fünftaktigen Schemas um einen Takt verkürzt ist.

*

Wenn man im Englischen sagt «Say it with flowers», versteht man darunter die Mitteilung von Empfindungen oder Gesinnungen nicht auf dem Wege sprachlicher Formulierung, sondern durch die

---

7 Man erinnere sich der merkwürdigen Stelle im Helena-Akt von Goethes *Faust*, wo Phorkyas-Mephisto der heimgekehrten Herrin berichtet, es habe sich eine Schar nordischer Krieger im Gebirge oberhalb Spartas festgesetzt. Von deren Führer sagt er, er habe das Land nicht gebrandschatzt, vielmehr er «... begnüge sich / Mit wen'gen Freigeschenken, nannt' er's, nicht Tribut.» (Verse 9008-09). Es kostet einige Übung im Vortrag, bei dem Wechsel der Konstruktion in *mediis rebus* nicht über den Dativ zu stolpern, der sich im Handumdrehen in einen Akkusativ verwandelt.
Ein ergötzliches Spiel derselben Art findet man in Christian Morgensterns Gedicht «Korfs Verzauberung» (Alle Galgenlieder, S. 134). In der vierten Strophe erscheint das Wort «Töne» als kunstvoll verzögertes Objekt beredter Ausmalung, dabei schießt es einen Purzelbaum und entpuppt sich als Subjekt des angefangenen Verses, folgendermaßen:

«Und die Kugel löst sich los vom Halme,
schwebt gelind empor,
dreht sich um und mischt dem Sphärenpsalme,
mischt dem Sphärenchor
Töne, wie aus ferner Hirtenschalme
dringen sanft hervor.»

Überreichung einer Gabe, die den Symbolwert der Neigung oder Erkenntlichkeit in sich trägt. Wenn man im Deutschen sagt, man muß es ihm bzw. ihr durch die Blume beibringen, so handelt es sich um eine verschlüsselte Mitteilung, nicht notwendigerweise angenehmer Art, die damit rechnet, daß der gewitzigte Empfänger das Angedeutete kapiert. Wie in der lateinischen Wendung «sub rosa» spielt die Blume dabei bloß die Rolle eines völlig verblaßten Klischees. In unserem Gedicht ist die Blume in prangender Körperlichkeit vorhanden; zugleich aber wird das Wesen der Pflanze in der Schilderung ihrer organischen Entfaltung in Worte übertragen, die das pflanzliche Sein als gültige Entsprechung leidenschaftlicher Liebkosungen feiern. Der Dichter sendet die Blume als den Text, und das begleitende Gedicht bildet dazu den Kommentar, nicht anders als seinerzeit des jungen Goethe «Mit einem gemalten Band». Wie schon oben bemerkt, gliedern sich die acht Verse unseres Preisliedes in zwei Vierzeiler, die einander als die Schenkel eines Gleichnisses entsprechen. Dabei ist ihre Anordnung die weniger übliche. Man würde erwarten, daß zuerst die Momente der blühenden Pflanze zur Sprache kämen und daß dann deren Entsprechung in den Liebkosungen des Senders angedeutet würde. Hier verfährt der Dichter in umgekehrter Reihenfolge. Halten wir aber gleich das Wesentlichste fest: der Dichter spricht nicht eigentlich von der Umarmung, nicht von der Abwandlung erlesener Liebkosungen, er spricht von Worten. Das Liebesgeflüster, die Worte sind das eigentliche Tertium comparationis, das die erste der zwei Gruppen vollkommen ausfüllt. Worte sind der Kern dieser Aussage, aber das ganze *ambiente* der Situation wird dabei sinnlich leibhaft ausgekostet: Nacht, das doppeldeutige Himmelbett, die Stille, die Bewegung der hindüftenden Worte. Die Worte, ein dringendes Geflüster, wie wir längst wissen, beileibe kein Gestammel. Wie sehr muß es dem Dichter darum zu tun gewesen sein, noch in der intimsten Liebessituation die Klarheit des Wortes zu präzisieren, häuft er doch in vierfacher Wiederholung den Charakter der Worte als «süß ... in Sätzen beisammenstehn... ganz dicht, ... durch nichts getrennt»! Geistig, seelisch, sinnlich vermitteln sie in untrennbarem Verein das Wesen der imaginierten Umarmung. Für den Kenner von Rilkes *Neuen Gedichten* hat die vierfache Wiederholung der Worte noch darüber hinaus den verschwiegenen Sinn eines Selbstzitats. Da finden wir in der allernächsten Nachbarschaft des «Persischen Heliotrop» ein Gedicht, betitelt «Die Entführung». Es entstammt demselben Zeitraum wie unser Gedicht.[8] Nacht, ein ganz unerfahrenes Mädchen, eine Strickleiter, ein schwarz ausgeschlagener Wagen, Angst sich verdichtend zum Geruch, dann endlich als letzter Vers die flüsternde Stimme des Liebenden: «ichbinbeidir», im Text als *ein* Wortgebilde von vier mal drei Buchstaben gesetzt. Man fühlt, die Worte transzendieren ins Kosmische, indem sie hindüften «aus der Vokale wachem Violett». Dieser Vers hebt sich aus dem tonlosen Geflüster als gesungen heraus durch seine dreifache Alliteration und seine Licht und Farben sprühende Vokalik. Ist es nicht so, daß der im dritten Vers mit vierfacher Volltönigkeit der Vokale genannte Name Heliotrop als prängender Antwortreim auf die verschwisterte Volltönigkeit von «der Rose Lob» dieses Wortwunder angeregt hat? Nehmen die Worte hier nicht den sonst nirgends erwähnten klar-violetten Farbenton der Blütensterne vorweg? Gehen wir zu weit, wenn wir das «wache Violett» als Grenztönung eines ins Unsichtbare hinüberschwingenden unsichtbaren Ultravioletts auffassen?[9]

Endlich nun in den vier Schlußversen kommt die Übertragung der Worte in sinnliche Liebkosungen. Alles wird ausgekostet, was die Momente des organischen Pflanzenlebens in den Bereich der Liebeserfüllung hinüberspielt. Da ist das «gesteppte Laub», weich aber rauh, nachgiebig, als Decke empfunden. Da sind die Blütensterne, einzeln deutlich gesehen, zugleich aber sich zur Traube zusammenschließend mit der Tastempfindung der Seide. Da finden sich die hindüftenden Worte, imprägniert von dem Duft und Geschmack von Vanille und Zimt. Auge und Ohr sind ja in der Erregung des inneren Sinnes immer primär angerufen. Hier kommen alle Sinnesbereiche zugleich zu ihrem Recht, Auge und Ohr, Geruch und Geschmack, und der so vielfach als Tast- und Temperaturreiz differenzierte Hautsinn. Haben wir hier nicht eine exemplarische Erfüllung dessen, was Rilke zehn Jahre später in seinem programmatischen Aufsatz «Ur-Geräusch» als ideale

---

8   Band I, S. 632. Nach Ernst Zinn entstanden vor dem 15. Juli 1909.
9   Ich kann nicht finden, daß unser Gedicht eine Anspielung auf Arthur Rimbauds berühmtes Gedicht «Les Voyelles» enthält, das den Klang bestimmter französischer Vokale mit bestimmten Farben assoziiert.

Forderung aufgestellt hat, daß nämlich das Gedicht alle Bereiche menschlichen Empfindens durchdringen müsse? Hier ist das ganze Sensorium in seiner instrumentalen Vollzähligkeit angerufen.[10]

Als letztes Moment eines mit dem inneren Sinn als vollkommen erlebten Augenblicks bleibt «die Stille». Die Stille wird empfunden nicht als etwas Negatives, Abstraktes, sondern als etwas Substantielles, als ein spürbares Medium wie die Luft, nur unendlich feiner. Bei dem geringsten Versuch, diesen Tatbestand zu exemplifizieren, führt ein Hinweis zum anderen, ohne daß der Zirkel der versuchten Interpretation je dazu käme, sich zu schließen. Hier sei nur daran erinnert, wie immer mehr für den späteren Rilke das Flüssige, Strömende, das Luftige, Wehende, das Sich-Verflüchtigende, als die Grenze des Materiellen Transzendierende, zum Medium einer Kommunikation wird, die den Weltraum durchpulst. In der Überzahl der Ausdrücke, die solches Gefühl kosmischen Bezugs in Rilkes Sprache greifbar zu machen suchen, macht die Stille Anspruch auf eine führende Stellung.[11] Schon in der ersten «Duineser Elegie» stoßen wir auf Wendungen wie «der Wind voller Weltraum», «das Wehende», «es rauscht», «die ewige Strömung ... übertönt sie in beiden». Schon hier haben wir in unendlich subtiler Unterscheidung einerseits «*die* Leere» als menschlich imprägniertes Medium und andererseits «*das Leere*»: «Wirf aus den Armen die Leere ...». Dagegen am Ende der Elegie heißt es, daß bei der Klage um den beinahe göttlichen Jüngling Linos «das Leere in jene Schwingung geriet ...». Hier ist eigentlich alles schon zusammen-

---

10 «Ur-Geräusch», Band VI, S. 1085-1093.
11 Merkwürdigerweise hat Rilke anscheinend die Bewegung eines flüssigen oder luftartigen Mediums als Masse und die Wellenbewegung des in Schwingung versetzten Mediums als irgendwie einander gleichwertig aufgefaßt. Dies tritt deutlich in Erscheinung in dem Gedicht «Absaloms Abfall» (Band I, S. 569/70, nach Ernst Zinn Sommer 1908, vor dem 2. August), wo es von der rauschenden Militärmusik heißt:
> «Sie hoben sie mit Geblitz:
> der Sturm aus den Hörnern schwellte
> seidene, breitgewellte
> Fahnen.»

War die Aussage, daß die überlaute Musik die Fahnen in Bewegung versetzt, als rhetorische Hyperbel gemeint? Oder war eine beobachterische Fehlleistung im Spiel, bleibt doch die Wellenbewegung, auch im flüssigen Medium, für den sinnenden, einfühlenden Beobachter ein unerklärliches Wunder!

gefaßt in der Aufforderung: « ... aber das Wehende höre, die ununter-
brochene Nachricht, die aus Stille sich bildet». Dieser unendlich er-
füllten Stille steht dann gegenüber in der zehnten Elegie, mit einem
Abstand von zehn Jahren, die «falsche, aus Übertönung gemachte /
Stille ... der Leid-Stadt», die in dem «vergoldeten Lärm» zuerst op-
tisch, dann in dem «platzenden Denkmal» akustisch zu verstehen ist.
Doch diese flüchtigen Andeutungen beweisen schon zur Genüge, daß
wir die Grenze unseres Interpretationsfeldes bereits überschritten
haben.

12.
RAINER MARIA RILKE: DAS BETT
A SEMINAR LECTURE

LASS sie meinen, daß sich in privater
Wehmut löst, was einer dort bestritt.
Nirgend sonst als da ist ein Theater;
reiß den hohen Vorhang fort —: da tritt

vor den Chor der Nächte, der begann
ein unendlich breites Lied zu sagen,
jene Stunde auf, bei der sie lagen,
und zerreißt ihr Kleid und klagt sich an,

um der andern, um der Stunde willen,
die sich wehrt und wälzt im Hintergrunde;
denn sie konnte sie mit sich nicht stillen.
Aber da sie zu der fremden Stunde

sich gebeugt: da war auf ihr,
was sie am Geliebten einst gefunden,
nur so drohend und so groß verbunden
und entzogen wie in einem Tier.

Sämtliche Werke I, 626
Insel Verlag, 1955

This sixteen-line poem, one of the nearly two hundred poems from Rilke's middle period, collected under the significant title, *Neue Gedichte*, presents a challenge to the interpreter. It raises questions as to its structure, its symbolism, its grammatical coherence, its time frame, its inner sense of proportion that make it a model for the application of what James Russell Lowell once referred to as "enucleating sagacity." The poem has a masterly preamble extending into line four, defining the locale, the parameter of the theme, and eventually the mood of the poet. It plunges us into *medias res*. As is the case with almost all of the *Neue Gedichte*, its title focusses the reader's attention upon the object, *das Ding*, — a felicitous measure of economy dispensing with the cumbrous need of naming the object. The preamble is of a density that calls upon the experienced reader's imagination to weigh every word as a shorthand term for complex associations. Lines one and two present human life as a whole under two contrasting aspects. There is a private world, the world of the bed, and there is a public world out there — *dort*. This contrast is reinforced in the third line by *da,* right here, suggesting a thrust out forearm and a pointing index finger, aimed of course at the bed. I cannot resist quoting the opening lines of two other poems of our collection which employ the same device to orient the reader.

In *Der Reliquienschrein* it is the contrasting pair of *Draußen* and *Drinnen* — out there and in here — differentiating the human world of emotions and passions associated with the use of jewelry from the function of these precious materials in the artificer's workshop, where they figure only as the malleable objects of his shaping hand.

> DRAUSSEN wartete auf alle Ringe
> und auf jedes Kettenglied
> Schicksal, das nicht ohne sie geschieht.
> Drinnen waren sie nur Dinge, Dinge
> die er schmiedete; . . .

In the same way the poem entitled *Die Fensterrose* teases us with an opening beat, *Da drin,* followed by a colon. It begins by recording the poet's fascination by the lethargic tread of fierce panther cats in the cage of the Paris zoo, this followed by the hypnotic spell cast by the eye of one of the beasts — a spell followed out to the point of vertigo and annihilation and equated only three lines from the end with the religious spell cast by the rose window of the cathedral in an age of faith. The parallels quoted offer too striking a proof of our reading of *da* and *dort* as the prime points of orientation to permit of any doubt.

Now for the substance of the contrast. We begin with the easier member: *was einer dort bestritt* — what one had to contend with out there. Does not this simple formula include everything that transpires in the public world, the daytime world, the active world involving the exercise of strength, energy, stratagem, like a contest in the lists or in the arena, involving blows, contusions, wounds, exhaustion — you name it, as our saying goes? Now, on the other side, the "inscape" of the bed, to quote a felicitous term of Gerard Manley Hopkins, every word conjures up a web of intimate associations which we can spin out at will. The privacy of the bed spells out quiet, security, shelter, warmth, peace. *Wehmut* is a state of mind suggestive of elegiac melancholy. It has ingredients of both pain and pleasure. It is a dreamy, soothing sadness. *Lösen* is the undoing of tension, the untying of knots, a mood of solace during convalescence. Since strife is of the essence of the world out there — the *vita activa,* the *vita contemplativa* offers a galaxy of opposites as its counterpart.

Having caught the points of orientation and glimpsed the values of the dichotomized world, we have not yet done with the prologue. We passed over the first three words, *Lass sie meinen* — let them fancy —, without comment, not because of indifference but because things could not be said all at once. These words begin to express the poet's mood. If the strains of a famous Goethe poem, *"Selige Sehnsucht,"* echo in our ear —

> Sagt es niemand, nur den Weisen,
> Weil die Menge gleich verhöhnet,

we may expect a mood of controlled insouciant tolerance. Goethe's first lines are addressed to an invisible audience of like-minded friends; the next strophe addresses the moth about to immolate itself in the candle; the final strophe addresses the poet's own self as *du,* turning it into an inner monologue. Rilke's poem differs slightly in being cast as an inner monologue from beginning to end, the imperative singular occurring also in line four. Goethe's reference to *die Menge* is disparaging, of course. The multitude smacks of Horace's *profanum vulgus.* The plural *sie* of Rilke's opening similarly dismisses the opinions of the populace as illusory. However, without some cunning in the art of lip-reading, we are unprepared for the outburst of line three — Nirgend sonst als da ist ein Theater — nowhere but here is anything deserving the name of theater — an overstatement maximized by exclusivity. It is a vehement repudiation of the multitude. Obviously the poet is out of control. We sense the bitter bile rising in his gorge, leading to an act of impulsive fury in line four: *reiß den hohen Vorhang fort* — yank away the high curtain. Strong language, this. He is beside himself with rage. For Rilke, the Rilke of *Neue Gedichte,* this is startling indeed. We are certainly accustomed to extremes of passionate language in some of these poems, but they are attributes of characters portrayed as in *"Die Versuchung,"* a temptation of Saint Anthony worthy of the brush of a Breughel.

We think of the poet rather in terms of Wordsworth's formula, "Emotion recollected in tranquillity." To complete this discussion of the poet's mood we should note that there is a point-counter-point relation between the *sie* of line one and the *einer* of line two. *Einer* replaces the general *man* to indicate a select individual, an elitist. It would be difficult if not impossible to find an appropriate synonym for *one* in English. Rilke's fury of self-abandonment in this exquisitely dense prologue is a case *sui generis*.

Having disposed of the preamble, Rilke is now in such a hurry to put on his own night-time show and make it run its course from the beginning through the middle, to the finish line, all in one lungful of breath that, having barked the command, he completes the line with *da tritt* — when there emerges — to take her stance in the proscenium in front of the chorus of nights which has already begun its interminably tedious litany — the hour that supervised their coupling and ... and ... Strain our attention as we may, we do not find a genuine full stop before the end despite the period before *Aber*.

Theater, he calls the spectacle, produced and stage-managed by the articulation of his inner vision. Drama? Tragedy? Impossible as a stage sequence. We do not see a Johannes Rosmer and Rebecca West plunge into the mill race clasped in each other's arms in an opening scene, to be followed by a long post mortem explaining how this came about. This is a show, a spectacle of violence, guilt, and horror conjured up by the narrator's voice with not one syllable of spoken dialogue. We see a pantomime, a night-time vision acted out at breakneck speed, hedged nevertheless most paradoxically by ambiguities and retardations — surely the stuff of nightmare, defying the racing of the second hand as a standard of experienced time.

Without knowing where to begin in attempting to grasp the sense of this nightmare, let us look at the disposition of the stage. The middle ground is filled with clusters of phantom figures — the nights and their component elements, the hours — all of them pictured as females in accordance with their grammatical gender in the classical languages and in German. I see them stretched all across the stage. The background is vacant for the time being, while at the edge of the proscenium the poet is stationed as producer, narrator, and sole audience. The nights present no problem of interpretation. They are engaged in chanting their interminably tedious song — *ein unendlich breites Lied zu sagen* —. What is it but the torment of insomnia experienced night after night! The chorus has already begun its litany when the action proper begins. Does not the text say *"begann?"* Indeed, we have a preterite. However, the poet allows himself a very liberal license in this regard. Unless we readjust the tenses to an understandable time scheme we shall find ourselves in a hopeless muddle. The moment the curtain is yanked aside, a phantom step emerges — held in abeyance to be sure by the two lines required for the presentation of the chorus. This studied retardation provides suspense. Now we behold a Phantom Hour emerging from the chorus and taking her stance in the proscenium to face the poet. With the help of hindsight, we shall be able to put the manner of her entry more precisely, as barging through the diaphanous chorus from the rear. She is cryptically introduced as that hour which supervised their coupling — *bei der sie lagen*. The language introducing the lovers is spare to the point of exasperation — of emaciation I am tempted to say. The words have an abstractness suggestive of a linguistic shorthand. *Sie*, a pair of lovers; *lagen*, embracing, making love. *Bei der*, — it defies language to express the function of the Phantom Hour regarding the human pair. Let us content ourselves with translating: the hour that had witnessed their coupling. To put even this bit of translating into perspective we had again to rectify Rilke's tense, to avoid grammatical pedantry, to read: *bei der sie gelegen hatten*. If we had perhaps entertained the idea that the Phantom Hour's present tense — *da tritt* — is simultaneous with their *lagen*, this will not make sense. The two unknown humans are not lying at her feet as a package. Their coupling is the Phantom Hour's reminiscence. This stage is no abode for human couples. It is reserved for pure phantoms only. What does it mean to have the Phantom Hour dignified by a noun label to be twice repeated in the few lines remaining, whereas the human couple are disposed of with a flimsy pronoun? To be sure there is one late allusion to the male partner: *"am Geliebten,"* but that is a recollection of a poetic long ago — *einst*. To put it boldly: is Rilke here experimenting with a para-Platonic transvaluation of values, lending substantial weight to the phantoms while dismissing

the world of men as mere fortuitous instances of the type? At long
last we are ready to focus on the Phantom Hour's pantomime — a
one-scene pantomime acted in a single line, and its presentation as
part of the sentence that told of her entry gives it that breathless
quality that we have remarked upon. She rends her dress, an expression of violence and horror, and she utters self-accusations. The rending of one's garments has come down to us in Christian tradition as a
gesture of maximum intensity. When Caiaphas adjures Jesus in the
name of the living God to say whether he is the Christ and Jesus
answers in a quasi-affirmative, the High Priest rends his garments in
the face of the ultimate blasphemy (Matthew 26). Students of German literature may remember another instance of this gesture in
Heinrich von Kleist's *Das Käthchen von Heilbronn*. When Graf Wet-
ter vom Strahl, charged by the secret underground court, the Fehme,
with having perverted the mind of the girl by infernal magic, protests
his total innocence despite what appears like convincing evidence to
the contrary, the judges run out of the caves rending and scattering
their robes in horror. The next three lines continue the sentence
detailing the Phantom Hour's dereliction. It shows her involvement
with another Phantom Hour and motivates her sense of guilt in her
failure to assuage the agitation of the other. Whether her sympathy
was too slack or whether the other was a hopeless case never becomes
clear. Tenderness there certainly was as indicated by Rilke's use of
the word *stillen*, suggesting a mother's offer of her breast to quell
the tantrum of an infant. Let us recall two lines in the first of the
Duino Elegies:

> Jene, du neidest sie fast, Verlassenen, die du
> so viel liebender fandst als die Gestillten.

> Those you all but envy, the abandoned ones, whom you
> found so much more loving than those who had their fill [of love].

The way I read the three lines discussed, they contain altogether too
much circumstantial matter. Only the middle line presents a very
vivid image of the second Phantom Hour flailing and writhing in the
background. The chorus of the hours must have become diaphanous
for us to see her; for we do see her even though her image is only a
flashback. The attempts to soothe the sister hour — the alien hour

she is called later — antedate the one-line pantomime, and all that follows continues the progression of the same flashback. In this same context we again bring the tenses into focus with the time scheme. *"Wehrt"* and *"wälzt"* may be read as a sort of progressive present continuing after our phantom hour has made her way to the proscenium; the *"konnte"*, on the other hand, stands for a pluperfect: she *had* not succeeded in pacifying her paroxysm. The whole passage leaves one cold, crowding out empathy by curiosity, contributing nothing to the solution of the mystery.

The transition to the flashback is accomplished in three lines. I said above that the lines continue the sentence that began *"da tritt."* But you tell me that these lines end with a period. True, a grammatical period, a major device reducing the speed, but a full stop? No. The voice does not drop as it should in approaching a full stop. It continues suspended, suspended with a considerable pause before the fatal *aber* that introduces what the Greeks called the peripeteia, the turning point, the *Abgesang*, the resolution in musical terms. We are apprised of a radical shift of course. This device, ever the same for its inexhaustible variants in *Neue Gedichte*, was destined to receive its theoretical formulation in one of the *Sonette an Orpheus*, a decade and a half later (Part II, number 12). There we read:

> jener entwerfende Geist, welcher das Irdische meistert,
> liebt in dem Schwung der Figur nichts wie den wendenden Punkt.

> That designing spirit who is in charge of earthly matters
> loves nothing so much in the sweep of the line as the turning point.

("Nothing so much as" — never: "nothing but." For "nothing but" Rilke always writes "nichts als.") This defines, of course, the credo of that spirit's disciples — the poet, the graphic artist, the painter, the sculptor. Frequently marked by an initial *aber, a doch, a denn*, an *auf einmal*, a *nur*, it is often reinforced by a *plötzlich* that may follow on the heels of the signalling word or require as much as ten lines of preparation before coming out into the open. Such is the case in *Der Reliquienschrein*, as also in *Archaïscher Torso Apollos* where there is a one hundred eighty degree shift of course achieved, a shift from subject to object, a human being quailing under the scrutiny of a human artifact that has suddenly come to reveal an

inner life of its own — an ethical imperative of absolute dominion.
Often it ends with a shock, a threat, a terror, a vivid surprise, or even
a beatific strain of heavenly music as in *Sankt Georg*. Now, resisting
the temptation to adduce further examples, let us explore the situation in hand. Let us remind ourselves that what is still to come is all
part of the flashback. The image of the flailing supine form that the
poet's eye has compelled us to see in the rear of the diaphanous
chorus of the nights, has given way to a group image as our Phantom
Hour has stooped down to this alien hour. After the movement that
accomplished this shift the text confronts us with a colon, a most
unusual mark of punctuation, the second one as a matter of fact in
our short poem.

What can such a mark, separating a temporal clause from its main
sentence, be but a signal to stop and listen — a retardation of prime
importance. Now four staccato monosyllables confront us: *da war
auf ihr* — there was on her — all cold, sober, factual reporting without a touch of human warmth, reminding us of the more than lenten
leanness of "*bei der sie lagen*" and most certainly involving a second
retardation.[1] We are already in a thicket of ambiguous female personal pronouns; but the "ihr" — her — of this statement surely refers
to the supine Phantom Hour. Next we take note of the fact that this
line falls short by one full measure of the rhythmical scheme underlying this poem. Such a reduction spells another retardation, a third.
The most enigmatic peculiarity of this line must have escaped our
scrutiny completely unless we caught a glimpse of the line that follows. The "*auf ihr*" is unquestionably correlated with the "*am Geliebten*" of the next line. What can this mean but a fourth retardation, another problem to puzzle out. As we ponder the line "*was sie
am Geliebten einst gefunden*," it stands in sharpest contrast of quality
to the line preceding. Every one of its syllables pulsates with human

---

1   The sparseness of some of the language, a sort of skeletal emaciation that we
    noted in the phrase, *die beiden* and again in *da war auf ihr*, seems also dis-
    cernible in the four-fold use of *da* with a variety of functions: (a) line three
    — *nirgend sonst als da* — a very strong demonstrative adverb; (b) line four
    — *da tritt*, an adverbial expletive, a filler; (c) line twelve — *aber da sie* —
    a temporal conjunction, a synonym of *als*; (d) line thirteen — *da war auf
    ihr* — another expletive with local and temporal overtones.

warmth in contrast to the glacial line above. She, the stooping figure, had found something on the lover in the long-ago. The lover may be the male partner of the couple referred to above. *"Einst"* is a word of lyrical overtones, the long ago of romantic sentiment. *"Gefunden"* is something discovered, found – a treasure? The *"am"* of *"am Ge-liebten"* must refer to an organic part of the lover, a treasurable something, in contrast to the *"auf ihr"* of the preceding line, which would also be rendered by the unsuspecting reader as "on her" be-cause there is no preposition in English to mark the difference. This something *"auf ihr"* can not be anything organic, it must be some adventitious adjunct atop her. We could phrase it more smoothly by saying "there bulged on her" or "there loomed on her." By now the reader will understand that I translate *"was sie am Geliebten einst gefunden"* by "what she had been wont to treasure in the lover," a startling circumlocution for his genitals. My whole reading of the scene as a fiendish nightmare stands and falls with this interpretation of the two enigmatic lines. *The* lover may plausibly refer to the male partner of the couple mentioned above. That now the female alien hour is described as wearing a counterpart of his sex affixed to her should not trouble us. We are here dealing with phantoms.

We are now poised for the annihilating blow to come. "Nur" begins the line next to the last. As the correlate of the *aber* and the *einst, nur* can only mean "but now" or "only now". It introduces a reservation of the gravest sort. By its sound *nur* can lend itself to very deliberate articulation, suggesting the long drawn-out growl of a vicious dog about to spring.[2] The mysterious appendage is character-ized as threatening – *so drohend.* – And whom is this looming some-thing threatening? It can only be the stooping Phantom Hour looking at the body of the supine figure. To be sure, we are not told that she is looking. In fact the line with the staccato monosyllables studiously

---

2   I had found myself on the wrong track for a long time regarding the *nur* of line fifteen. This I had regarded as redundant, being synonymous with *nun* in its context. Thanks to a very welcome and exhaustively specific letter of Dr. Zinn to my friend Professor Herman Meyer of Amsterdam, graciously passed on to me, I came to realize that owing to the onomatopoeic quality of a drawn-out *nur* this word contributes a final retardation to the cluster of obstacles encountered in the previous lines.

avoided taking any note of her. Instead of *"da war auf ihr"* it would
have been so much easier to say *"fand sie auf ihr."* We must think of
her gaze as wandering at first. Whom can the looming adjunct be
threatening but her? But how can it threaten? It must have developed a cyclops eye, catching her roving gaze and hypnotically holding it as in a vise. Do not all human artifacts develop a power in
Rilke's poems of participating in human consciousness, will, and
emotion? Let us recall the artificer of the *Reliquary* overcome by the
power of his own handiwork, on his knees, fascinated by the great
central ornament, the quiet ruby which suddenly looks him through
and through with the authority of all the ages. Or, remember the
crescendo of the dazzling light gradually emanating from all the
fracture-surfaces of the *Archaic Torso of Apollo*, turning its starlight
on the beholder, making him quail on finding himself weighed and
found wanting. In its threatening aspect the sinister surrogate of the
lover's genitals is visualized as *groß verbunden* — hugely bandaged —
and *entzogen wie in einem Tier* — impossible to relate to as in a
beast.

We are left to brood over a group image of frozen horror. Some-
how, it does not satisfy. The emotional outburst that starts the headlong run to the finish is paradoxically at variance with all the hurdles
blocking the course of the runner. This puts an exorbitant strain on
the effort to grasp the microcosm of these lines as a totality.

Doubts arise on another score. The frozen group image, being the
end of a flashback, cannot maintain itself indefinitely. Must not
there be a moment when our Phantom Hour leaps up, elbows her
way through the chorus to face the poet and put on her one-line
pantomime? But as the pantomime glides into a series of non-visual
flashback explanations projecting a new scene that almost instantly
crystallizes into a group image frozen in shock, we have retraced the
mental cinema all the way through a second time. And why not a
third time? There is a built-in impulse for the spindle of the frame to
move at the slightest touch, Carrousel, Carrousel, it hums. A whole
round lasts but a minute. Do we have a show, a visual spectacle, to
accompany the interminably tedious litany of the chorus all night
long? Could this have been Rilke's intention? I do not know.

My mind drifts from this poem to another a seventeen-line member of the series, which is also concerned with a bed and a pair of lovers clasped in embrace. Written possibly as a realistic counterpart to the spooks of *Das Bett*, its title, *Östliches Taglied* (see text below), embodying a cautionary signal reminiscent of the old adage, *ex oriente lux*, it is a serious parody of the Provençal and French *aubade*, also a favorite of the German minnesingers. Here there is no cursing of the dawn and of the malevolent guardians of the conventions, no planning of the next tryst, no tearful last embrace. Our lovers are not romantics but sophisticated children of the modern age. While the woman is still asleep, the lover is engaged in reveries that try to sort out the chaos of his mind after a night of abandenment to sexual passion. He is totally disoriented in an ambience of strange contours. They are like castaways exposed on a bit of coastline, and the sounds of nighttime mating and devouring echo in his ears. Of a frail, neurasthenic constitution, he is a victim of total alienation. Spent in body as in spirit, he conjures up an idyll of the Golden Age of innocence and pristine purity: would that our embrace could be as self-contained as the petals of blossom buds enfolding the mysteries of pollination. But the romantic wish-dream straight-way evokes its counterpart in a glimmer of light that has the flash of an epiphany: for as we huddle together more closely so as not to see the eerie wisps advancing upon us round about, what if the lethal virus may already be rampant from within you — from within me, for our souls thrive on treachery? Treason breeds within the citadel of the self!

ÖSTLICHES TAGLIED

IST dieses Bette nicht wie eine Küste,
ein Küstenstreifen nur, darauf wir liegen?
Nichts ist gewiß als deine hohen Brüste,
die mein Gefühl in Schwindeln überstiegen.

Denn diese Nacht, in der so vieles schrie,
in der sich Tiere rufen und zerreißen,
ist sie uns nicht entsetzlich fremd? Und wie:
was draußen langsam anhebt, Tag geheißen,
ist das uns denn verständlicher als sie?

Man müßte so sich ineinanderlegen
wie Blütenblätter um die Staubgefäße:
so sehr ist überall das Ungemäße
und häuft sich an und stürzt sich uns entgegen.

Doch während wir uns aneinander drücken,
um nicht zu sehen, wie es ringsum naht,
kann es aus dir, kann es aus mir sich zücken:
denn unsre Seelen leben von Verrat.

Sämtliche Werke I, 486

13.
FRANZ KAFKA'S "THE BURROW" ("DER BAU"):
AN ANALYTICAL ESSAY

Every reader of "The Burrow" who is even moderately familiar with Kafka's life and work cannot fail to be struck by the realization that there is an intimate relation, often amounting to identity, between the author and the persona of his story.[1] A symbolical interpretation is fully warranted and has often been undertaken, with varying success. It is not my purpose, however, to take such an approach in this essay. I have been intent on analyzing the story in terms of its own data. The reader will be well rewarded by supplementing this account with a study of many others, including those listed in brief notes.

"I have made the burrow habitable, and I think it has shaped up well."[2] This, the first sentence of what is probably Kafka's last story, prompts us to examine the blueprint of the structure in question.

Having taken precautions against flooding from the outset, the speaker has built in a dry, sandy spot, deep underground, a central stronghold, spacious, smooth, and elegantly vaulted, large enough to accommodate provisions to last him for half a year without crowding. From this stronghold ten tunnels radiate, rising, dipping, curving to conform to functional needs and to features of the terrain. At intervals of one hundred meters, each of the tunnels expands to a platform suitable for rest or storage. There are more than fifty of these platforms, each of them individually designed and distinguishable by feel and sight. The tunnels are again crisscrossed by a network of connecting galleries or corridors. One of these has the function of communicating with the world above ground. Before leading to a vent, thinly covered by a layer of moss, it expands into a maze of intricate design, a feature intended to baffle and impede any

---

1   This essay is based on Franz Kafka's "Der Bau" as contained in *Gesammelte Schriften*, ed. Max Brod (New York: Schocken Books, 1946), V, 172-214. The English renditions are mine.

2   Ich habe den Bau eingerichtet und er scheint wohlgelungen (p. 172).

potential prowler who might have stumbled upon the well-concealed vent. This underground habitat, serving the material needs of security, shelter, and sustenance, a self-contained world as it were, is beautifully air-conditioned, thanks to the channels dug by the wood mice and other small fry. The master-builder prides himself on having incorporated these small animals into his plans, not only for regulating the ventilation but also letting them serve as an unfailing if modest food supply. While there is no reason to doubt the truth of the account as respects all other features of the burrow, we detect a note of swagger in his reference to the ventilation: he is claiming credit for a feature that resulted as an automatic by-product of any burrower's layout.

The underground structure, planned on so vast a scale and requiring years of unremitting effort to execute — can it have been undertaken merely to provide for the material needs of security, shelter, and sustenance? Of course not. Every page of the account tells us rather that it was designed to answer its creator's craving for self-glorification.

For our story to cohere, we have to venture into the realm of unreality. What kind of creature is the builder of this burrow? Generically speaking, he is a hybrid of man and animal, a large, furry, tailless carnivore with a powerful dome of a forehead that constitutes his chief tool. His wants and needs are strictly those of an animal. However, his powers of abstract reasoning and introspection and the sensitive differentiation of his emotional life are on a high human level. He is an artist-engineer, skilled in discussing the problems of his craft, with a passion for meticulous and often irritatingly pedantic exactness. This master-builder has no supernatural endowment, no innate knowledge. He is totally devoid of curiosity or imagination concerning anything except himself and his burrow. In his capacity of both man and animal, the master-builder is a loner. Without clan, family, or overt sex life, he is asocial and antisocial. Engrossed entirely in his own problems, he has no rapport with any possible audience. Society as complement and self-fulfillment is replaced by the burrow, the product of his brain and muscle. The burrow comes to assume the status of the self objectified, bearing the same relation to its designer as body and soul in ordinary parlance. The master-builder and his burrow are one.

What about the living social world outside the burrow? Has it ceased to exist for him? Not at all. Its presence on the other side constantly makes itself felt. It is perhaps never wholly absent from his consciousness, but it exists only as a foil, generating a state of tension within him. It turns out that this state of tension is necessary to his well-being as the fulfillment of his desire for isolation and security.

Not being a synthetic creature, although a loner, our master-builder must have sprung from a social background. We probe the texture of his self-revelation for every hint of its specific character and we scan the record with eagerness for some clue to the mystery of his withdrawal from society. Although we shall never get beyond very general surmises, let us see what we can learn of his social background, both human and animal.

To begin with the human side, at an early point of the account he speaks of legends regarding mysterious, inconceivably powerful creatures that dwell in the interior of the earth; their powers render null any attempt to arrive at absolute security. He must be the beneficiary of a tradition in this respect. The same applies to a later reference to a Providence as a feature of religious instruction. As for his technical education, he makes his calculations in terms of the metric system. If I speak of his design as a blueprint, this would seem to be justified in its literal meaning. And there is a hint of his familiarity with delicate machinery when he remarks on the enormous acuity of his hearing. At a late point of his account, a remark slips out of his mouth to the effect that he now works like a laborer, going through the motions of the act under the eye of a foreman, thus betraying some familiarity with human labor conditions. Earlier, upon the return to his burrow after a prolonged sojourn and exile aboveground, he greets his tunnels and chats with them "as with friends," then checks himself because the ring of the word "friend" awakens emotions he is determined to suppress. Twice we come across a turn of speech that seems to reflect a background of literary education. "There in the dark moss is the spot where I could be destroyed."[3]

---

3   ... dort an jener Stelle im dunklen Moos bin ich sterblich ... (p. 172). Cf.

To a German ear this sounds like a quotation from Schiller's *Don Carlos*. The second passage of this sort, expressing his confidence that he is not destined or doomed to spend the remainder of his life in the open, away from his burrow, reads, "Someone will call me to him and I shall not be able to resist his invitation."[4] The somewhat ironic humor of this context tends to disguise the fact that this sounds like a reminiscence of the sinister role of the commendatore in Mozart's *Don Giovanni*. But I would not labor the meaning of these passages because their quotational quality seems to attach to Kafka rather than to his hero. This exhausts the list of reminiscences that tend to shed light on the hero's background conceived in human terms.

On the animal level, basking in the first flush of pride at the achievement of his master burrow, his memory ranges back with mock sympathy to contemplate the packs of forest roamers dependent on improvised shelter and subject to the vicissitudes of chance. At some time or other he must have shared in this life of vagabondage. Much later, while outside the burrow, tormented by inhibitions and hoping against hope to overcome the frustration that bars him from returning home, his rage at the thought of one of his own kind, a connoisseur of building but a marauder, snooping about his burrow and threatening to dispossess him, arouses him to an orgiastic pitch of lust and fury. I cannot help wondering whether this murderous fantasy is not the reactivation of some hostile encounter with one of his fellows, an outrage perpetrated against himself. Was it this, perhaps, coupled with a humiliation too painful to avow to himself, that made him decide to go it alone for the rest of his life?

Before turning to an analysis of the content, we must come to grips with the formal pattern of the discourse. We first meet the speaker at the prime of his life, after he has just completed the object of his ambition. We hear his voice, coming, as we subsequently learn, from the interior of the burrow. He engages in a progressive recital, not meant as a communication because all social contacts have

---

Schiller's *Don Carlos*: Hier ist die Stelle, wo ich sterblich bin (I.VI. 865).

4   ... daß mich ... jemand zu sich rufen wird, dessen Einladung ich nicht werde widerstehen können (p. 183).

ceased to exist for him.[5] Nevertheless, in its character of human speech, it comes through to us as a communication. From the moment of his first utterance, the recital has the character of an emerging present, continuous with the flow of his life. There is no narrative element in the strict sense of the word. Only as occasional reminiscences, dating back beyond the achievement of his building project, the preterite tense, hallmark of narration, is used.[6] The flow of his recital, a matter of ninety minutes, is synchronous with the flow of his life, condensing a span of experience that extends over many years. His speech flows forward as his life flows forward, encountering unforeseen troubles of a psychological nature. It flows on as he finds himself beset by restlessness and anxiety, inhibitions, phobias, and all the symptoms that add up to a state of psychoneurosis. It flows on, recording its progression from virility to advanced age; it flows on, the speaker's strength of mind giving way to senile dementia and exhaustion. Some patterns of life tend to repeat themselves and words like "occasionally," "sometimes," "now and then," (*"öfters," "manchmal," "zu Zeiten"*) have to be employed, but these are always followed by an iterative or durative present. The ninety-minute recital and the life span of many years run on two parallel but qualitatively different rails, beginning and ending, mirabile dictu, at the same point of time. This is one way of equating enacted time with imagined time. The monologue is strictly grammatical, a discourse composed of precisely organized, often infinitely complicated sentences, never interrupted by those abrupt and fragmentary musings that carry the flavor of what we term interior monologue. This is altogether different from stream of consciousness thinking, which abounds in broken off phrases, unfinished sentences, incoherent terms, and helter-skelter associations. In this recital there is not a sentence that fails to reach the objective of its grammatical aim.[7]

---

5   There is one exception. On the first page he defends himself against the imputation of cowardice. This presupposes his having a mental *Gegenüber* in mind. But this aspect is dropped, never to be taken up again.

6   An exception to this occurs on p. 184, when he sums up the experiences of the first week spent above ground after leaving the burrow.

7   Most critics are completely silent about the form of the recital. These include Wilhelm Emrich, "Der Bau und das Selbst des Menschen," in *Franz*

This sense of our participating in an unbroken time continuum is all
the more remarkable because the greater part of its forty-two pages
is devoted not to events and actions, but rather to speculations,
problems, working hypotheses put forward, modified, rejected, reversed, and taken up afresh. There is a zigzag motion of ratiocination
based on premises that look sound enough but shift like quicksand.
For the attentive listener, all this verbalizing is full of ominous overtones to whose wavelength the speaker's ear is not attuned. And the
deeper, often tragic meaning of its formulation never seems to rise to
the threshold of his consciousness.

Let us try to envisage this piece of Kafka's prose in terms of its
structural articulation. Several avenues to this end suggest themselves.
One of the easiest lines to follow is to see the story in terms of the
changes of locale. This approach would yield five major divisions:
(1) The speaker is inside his burrow at the outset and he continues to
speak from inside it for about one quarter of the whole. (2) The
speaker has emerged into the open for a relatively brief change of air
as he thinks, but this excursion takes on the character of a period of
exile lasting for weeks, at the very least. All this time he is subject to
extreme mental agitation. He wants to go home but insurmountable
inhibitions bar his return. This, for me the most striking and imagina-
tively executed part of Kafka's story, also accounts for about one
quarter of the whole. (3) Back in the burrow once more, the stillness
of which he has praised as its most beautiful feature, he finds himself
disturbed by faint, intermittent sounds suggestive of hissing or

---

Kafka (Bonn: Athenäum, 1958), pp. 172-86; Walter F. Sokel, "Das Schweigen des Baus," in Franz Kafka: Tragik und Ironie (München: A. Langen-G.
Müller, 1964), pp. 371-87; Heinrich Henel, "Kafka's 'Der Bau,' or How to
escape from a Maze," in The Discontinuous Tradition: Studies in German
Literature in Honour of Ernest Ludwig Stahl (Oxford: Oxford Univ. Press,
1970), pp. 224-46; Heinz Politzer, Franz Kafka: Parable and Paradox
(Ithaca, N.Y.: Cornell Univ. Press, 1962), in his chapter "The Castle Within"
(pp. 318-33) has a lapse of memory in speaking of the story as told by an
old master-builder. To my knowledge, the only study including a precise
description of Kafka's narrative technique in "The Burrow," but limited to
technical matters exclusively, is to be found in Hartmut Binder's brief
chapter, "Der Bau," in Motiv und Gestaltung bei Franz Kafka (Bonn: H.
Bouvier, 1966), pp. 340-46.

whistling. These torment him in ever increasing measure. This part of the story, constituting the longest section, deals with his attempts to define the sound, to locate its point of origin, to speculate upon its possible causes and on possible means of eliminating them, in the course of which he becomes worn down and enfeebled. This process of progressive attrition is measured in terms of years. (4) When mental torture and enfeeblement have reached a certain point, he yields to an automatic urge to escape. Having threaded his way through the maze, he settles down at the bottom of the vent that leads into the open. Here, at last, the tormenting sounds of the interior no longer haunt him. He finds a degree of relief, and in continuing to brood over his problem, his memory comes upon a remarkable incident that occupied his mind while he was at work on the maze. Having correlated that incident with the torturing images that presently haunt him, he feels an irresistible urge to return to the locale of his woes, wishing at the same time that his enfeeblement were too great to permit it. This fourth part is rather short. (5) He resumes his restless wanderings through his passageways and finally settles down in the stronghold to speculate on the principles of an efficacious defense and on the chances of negotiating with a potential intruder. Beset by futile speculations, he concludes, the only practical course to pursue is to consume as great a portion of his provisions as his strength still permits. This, the last part, is also short. Summing these up by captions, we have (1) inside the burrow, (2) in exile above the ground, (3) back in the burrow, (4) down in the vent between two worlds, (5) once more in the burrow.

Another approach to the structure would see the story in two parts, the first being not much more than a takeoff point, showing the speaker in his prime, and at the height of his achievement, presenting some fairly precise personality traits and letting us glimpse the disposition of the adolescent at the time the great project got under way. Beyond that point no early memories are overtly acknowledged. Part two would then comprise all the rest of the story. It would be a story of a progressive mental illness, of creeping nervous tension and anxiety, of inner conflict and tribulation, leading by way of various crises to eventual senility and collapse. This would be the clinical view. It might be reduced, perhaps too simply, to the

formula: having spent his adolescence and the early years of his manhood in the execution of a grandiose original idea, the designer,
artist, and engineer in one still has a great surplus of mental and animal energy, but he does not know what to do with it. His simple
wants — security, shelter, sustenance — are more than adequately
provided for and the great structure is a tangible symbol of his sense
of self-glorification. Now his excess mental and physical energy, finding no rewarding outlet, in the total absence of any social life, turns
sour. The stages in the decline of his mental health, corresponding to
stages of the aging process, might warrant the following labels: (1)
creeping neurosis, (2) aboulia (paralysis of the will) in exile, (3) a
psychosis, a haunting hallucination, (4) religion, (5) senile dementia
and total enfeeblement of animal energy. I trust that these labels will
become meaningful in the course of our analysis. I see the most important qualitative escalation of his mental illness in the emergence
of the hallucination — the hissing and whistling noise.

Another approach would stress a structural dichotomy in terms
of the great *Umschlag*, the total turnabout of the inner center of
gravity which takes place during his exile. From being the beneficiary
of the burrow's protection, he reverses the roles to fancy himself its
guardian. This attitude, developed in great detail, carries over into
the later phase of psychotic hallucination, with great imaginative
intensity. All the foregoing approaches are proper and should be
turned to as mutually complementary in analyzing the story.

The opening paragraph furnishes an abundance of leads from
which to form a precise image of the personality traits and temperament of the hero-antihero. With the hindsight afforded by knowing
the whole course of the story, a skilled psychiatrist should, in fact,
be able to predict the terminal stage on the basis of the introductory
statements. He would soon detect the almost imperceptible curve of
a large, systematically inward-turning mental spiral that must eventually end up in a point. In introducing his burrow, the speaker intones a note of serene satisfaction. His voice is calm and precise, his
account of the problems he encountered is meticulously lucid; he
speaks with the air of one in command who deserves unqualified
credence. Ends and means have been brought into focus, everything
has been achieved in accordance with precise calculations, it is a

triumph of the reasoning mind over a challenging environment. With the knowledge of innumerable potential enemies to endanger his life, he has steered a course of firm caution, the rational counterpart of fear. Caution tells him that absolute security can never be achieved in this world. By way of legends he has learned that there are sinister, irrational forces within the earth too powerful for any individual to cope with, they can annihilate without a trace of warning. (We might think of earthquakes, by way of example.) Caution requires such knowledge, but it must never be allowed to intrude into rational calculations.

The first material detail to catch our eye is a hole that leads nowhere. After countless false starts in the vicinity, all of them carefully obliterated, this hole has been left at a distance of a thousand paces from the point where he began to establish his burrow. Why did he leave that hole for some potential enemy to pry into? From the very outset there is an ambivalence about his motives. By leaving this hole, the hero exhibits a dash of recklessness, an overweening sense of security, an air of bravado. Repudiating the insinuation of cowardice,[8] he wants to be thought of as bold (*kühn*). The hole is left to potential enemies as a lure and a decoy. Someone coming upon it unaware is intended to surmise that something worthwhile is waiting for a discoverer's ingenuity; at the same time there is only a minimal possibility of his ever finding it. By this device our hero has staked out the position of a game of hide-and-seek. There are innumerable potential players, but no second player ever materializes to lead him a chase or make him face up to a confrontation. To make his life worth living, the excitement of danger seems as necessary as the need for security. Since his subsequent experience never converts the potential threat to a real threat, his imagination will be called on to supply the deficiency. Fear of a confrontation neatly balances his wish to be discovered. This ambivalence is the field of force in which the whole story has its being. Intuitively aware of this, he delights in aphorisms to give it polished expression: "... some acts of cunning are so subtle as to work their own destruction."[9] At this point he

---

8   Cf. n. 4.
9   ... manche List ist so fein, daß sie sich selbst umbringt ... (p. 172).

knows the concept of tragic irony without feeling the shudder of his
own tragic involvement. Another aphorism: "As is so often the case,
the very stance of caution requires the risk of life."[10] Another: "...
and the pleasure which an ingenious brain takes in its own operations
is sometimes the only reason for continuing on one's calculations."[11]

The very design of his structure reveals the same basic ambivalence of purpose. It is all so well coordinated, with its tunnels radiating from the central stronghold, as to seem an exemplary instance of
the principle, form follows function. Yet the vastness of its design
makes it disproportionate to his simple animal needs. To be sure, the
scale of the blueprint makes its execution a symbol of the designer's
demand for self-glorification, but this caters to the wants of the
brain, not those of the animal. He tells us repeatedly of his dislike for
hard physical labor, and on this score he concedes his contruction to
have proved disproportionately costly. We think of the thousands of
hammer blows delivered by his forehead to firm up the vault of his
stronghold, with the ooze of his own lifeblood serving as the binder.[12] The idea of function is self-defeating in another respect: the
number of his tunnels and that of the channels crisscrossing them is
so great as to increase by very large odds the danger of a potential
enemy stumbling by accident upon the burrow in the course of its
own digging. Such an accident would get the game of hide-and-seek
agoing.

There is ambivalence, of course, in staking everything upon maximum security while realizing that total security is impossible. Thus,
at an early point, his allusion to legends prompts him to admit that
the exit, though his only hope, is more likely than not to work his
ruin. I think this marks the first strong indication of a pessimistic

---

10   ... gerade die Vorsicht verlangt, wie leider so oft, das Risiko des Lebens
     (p. 173).
11   ... und die Freude des scharfsinnigen Kopfes an sich selbst ist manchmal
     die alleinige Ursache dessen, daß man weiterrechnet (p. 173).
12   Sokel puts the main emphasis on charging the hero with narcissism and self-
     indulgence. To my way of thinking he vastly overstresses the hero's indul-
     gence in a sense of ease. I think of him as driven and on the go practically
     all the time. As to his protestation that he has always taken off too much
     time, instead of working, I regard these self-reproaches as morbid.

foreboding. Ambivalence is found again in the statements concerning his life within the burrow. The most delectable thing about the burrow is its stillness, radiating an atmosphere of peace, but it is deceptive and can be broken at any moment. And there is his admission in the opening paragraph that life within the burrow rarely affords a really quiet hour. If we take this as referring to the struggle for survival which goes on unabating as long as there is life, we now find his sense of uneasiness taking on very specific forms. He has dreams, worries, anxieties, nightmares, his sleep is fitful, and he is apt to wake up with a violent start. "Aufschrecken" is a word repeatedly used to describe it. Ever since "moving in" he has busied himself with relocating his provisions with a view to greater security, trying now this, now that, performing a vast amount of backbreaking work, sometimes in a nightmarish state of panic, all to no purpose, as he finds after restoring his supplies at last to their original locale. It is to the credit of his personality, to be sure, that his temperament forbids his vegetating in the peaceful possession of a house like any bourgeois grown fat, but this does not alter the fact that he is by this time a very sick animal. Ruefully and irrationally he tells himself that his blueprint should have made provision for a number of strongholds (although we cannot for the life of us see how this would have increased his security). He realized this need dimly while at work on the structure, but then it was too late to fit this enlargement into his plan, and in any case it would have required an amount of physical energy beyond his capacity. So he finds that his blueprint has an irremediable flaw and he contents himself with the aphoristic reflection: "There is bound to be a flaw in everything of which there is but a single model."[13]

This admission is a formulation of what we may call existential guilt as a shortcoming implicit in the conditions of life itself. It is reinforced by a more specific, passive guilt, a refusal to implement maturing insight with corresponding practical improvements in detail,

---

13 ... wie überhaupt dort immer ein Fehler ist, wo man von irgend etwas nur ein Exemplar besitzt (p. 178). Politzer persuasively argues that words like *Exemplar* and *Erstlingswerk* carry overtones of literary activity, rendering plausibility to his interpretation of "The Burrow" as a symbol of Kafka's literary work.

as in his criticism of the maze. This sense of guilt continues to haunt
him. Without doubt he also feels an active sense of guilt in the wake
of those rare gluttonous orgies which, leaving him in a state unfit for
defense, seem rather like a symptom of nervous exhaustion than an
ingrained vice.[14] In a later stage, when he speaks of himself as suffering punishment for guilt that he is not aware of, all the above factors
must have coalesced into a vague feeling which his logical analysis
cannot fathom.

The most startling sentence to have reached our ears up to this
point comes as part of his speculation for the need of several strongholds. As a rule, one does not suffice; however, he hopes that in his
case one will suffice "by way of exception, by way of grace, probably because Providence has a special stake in the preservation of my
forehead, the stamping-hammer."[15] It is surprising as such to realize
that he should have a concept of a Providence, but we cannot undertake to interpret its application to his case at this particular point
with any assurance of being right. It is phrased in the low key of a
rational proposition that is accepted as probable. Only the word
"gnadenweise" rises above the level of the phrasing to express an attitude of faith. He is favored, but if Providence has a stake in the preservation of his forehead, the relation is a reciprocal matter of interdependence. Is it possible that he could have kept under cover a layer
of mystical feeling akin to the epigram of Angelus Silesius?

> Ich weiss, dass ohne mich Gott nicht ein Nu kann leben,
> Werd' ich zunicht, er muss sofort den Geist aufgeben.

> I know that without me, God cannot live for a moment,
> If I am annihilated, he must at once give up the ghost.

If Providence has its eye upon him, he must be instrumental in the
working out of a higher design. Perhaps the reference to Providence
is only a belated echo, possibly a bitterly cynical echo, of a great
wave of optimism that animated him during his adolescence. Does

---

14 Sokel to the contrary.
15 ... ausnahmsweise, gnadenweise, wahrscheinlich, weil der Vorsehung an der
    Erhaltung meiner Stirn besonders gelegen ist, des Stampfhammers, ...
    (p. 178).

not many a young man of genius instictively feel himself to be a darling of the gods — witness Goethe, in whom the feeling was very strong, more than traces of it persisting into his old age — and was our builder not a genius, the designer of a structure that deserved the admiration owing to a priceless work of art! I confess my inability to fathom the emotional overtones that accompany this statement. Unless everything deceives me, the existence of a Providence and the existence of himself as being assigned a special role in the pursuance of its purposes are stated as matters of fact, whereas the aspect of probability applies only to the present means, sufficing in his own particular case by way of exception and by way of grace.

Reduced by humiliating reflections, by senseless physical toil, by the alternation of compulsive fasts and orgies, and driven by a persecution complex only dimly avowed at this point, he looks for a change of environment to restore his mental balance. According to his phrasing, to absent himself for long would seem "too severe a punishment." This curious statement becomes clear only in the light of his admission, when out in the open, that he was seriously troubled at the time: "And I find, strangely enough, that I am not in as bad shape as I often believed to be the case and as I shall probably again believe when I descend into my house."[16]

He has been in the habit of leaving his burrow from time to time to engage in the hunt and replenish his supplies, and for all we are told, everything went well. But now he has got himself into a state which opposes great obstacles to such a maneuver. For the first time we hear of the maze, located this side of the hole of ascent, on the construction of which he lavished all the enthusiasm of his youth and which he has now come to look upon with a mixture of condescension, admiration, and fears regarding its solidity. Forgetting all his brave talk of a rational pursuance of well-calculated ends, his speech shifts to the exposure of feelings with which he cannot cope. The maze has become a symbol of something to be dreaded. He deliber-

---

16 Und ich finde, daß es merkwürdigerweise nicht so schlimm mit mir steht, wie ich oft glaubte und wie ich wahrscheinlich wieder glauben werde, wenn ich in mein Haus hinabsteige (p. 183).

ately avoids it on his daily walks. He tries to suppress his awareness
of its existence. It has become a terror zone, the mere approach to
which makes him feel skinned alive. Why this should be so we do not
clearly understand, because all the reasons he advances to explain his
dread are prima facie rationalizations, suppressing something that lies
beyond. Is it that he is tormented by an unconscious tension between his underground habitation and the world above? Is it that he
feels himself a captive of his burrow, yet so acclimatized to its walls
that he dreads the prospect of the unfamiliar? Is it that he fears that
once having escaped, he will never have the courage to return, thereby forfeiting all that his life has stood for? He expatiates on the distress in a way to create the impression that he has been a prey to
these neurotic torments on previous occasions when he felt the urge
to have a change of air. To this purpose he makes free use of expressions like "sometimes," "occasionally," "at times." In shifting from
these iteratives to "today" (*heute*)[17] and successfully taking us with
him over the hurdle and up over the "trapdoor" (*Falltür*)[18] he is
ignorant of the dimensions of the neurosis awaiting him on the other
side. He — and the reader as well — is ignorant of the fact that this
self-imposed period of exile is destined to mark his last communication with the world outside.

　　Not all his dread of entering the maze was a matter of rationaliza-
tion. He was clearly aware that it was of too flimsy a construction to
withstand a determined attack, but contenting himself with this insight he has stubbornly refused to undertake the work of rebuilding
it, thus incurring the guilt of negligence. Of course, as usual, he
stifles the inner voice of self-reproach by the reflection that it is now
too late to undertake so extensive a change — he could not escape
observation if he were to do so now. Moreover, he compensates by a
recurrent wish-fulfillment dream, that he has succeeded in making
the maze impregnable (*uneinnehmbar*). The tears of joy that stream
down his whiskers on awakening from this dream are sweeter evi-

---

17　This is the only instance of *heute* occurring in the sense of "today," in con-
　　trast to other passages where it has the meaning of "nowadays."
18　Politzer, relying on a faulty recollection, speaks of "trap doors" and "forti-
　　fications."

dently than the drops of sweat that would have been the by-product of actual labor.

The moment of decision, of actually lifting the moss cover and slipping out, is built up as a dramatic episode. The suspense takes the form of a series of questions addressed to himself in which reluctance is balanced by a desire to escape. Even the impulse to leave everything behind for good is entertained for a moment, only to be repudiated later.

Once he is outside, the web of anxieties is dissipated for a moment. He feels a resurgence of vital energies. His voice has the old ring of mastery. The concern for the hunt is the first thing to engage his attention. The strenuous life agrees with him. Everything considered, spartan fare outside is better than luxury at home. It is great to be roughing it, because this is a vacation freely chosen and to be terminated whenever he tires of the game. This is where he says, "Someone will call me to him and I shall not be able to resist the invitation." For him this phrasing expresses an exuberance of animal spirits at variance with the ominous overtones that strike our ears. This is the first time that he personifies his burrow by referring to it as "someone" (*jemand*). Here he does so playfully, without realizing what a deeply obsessive fixation this personalization is destined to become.

The joy of being on his own, away from the burrow, is short-lived. He soon yields to an impulse to return to its vicinity and lie in wait, keeping his eye fixed on the entrance. Up to the point of his exile, he had persuaded himself that he had built the great structure primarily as a means for his protection, but now that he is on the other side, the roles become curiously reversed. His inner compass swings around by 180 degrees: it is the burrow which must now be protected at all costs, and the role of protector has devolved on him. What was designed to be the instrument of his protection has become the object of his solicitude. He and his burrow are now like two poles of an elliptical field of force.

At once his morbid anxiety returns. He has already spent a week with his eye trained on the trapdoor. If we are to believe him, there is a great deal of traffic passing through the area, much of it potentially hostile, but no chance passerby has evinced any curiosity to investigate the spot. He keeps on the watch, prepared for a ferocious defense, alternating with impulses toward flight. As the time continues to pass without any untoward incident, he ruminates on the possibility that the world's hostility toward him may have abated, or that his structure radiates a mysterious power exempting him from the universal struggle for survival. (This is the second time that he manifests an attitude of mystical faith.) We see in this how the personalization of the structure has taken root in its builder. He develops what he calls a childish fantasy to the effect that he might find his greatest happiness in being on the watch forever and ever, guarding his house against attack and imagining himself as cradled inside it.[19] From such daydreams he starts up in sudden terror, finding himself deluged by new anxieties regarding the tenuous security afforded by the burrow when he is inside it. There comes a time when he leaves his place of observation, tired of life in the open, persuaded that there is nothing more to be learned here, either now or later. "And I am inclined to take leave of everything here, to descend into the burrow and never to return."[20] His choice of phrasing in the passage quoted surely reveals an unconscious death wish. However, this yearning for return needs but to be expressed for the shuttle of his mind to dart in the opposite direction and cancel out his impulse. The web of reasons to motivate his reluctance is too tangled for us to understand — at least for the present: the act of descending would be designed to focus attention upon him, "a procedure nothing short of spectacular,"[21] a thought he finds eminently painful (*sehr quälend*). This would be, he tells us, because he would not know who is watching as he descends and replaces the trapdoor.

But why should this be so painful? He admits to having been spoiled (*verwöhnt*) by having been so long an observer of everything

19 Emrich ably develops the metaphysical implications of the hero's ruminative introspection, but in doing so he ignores many other features of great importance.

20 Und ich habe Lust, Abschied zu nehmen von Allem hier, hinabzusteigen in den Bau und niemals mehr zurückzukommen ... (p. 185).

21 ... die an sich geradezu Aufsehen machende Prozedur des Hinabsteigens ... (p. 185).

that transpired above ground. But has he remarked an anything to interest him while lying guard? Has anyone taken the slightest notice of *his* presence? For all the attention paid to him, he might have been wearing a *Tarnkappe*, a cloak of invisibility, in the stream of traffic. We can say, to be sure, equating the creature's position with Kafka's own: in the context of the unconscious death wish, he would find dying very painful and the funeral arrangements would be designed to call attention to one who had long gone unnoticed. Such an interpretation would make sense when applied to the author during the last stage of his long illness, when he was writing this story, but it does not carry the ring of conviction in the context before us. In contrast to many other passages which expose the fallacy of the speaker's reasoning at a glance, the present train of thought, so heavily saturated with emotion, remains obscure in its bearing: "... behind my back and after that, behind the readjusted trapdoor."[22] In line with this personal interpretation, the enigmatic remark that follows would be read as Kafka's speculation on the possibility of an afterlife. "It will be made manifest, but no longer to me, or possibly to me also, but too late."[23]

The next stages of sojourn above ground can be quickly summarized. As a preliminary to his own descent he stuffs the collected booty down the entrance hole. Finding himself psychologically unable to follow, he constructs a very short observation trench and as time passes, days and weeks going by at the very least, the urge to return home becomes more insistent. During this long spell of inactivity, he is seriously beset by the temptation to abandon his burrow for good and resume a life of roaming in the open. At no time does any sentimental attachment to nature appear as an element of this wish; neither is there any hint throughout the whole account of any thought of returning to society. The diffused dangers to be encountered in such a life everywhere seem preferable to the specific danger which his entrance hole presents. Dismissing this as nonsense, he tries

---

22   ... hinter meinem Rücken und dann hinter der wieder-eingefügten Falltür ...
    (p. 185).
23   ... es wird sich zeigen, aber nicht mehr mir, oder auch mir, aber zu spät
    (p. 185).

to force a showdown. By running at top speed in broad daylight, he
plans to make a dive for his hole, but unnerved, he overshoots it and
flings himself into a thicket of briars.[24] Self-inflicted pain, as punishment for what? he muses. But on further thought he justifies his
avoidance of the hole by the reflection "that it is really impossible
to descend without exposing the most precious thing I have, at least
for a little while, to the full view of all those around me, on the
ground, in the trees, in the air."[25] "The most precious thing I have..."
(*das Teuerste, was ich habe* ...) — this phrase, charged with a high
emotional content, is it not a strange designation for a hole stuffed
with booty? Yet to relate the phrase to the whole system of underground construction sounds even more improbable because the burrow represents the sum total of what he cherishes, not the most precious part of it. *Preisgeben* is an ambiguous word. It can mean either
"abandon" or "expose to view." In this context the latter meaning
makes better sense, in fact the only sense. To expose to view the
most precious thing he has for even a little while to everything on the
ground, in the trees, in the atmosphere — can he have something else
in mind? He must have something else in mind, that something which
he referred to as making the act of his descent nothing short of spectacular.

If I may be personal for a moment, I remember, after weeks of
preoccupation with this story, the exact day and hour on which it
struck me in a flash: this passage, and the passage above, as well as a
number of passages to follow, must have a sexual meaning, fastidi-
ously concealed because intolerably humiliating to the creature's puritanical code. The fear of indecent exposure, and exhibitionism as
its counterpart, beset him as manifestations of a libido that torments
him. They add an emphatic note of sexual anxiety to those other
sources of guilt which we have designated as existential, positive
(active), and passive (negative). To imagine his hinder parts exposed

---

24 Politzer sees in this an allusion to the burning bush of Exodus, an idea alto-
    gether too fanciful for me to entertain.
25 ... daß es wirklich unmöglich ist hinabzusteigen, ohne das Teuerste, was ich
    habe, allen ringsherum, auf dem Boden, auf den Bäumen, in den Lüften
    wenigstens für ein Weilchen offen preiszugeben (p. 186).

for even the little while of his descent is too shameful an idea to bear. He might be followed down, in his rationalizing of the situation, by "some harmless little minx," *eine beliebige kleine Unschuld*, who might unwittingly attract a real enemy (presumably by her scent). The abstract term *Unschuld* he invests with concrete personality, in line with its grammatical gender, as a female, and its two qualifying attributes express both contempt and attraction, whereas in the phrase to follow, "some nasty little creature," *ein widerliches kleines Wesen*, only the former persists. The whole thought could stand for some trifling illicit adventure. If we remember that the heroes of Kafka's long novels yield to sexual lust under conditions to be described as unsavory by any standards, is it not surprising that the overt manifestation of the libido should have been omitted from the account of a life so filled with psychological torment as that of our hero? He refers to the distasteful female as motivated by curiosity. In its train, the fantasy of the little female leads to a second fantasy of overwhelmingly formidable proportions: supposing the very worst, there might be attracted in her wake

someone of my own kind, some connoisseur and fancier of structures, some forest vagabond, a lover of peace but a shameless bum who wants to dwell without building. If only he would come now, if only with his filthy greed he would discover the entrance, if only he would begin working to lift up the moss, if only he would succeed, if only he would wedge himself inside there for me, having got in there far enough for his hinder parts still to show for a moment, if only all this were to happen so that finally, in a mad dash after him, all inhibitions tossed aside, I could leap upon him, bite, tear, and mangle him to pieces, suck his blood to the last drop, and immediately pack his carcass with the rest of my booty, but above, all — this would be the main thing — be once more in my burrow.[26]

---

26 ... irgendjemand von meiner Art, ein Kenner und Schätzer von Bauten, irgendein Waldbruder, ein Liebhaber des Friedens, aber ein wüster Lump, der wohnen will ohne zu bauen. Wenn er doch jetzt käme, wenn er doch mit seiner schmutzigen Gier den Eingang entdeckte, wenn er doch daran zu arbeiten begänne, das Moos zu heben, wenn es ihm doch gelänge, wenn er sich doch für mich hineinzwängte und schon darin soweit wäre, daß mir sein Hinterer für einen Augenblick gerade noch auftauchte, wenn das alles doch geschähe, damit ich endlich in einem Rasen hinter ihm her, frei von allen Bedenken, ihn anspringen könnte, ihn zerbeißen, zerfleischen, zerreißen und austrinken und seinen Kadaver gleich zur anderen Beute stopfen könnte, vor

The terrible imagery of this wish-dream is so gripping that its motivation may dwindle into a hypnotic blank in the reader's mind. This was, indeed, my own case. Was this contingency not introduced as the most dreaded thing of all? What then transformed it in a flash into a wish-dream? It was the thought of getting home by this device, where all devices toward this end had failed, which makes him turn berserk. So all the lustful outrage is imagined as the one sure means of achieving salvation!

Of all the passages in the story, this sentence has the greatest accumulation of graphic detail. How these six steeply mounting wish-clauses reveal an escalation of passion involving voyeurism, rape, murder, and cannibalism.[27]

After this explosion of animal passion, the speaker's tone again becomes subdued. He develops a new fixation. His favorite pastime now is to move in circles about the entrance hole, heedless of observers, playing the game of himself being the enemy that is stalking the area in order to penetrate into the inner sanctum. Now the wish to have a trusty to stand guard in his place is taken up by his imagination and developed at great length, only to be rejected because he is antisocial, and his definition of trust is a contradiction in terms. Having dismissed this line, and still finding himself prevented by a psychological block from returning home, he dreams up new ways of insuring greater safety of exit and reentry. To have two entrances

---

allem aber, das wäre die Hauptsache, endlich wieder in meinem Bau wäre ... (p. 187).

27 Many commentators have observed discreet silence on this passage, Emrich and 'Sokel among them. Politzer protests that the episode, in its violence, is out of keeping with the rest and contributes nothing to the story. It is to his credit that, having felt the shock without understanding it, he did not pass it over in silence. As for Henel, he does some very curious things. To begin with he reverses the order of the two imaginary encounters, and his blurred references to the first do not even make it clear that a female is involved. As for the male marauder, who is imagined as wanting to dispossess the hero of his burrow, Henel quotes the colorful sentence, but unaccountably leaves out the key phrase: "einer der wohnen will ohne zu bauen." Without realizing how threatened the creature felt, he chides him for his cruelty and brutality toward harmless creatures and those of his own kind, and in sum finds the colorful language hilariously funny.

instead of one, one of them very narrow, just for observation purposes, would seem a decided improvement. Its technical advantages appeal to him, but after deliberating on the pros and cons, he dismisses the whole idea in extraordinarily resolute language. The advantages are undeniable, "but only as technical achievements, not as real advantages. For, this unhindered slipping in and out, what good is it? It points to a restless disposition, to an uncertain estimation of one's own worth, to unclean appetites, bad qualities that become even worse in the face of the burrow."[28] Every reader who is not forewarned must find it strange that this project is dismissed not on technical but on moral grounds. Five successive phrases condemn the project in the severest moral terms. The last of these phrases suggests the burrow is something hallowed and suffering desecration at the thought of such a device. After the foregoing analysis, can there be any doubt that the two entrances, very close to each other, easy to slip into and out of, suggest to the speaker specific forms of libido? Not long ago he had allowed himself to be sucked into the vortex of lustful, murderous aggression. Now that he has himself in hand again, he definitely rejects easy lubricity as a way of life.

When the tug-of-war between his yearning to return home and its compulsive interdiction is finally decided in favor of the former by a tour-de-force of autohypnosis, he does something very curious. In a trancelike daze, he detaches the cover of moss and descends. Then, remembering that he has absentmindedly forgotten to replace the cover, he reascends to the surface to correct the oversight, quite unnecessarily and quite deliberately, the word *langsam* (slowly), followed by "much too long," appearing twice in this context. This is surely a classical case of a Freudian slip (*Fehlleistung*). He blames his confusion on absentmindedness (*Zerstreutheit*)! Is he not thereby performing an exhibitionistic ritual before his final return underground?

---

28   ... aber doch nur als technische Errungenschaften, nicht als wirkliche Vorteile, denn dieses ungehinderte Aus- und Einschlüpfen, was soll es? Es deutet auf unruhigen Sinn, auf unsichere Selbsteinschätzung, auf unsaubere Gelüste, schlechte Eigenschaften, die noch viel schlechter werden angesichts des Baues ... (p. 189).

Let us pause for a moment to summarize all the sexual anxieties we have encountered. First, in his longing to take one of the necessary excursions to the outside world, there was the inhibition against entering the maze, when he felt his pelt thinning and his fantasy pictured him as standing naked, hairless, and raw, surrounded by a mob of jeering enemies.[29] The second, like all the following inhibitions, he faces in the world above, when the wish to reenter his burrow is blocked by the thought that his act of descending would be too conspicuous to go unnoticed. The third was a recurrence of the same fantasy expressed in poignantly emotional though veiled language, how the eyes of everyone, on the ground, in the trees, in the air, would be riveted, if only for a short moment, upon "the most precious thing I have." Number four was his fantasy of some little minx, meaning no harm, a nasty little snooper whose entering would leave her scent as a trail for the world to follow. Five: directly in the wake of this there materialized his wish-dream of one of his own kind, a male, in a posture precluding defense — the grandiosely uninhibited vision of a fellow burrower, a male marauder, whom he annihilates with berserk fury. Number six concerns his speculations about the advantages of two holes to slip in and out of at will, but these, following upon the unrestrained assertion of his overpowering libido, though technically advantageous, are rejected on moral grounds as he regains his composure. Finally, seventh, the libido, having been checked by the puritanical censor, reasserts itself in a curious Freudian slip when, in a trancelike state, having gone down into the entrance hole, he remembers that he has absentmindedly forgotten to close the trapdoor. Instead of reaching up with his paw to close it, he reemerges all the way in order to descend again, and carries out the necessary maneuver, all of this slowly and deliberately.

The return to his burrow has affected his spirits as a reviving tonic. In following his movements we are very soon struck by his

---

29   ... mir ist manchmal, als verdünne sich mein Fell, als könnte ich bald mit bloßem, kahlem Fleisch dastehen und in diesem Augenblick vom Geheul meiner Feinde begrüßt werden (p. 181).

use of a word that sounds odd in the mouth of a loner. The long inspection tours awaiting him are not to be rated as work, he says. Moving along those passageways is more like "a chatting with friends, the way I used to do in olden times or — I am not yet what one would really call old, but my memory has already become completely hazy as regards many things — as I used to do, or as I heard that it is usually done."[30] As a loner he has no friends. Has he not banished from his vocabulary all memories of social intercourse? Without doubt the joy of being able to let himself go accounts for a slip of the tongue. The word "friends" (*Freunde*) having escaped his lips, he must pause with the intent of blurring it and rendering its application to his own circumstances meaningless. The syntactical twists he performs in his attempt to repudiate any admission as to erstwhile social relations of his own are a remarkable example of the inner censor at work.[31]

The word "friends" (*Freunde*) finds us involved in the emotional climax of his homecoming. He laughs for joy and having assured himself while still outside, in sober and solemn tones, that he and his structure are one and indivisible, he now raises his voice in a paean to his tunnels and above all to his stronghold. "On your account, you tunnels and platforms, and on your account above all, my stronghold, I have come at the risk of my life, after I had long been so idiotic as to tremble on its account and delay the return to you. What do I care about the danger now that I am with you? You belong to me, I to you, we are united, what can happen tu us?"[32]

---

30 ... ein Plaudern mit Freunden, so wie ich es tat in alten Zeiten oder — ich bin noch garnicht so alt, aber für vieles trübt sich die Erinnerung schon völlig — wie ich es tat oder wie ich hörte, daß es zu geschehen pflegt (p. 193).

31 Nobody, to my knowledge, has commented on the tortuous gyrations of this sentence.

32 Euretwegen, ihr Gänge und Plätze und deinetwegen vor allem, Burgplatz, bin ich ja gekommen, habe mein Leben für nichts geachtet, nachdem ich lange Zeit die Dummheit hatte, seinetwegen zu zittern und die Rückkehr zu euch zu verzögern. Was kümmert mich die Gefahr, jetzt, da ich bei euch bin. Ihr gehört zu mir, ich zu euch, verbunden sind wir, was kann uns geschehen (p. 194).

I have changed the text to read "deinetwegen" in place of "deine Fragen" (l. 9, p. 194). "Deine Fragen" is both illogical and ungrammatical in the

This apostrophe marks the greatest departure from the low-key approach of the story's beginning. Here for once there is a purely spontaneous flow of high-pitched joyous emotion without hedging, backtracking, or ambivalence, but this crest of the wave is of only momentary duration, for now we are on the threshold of a wholly new phase of anxiety and torment, a phase that will pursue its relentless course all the way to the point where the voice comes to a stop.

The stillness of the burrow, he has told us at the outset, was its most blissful feature, but now, after his return, something has happened to destroy this bliss. He becomes aware of a faint hissing or whistling, coming from he knows not where. Curiosity gives way to alarm. Its persistence and ubiquity are the only known elements in a multitude of unknowns which he must identify, first to account for the phenomenon and then, if possible, to remove it. We pause to note that he, the speaker, has ingeniously prepared the ground for his "psychosis," if we may use this term to denote a much more deep-seated disturbance than the anxieties that proliferated during the first half of the "story." From the start he had shown a marked anxiety regarding the continuation of the stillness. "To be sure, it is deceptive. Suddenly, at some moment, it may be broken."[33] He also anticipated what becomes his fixation as to the cause of the noise. In commenting on the advantages deriving from the presence

---

context of the sentence. Preceded by "euretwegen" and followed by "seinetwegen" in the same sentence, "deinetwegen," involving a change of only three letters, makes perfect sense. Yet many writers on "The Burrow," Politzer, Emrich, and Sokel among them, have quoted the sentence as it stands in print, without being aware of the misreading of the manuscript. J.M.S. Pasley has put out a college edition, with an introduction and notes, of three stories: *Franz Kafka, Der Heizer, In der Strafkolonie, Der Bau* (Cambridge, Eng.: Cambridge Univ. Press, 1966). In preparing his text he had the benefit of using the manuscript of "Der Bau." His version of the sentence in question replaces the senseless "deine Fragen" by a simple "Du." This indeed makes sense, even if its rhythm leaves something to be desired, but Pasley has given us no note to account for a change which is arbitrary and by no stretch of the imagination a correction of a misreading of the manuscript. Extreme skepticism as to his editorial procedure is in order.

33 Freilich, sie ist trügerisch. Plötzlich einmal kann sie unterbrochen werden und alles ist zu Ende (p. 174).

of the small fry in his burrow, he had checked himself to add, "Such nonchalance may perhaps not be without danger for other reasons."[34] Is this not as if he had had an unconscious foreknowledge of both the noise and its origin? Clearly the germ of the cancer was dormant within him, biding a favorable climate to grow. When the proper moment has come to unhinge his precarious mental balance, these two built-in points are at hand for him to grasp and on which to hang, as on pegs, his psychotic hallucinations. It is as if he had, paradoxically speaking, taken out mental health insurance in reverse. As if he had known that his fundamental balance was going to be upset, he prepared in advance for local symptoms to occupy his mind and fuss over and to divert his attention from the basic issue.

Throughout the rest of the story all his ingenuity is put to work in efforts to probe into an unknown which by its nature is unknowable. His reasoning becomes overtly paranoid as one conjecture gives place to another. A remarkable illustration of this comes as he reasons, at one point, that in order to persist with the same intensity at every point of the walls and wherever he puts his ears to the ground, the sound must have two points of origin at opposite ends of his burrow. In this way, no matter how he shifts his location, the sound maintains the same degree of intensity, the diminution of one source being compensated by the augmentation of the other. Many a reader will be quick to observe that this application of the general hypothesis would hold true only if the master-builder kept moving along the straight line extending between the two poles from which the noise originates, but it is nonsensical in any case because sound does not travel at an arithmetical ratio. It is part of Kafka's peculiar humor to set such traps for the unwary reader.

The hypotheses the hero successively entertains as to the where, the how, the who, and the why of the hissing would be wearisome to recapitulate in all their turns. The extraordinarily explicit detail of their presentation serves the primary purpose of making us feel that a very long time is spent in these futile exercises of the brain. In the course of our wandering through the tortuous maze of his reasoning,

---

34   ... was allerdings aus anderen Gründen vielleicht unvorsichtig ist (p. 176).

we come across a couple of strikingly beautiful images regarding the
stillness. Hoping to find it again he says, "It is as though the source
were opening out of which the silence of the burrow flows."[35] A
little later he explores a passageway "whose stillness wakes up at my
coming and envelops me from above."[36]

The imaginative high point of emotional involvement during the
process of attrition concerns "a favorite plan of my youth and ma-
turity" (*ein Lieblingsplan meiner Jugend- und Mannesjahre*) to hollow out a spherical area around his stronghold, leaving only a column
for gravitational support to connect it with the earth. This done, he
would have cavorted all over the global surface, caressing it, feeling
it most intimately his own, and the delight of holding it, as it were in
the hollow of his embrace, outside it, protecting it, being its guardian,
would have surpassed the pleasure of being cradled inside it and en-
joying its protection. Here again we happen upon that most fundamental ambivalence which provided the dominant tension during his
long period of exile — the reversal of roles of protector and protégé.
This is surely another manifestation of his libido, applied not to a
living thing, as during his exile, but this time to his own creation.
We note the ambivalence between choice of belly and womb as characteristic of his whole personality. Literally taken, this fantasy would
seem to involve a total death wish, because with the ten avenues of
the stronghold presumably plugged up, he would be left to perish
without food and air.[37]

It is almost embarrassing to state the obvious. During the whole
declining phase of his life, that is, after his return to the burrow, the
hero is the victim of a haunting hallucination. We note that the paranoid, ever-present preoccupation with the sound, while taking the
predominant form of theoretical explanation, also expresses itself in
senseless and self-destructive activity. Exasperated by the elusiveness

---

35   ... es ist, als öffnete sich die Quelle, aus welcher die Stille des Baues strömt
     (p. 204).
36   ... deren Stille aufwacht bei meinem Kommen und sich über mich senkt
     (p. 206).
37   Politzer has blurred the account of this hermetic-hollow fantasy beyond
     recognition. His memory apparently confused it with the hero's earlier
     craving to have several strongholds.

of the noise, he claws at the walls of his tunnels, digging holes at random and reducing the beautifully smooth design of his passage-ways to a shambles. Realizing the self-destructive futility of these acts at last, he resolves, as the preliminary to another grandiose and harebrained thrust into the unknown, to repair the damage; but to the extent that he sets about doing so, instead of merely thinking about the project, his heart is not in the work. He performs it list-lessly as though under the eyes of a foreman (*Aufseher*). How things have changed again! For all its drudgery, the work of executing his blueprint was the self-imposed goal of self-glorification; now he feels reduced to the status of an employee, laboring reluctantly under another's direction.

The long phase of paranoid hallucination takes a new turn when, not far from the end of the story, he seeks to escape from the haunt-ing sound by approaching the maze, threading his way through its labyrinthine walls, and settling down inside the exit hole. By another ambivalent turn, the din of the world's traffic outside affords relief to his harassed mind from the obsession of the hissing sound. Here he can concentrate afresh on theorizing as to the trouble within. By all odds, the most remarkable theory to which he now attaches himself is that of a monstrously large and powerful animal, ploughing its way through the earth at a swinging stride, spirally encircling the burrow to which it has already drawn nearer by several loops. The hissing he interprets as nothing but the echoing tremor of his relentless ap-proach. "Someone is coming." ("Es kommt jemand heran.") The symbolism of this projection as the inescapable doom of death is too obvious for us to miss. But instead of his facing it for what it is, it awakens in him a memory of his adolescent days when his work on the burrow was still tentative and subject to change. He remembers having heard the sound of a fellow burrower.[38] At that time he responded to it with curiosity mixed with indifference, but without fear. The noise would alternately be felt as nearer or more distant, and there came a time when he no longer heard it. During all of that

---

38 Strangely enough, Sokel regards the hissing as actually emanating from with-in the earth.

time he was equally prepared to face an intruder in a clean-cut fight, or to move his own operations to an area where he would not be disturbed by neighbors.

To us, this reminiscence shows the difference between the sound mind of the vigorous adolescent and the diseased mind of the creature grown old.[39] Ironically, he puts a different interpretation upon it. "Admonitions were not wanting." (*An Mahnungen hat es nicht gefehlt.*) He sees this incident of his youth as a warning, an admonition which he should have heeded in order to avoid the inexorable burrower who will be getting him at last. The term "admonitions" (*Mahnungen*) is one of those peculiar words that we sense as a religious element of his experiences. We remember that casual but altogether enigmatic remark about his protective devices having worked "by way of exception, by way of grace, because Providence has a special stake in the preservation of my forehead, the stamping-hammer," where he voiced his conviction that he enjoyed the special protection of Providence, and claimed a relationship of interdependence with it. The level of this wording left it an open question whether this expressed the buoyancy of youthful genius, a whimsical bit of pragmatic philosophy, a cynical witticism, or the deep conviction of a mystical bond obtaining between him and higher powers. During his prolonged exile there emerged a feeling regarding his structure as radiating a mystical power to keep him from harm, exempting him, as he then put it, from the universal struggle for suvival.

Now, with the word "admonitions" still sounding in our ears, we listen to a series of rhetorical questions, couched in the language of genuine religious emotion: "How did it happen that for so long a time tranquillity and happiness pervaded my burrow? Who was it that guided the paths of my enemies that they skirted my domain by a great curve? Why was I protected so long only to be so terrorized

---

39 Hans Bänziger's essay, "Der Bau," *Merkur, Deutsche Zeitschrift für Europäisches Denken*, 11 (Jan. 1957), 38-49, in attempting to bridge the gap between literary and scientific studies, has interesting things to say on the well-known concept of animal territorialism. However, to a wholly nonaggressive loner, who thinks only of security in terms of concealment, delaying devices, precipitous flight or, at worst, a defensive fight to the death, its applicability seems minimal.

now?"[40] This is the conversion (*das Insichgehen*) of the repentant sinner, humbly acknowledging the error of his ways in having turned a deaf ear to divine guidance. We ask the question: are all these successive stages of a religious turn of mind to be interpreted as progressive phases of a mind coming apart? Whatever one may think of Kafka's own religious development, the religious factor in the context of this story must be taken as a symptom of a progressive mental deterioration. This humility is not old age mellowing to wisdom; it is the pragmatism of a creature grown bewildered and feeble. To put it another way: the pragmatism of self-conscious youth has yielded to a senile will-to-believe.[41]

Only one short phase remains to be reviewed. Lying just below the moss cover of the exit vent, separated from his tunnels and the central stronghold by the maze, he again feels the urge to betake himself off. Subject as always to the tension of ambivalent desires, he wishes he were too feeble to respond to the homing urge. He does get back to the stronghold. Now he speculates on the guidelines that should have dictated its construction. From the outset he has referred to it in terms of defense; the word "Verteidigung" has frequently occurred in this context. However, we must have felt all along, supposing that we gave any thought to the matter, that what he calls his "*Burgplatz*" — rendered by us as stronghold — is a grandiose misnomer. It is a place of shelter and protection and its spaciousness would make it a fine status symbol if its possessor were part of any social order, in the absence of which it is an expression of self-aggrandizement. But of defensive devices in the proper sense of the word there is not a trace. This insight has come to him very late and he now thinks of guidelines to be translated into engineering know-how for the purpose of confusing and annihilating a potential foe. But self-criticism has long ceased to have any relation to practical

---

40 Wie kam es nur, daß so lange Zeit alles still und glücklich verlief? Wer hat die Wege der Feinde gelenkt, daß sie den großen Bogen machten um meinem Besitz? Warum wurde ich so lange beschützt, um jetzt so geschreckt zu werden? (p. 209).
41 Henel intimates that "a friendly encounter" was in order because the creature was in "the house of God."

initiative. The dissociation of theoretical reason from practical living, of the brain from the body, is complete. Barren introspection has totally replaced reason in the service of life. From the vantage point of a higher perspective, as he now realizes, all his life has been play. Fear being everpresent, he deliberates on the chances of negotiating with an intruder, but he still has sense enough to realize that his proposals are silly. Things finally boil down to a single item of animal instinct: let him reduce the store of his supplies by consuming as much as possible while there is time. We see him last, in his mutilated stronghold, under a pile of rubble with a piece of flesh between his teeth. He has stopped talking. His last sentence, though complete enough, could have involved an about-face. But for all practical purposes he is finished, his life and strength are played out. We may think of him as having died in his sleep, without any conscious struggle. Confrontation, torture, and pain are related to strength. This speaker's strength is gone.

There is a final question to be answered: is "The Burrow" complete or is it a fragment? Many critics, Emrich among them, hedge their aswer by referring to the assertion of Kafka's friends, Max Brod and Dora Dymant, that there was to be an encounter which would have ended with the hero's death. Pasley (see Notes), who had the benefit of Kafka's manuscript in preparing his college editions, asserts that the final page is completely filled without any terminating punctuation mark. This he takes as proof that there was more to follow. There is the fact, moreover, pointed out to me by Professor Steven Scher, that in Pasley's version, the last four words are separated from what precedes by a mere semicolon, whereas Max Brod's heavy-handed editing saw fit to set them off by a period and a dash. Now it is perfectly conceivable that the hero might have gone on verbalizing for a number of paragraphs, but it is difficult to imagine what more he could have had to say. If, as I believe, Kafka thought of his hero as destined to die of a heart attack or other natural causes, he could have snapped his life cord right then and there by stopping his pen in the middle of the last word of the final phrase, but he did not choose to do so.

But what of the alleged violent confrontation that was to end the hero's life? This is improbable, even impossible, on a variety of grounds. To begin with, the ruminations of our hero regarding the relentless approach of a silent predator can be dismissed as the figments of a feverishly hallucinating brain. Beyond this, surveying our hero's whole life span, we find not a single instance of any overt attempt on the part of any living creature to invade his stronghold. To introduce such an event now, when the burrower's life has entered its twilight zone, would be tantamount to using the device of a freak chance to end matters — a device contrary to all esthetic logic and unworthy of Kafka.

But the idea of a terminal fight is untenable on other grounds. Have we forgotten that this "story" unfolds as the synchronous reeling off of the hero's life and his voice? He has talked his life away without any break in the flow. But how could he continue to speak with his teeth engaged in snapping at his opponent's throat? In other words, the author would have been compelled at a certain point to introduce the voice of a second speaker, the voice of the "omniscient author." Such an abrupt change of focus is unthinkable in the sophisticated atmosphere of Kafka's art.

Is there, then, no possibility of any definitive ending to a story built on such premises? No creature, however miraculously endowed or engineered, can report on its own death. Very well; but I think there is a way of contriving to have the hero speak to his very last heartbeat and for us to know that it is his last. Suppose we let him experience his death by heart failure to an accompanying nightmare. This could have been put into words that finally echo from the land of no return. Seizing Kafka's pen, we have the temerity to write:

Da, was ist das? Ein Geräusch, das mich aufschreckt und mich zwingt die Augen aufzuschlagen. Aus der zerschlissenen Wand hervor, mir entgegen, schiebt sich ein riesiges Gebiß, und indem ich den Abgrund seines dunklen Schlundes hinuntergleite, höre ich noch das Knacken meiner Kniescheiben und Knöchel zwischen seinen Kiefern.

There, what's that? A noise that startles and forces me to open my eyes. Out of the crumbling wall there reaches toward me an enormous set of jaws, and as I feel myself slide down the dark abyss of his gullet, I can hear the crackling of my kneecaps and ankles between his grinders.

Since Kafka did not give this version the sanction of his Imprimatur, choosing rather the ambiguity of open-endedness, "the rest is silence."

14.
ZU THOMAS MANNS ANTEIL AN SERENUS ZEITBLOMS BIOGRAPHIE VON ADRIAN LEVERKÜHN

Wir haben von kundiger Hand[1] so viel über die unerhört detaillierte Montagearbeit des *Doktor Faustus* erfahren, daß es sich nachgerade lohnt, den naiven aber aufmerksamen Leser zu spielen und mit gleichsam neugewaschenen Augen das Werk als geschlossene Einheit in uns aufzunehmen als authentischen biographischen Versuch über Leben und Werk eines dem Biographen sehr nahestehenden Komponisten. Der Name Thomas Manns steht freilich auf dem Titelblatt, was uns als Leser veranlaßt, in unserem Unterbewußtsein immer das Mitschwingen der Tatsache zu spüren, daß sich Thomas Mann im *Doktor Faustus* in den Darsteller Zeitblom und den dargestellten Helden Adrian Leverkühn aufgespalten hat. Mit diesem Vorbehalt lesen wir das Werk, als trüge es den Titel: Serenus Zeitblom: Das Leben des deutschen Tonsetzers Adrian Leverkühn, erzählt von einem Freunde. Wir geraten sehr bald in den Bann des Erzählers, wir verspüren sofort die lebenslängliche, leidenschaftliche, aber durch ein strenges Ethos gezügelte Bindung des Erzählers an seinen Freund. Wir verspüren seine intime Vertrautheit mit Leben und Werk des Freundes, seine Aufrichtigkeit, seine tiefe, überaus fühlsame Witterung für alles, was im Inneren seines Freundes vorgeht. Wir billigen seinen klar ausgesprochenen und an vielen Stellen zum Vorschein kommenden Verzicht auf jede Art romanhafter Spannung, das Was der Ereignisse betreffend, die er erzählt. Wir bewundern dabei eine Darstellungsgabe, der es gelingt, ein in gewollter Absonderung sich abspielendes asketisches Künstlerleben in den Mittelpunkt einer Erzählung zu stellen, die eine Fülle lebenatmender Gestalten dank der Doppelpoligkeit von Darsteller und dargestelltem Helden an der Peripherie ihr Wesen treiben läßt, ohne die zentripetale Spannung zu schädigen. Von Stau-

---

1 Bergsten, Gunilla, *Thomas Manns Doktor Faustus: Untersuchungen zu den Quellen und zur Struktur des Romans* (1963, 1974); Voss, Lieselotte, *Die Entstehung von Thomas Manns Roman Doktor Faustus: dargestellt anhand von unveröffentlichten Vorarbeiten* (1975).

nen eingegebene Zweifel überkommen den Leser, wenn er sich fragt,
wie es möglich sei, daß ein in bescheidenen Grenzen wirkender Hu-
manist und Lateinlehrer eine so erstaunliche Fülle von Kenntnissen
an den Tag legt, vor allem auf musiktheoretischem Gebiet, das doch
außerhalb seines Faches liegt. Was für eine geradezu tolle Gedächtnis-
leistung stellen nicht gewisse Referate dar, die die in früher Jugend
von den Vorträgen Wendell Kretzschmars erhaltenen Eindrücke mit
einer Lebendigkeit und Treue wiedergeben, die das menschliche Ver-
mögen doch wohl übersteigen. Oder man denke an die große philo-
sophisch-politische Debatte der Winfried-Theologen auf ihrer Wan-
derung, der sich Zeitblom seines Freundes wegen als Außenseiter
angeschlossen hat. Ein weiteres Beispiel unerhörter Gedächtnislei-
stung referiert-zitiert Zeitblom ohne Adrians Brief an seinen Lehrer
Kretzschmar zur Hand zu haben, jene berühmt gewordene Charakteri-
stik eines nicht mit Namen genannten Orchesterstücks, welches für
den Eingeweihten die unverkennbare Signatur des Vorspiels zum
3. Akt der *Meistersinger* trägt (207ff).[2] Nicht weniger zweifelnde
Bewunderung erregt die Darstellungsgabe des Biographen, dessen
beobachtende Einfühlung und stilistische Meisterschaft in der klaren
Formung labyrinthisch gewundener Satzgefüge einem sein Leben lang
auf die Vervollkommnung des Wortes bedachten Künstler Ehre machen würde. Dabei erlaubt er sich Freiheiten, die der Form nach von
jedem Novellisten beansprucht, aber von jedem strengen Biographen
verpönt wären. Er stellt zum Beispiel gewisse Vorgänge szenisch dar,
bei denen er nicht zugegen gewesen, wie etwa Adrians zufälligen ersten Erkundungsbesuch in Pfeiffering, bei dem wir nicht nur die ganzen Liegenschaften des Hofes besichtigen, sondern auch an dem teils
direkt, teils indirekt geführten Wechselgespräch der beiden Herren,
Adrians und Schildknapps, mit Elsbeth Schweigestill teilnehmen.
Solche Freiheit szenischer Darstellung erklärt sich ganz natürlich aus
der Tatsache, daß Zeitblom wenige Jahre später das Milieu des Hofes
der Schweigestills durch seine häufigen Besuche bis ins minutiöseste
kennenlernt. Ganz andere Kräfte sind im Spiel, wo Zeitblom sich als
unsichtbaren Teilnehmer der verhängnisvollen Szene beglaubigt, in

---

2   Stellennachweise aus dem *Doktor Faustus* beziehen sich auf die erste, die
    Stockholmer Ausgabe des Jahres 1947, vom Bermann-Fischer Verlag.

der Adrian sich seines Freundes Rudi Schwerdtfeger bedient, seine Werbung um Marie Godeaus Hand vorzubringen. Diese Zumutung an den Freund, der sich seine intime Ausnahmestellung zu Adrian durch eine viele Jahre lang geübte Geduldprobe des Ausharrens um Erhörung erkämpft hat, spiegelt die abstrakte Gefühllosigkeit Adrians in grellem Lichte. Hier ist es Zeitbloms eigener Versicherung gemäß die schmerzlich brennende, aber durch sein Wissen um den tragischen Ausgang ethisch gezügelte Eifersucht, die ihn hellsichtig macht. Kein Leser, der über die Vertrauenswürdigkeit des Biographen nachdenkt, könnte sich veranlaßt fühlen, an solcher Lizenz Anstoß zu nehmen.

Gewiß wird das Vertrauen des Lesers zum Biographen auf manche Probe gestellt. Allgemein gesprochen verflüchtigen sich die Zweifel in der Erwägung, was Serenus Zeitblom zu einer Leistung von nahezu unfaßbarer Schwierigkeit befähigt, ist seine Liebe zu Adrian als lebenslange Passion, ist die Steigerung seiner Persönlichkeit durch den indirekten Umgang mit dem Dämonischen. Diese Steigerung durch eine homosexuell bedingte lebenslängliche unerwiderte Bindung an den Freund – läuft sie nicht völlig parallel zu der Steigerung Hans Castorps im *Zauberberg*? Dort hatte ein unverstandenes, ein Jahr andauerndes Gefühl für den kirgisenäugigen Schulkameraden Przibislav Hippe Hans Castorp beherrscht, um zuerst in Vergessenheit zu geraten und dann in der unter dem Antrieb der Krankheit von Clawdia Chauchat ausgeübten Faszination neu aufzuleben. Diese Leidenschaft hatte die Aufnahmefähigkeit des "einfachen" jungen Mannes ins Grenzenlose gesteigert, wir waren einer Einweihung in hermetische Sphären gefolgt. Steht es nicht ähnlich um Zeitblom, doch mit dem beachtenswerten Unterschied, daß Hans Castorp in dem Bereich der Rezeptivität beharrt, während im Fall Zeitbloms die Erinnerung an das Leben und das furchtbar tragische Schicksal des Freundes in ihm den Trieb zur Gestaltung auslöst? Bei ihm bedeutet die Steigerung nicht nur ausgedehnteste Rezeptivität in Bezug auf alles Menschliche, sondern darüber hinaus den Drang festzuhalten, zu fixieren, zu gestalten.

Bei alledem gibt es Stellen in der Biographie, wo der kritische Leser mit dem Bleistift in der Hand sich versucht fühlt, durch eine Randbemerkung sein Bedenken über einen Punkt zu äußern, wo nicht gar ein kräftiges Fragezeichen zu setzen. Wir denken bei diesem

Vorbehalt nicht an Meinungen und Deutungen, sondern an das bio-
graphische Tatsachenmaterial. So ist von verschiedenen Seiten, u.a.
von Gunilla Bergsten und Lieselotte Voss,[3] längst bemerkt worden,
daß es mit der Chronologie von Adrians Leben an gewissen Stellen
hapert, was sich leicht daraus erklärt, daß der Biograph aus dem
Schatz seiner Erinnerungen schöpft, statt sich auf Dokumente zu verlassen. Um ein Beispiel zu nennen: wir hören, daß Adrian im Jahre
1905 als Student nach Leipzig kam (212); aus dem Wortlaut seines
hochwichtigen Briefes über das Bordellerlebnis erfahren wir, daß es
die Zeit der Herbstmesse war (216). An späterer Stelle teilt uns Zeitblom mit, daß mehr als ein Jahr verging, ehe Adrian sich entschloß
das Mädchen, dessen Arm seine Wange gestreift hatte, aufzusuchen
(236) und daß dies im Mai 1906 war, wie wir an anderer Stelle lesen
(238). Bis zum Mai 1906 könnten höchstens sieben bis acht Monate
verstrichen sein. Ähnlichen Widersprüchen begegnen wir in bezug auf
die Dauer von Adrians Aufenthalt in Leipzig. Nach Seite 273 beläuft
sich Adrians Aufenthalt auf vier Jahre; Seite 278 hören wir von vier
und ein halb Jahren; später heißt es, er verließ Leipzig im September
1910 (287), was zu dem Datum seiner Übersiedlung nach München
stimmt. Es handelt sich danach um volle fünf Jahre. Wir gehen nicht
weiter auf Bedenken dieser Art ein, denn in allen Hauptpunkten ist
der Verlauf von Adrians Leben genau zu errechnen.

Ganz anders steht es um die Mitteilung, der Dom von Kaisers-
achern berge die Gruft Kaiser Ottos III. (56), eine Aussage, deren
Erinnerung noch an zwei späteren Stellen aufgefrischt wird. Der Leser hat längst vermutet, Kaisersaschern, die Heimatstadt des Biographen, in der er mit Adrian seine Schuljahre verbringt, sei ein fingier-
ter Name, aber die Landschaft, in der sich diese Stadt befindet, ist
durch eine Fülle von Stadtnamen als Thüringen gesichert. Mehr als
ein Dutzend Städtenamen, darunter Halle, Merseburg, Naumburg,
Wittenberg, bezeugen dies. Es ist das Land der sächsischen Kurfürsten

---

3　Voss, 83ff geht sehr genau ein auf eine ganze Reihe von kleinen Widersprü-
　chen in bezug auf die Chronologie von Adrians Leben. Sie zeigt, wie stark
　Thomas Mann in Verwirrung geraten ist. Sie erörtert viele Beispiele, nicht
　aber den Widerspruch in bezug auf die Dauer von Adrians Aufenthalt in
　Leipzig.

und der Ausgangspunkt von Luthers Reformation. Wenn wir uns aber in einem Nachschlagewerk über Otto III. informieren, um der gemeinten Stadt ihren Decknamen abzustreifen, so erfahren wir zu unserer Bestürzung, daß Otto III. im Dom zu Aachen beigesetzt ist, wie schon zweihundert Jahre vor ihm Karl der Große. Wir wissen nun also, nicht nur der Name, sondern die Stadt selbst ist eine Fiktion. Wie ist es möglich, fragen wir, dem seit Generationen seiner Heimatstadt verbundenen Zeitblom, dem Humanisten und Mann der Bildung, solche eine unerhörte historische Fälschung in den Mund zu legen? Solche Zumutung ist radikal indiskutabel. Serenus Zeitblom ist ein Ehrenmann, kein Memoiren schreibender Hochstapler. Also — wir können uns dieser Schlußfolgerung nicht verschließen — muß Thomas Mann, den wir ganz ausgeschaltet zu haben glaubten, verantwortlich sein für dieses so leicht zu entlarvende historische Falsum. Wie er dazu kam ist einerseits leicht zu erklären: er wollte damit der tausend Jahre alten Stadt einen Nimbus verleihen, in dem uralte historische Traditionen vibrieren, aus denen sich Träume zukünftiger Wiedererstehung und Weltherrschaft gestalten könnten. Andererseits enthält dieser willkürliche Eingriff in eine gesicherte jahrtausendalte Überlieferung etwas beunruhigend Fragwürdiges. Was hätte Thomas Mann wohl geantwortet, wenn man ihn darüber zur Rede gestellt hätte? Äußert sich in diesem Verstoß gegen die historische Wirklichkeit ein radikaler Nihilismus, der die deutsche Geschichte in ihrer ganzen Entwicklung ins Nichts zerstieben läßt? Oder ist der gefälschte Zug dahin berechnet, daß das Buch in erster Linie als Ware auf dem ausländischen, spezifisch amerikanischen Markt erscheinen wird für einen Leserkreis, dem die Voraussetzungen für ein tiefgehendes Verständnis der Problematik dieses Werkes fehlen und dessen eigenes Staatsgebilde kaum zweihundert Jahre zählt? Das historische Falsum wäre in dieser Beleuchtung ein Ausdruck von Menschenverachtung nach beiden Seiten hin, denn Thomas Mann konnte sich keinen Illusionen darüber hingeben, daß die junge Generation, die den Aufstieg des nationalsozialistischen Mythos und den Zusammenbruch Deutschlands erlebt hatte, den Zugang zu den Problemen und dem Stil seines Buches finden würde.

Ein Zweifel völlig anderer Art wird laut im Zusammemhang mit dem erschütternden Freitod Clarissa Roddes durch Zyankali, nachdem der aus einem Verführer zu einem verfluchten Erpresser gewordene Rechtsanwalt ihr durch einen anonymen Brief an den Bräutigam die erhoffte Rettung durch die Ehe mit diesem vereitelt hatte. Statt zu kommen, hatte ihr der Bräutigam den Brief geschickt und sie hatte ihm in ihrem Stolz und ihrer Verzweiflung einen Zettel hinterlassen, der die Worte enthielt: "Je t'aime. Une fois je t'ai trompé, mais je t'aime" (586). Daraufhin hatte sie das Gift genommen. Es ist unwahrscheinlich anzunehmen, daß ihr Stolz es ihr erlaubt hätte, sich der etwas leichtfertigen Mutter oder der anders gearteten Schwester anzuvertrauen. Dennoch schreibt der Biograph:

> Nach allem, was wir später in Erfahrung gebracht, müssen verzweifelte Szenen sich zwischen dem Mörder und seinem Opfer abgespielt haben. Vergebens flehte das Mädchen — zuletzt auf den Knien — ihn an, sie zu schonen, sie freizugeben, sie nicht zu nötigen, ihren Lebensfrieden mit dem Verrat an dem Manne zu bezahlen, der sie liebte, und dessen Liebe sie erwiderte. Eben dies Bekenntnis reizte den Unhold zur Grausamkeit. (583)

Wir fragen uns daraufhin, wie kann der Biograph von diesen verzweifelten Kämpfen erfahren haben, da sich alles, so weit wir wissen, im Geheimen zwischen dem Erpresser und seinem Opfer abspielte. Hier hat Thomas Mann offensichtlich auf die Schicksale seiner eigenen Schwester Carla zurückgegriffen, die er in seinem *Lebensabriß* (1930) streng sachlich geschildert hatte, großenteils mit den nämlichen Worten des *Doktor Faustus*, über deren Hintergrund er selbstverständlich genauer Bescheid wußte, als dies bei Zeitblom der Fall sein konnte. Wir stellen hier eine gewisse Flüchtigkeit in der Redigierung des *Doktor Faustus* fest. Hätte Thomas Mann über die oben angeführten Sätze weiter gesonnen, so hätte er sie vermutlich entweder ausführlicher motiviert oder gestrichen.[4]

Wenn Zeitblom in der eben behandelten Episode uns mehr gesagt hat, als er hat wissen können, so kehrt sich der Sachverhalt um, wo

---

4 Einer ähnlichen Flüchtigkeit begegnen wir in der Schilderung der Besucher bei Adrians Rede vor seinem Zusammenbruch. Unter anderen verlassen die Nottebohms den Saal. Bei Erwähnung Frau Nottebohms fällt der Nebensatz, "die wir 'die mütterliche Brust' zu nennen pflegten" (760). Diese Wendung, hier zum einzigenmal gebraucht, ist offenbar fehl am Platze mit ihrer humoristischen Wirkung. Wir erfahren ja durch Voss, daß Tochter Erika beauftragt worden war, den Text durch Streichungen radikal zu verkürzen.

das Verhältnis der Frau von Tolna zu Adrian Leverkühn zur Sprache
kommt. Wir stehen auf festem Boden, wenn wir sagen, Zeitblom hat
es für gut befunden, uns mit ganz spärlichen Indizien über die geheimnisvolle Dame abzuspeisen, die durch ihren sagenhaften Reich-
tum zur Vermittlerin zwischen Adrians Werk und der Welt wird. Wir
wissen, daß Adrians Nachlaß in Zeitbloms Hände überging, daß sich
die Briefe der Frau von Tolna darunter befanden, und daß er sie
nicht etwa ungelesen verbrannt hat. Denn wie hätte er sonst in Erfahrung bringen können, daß sie nicht nur allen Aufführungen seiner
Werke beigewohnt hatte, sondern daß sie darüber hinaus zu allen
Stätten gepilgert war, die seine Lebensspur bewahrten. Nicht nur sein
Vaterhaus Buchel, nicht nur die Familie Manardi in Palestrina hatte
sie aufgesucht, hatte sie doch unter dem Fenster von Adrians Arbeits-
raum in Pfeiffering gestanden, wie sie sich denn auch als verschleierte
Dame bei Adrians Begräbnis gezeigt hatte und dann wortlos verschwunden war. In der *Entstehung*[5] teilt uns Thomas Mann mit, daß
er diese Gestalt nach dem Muster von Frau von Meck, der Gönnerin
Tschaikowskys, eingeführt habe. Das mögen ihm andere glauben.
Hier hat Thomas Mann mit dem Leser sein Spiel getrieben, indem er
eine Motivierung vorschützte, die den Charakter banalster Kolportage
trägt. Ich bin nicht der erste, der so urteilt. Schon ein Jahr nach Erscheinen des Romans veröffentlichte Viktor Oswald[6] einen Aufsatz,
wo er es für selbstverständlich erklärt, daß die geheimnisvolle Fremde
keine andere sein könne als die Hetaera Esmeralda, deren Chiffre
h-e-a-e-s sich in Adrians musikalischen Werken seit seinem Besuch in
Preßburg im Mai 1906 immer wieder findet. Als der Musikagent Saul
Fitelberg (1923) Adrian für das persönliche Auftreten in der großen
Welt zu gewinnen sucht, fragt er, ob Adrian Frau von Tolna kenne.
Dieser verneint die Frage, aber ohne irgendwelche Neugier über die
Bewandtnisse dieser Freundin der neuen Musik an den Tag zu legen.
Der Briefwechsel mit Frau von Tolna muß spätestens 1918 begonnen
haben, als Adrian sich an die Komposition der "Apocalipsis cum fi-
guris" herantastete, denn wir erfahren, daß der erste Brief der Dame,

---

5   Mann, Thomas, *Die Entstehung des Doktor Faustus* (1949), S. 34.
6   Oswald, Victor A., Jr., "Thomas Mann's *Doktor Faustus*: The enigma of
     Frau von Tolna," *Germanic Review*, 23 (1948), 249-253.

aus Brüssel datiert, von der Sendung eines Ringes begleitet war, jenes großflächigen Ural-Smaragds, dem die zwei Verse des Kallimachos und die Umrisse des geflügelten Fabeltieres mit dem symbolischen Zungenpfeil eingraviert waren. Diesen Ring, den außer Zeitblom niemand zu sehen bekam, habe er während der Arbeit an dem apokalyptischen Werk stets getragen (599ff), und wir hören, daß dieses Werk in der ersten Hälfte des Jahres 1919 fast vollständig zustande kam (539 und 549). Wenn also der Briefwechsel zwischen Frau von Tolna und Adrian im Jahre 1918 einsetzte, so wären zwölf volle Jahre seit jenem Besuch in Preßburg verstrichen gewesen, wo er in irgendeinem Freudenhaus das begehrte Mädchen gefunden und trotz ihrer Warnung vor der Vergiftung die Süßigkeit ihres Leibes genossen hatte. Es bleibt der Phantasie überlassen, sich alles Übrige auszumalen – eine überwältigende Ergriffenheit beiderseits, der Schwur, einander nie wieder zu sehen. Wohl sehr bald darauf geschah der große, aber überaus nicht unvorstellbare Glückswechsel des Freudenmädchens, die Heirat mit dem ungarischen Lebemann, der dann im Sportrennen tödlich verunglückte und seine Witwe als Erbin eines Riesenvermögens zurückließ. Was können nicht diese zwölf Jahre zwischen Preßburg und jenem Brief aus Brüssel aus ihr gemacht haben? Von Adrians Antworten auf Frau von Tolnas Briefe können wir uns keine Vorstellung machen; vielleicht hatte der satanische Pakt auch diese Seite seines Seelchens unter einem Siegel verschlossen. Aber über Frau von Tolnas Briefe hätte uns Zeitblom Aufschluß geben können. Warum er mit keiner Silbe auf die Äußerung ihres Seelenlebens eingeht? Fehlte ihm, dem Mann klassischer Bildung, der Sinn für die seelischen Entwicklungsmöglichkeiten eines auf solcher Grundlage angesponnenen Verhältnisses? War seine Eifersucht auf die Begünstigte des anderen Geschlechts mit im Spiel? Oder bewahrte ihn ein Gefühl von Takt, Diskretion, Pietät vor der Enthüllung des Geheimnisses? Machte er sich den Denkspruch zu eigen, mit dem Adrian die Aufzeichnung des Teufelsgesprächs begonnen hatte: "Weistu was, so schweig."? Wir wissen es nicht. Ein Vorwurf ist Zeitblom aus diesem Schweigen nicht zu machen. Ich sehe Thomas Mann und Zeitblom sich mit einem vielsagenden Blick die Hände reichen zur Besiegelung des Geheimnisses.

Alles was wir hier angeführt haben als Bedenken erregend über die absolute Zuverlässigkeit des Biographen — die nicht ganz verläßliche Chronologie von Adrians Leben, die unmögliche Tatsache von der Kaisergruft in Kaisersaschern, die Kämpfe, die dem tragischen Untergang Clarissas vorausgehen, das ungelüftete Geheimnis um Frau von Tolna — betraf das Tatsachenmaterial. Wir fanden, daß der Autor dabei seine Hand mit im Spiele gehabt haben muß. Mit diesen Betrachtungen sind wir bei dem Punkt angelangt, der den eigentlichen Gegenstand dieser Untersuchung bildet und sie von vornherein veranlaßt hat. Es handelt sich um einen bestimmten Zusammenhang, um die Zurschaustellung eines bestimmten Namens, bei der dem im Grunde nichtsahnenden Biographen Zeitblom Thomas Mann die Feder geführt haben muß. Es handelt sich um den Namen des Barons Alexander von Gleichen-Rußwurm. Um es gerade heraus zu sagen, es handelt sich um Thomas Manns Abrechnung mit einem ihm bekannten Münchner Literaten dieses Namens. Da ein solches Verfahren ein Unikum im *Doktor Faustus* darstellt und auf raffiniert subtile Weise mit der Erzählung verflochten und in die Wege geleitet wird, ist es geboten, mit ausführlicher Gründlichkeit darauf einzugehen.

Zu Eingang wurde erwähnt, daß wir bei aller Nachprüfung des exakten Sachverhalts uns immer der Tatsache bewußt bleiben, daß Thomas Mann im *Doktor Faustus* sich in die zwei Figuren des Helden und seines Biographen aufgespalten hat, diese Figuren mithin fiktiv sind, und daß die private Sphäre, in der sich die beiden polaren Gestalten bewegen, in ihren Einzelheiten ebenfalls fiktiv ist. Selbstverständlich gilt dies auch für den ganzen Komplex privater Personen, deren Leben in das von Held und Biograph verflochten ist. Der Technik Thomas Manns gemäß, die er seit seinen Anfängen übt, hier aber in größtem Ausmaß befolgt, sind viele der unter dem Schleier von Decknamen begegnenden Gestalten dem eingeweihten Leser als mehr oder weniger genaue Abbilder von Personen aus Thomas Manns Familien- und Bekanntenkreis erkennbar. Es versteht sich von selbst, daß wir über etwa die Roddes und ihren Bekanntenkreis oder die Gelehrten und Künstler, die sich bei Sixtus Kridwiss zu Diskussionsabenden versammeln, im Adreßbuch keine Auskunft finden würden. Eine Ausnahme von dieser axiomatischen Regel der Verschleierung

bilden die Namen von Personen, die der breiten Öffentlichkeit ange-
hören, und deren Nennung genügt, dem mit der Zeitgeschichte ver-
trauten Leser die Erinnerung an die gemeinten Personen wachzuru-
fen, ohne daß der Autor genötigt wäre, die Genannten mit einem
Wort zu charakterisieren. So erfahren wir, daß Ansermet (277),
Bruno Walter, Klemperer und andere die Hand mit im Spiel hatten
bei der Erstaufführung von Adrian Leverkühns fiktiven musikalischen
Kompositionen. Die Kenntnis, beziehungsweise das Schwergewicht
dieser Namen, wird bei dem Leser vorausgesetzt. Dieselbe Orientie-
rung des Lesers wird erzielt, wo es sich im musikalischen Bereich um
fiktive Namen handelt. Wo aber Thomas Mann die eben genannten
Dirigenten mit ihrem bürgerlichen Namen einführt, bedeutet dies eine
Geste der Huldigung des Autors für ihm befreundete Meister. Ein
Fall besonderer Art liegt vor in der Person von Richard Strauss, wohl
der berühmtesten musikalischen Größe seiner Zeit, einem Mann, dessen Leben in München die ganzen zwanzig Jahre von Adrians Ver-
bleib in Oberbayern überspielt, und der doch nie mit Namen genannt
wird und Adrians Wege nirgends im Leisesten kreuzt. Es wird dafür
gesorgt, diese möglicherweise auffällige Lücke zu tilgen, indem, wie
wir uns erinnern, Adrian der Erstaufführung der *Salome* in Beglei-
tung seines Lehrers Wendell Kretzschmar in Dresden beiwohnt. Angeblich oder wirklich unternimmt Adrian einige Monate später eine
Reise nach Graz, um sich die Oper ein zweites Mal anzuhören. Von
der Begegnung mit der Hetaera Esmeralda in Preßburg zurückgekehrt,
wozu ihm die angebliche Reise nach Graz als Vorwand gedient hatte,
äußert sich Adrian Leverkühn folgendermaßen über das Wesen des
erfolgreichen Komponisten, unter geflissentlicher Vermeidung seines
Namens:

"Was für ein begabter Kegelbruder! Der Revolutionär als Sonntagskind, keck
und konziliant. Da waren Avantgardismus und Erfolgssicherheit vertrauter bei-
sammen. Affronts und Dissonanzen genug, – und dann das gutmütige Einlenken,
den Spießer versöhnend und ihn bedeutend, daß es so schlimm nicht gemeint
war... Aber ein Wurf, ein Wurf..." (241)

Diese Charakterisierung von Richard Strauss genügt, um jede Frage
darüber abzuschneiden, wie es möglich sei, daß Adrian mit dem berühmtesten in seiner unmittelbaren Umgebung ansässigen Komponisten seiner Zeit nie in persönliche Berührung gekommen ist. Der Ge-

gensatz der musikalischen Richtungen, in denen sich beide bewegen, motiviert die Tatsache, daß Adrian eine persönliche Begegnung vermied. Das Nennen von authentischen Personen außerhalb des musikalischen Bereichs wird in der Hauptsache vermieden, gerade für die sichtbarste Sphäre, die der großen Politik. So werden zwar Kaiser Wilhelm II. und sein Kanzler Bethmann-Hollweg für die Erinnerung des Lesers durch wenige scharfe Striche kenntlich gemacht, aber ohne mit Namen genannt zu werden.

Mit Hinsicht auf das Gesagte mustern wir nun Adrians geselligen Privatverkehr nach seiner Übersiedlung von Leipzig nach München im Herbst 1910. Sein Freund, der Dichter und Übersetzer Schildknapp, der ihm nach München gefolgt war, hatte von Berufs wegen Beziehungen zu einigen ansehnlichen Häusern angeknüpft, in die er auch Adrian einführte. Am repräsentativsten war der Verkehr mit den Schlaginhaufens,

einem älteren, vermögenden und kinderlosen Ehepaar, welches, der Mann von schwäbischer Herkunft und Privatgelehrter, die Frau aus Münchener Familie, in der Briennerstraße eine etwas düstere, aber prächtige Wohnung innehatte. Ihr säulengeschmückter Salon war der Treffpunkt einer das Künstlerische und das Aristokratische umfassenden Gesellschaft, wobei es der Hausfrau, einer geborenen von Plausig, das Liebste war, wenn beide Elemente sich in ein und derselben Person vereinigten, wie in der des Generalintendanten der königlichen Schauspiele, Exzellenz von Riedesel, der dort verkehrte. (312)

Exzellenz von Riedesel, München, 1910, den muß es gegeben haben, freilich unter anderem Namen.[7] Schon bei diesen einführenden Sätzen wittert der Leser, daß es bei den Ambitionen der Dame nicht an Stoff zu sozialer Satire fehlen dürfte. Fast unmittelbar anschließend heißt es dann:

Bei Schlaginhaufens hatte Rüdiger auch Adrian eingeführt, der dort denn also, ein einsilbiger Fremdling, mit geadelten Malergrößen, der Wagner-Heroine Tanja Orlanda, auch noch mit Felix Mottl, bayerischen Hofdamen, dem "Urenkel Schillers", Herrn von Gleichen-Rußwurm, der kulturgeschichtliche Bücher schrieb, und mit solchen Schriftstellern, die überhaupt nichts schrieben, sondern sich nur als Sprechliteraten gesellschaftlich interessant verausgabten, oberflächlich und folgenlos zusammentraf. (312)

---

7   Der Name Riedesel stammt nach Voss (75) aus Luthers Briefen wie eine Unzahl anderer Namen.

Mit diesem Satz sind wir auf das Kernstück eines behutsam im Verborgenen angelegten Aktes der Animosität Thomas Manns – beileibe nicht Zeitbloms – angelangt. Möglicherweise, sogar wahrscheinlicherweise, hat sich der nicht alarmierte Leser, dem die langen Satzperioden Thomas Manns im Gehör schwingen, beim Überfliegen dieses labyrinthisch gewundenen Satzes keiner verborgenen Fußangeln versehen, doch enthält dieser Satz eine höchst sorgfältig verborgene Zeitbombe, die bestimmt ist, erst mehr als ein Jahrzehnt später zu explodieren.[8] Anders gesprochen, es geht hier zu wie in einem Kartenspiel, wo von einem in allen Praktiken der Kunst erfahrenen Spieler unter der Hand eine falsche Karte in das Spiel eingeschmuggelt wird, ohne daß der Trick von den Mitspielenden bemerkt würde.[9] Wir müssen den genannten Satz einer gründlichsten Analyse unterziehen, um zu erfahren, auf wie raffinierte Weise Thomas Mann sich darin etwas Ungeheuerliches geleistet hat. Man denke, Thomas Mann führt in das Schlaginhaufensche Haus einen Herrn von Gleichen-Rußwurm, den Urenkel Schillers, noch dazu in Gänsefüßchen, noch dazu einen Schriftsteller, den muß es doch leibhaftig geben, nicht bloß als

---

8   Voss (91) zitiert die Vorform des Kernsatzes in dem großen Konvolut, das ihre Hauptquelle bildet. Darin findet sich unter anderen der Name Gleichen-Rußwurm, aber ohne die beiden Prädikate "Urenkel Schillers, der kulturgeschichtliche Bücher schrieb." Da die Verfasserin gleich darauf den ausgeformten Satz ohne Kommentar zitiert, scheint ihr das Einmalige der Nennung eines Münchener literarischen Kollegen Thomas Manns mit seinem bürgerlichen Namen nicht aufgefallen zu sein. Ähnlich verhält es sich gegen Ende bei Aufzählung all der Geladenen zu Adrians Vortrag. Zeitblom selber zählt die Gleichen-Rußwurms an letzter Stelle auf und ist überrascht über ihr Kommen. Voss dagegen zitiert aus dem Konvolut Thomas Manns Zusammenstellung der Liste der Geladenen, wo Gleichen-Rußwurm ohne Erwähnung seiner Frau wahllos in der Mitte untergebracht ist (203). Daß Voss diese Liste ohne Kommentar zitiert ist wieder ein Anzeichen dafür, daß sie nichts gemerkt hat.

9   In der *Entstehung*, S. 33f, berührt Thomas Mann diesen Sachverhalt:
     Die Einschwärzung lebender, schlechthin bei Namen genannter Personen unter die Figuren des Romans, von denen sie sich nun an Realität oder Irrealität nicht mehr unterscheiden, ist nur ein geringeres Beispiel für das Montageprinzip, von dem ich spreche.
     Die leicht hingeworfene Meinung des Verfassers, die einmal ausgespielten wirklichen Namen unterschieden sich fortan nicht mehr von den fiktiven, erlaubt sich unsere Arbeit aufs Entschiedenste zu bezweifeln.

Romanfigur auf dem Papier, und diesen Herrn dürfte, wie seinem Zwillingsbruder Exzellenz von Riedesel, der gleicherweise das Aristokratische wie das Künstlerische in ein und derselben Person verband, eine interessante Rolle im Verlauf der Erzählung zugeteilt werden. Der Satz, von dem wir sprechen, ist angefüllt von einer Reihe disparater Elemente, teils typisierender Art, wie die "geadelten Malergrößen" und die "bayerischen Hofdamen," teils werden Personen genannt wie die Wagner-Heroine mit dem prächtigen Namen Tanja Orlanda. Dann heißt es "auch noch mit Felix Mottl." Felix Mottl ist kein Deckname, sondern der Name eines seinerzeit berühmten Wagnerdirigenten, der wie Bruno Walter und Klemperer der Musikwelt angehört und keiner weiteren Bezeichnung bedarf. Sein Name kommt nur dies eine Mal vor, und zwar mit gutem Grund, denn er starb im Jahre 1911, während Adrians ersten neunmonatigen Aufenthaltes in München. Darum also das "auch noch"! Vielleicht aber spüren wir auch noch einen leise mitschwingenden Tadel über den Geist Münchens "mit seiner stehengebliebenen Wagnerei" (314). Gleich nach diesem für die damaligen Zeitgenossen wohlbekannten Namen Felix Mottl wird der Name des Barons von Gleichen-Rußwurm ausgespielt mit einer Unschuldsmiene, als ob nichts geschehen wäre. Und doch hat Thomas Mann mit der Nennung dieses Namens mit vollem Wissen einen Verstoß gegen die allgemein befolgten Konventionen der Romantechnik begangen. Mit Alexander von Gleichen-Rußwurm stellt Thomas Mann einen ihm wohlbekannten literarischen Kollegen auf die Beine, der, 1865 geboren, den größten Teil seiner Mannesjahre in München verlebte und erst am 25. Oktober 1947 verstarb, vielleicht in demselben Monat, in dem der *Doktor Faustus* auf dem Büchermarkt erschien. Dieser Verstoß gegen das literarische Herkommen muß seine Gründe haben. Vorwegnehmend ist zu bemerken, daß dem Baron im Verlauf des ganzen Romans nicht ein einziges Wort in den Mund gelegt wird, und daß er über die Signalisierung als Urenkel Schillers und Verfasser kulturgeschichtlicher Bücher hinaus mit nicht einem Wort persönlicher Charakterisierung bedacht wird, während wir doch alle übrigen im Roman auftretenden Figuren zu *sehen* bekommen! Der Satz läuft wie ein dem Namen des Barons angegliederter glänzender Kometenschweif seinem periodischen Ende zu, indem wir von solchen Schriftstellern hören, "die überhaupt nichts" schrieben. Wir unterbrechen mit der Frage: warum das "überhaupt"? Sind die kulturgeschichtlichen Bücher des Barons etwa als ein Nichts zu verstehen, das immerhin von etwas mehr Gewicht ist als das "überhaupt nichts" der interessanten Sprechliteraten? Nun noch die Schlußkadenz des labyrinthischen Satzes: mit denen Adrian "oberflächlich und folgenlos zusammentraf". Und dieses Allerdings leitet die Schilderung einer Dame ein, Jeanette Scheurl mit Namen, deren Umständen der Biograph eine volle Seite widmet und von der es heißt:

> Zwischen den Sprachen aufgewachsen, schrieb sie in einem reizend inkorrekten Privatidiom damenhafte und originelle Gesellschaftsstudien, die des psychologischen und musikalischen Reizes nicht entbehrten und unbedingt zur höheren Literatur zählten. (313)

Es vergehen Jahre — wir befinden uns im letzten Halb-Jahr vor Ausbruch des ersten Weltkrieges 1914 — bis wir uns wieder im Hause Schlaginhaufen einfinden, diesmal nicht nur im Beisein Adrians, sondern auch seines Biographen Zeitblom, der nicht darauf hinzuweisen vergißt, daß es ein viel weiterer und gehobenerer Kreis als bei den Roddes ist —,

> den der Ehrgeiz der Frau Dr. Schlaginhaufen, geb. von Plausig, um sich und ihren schwäbelnden, dabei sehr schwerhörigen Gatten zu versammeln wußte... (425)

Es kommt hier zu einer virtuosen Szene von 13 Seiten (425-37), in der die Glanzrolle zuerst dem bereits erwähnten Intendanten der königlichen Schauspiele, Exzellenz von Riedesel, zufällt, während er im zweiten Teil, immer noch sichtbar, von Chaim Breisacher, dem rabulistischen Verfechter eines Neuprimitivismus, in den Schatten gedrängt wird. Herr von Riedesel vertritt, wie es dem Geist des Hauses gemäß ist, einen Standpunkt durchaus konservativer Art.

> Dieser Hofmann, ein ehemaliger Reiteroberst, der auf seinen gegenwärtigen Posten einzig und allein aus dem Grunde befohlen worden war, weil er dafür bekannt gewesen war, ein wenig Klavier zu spielen (wieviele Jahrhunderte scheint heute die Zeit zurückzuliegen, wo man Generalintendant wurde, weil man von Adel war und dabei etwas Klavier spielte!) — (426)

Er war ohne Verständnis für das Neue, Aufkommende. Er protegierte das Ballett,

> und zwar, weil es "graziös" sei. Das Wort "graziös" bedeutete ihm ein konservativ-polemisches Schiboleth gegen das Modern-Aufrührerische. (426)

Vom russischen Ballett, von Tschaikowsky, Ravel und Stravinsky wußte er nichts. Was ihm beim Ballett vorschwebte, waren "Gazeröckchen, Spitzengetrippel und 'graziös' über den Kopf gebogene Arme – ..." (426). Dabei gelang es ihm, sogar Wagner in den Bereich des Konservativen, will sagen des Feudal-Graziösen, mit einzubeziehen. Es kommt an dem Abend zu improvisierten musikalischen Darbietungen, zu welchen auch Zeitblom, vom Intendanten aufgefordert, auf seiner Viola d'Amore verschiedenes beiträgt. Im folgenden tritt das Bild dieses Mannes ganz nahe vor unser Auge mit

seiner zwar süddeutsch gefärbten, aber vom Offizierston geschärften Sprechweise...

Wie schwach ist der Mensch! Ich war ihm dankbar, ich vergaß völlig meinen Widerwillen gegen seine glatte und leere, ja vor unverwüstlicher Unverschämtheit gewissermaßen klare Aristokratenphysiognomie mit dem gezwirbelten blonden Schnurrbart vor den rasierten Rundbacken und der blitzenden Monokelscheibe im Auge unter der weißlichen Braue. Für Adrian, das wußte ich wohl, stand die Figur dieses Ritters sozusagen jenseits jeder Bewertung, jenseits von Haß und Verachtung, ja jenseits des Gelächters; ... (428)

Nun ergreift Chaim Breisacher das Wort als Apologet eines wahrhaft radikalen Konservatismus, der alles, was bisher als Fortschritt gegolten, als Verfall bezeichnet, sei es auf dem Gebiet der Malerei, der Musik, der Religion. Daß er sein Programm der Rebarbarisierung mit Geist verficht, versteht sich von selbst. In unserem Zusammenhang muß es genügen, auf den Eindruck zu achten, den seine Suada auf den Intendanten macht, aus dessen Gesicht beim Entfallen seines Monokels jede Spur von Intelligenz geschwunden ist. Die ganze Szene in ihrem doppelten Aspekt als Satire auf den verknöcherten Konservatismus einerseits, und auf die Propheten einer kulturfeindlichen Erneuerung andererseits, gehört zu den lebendigsten Szenen im *Doktor Faustus*. Daß wir aber überhaupt auf diese Szene eingegangen sind, ist nicht ohne weiteres einleuchtend und kann an dieser Stelle nur andeutend begründet werden. Wir erinnern uns, daß Exzellenz von Riedesel, ein kapitaler Esel, wie wir jetzt zur Genüge wissen, als eine der Koryphäen des Hauses Schlaginhaufen eingeführt worden war, da er durch seinen altadligen Namen und seinen Beruf das Aristokratische und das Künstlerische in ein und derselben Person vereinigte, zur besonderen Genugtuung der Hausfrau, der geb. von

Plausig. In unmittelbarer Nähe war neben ihm der Name des "Urenkel Schillers," Herrn von Gleichen-Rußwurms, der kulturgeschichtliche Bücher schrieb, aufgetaucht, weil dieser Herr sich aus den gleichen Gründen der besonderen Gunst der "hochbeinig eleganten"
Hausfrau erfreute. Es wird noch sehr lange dauern, bis wir ein weiteres Wort über diesen erfahren. Kann man uns aber einen Vorwurf daraus machen, wenn wir mit der Witterung von *hindsight* die beiden
Herren als Pendants und Zwillingsbrüder bezeichnen? Bei der geradezu vernichtenden Satire, die Seine Exzellenz trifft, darf man an das
deutsche Sprichwort denken, das mit wortspielender Umkehrung am
Platze wäre: Man schlägt den Sack, aber meint den Esel. Es wird sich
an späterem Ort herausstellen, daß der Zwillingsbruder übertragener
Weise hier sein Teil abbekommen hat.

Wir überspringen nun ein ganzes Jahrzehnt, um die Namen der
beiden Herren, der Exzellenz von Riedesel und des nun mit gewollter
Lässigkeit als "Enkel Schillers" bezeichneten Barons, diesmal wirklich nachbarlich verkoppelt noch einmal zu vernehmen. Der Zusammenbruch Deutschlands im Jahre 1918 liegt bereits weit zurück, die
verheerende Inflation ist über das Land gegangen, wir befinden uns
am Ende des Jahres 1924, wo Adrian das Violinkonzert für Rudi
Schwerdtfeger bereits komponiert und sich Hand in Hand mit dem
Geiger in Bern und Zürich dem Publikum präsentiert hat. Eine unge-
heure Veränderung im Leben Adrians hatte damit bereits ihren Anfang genommen. Die Theaterdekorationskünstlerin Marie Godeau ist
jetzt in Adrians Gesichtskreis getreten, und er ist dem Zauber ihrer
schwarzen Augen und ihrer erzsympathischen Persönlichkeit in dem
Maße verfallen, daß er im Begriff ist, seinen Freund Rudi an eigener
Statt als Freiwerber zu ihr zu schicken. Soviel zur Kennzeichnung der
Situation. Es ist wieder ein Empfangsabend bei den Schlaginhaufens,
von dem Zeitblom berichtet:

> Das gesellschaftliche Bild hatte sich seit dem Kriege wesentlich geändert.
> Kein Baron Riedesel trat länger hier für das "Graziöse" ein; längst war der Kla-
> vier spielende Reitersmann in der Versenkung der Geschichte verschwunden, und
> auch den Enkel Schillers, Herrn von Gleichen-Rußwurm, gab es nicht mehr, da
> ein mit närrischer Ingeniosität erdachter, aber mißglückter Betrugsversuch,
> dessen er überwiesen war, ihn aus der Welt verscheucht und ihn zum quasi-frei-
> willigen Arrestanten auf seinem niederbayrischen Gute gemacht hatte. Die Sache

war fast nicht zu glauben. Der Baron hatte, angeblich, ein wohlverpacktes und sehr hoch, über seinen Wert, versichertes Schmuckstück zur Umarbeitung an einen auswärtigen Juwelier gesandt, — welcher, als das Paket bei ihm eintraf, nichts darin fand, als eine tote Maus. Diese Maus hatte untüchtigerweise die Aufgabe nicht erfüllt, die der Absender ihr zugedacht hatte. Offenbar war die Idee gewesen, daß der Nager sich durch die Hülle beißen und entkommen sollte, — die Illusion erzeugend, daß das Geschmeide durch das Gott weiß wie entstandene Loch gefallen und verloren gegangen sei, womit die Versicherungssumme fällig gewesen wäre. Statt dessen war das Tier verendet, ohne den Ausgang zu schaffen, der das Abhandenkommen des nie hineingelegten Colliers erklärt hätte, — und aufs lächerlichste sah der Erfinder des Schelmenstückes sich bloßgestellt. Möglicherweise hatte er es in einem kulturhistorischen Buche aufgepickt und war ein Opfer seiner Lektüre. Vielleicht aber auch trug ganz allgemein die moralische Verwirrung der Zeit an seiner verrückten Eingebung die Schuld. (644-5)

So haben wir denn Recht behalten mit unserer oben geäußerten Vermutung, der Theaterintendant und der kulturgeschichtsbücherschreibende Baron wären von Anfang an als Pendants, als ungleiche Zwillingsbrüder konzipiert worden. Den einen hatte der Biograph in der großen Szene, wenn das Wort erlaubt ist, durch den Kakao gezogen, der andere hatte jetzt sein Fett bekommen durch die mit behaglicher Breite vorgetragene Erzählung von dem Schelmenstück mit der untüchtigen Maus. Schadenfreude und Spott könnten nicht unverhüllter zu Tage treten als es hier geschieht, mit der humoristischen Motivierung und dem bewußten Anglizismus "aufgepickt." Es dauert eine Weile, bis man sich von dem Schock erholt, den dieses Losgehen der Zeitbombe bewirkt. An der Tatsächlichkeit des Berichteten ist keinen Augenblick zu zweifeln. Die Aufdeckung des kompromittierenden Schelmenstücks muß sich im Lichte der Öffentlichkeit abgespielt haben, vermutlich im Jahre 1923, jedenfalls nicht später als 1924. Unter dem Aspekt der Montagetechnik[10] bietet dieses Stück krassester Wirklichkeit eine Antwort auf die Frage: Wie wird man aus einer Privatperson zu einer öffentlichen Person? Antwort: durch einen öffentlichen Skandal. Man erinnere sich: der Baron war noch am Leben, als der *Doktor Faustus* auf dem Büchermarkt erschien.

---

10 Warum weder Bergsten noch Voss sich veranlaßt gesehen hat, dieses Stück Montage mit seinem Wirklichkeitssubstrat zu vergleichen wüßte ich nicht zu sagen.

Man bedenke ferner, das mißglückte Schelmenstück lag um zwei Jahr-
zehnte zurück, als Thomas Mann den *Doktor Faustus* schrieb. Mithin
kann von einer Entstellung der Tatsachen, durch Gerüchte, die während des Krieges nach Amerika gelangten, wo Thomas Mann schrieb,
nicht die Rede sein. Man erwäge ferner, wie leicht es möglich gewesen wäre, den kulturgeschichtliche Bücher schreibenden Münchner
Kollegen unter einem Decknamen anzuprangern, was die Ergötzlich-
keit der Entlarvung des Schwindels um keine Spur verringert hätte;
aber freilich den "Urenkel Schillers" als steckbriefliche Bezeichnung
des Täters hätte Thomas Mann dann fallen lassen müssen, was offensichtlich seinen Absichten zuwider gewesen wäre. Um das Kind beim
rechten Namen zu nennen, müssen wir sagen, es geht bei der Einführung des Urenkels Schillers in den Roman um eine Abrechnung, um
eine Züchtigung, um einen Akt kalter Rache. Wenn wir aber nach
den Gründen fragen, die Thomas Mann zu dieser unerhörten Anpran-
gerung eines literarischen Kollegen und zweifellos persönlich Bekannten bewogen haben dürften, falls keine Zeugnisse von Überlebenden
bzw. aus Briefen und Tagebüchern zum Vorschein kommen, so sind
wir auf Vermutungen angewiesen. Thomas Mann hat bekanntlich das
Wort geprägt, Schriftsteller seien Menschen, denen das Schreiben
schwerer fällt als anderen Leuten. Hatte es seinen Spott gereizt, daß
des Barons Ergiebigkeit mehr als achtzig Bände auf dem Büchermarkt
abgesetzt hatte? Hatte der Baron sich seines berühmten Urgroßvaters
als Aushängeschild bedient, um die Qualität seiner eigenen Produktion in ein günstiges Licht zu stellen? War er, der Besitzer des Binde-
strich-Adelsnamens und des alten Schlosses Greifenstein, dem bloß
bürgerlichen Kollegen herablassend begegnet? Hatte der Baron bei
persönlicher Begegnung es Thomas Mann deutlich, vielleicht über-
deutlich zu verstehen gegeben, daß er durch seine Einheirat in eine
jüdische Familie für die maßgebenden Kreise als deklassiert zu betrachten sei? Hatten politische Differenzen der Nachkriegszeit das
Feuer von Thomas Manns Animosität geschürt? Wir wissen es nicht.[11]

---

11 Mir ist ein einziger dokumentarischer Hinweis bekannt, der die Feindselig-
    keit Thomas Manns gegenüber dem Baron bestätigt. In den wiederholt ver-
    öffentlichten Tagebuchaufzeichnungen "Leiden an Deutschland," die Tho-
    mas Mann 1933 bis 34 aus dem Exil schrieb, hat er stichwortartige Eintra-

Sind wir jetzt fertig? Ist der Baron mit der Mauseepisode endgültig von der Bildfläche verschwunden? Keineswegs, zu unserer wie
auch des Biographen Überraschung. Neben seiner Bestimmung, dem
Autor die Genugtuung einer grausamen Abrechnung zu verschaffen,
ist ihm eine zweite Funktion zugewiesen, der er mühelos gewachsen
ist. Es ist Mai 1930, Adrian hat sein symphonisches Chorwerk "Doktor Fausti Weheklag" vollendet. Ganz entgegen seiner üblichen Scheu
vor der Öffentlichkeit, trifft er Vorkehrungen, einem Kreis von
Freunden und Bekannten Proben aus dem Klavierauszug mit Erläu-
terungen vorzutragen. Dies ist der Rahmen für die Schlußszene mit
Adrians Beichte und seinem Zusammenbruch. Es handelt sich um

---

gungen zu der sogenannten Säuberungsaktion vom 30. Juni 1934 gemacht,
in der Ernst Röhm, der Begründer und Führer der SA, der General von
Schleicher nebst einer großen Anzahl führender sowohl rechts wie links
stehender Persönlichkeiten liquidiert wurden. Ich zitiere aus dieser Eintra-
gung:

Die Zahl der Getöteten liegt im dunklen. Sie ist sicher sehr groß. E. Jung
ist erschossen — er schrieb die "Herrschaft der Minderwertigen". General
von Bredow, der Katholik Klausener, zehn, zwölf weitere konservative
Patrioten ermordet. Schleicher glaubte, daß sie es nicht wagen würden; er
irrte. Die Reichswehr hat ihn geopfert, nachdem Blomberg sich mit Hitler
und Göring verständigt, und Neudeck, der ihn haßte, deckte ihn nicht, wie
Papen, der entrann. — Der "Herrenklub", nationalistisch und reaktionär
genug, ist aufgelöst, v. Gleichen und andere ins Ausland entkommen. Ich
bemitleide diese Schrittmacher des Elends nicht, ... (*Gesammelte Werke*,
Bd. XII, 1960, S. 736)
(Die Notiz über das Entkommen von Gleichens ins Ausland beruht offensichtlich auf einem falschen Gerücht, denn der Baron hat Deutschland nie
verlassen.) Wie ich jetzt sehe, beruht mein Hinweis auf den eben angeführten
Passus auf falschen Voraussetzungen. Das Generalregister in Band XIII der
Gesammelten Werke verweist unter dem Namen Alexander Freiherr von
Gleichen-Rußwurm auf unsere Stelle Band XII, 736. Da ich mich veranlaßt
fühlte, mich näher über den Herrenklub zu informieren und dabei den
Brockhaus und den großen *Meyer* zu Rate zog, fand es sich, daß der in unserem Passus genannte v. Gleichen nicht mit Alexander von Gleichen-Rußwurm identisch ist. Gemeint ist vielmehr Raimund August Heinrich von
Gleichen, führendes Mitglied des Berliner Herrenklubs, der nach der Regierung Papen 1932 an Bedeutung verlor. Dem *Brockhaus* zufolge wurde der
Herrenklub 1944 aufgelöst. Bei Thomas Mann, der seine Quelle nachschreibt,
steht das Datum der Auflösung 1934, was stimmen dürfte. Der ganze Hinweis im Register Band XIII beruht auf einem Irrtum. Ob Thomas Mann
selbst den von Gleichen des Herrenklubs mit seinem Münchner Bekannten
verwechselt hat, entzieht sich meiner Beurteilung.

etwa dreißig Personen. Teils bestellt Zeitblom die Einladungen, teils läßt er dies durch Rüdiger Schildknapp besorgen. Alle sagen ihre Beteiligung zu; sogar manche nicht Geladene, die von der Veranstaltung gehört haben, bemühen sich um Zulaß, was ihnen gewährt wird. Beim Überdenken der Situation regt sich in mir der verrückte Wunsch, Zeitblom möchte seine Biographie durch Einfügung etwa des folgenden Satzes bereichert haben: 'Unter diesen letzteren, die um eine Einladung baten, befand sich auch der bekannte Romanschriftsteller und Essayist Thomas Mann, von dessen reger Aufgeschlossenheit für neue Musik ich bis dahin nicht einmal von Hörensagen wußte. Er erschien wie alle übrigen'. Daß es einen solchen Satz in dem biographischen Werk des Humanisten, der das Leben Adrian Leverkühns zwischen Mai 1943 und August 1945 schrieb, nicht gibt, ist kennzeichnend für die literarischen Konventionen jener Epoche, und trägt dazu bei, die Verletzung der Konventionen im Falle Gleichen-Rußwurms in um so grellerem Lichte erscheinen zu lassen. Heute — ich schreibe im Jahre 1976 — ist man an eine solche Vermischung der Sphären schon zu sehr gewöhnt, um besonderes Aufheben darüber zu machen. Zeitblom zählt nun die Geladenen in wahlloser Reihenfolge auf, wie sein Gedächtnis es ihm eingibt. Anscheinend mit seiner Aufzählung zu Ende gekommen,[12] fährt er fort:

Wer sich, zu meiner völligen Überraschung, und wohl nicht nur zu meiner, ebenfalls eingefunden hatte, war Baron Gleichen-Rußwurm, der sich, so viel mir bekannt, seit der Geschichte mit der Maus zum allerersten Mal wieder mit seiner fülligen, aber eleganten Gemahlin, einer Österreicherin, gesellschaftlich blicken ließ. Es stellte sich heraus, daß Adrian ihm schon acht Tage im Voraus eine Einladung auf sein Schloß gesandt hatte, und wahrscheinlich war der so sonderbar kompromittierte Schiller-Enkel der eigenartigen Gelegenheit zu sozialer Wiederanknüpfung recht froh gewesen. (748-9)

Die Baronin Gleichen ging umher, Sympathie nachsuchend für das abstruse Mißgeschick, von dem ihr Gatte und sie betroffen worden. "Sie wissen doch, wir haben ja dieses ennui gehabt", sagte sie da und dort. (749)

Damit verschwindet das gräfliche Paar endgültig aus unserem Blickfeld. Blickfeld ist übrigens ein fragwürdiger Ausdruck, da wir den Baron ja nie zu Gesicht bekommen, geschweige denn, daß er den Mund zu einem einzigen Wort geöffnet hätte. Diesen Tatbestand vielleicht

---

12 Vgl. Anmerkung 8.

nicht überflüssigerweise unterstreichend, zeichnet der Verfasser mit ein paar Strichen die Umrisse der Baronin. Füllig aber elegant nennt er sie, eine geborene Österreicherin.

Dies ist das einzige Mal, daß Baron von Gleichen-Rußwurm, allerdings völlig gesichtslos, am Arm seiner Gattin Zutritt zu einer Szene erhält, und zwar zu der erschütterndsten Szene des ganzen Werkes. Was hat Thomas Mann dazu bewogen, dem des mißglückten Schelmenstreichs überwiesenen, dem öffentlichen Gelächter preisgegebenen Herrn, der sich, wie sein großer Ahnherr gesagt haben würde, "in seines Nichts durchbohrendem Gefühle" daraufhin von der Gesellschaft zurückgezogen hatte, einen Platz in dem Nikesaal zu gönnen?

Fragen wir lieber zuerst, was vermochte Adrian Leverkühn, dem übelbeleumdeten Herrn bereits acht Tage vorher eine persönliche Einladung zu schicken? Die Antwort auf diese Frage hebt unsere Betrachtungen in eine höhere Sphäre. Was war der Kern von Adrians Satanismus gewesen? Es war die Superbia, der Hochmut, der den Satan dazu getrieben hat, sich gegen Gott zu empören. In Adrians Fall ist es der Hochmut gegenüber allem Göttlichen und Menschlichen, es ist die Kälte, das Abstandnehmen, das sich bei allen feierlichen Gelegenheiten regende spöttische Gelächter, der unwiderstehliche Drang, das Heilige zu parodieren. Ist aber Adrian derselbe geblieben, wie wir ihn seit seiner Kindheit kannten? In den letzten Jahren haben ihn eine Reihe schwerer Schicksalsschläge getroffen — der Abfall des Freundes und dessen jäher Tod, der Verlust der geliebten Frau, endlich der schreckliche Tod des engelgleichen Knaben Echo — die darauf angelegt waren, ihn entweder zu unentrinnbarer Verstocktheit eines zur Hölle Prädestinierten, oder zur Lösung seiner seelischen Starrheit zu führen. Dies ist ja das theologische Dilemma, und wir erinnern uns aus dem Satansgespräch, daß der Teufel Adrian auf das Bündigste demonstriert hatte, es würde ihm nie gelingen, über seinen Intellektualismus hinwegzukommen und sich der göttlichen Unerforschlichkeit auf Gnade und Ungnade zu unterwerfen. Immer würde er bei allen Versuchen, sich zu unterwerfen, die Initiative dabei wahren wollen, wie ein Hazardspieler, der den Gegenpart stets zu überbieten sucht, um das göttliche Wesen zu zwingen, auf seine Gebärde zu *reagieren*, was natürlich das Gelingen eines sol-

chen Experiments von vornherein zum Scheitern verurteilen würde.
Nun meine ich, es gibt in unserem Roman eine Reihe von Anzeichen,
die dafür sprechen, daß "Das Verlangen nach Seele ... eine inständige
Bitte um Seele" (576) in Adrian lebendig geblieben ist. Hatte er nicht
seinerzeit die Komposition von Klopstocks "Frühlingsfeyer" als
Sühneopfer unternommen, als Gegenstück zu der blasphemischen
Ironie, die in dem Titel der Symphonie "Wunder des Alls" zum Ausdruck kommt? Oder man denke an den Wutanfall, der ihn während
der Marterung Echos ergriff, wo er dem Teufel zurief:

> Nimm ihn, Auswurf! schrie er auf und trat wieder zurück von mir, wie ans
> Kreuz. – Nimm seinen Leib, über den du Gewalt hast! Wirst mir seine süße Seele
> doch hübsch zufrieden lassen müssen, und das ist deine Ohnmacht und dein
> Ridikül, mit dem ich dich ausspotten will Äonen lang. Mögen auch Ewigkeiten
> gewälzt sein zwischen meinen Ort und seinen, ich werde doch wissen daß er ist,
> von wo du hinausgeworfen wurdest, Dreckskerl, und das wird netzendes Wasser
> sein für meine Zunge und ein Hosianna dir zum Hohn im untersten Fluch! (724)

Man denke auch an sein verstörtes Grübeln über den unfaßbaren göttlichen Ratschluß der Prädestination zur Verdammnis, dies nach
Dante das Schicksal aller derer, zu denen die Botschaft des Heils nie
gedrungen war. Oder an das Grübeln, in das Adrian verfällt bei dem
Auftauchen des Prädestinationsgedankens in den Nachtgebeten des
kleinen Echo.

Alles dies erwogen, scheint es mir, rein subjetiv gesprochen, unzweifelhaft, daß Adrian in, mit und unter seinem Zusammenbruch
das Heil gefunden hat. Die herzbewegende Rede der Frau Schweigestill, die, wie schon an früherer Stelle (320-324) das Stichwort vom
"menschlichen Verständnis" umkreist, ist wie ein antiker Chorus,
wie der Engelchor am Ende von *Faust II*. Aufgrund des Wortlautes
des Textes der Beichte allein, ohne auf das, was Thomas Mann in
der *Entstehung* und späterhin Adorno darüber berichtet hat, einzugehen, ist es für mich einwandfrei klar, daß die Gottheit ein min-
destens ebenso großes Verständnis für den Fall Adrian aufbringen
müßte, wie Elsbeth Schweigestill menschlicherweise voraussetzt.[13]

---

13 Der ganze Streit über Seelenheil oder Verdammnis Adrians scheint mir da-
    durch verursacht, daß man dabei sich immer der Tatsache bewußt bleibt,
    daß unter dem Symbol des Doktor Faustus nicht nur Adrian, sondern im-
    mer auch Deutschland mitverstanden wird. So lautet die Frage das eine Mal:

Für Adrians Absage an seinen Satanismus spricht jeder Satz seiner Beichte, jeder Atemzug seines langen Besinnens, wie auch der auf sein Inneres konzentrierte Blick des Vortragenden, der mit keiner Miene, keinem Wimpernzucken auf das Dreinreden der teils amüsierten, teils schockierten Zuhörer und das Verschwinden eines Teils der Geladenen eingeht. Seinen Biographen, den Freund seiner Jugend, hatte er mit überraschend herzlichen Worten zu Anfang erwähnt, was diesem die Tränen in die Augen getrieben. Den Kreis der Geladenen angehend, hatte Adrian mit würdigem Freimut von ihnen Abstand genommen.

"Nun habe ich zu euch eine freundliche christliche Bitt, ihr wollet mein Fürtragen nicht in Argem auf- und annehmen, sondern es zum besten verstehen, denn ich ein wahrhaft Verlangen habe, euch Guten und Harmlosen, wenn nicht Unsündigen, so doch nur gewöhnlich und erträglich Sündigen, die ich darum herzlich veracht, aber inbrünstig beneide, ein voll, mitmenschlich Geständnis zu tun ..." (753)

Dies ist sachliche Feststellung, weder überheblich noch hysterisch verzückt. Es gibt auch eine "stolze Zerknirschung" (382), hören wir Adrian am Ende des Teufelsgesprächs dem Unterredner entgegenhalten, der ihn schon in der Tasche zu haben glaubt. Das Sündenregister, dessen er sich zeiht, einschließlich des vorbedachten Mordes an seinem Freund, ist, wie ich meine, als ein Fall metaphysischer Erkenntnis zu deuten, die alle psychologische Selbsterforschung hinter sich läßt. So deute ich denn auch die handschriftliche Einladung, die er dem kompromittierten Baron zugeschickt hatte, als Zeichen aufkeimender Demut: dieser Herr, der sich das kalte Gelächter der Welt wegen seines mißglückten Schelmenstreichs zugezogen hat, was ist er anders als ein harmloser, mittelmäßiger und erträglicher Sünder, und wie sollte ich es mir zukommen lassen, ihn von dem Anhören meiner Beichte auszuschließen? Diese einfache Erwägung zeigt, wie mir scheint, in voller Deutlichkeit, daß der Figur des Barons mit dem hohen Ahnen über das persönliche Rachegelüst des Verfassers hinaus eine Funktion zugedacht ist, die den Gestaltlosen zu einem wichtige-

---

gelangt Adrian zum Heil? und zum anderen Mal: entgeht Deutschland der völligen seelischen Vernichtung? Je nach den Umständen haben sich Serenus im Doktor Faustus und Thomas Mann in Aufsätzen und Briefen verschieden darüber geäußert.

ren Element der Erzählung macht als so viele andere, die im Besitz voller Leiblichkeit vor unseren inneren Augen stehen. Es wäre allerdings möglich, daß diese zweite Funktion des Barons einem späten, sozusagen inspirierten Einfall entsprungen sei außerhalb aller berechnenden Planung. Aber selbst wenn dies der Fall wäre, täte es der genialen Verwendung dieser Figur an dieser Stelle keinen Eintrag. Daß Adrian den Baron eigenhändig bereits acht Tage vor der Veranstaltung eingeladen hat, bestätigt den Eindruck des Vorbedachten in Ton und Wortlaut von Adrians Beichte.

Wenn wir nun die zwei Funktionen bedenken, die dem Baron zugefallen sind – für Thomas Mann die Befriedigung eines lang genährten Rachegelüsts, für Adrian Leverkühn die Bestätigung der radikalen Absage an seinen hochmütigen Satanismus – so finden wir uns versucht zu sagen: nicht nur die erste Funktion hat Teil an der Prägung des Bildes, das der Verfasser des *Doktor Faustus* von seiner eigenen Persönlichkeit wissentlich und willentlich entwirft; er ist zwar der Mann des zähen Gedächtnisses, der keine Verletzung seines Selbstgefühls ungestraft hingehen läßt, er ist aber zugleich der human tolerante Weise, der für die Schwächen des Durchschnittsmenschen ein lächelndes Verständnis aufbringt. Thomas Mann hat selbst dafür gesorgt, daß diese Auffassung der zwei Funktionen sich uns aufdrängt. "Alles haben wollen" ist ein Leitmotiv, das an verschiedenen Stellen auftaucht. Es findet seine Anwendung auf den Typus des Deutschen, der mit seiner Dialektik nach beiden Seiten hin alles haben möchte.

"Die Deutschen, sagte der neugebackene Student [Adrian], einen Grashalm im Munde, – haben eine doppelgeleisige und unerlaubt kombinatorische Art des Denkens, sie wollen immer eins und das andere, sie wollen alles haben. Sie sind imstande, antithetische Denk- und Daseinsprinzipien in großen Persönlichkeiten kühn herauszustellen. Aber dann vermantschen sie sie, ..." (135)

Ines Rodde warnt während der Faschingswoche 1911 Adrian davor, sich von Rudi Schwerdtfeger bestricken zu lassen. "Sie sollten ihm den Gefallen nicht tun. [ein Violinkonzert für ihn zu schreiben] Er möchte alles haben." Worauf Schwester Clarissa einfällt, "Vielleicht möchte auch Herr Leverkühn alles haben" (316). So dürften wir wohl berechtigt sein, dieses Wort auch auf den, der es geprägt hat, anzuwenden. Auch Thomas Mann möchte alles haben.

Nachtrag

Wir haben uns am Abschluß dieser Arbeit in aller Kürze mit dokumentarischem Material zu befassen, das über den Baron von Gleichen-Rußwurm Aufschluß gibt. Da ist der Nachruf von Linus Birchler (1947), der Artikel im Kosch, *Deutsches Literatur-Lexikon* (1949) und die Biographie in der *Neuen Deutschen Biographie* in dem Band des Jahres 1964. Der Nachruf von Linus Birchler erschien in Nr. 261 der *Neuen Zürcher Nachrichten* (1947). Eine Photokopie dieses Schriftstücks verdanke ich der Freundlichkeit Herrn Prof. Dr. Hans Wyslings vom Thomas Mann Archiv in Zürich. Ich setze eine Abschrift im vollen Wortlaut hierher.

† Alexander von Gleichen-Rußwurm

Der Urenkel Friedrich Schillers

Mit der im Zeitalter des rasend schnellen Verkehrs üblichen Verspätung gelangt in die Schweiz die Nachricht, daß am 25. Oktober 1947 in Baden-Baden der Urenkel Friedrich von Schillers im Alter von 82 Jahren entschlafen ist. Schillers jüngste Tochter, Emilie, 1804 in Weimar geboren, vermählte sich 1828 mit dem bayerischen Kammerherrn Adalbert von Gleichen-Russwurm; sie starb 1872 auf Schloss Greifenstein in Unterfranken, wo ihr Enkel, nachdem er den Hauptteil der Hinterlassenschaft seines erlauchten Ahn dem Goethe-Schiller-Archiv in Weimar geschenkt hatte, aus besonders wertvollen Erinnerungsstücken ein exquisites kleines Schillermuseum eingerichtet hatte.

Alexander von Gleichen war im Wesen kulturhistorischer und philosophischer Schriftsteller, obwohl er auch Verse, Dramen und Romane hinterläßt. Sein Hauptwerk ist die sechsbändige "Geschichte der europäischen Geselligkeit", ein Werk, das von enzyklopädischem Wissen zeugt. Die Gesamtzahl seiner Bücher beläuft sich auf über achtzig.

Alexander von Gleichen ist nicht dem "Los der Epigonen" verfallen gewesen; er verstand es, im gigantischen Schatten des Ahnherrn ein Eigener zu sein. In reizvoller Art verkörperte er den Typus des in der deutschen Literatur seltenen Dichter-Gelehrten, mit den französischen Kulturphilosophen und den Brüdern Goncourt verwandt. Er wusste sein erstaunliches Wissen nicht mit der Pedanterie des deutschen Gelehrten, sondern im geistvollen Stile des "écrivain" auszubreiten. Dies gilt nicht nur von seinen kulturgeschichtlichen Arbeiten, sondern auch von seinen philosophischen Büchern. Von diesen letzteren haben "Sieg der Freude", "Freundschaft" und "Der freie Mensch" besonderen Erfolg gefunden. Vielleicht das köstlichste Buch Alexander von Gleichens ist seine

"Weltgeschichte in Anekdoten und Querschnitten". Die historische Anekdote kann dem Wissenden blitzartig Menschen, Geschehnisse und Zeitsituationen enthüllen. Das letzte Werk Alexander von Gleichen-Russwurms liegt im Manuskript vor, "Lob der Armut". Es steht zu hoffen, dass dieses Buch, das dem wahren Geiste der Schweiz vielfältig huldigt, in unserem Lande bald erscheinen wird.

Der Heimgegangene war politisch sehr unabhängig. Bei den braunen Bestien war er schlecht angeschrieben, obwohl er im Buche "Das wahre Gesicht, Weltgeschichte des sozialistischen Gedankens", nach der Diktatur Ludendorffs auch die Gefahr von links aufgezeigt hatte. Dem Nationalsozialismus missfiel heftig sein prachtvolles Büchlein "Der freie Mensch", und nicht besser behagte den Herren der gedruckte Vortrag "Diplomatie". Vor allem aber stiess man sich am Europäertum des letzten Nachkommens Schillers. Die Herren des Tausendjährigen Reiches haben dem Dichter-Philosophen nach ihrer Weise mitgespielt, ihn mit einem plump-raffiniert aufgezogenen Postbetrugs-Schwindel zu kompromittieren versucht, was ihnen zum guten Teile leider gelungen ist, und ihn schliesslich hundertfältig schikaniert, weil er sich nicht anbiedern wollte. Frankreich hatte dem Nachkommen Schillers gegenüber sofort nach dem Zusammenbruch der tausendjährigen Herrlichkeit eine schöne Geste aufgebracht: Alexander von Gleichen-Russwurm wurde zum Ehrenbürger Frankreichs ernannt, gleich seinem illustren Urgrossvater. Die Todesanzeige führt diesen Titel neben dem eines Reichsfreiherrn. Die Franzosen sorgten seit 1945 für den Greis; in ihrer Zone, in Baden-Baden, ist er entschlafen, von seiner Gattin, einer geborenen von Thienen-Adlerflycht, seiner geehrten Mitarbeiterin, betreut.

Dass Gleichen-Russwurm sich zur S c h w e i z hingezogen fühlte, ist fast selbstverständlich. Schweizer Schriftsteller verkehrten gerne in seinem Münchner Heim, an der jetzt in den Boden gebombten Prinzregentenstrasse. 1927, als sich das Aufsteigen der braunen Wolken immer deutlicher erkennen liess, beschlossen Alexander und Sonja von Gleichen-Russwurm, den Bestand des Schillermuseums in Schloss Greifenstein ob Bonnland (in Franken) der Schweiz zu schenken. Wir dachten damals an Altdorf, dessen Tellspielhaus eine Weihestätte Schillers geworden ist. Aber die Reichsregierung, die von dem Projekt Wind bekam, legte Hand auf die Sammlung.

Alexander von Gleichen-Russwurm, physisch seinem mütterlichen Ahnherrn ähnlich, war eine aristokratische und zugleich sehr demokratische Natur. In einem Gedenkbuch zu seinem 60. Geburtstag schrieb ich 1925: "Das Trostvollste, was ich von einem düsteren Kriegswinter (1915-16) in München mit in unsere helvetische Insel zurücknahm, war die Erinnerung an Sie und Ihren Kreis. Das heute geschmähte Wort von der wahrhaft europäischen Gesinnung fand in Ihrem gastlichen Heim seine hellste Erfüllung: aus geläutertem Volksempfinden heraus erwuchs übernationales Verstehen. Unvergesslich, wie ich damals aus dem Munde Ihrer Gattin den ersten spontanen Nachruf auf den gefallenen Charles Péguy hörte, seine eigenen Verse: "Heureux ceux qui sont morts dans les grandes batailles." – R.I.P.

Linus Birchler.

Der Nachruf zeigt in jedem Satz, daß er von einem Freund und Verehrer des Barons, einem Schweizer, verfaßt ist. Der Anfang mit seinem Blick auf die Familiengeschichte ist unbeholfen stilisiert mit dem zweimaligen "hatte," das, wörtlich genommen, den Baron hätte sieben Jahre alt sein lassen, als er die Verfügungen über seine Schiller-reliquien traf. Dies ganz beiläufig. Er rühmt die Gastfreundlichkeit des Grafen, seine warme Menschlichkeit, die über die Schranken des Nationalen weit hinausging, seine politische Unabhängigkeit, seine außerordentliche literarische Produktion, — und macht eine beträchtliche Anzahl seiner Schriften namhaft. Seine Art der Produktion läßt ihn dem Typus des französischen écrivain verwandt erscheinen, nicht dem des deutschen Dichtergelehrten.

Wir fassen nun aus dem Bericht drei Punkte ins Auge, die zu kritischer Überprüfung auffordern:

(1) "Den plump raffinierten Versuch," den Baron durch einen "mißglückten Postbetrugsschwindel" zu kompromittieren, mit dem Eingeständnis, daß dies leider zum guten Teil gelungen sei und anschließend daran die hundertfältigen Schikanen von seiten der "braunen Bestien";

(2) Den Versuch, den kostbareren Teil seiner exquisiten Sammlung von Schiller-Reliquien der Schweiz zu "schenken";

(3) Die Erlangung des französischen Ehrenbürgerrechts nach dem deutschen Zusammenbruch.

Zum ersten Punkt ist zu sagen, Birchlers gewundene Erwähnung der Episode von der "untüchtigen Maus" scheint Thomas Manns Darstellung eher zu bestätigen als zu widerlegen, obgleich der Freund entschuldigend andeutet, der Baron sei in eine Falle gegangen. Über das Wann und Wie dieser skandalösen Episode müßten Zeitungen und Zeitschriften aus den Jahren 1923-24 ausführlich berichtet haben, falls Thomas Manns Einordnung der Episode in das Zeitschema des *Doktor Faustus* stimmt, und es gälte nun einfach, die betreffenden Organe aufzufinden und ihre jeweilige politische Färbung in Rechnung zu stellen, eine Aufgabe, der ich mich leider nicht unterziehen kann.

Zu Punkt zwei gestehe ich von vornherein, daß ich mich der Darstellung im Nachruf gegenüber skeptisch verhalte. Es war das Jahr

1927, vier Jahre nach der verheerenden Inflation, die den Besitz ganzer Gesellschaftsklassen vernichtet hatte. Da wäre man eher geneigt zu glauben, der Baron habe sich mit dem Gedanken getragen, seine Sammlung der Schweiz zum Kauf anzubieten, vielleicht mit einer geheimen Abmachung, den Preis in einem numerierten Züricher Konto zu deponieren. Daß die deutsche Regierung, als sie von den Verhandlungen Wind bekam, die Überführung nationalen Kulturgutes ins Ausland untersagte, entspricht dem in allen Ländern Westeuropas üblichen Brauch.

Der dritte Punkt, die Verleihung des französischen Ehrenbürgerrechts an einen Deutschen zu einer Zeit, wo die deutsche Bevölkerung der feindseligen Willkür der Besatzungsmächte wehrlos preisgegeben war, scheint auf den ersten Blick den Charakter des Barons zu kompromittieren, doch erklärt sich diese Auszeichnung vermutlich aus Umständen, die den Charakter des Barons in keiner Weise belasten. Man erinnere sich des Menschenverbrüderungsrausches, in dem das französische Volk während der ersten Jahre der Revolution schwelgte. Irgendwie war die Kunde von Schillers "Lied an die Freude" und das Freiheitspathos seiner Jugenddramen nach Paris gelangt, und auf den Antrag eines Mitglieds der Nationalversammlung wurde der deutsche Dichter durch einen Brief des Innenministers Roland vom 10. Oktober des Jahres eins (also 1792) benachrichtigt, Frankreich habe ihn in die Liste jener ausländischen Menschenfreunde eingetragen, denen laut eines Gesetzentwurfs vom 26. August desselben Jahres das französische Ehrenbürgerrecht zuerkannt worden sei. Dem Brief war eine Abschrift des Gesetzes beigefügt mit der Bitte um Empfangsbestätigung. Unten links stand der Name des Geehrten, wie ihn das französische Ohr aufgefangen hatte, als Monsieur GILLÉ. Der Wohnsitz des Empfängers war nicht beigefügt. Fünf und einhalb Jahre verstrichen, bis das Dokument in Schillers Hände gelangte. Er bespricht das Ereignis in zwei Briefen an Goethe vom 2. und 9. März 1798. Der zweite Brief meldet Schillers Entschluß, das Ehrendiplom dem großherzoglichen Archiv in Weimar zur Aufbewahrung zu übergeben. Er müsse sich aber vorher eine Abschrift davon machen lassen, für den Fall, "wenn etwa eins meiner Kinder sich einmal in Frankreich niederlassen und dieses Bürgerrecht reklamieren sollte." Es amüsiert, zu sehen, wie der praktische Sinn Schillers seinem ethischen Idealismus sekundiert, wo es sich um Realien handelt. Ich erinnere mich dabei an einen Brief Schillers vom 29. Nov. 1795 an Goethe, wo von einem Prinzen die Rede ist:

> Der Brief des Prinzen August hat mich unterhalten. Er hat, für einen Prinzen besonders, viel guten Humor.
> Könnten wir nicht durch diesen Prinzen Vergünstigung erhalten, die Diderotische Erzählung ... für die *Horen* zu übersetzen? ... Ich kann's nicht lassen: bei einem Prinzen fällt mir immer zuerst ein, ob er nicht zu etwas gut sei?

Es ist leicht zu erschließen, was 1945 geschehen sein muß. Der Baron war aus dem zerstörten München geflüchtet und hatte in Baden-Baden eine Unterkunft gefunden, möglicherweise befand er sich im Zustand völliger Verarmung. Mutmaßlich hat er um eine Audienz bei dem französischen Generalkommandanten nachgesucht, und sich ihm vorgestellt unter Aufweisung von Abschriften jener Dokumente, die seinen Urgroßvater zum französischen Ehrenbürger gemacht hatten. Der Kommandant hat daraufhin seiner Regierung darüber Bericht erstattet und es ihr nahegelegt, durch eine generöse Geste den anderhalb Jahrhunderte früher ausgesprochenen Wunsch Schillers als in Erfüllung gegangene Prophetie wahrzumachen.

Zu der Spalte in *Deutschen Literatur-Lexikon* von Kosch ist nur zu sagen, sie bringt die üblichen Personalien des Verfassers nebst Aufzählung einer großen Anzahl seiner Schriften mit Daten. Unter dem Stichwort "Behandlung" finden wir den Hinweis auf Thomas Manns Roman *Doktor Faustus*, 1947. Unter dem Stichwort "Literatur" finden wir einen Aufsatz von P. Wittko in der Köln. Volkszeitung Nr. 308, 1940 (den ich nicht zu Gesicht bekommen habe), und den hier wiedergegebenen Nachruf von Birchler. Vermutlich dürfte dieser Aufsatz eine Probe der oben erwähnten Schikanen abgeben, denen der Baron seitens der "braunen Bestien" ausgesetzt war. Meine Bemühungen, mir diesen Aufsatz zu verschaffen, sind leider erfolglos geblieben.

Wir haben nun noch in aller Kürze einen Artikel gez. Leonhard Lenk, zu referieren, der in der *Neuen Deutschen Biographie* für das Jahr 1964 (S. 445-446) über Leben und Werk Alexander von Gleichen-Rußwurms unterrichtet. Vorwegnehmend ist zu sagen, daß dieser Artikel kein Wort über die kompromittierende Affaire des versuchten Postbetrugs mit der Maus enthält, kein Wort über den mißglückten Versuch, den wertvolleren Teil der Schiller-Reliquien der Schweiz zu "schenken," kein Wort über die hunderterlei Schikanen seitens der "braunen Bestien." Ebenfalls unerwähnt bleibt seine Ernennung zum französischen Ehrenbürger. Allerdings wird mitgeteilt, daß der Nachlaß des Barons sich in Lyon befindet.

Der Bericht betont vor allem Alexander von Gleichen-Rußwurms Abstammung von einem alten weitverzweigten, fränkischen Adelsgeschlecht. Er entwirft das Bild eines altfränkischen Edelmanns, dem unter der Obhut seiner Großmutter Emilie, Schillers jüngster Tochter, die seine ersten sechs Lebensjahre betreute, die Pflege alter Tradition, die gleichsam bis in das ancien régime zurückreichte, zur zweiten Natur geworden war. Seine Liebe zur Natur, zur Heimat, zur angestammten evangelischen Religion, wird hervorgehoben. Er verband wahre Volksverbundenheit mit dem vornehmen Wesen eines Edelmannes, und in der Ausübung seines Berufs als Schriftsteller empfand er sich als eine Brücke zwischen der Pflege der Werte des klassischen Zeitalters und der heraufkommenden Massengesellschaft. Er war ein gern gesehener Gast in literarischen und künstlerischen Salons und an der Tafel des Prinzregenten Luitpold. Von seinen Schriften wird eine sehr große Zahl, zuerst chronologisch, mit Titeln und Daten, aufgezählt. Ein Zusatz liefert noch eine weitere große Anzahl, nach Kategorien geordnet. Eine ganze Reihe seiner Schriften habe er überdies von der Veröffentlichung zurückbehalten aus dem Gefühl, er wolle sie auf einen Zeitpunkt versparen, wo auf besseres Verständnis zu hoffen sei. Der Artikel ist im Ton vorbehaltlosen Wohlwollens abgefaßt. Über die Rezeption des Werkes fällt kein Wort. Das Stoffgebiet, das er behandelte, umfaßte alles von der Philosophie bis zu einem Werk über den guten Ton. Interessant ist die Erwähnung des Umstands, daß sich auf seinem Schloß Greifenstein eine Gruppe von Schriftstellern zum Zweck philosophischer Diskussionen zusammenfand. Genannt werden Heinrich Mann, Frank Thieß, Fedor von Zobeltitz und Schrenck-Notzing. Vermutlich bezieht sich dies auf die Jugendjahre Heinrich Manns. Damit wäre bereits ein Anhaltspunkt gegeben für Thomas Manns gereizte Ablehnung dieses literarischen Zeitgenossen. In der Bearbeitung des der Redaktion der NDB zur Verfügung gestellten Textes findet sich ein Hinweis auf einen Artikel von Walter Baum über die verhängnisvolle Rolle von Schillers Tochter

Emilie in der Betreuung der Herausgabe von Schillers Schriften (*Euphorion*, 1956, S. 217-227).

INDEX OF NAMES AND TITLES

The Index includes the names of all authors, including those mentioned in footnotes, as well as the titles of all works mentioned in the essays. The names of characters have been set in small capital letters to distinguish them from those of historical or mythological persons.